A Sourcebook on

Standards Information

education, access, and

development

A Sourcebook on
Standards Information

education, access, and

development

STEVEN M. SPIVAK
and
KEITH A. WINSELL

G. K. Hall & Co. • Boston, Mass.

First published 1991
by G.K. Hall & Co.
70 Lincoln Street
Boston, Massachusetts 02111

10 9 8 7 6 5 4 3 2 1

Library of Congress Cataloging-in-Publication Data

A Sourcebook of standards information: education, access, and
    development / [edited by] Steven M. Spivak and Keith A. Winsell.
        p. cm.
    Includes bibliographical references and index.
    ISBN 0-8161-1948-1
    1. Exchange of bibliographic information – Data
processing – Standards. 2. Cataloging of archival material – Data
processing – Standards. 3. Machine-readable bibliographic
data – Standards. 4. Library information networks – Standards.
5. Archives – Administration – Standards. 6. Information
technology – Standards. 7. Information science – Standards. 8. Data
bases – Standards. I. Spivak, Steven M. II. Winsell, Keith Andrew,
1940- .
Z699.35.E94S68   1991
021.6'5 – dc20   91-19207
                                                             CIP

The paper used in this publication meets the minimum requirements of
American National Standard for Information Sciences – Permanence of
Paper for Printed Library Materials. ANSI Z39.48-1984. ⊗™
MANUFACTURED IN THE UNITED STATES OF AMERICA

Contents

Publisher's Note

Producing a volume that contains both newly commissioned and reprinted material presents the publisher with the challenge of balancing the desire to achieve stylistic consistency with the need to preserve the integrity of works first published elsewhere. In *A Sourcebook on Standards Information: Education, Access, and Development,* essays original to the volume have been edited to be consistent with G. K. Hall's house style; reprinted essays appear in the style in which they were first published. Consequently, shifts in style from one essay to another are the result of our efforts to be faithful to each text as it was originally published.

Preface

PATRICIA R. HARRIS, EXECUTIVE DIRECTOR, NATIONAL INFORMATION
STANDARDS ORGANIZATION

The statement that we are living in an information age has become a cliché as
we all fight information overload in both our professional and personal lives.
It is staggering to be reminded that by recent count it is estimated that the
body of knowledge is now doubling every 15 years. As the supply of
information has increased, so has the demand for better tools and methods to
harness information so it can be organized, accessed, and shared. This boom
in the information world is putting tremendous strains on the information
professional trying to provide the interface between the information overload
and the information seeker. This book is being published at a very opportune
moment. Standards are clearly one of the tools that can and must be used to
shape our information future.

As *A Sourcebook on Standards Information* is being readied for
publication, we are anticipating final Congressional approval of and, one
hopes, appropriation of funds for the creation of a national network of fiber
optic data highways that will build a National Research Education Network
in the United States. The goal is to link all Americans with a high-speed
computer network that would extend to business and industry, universities,
schools, and even to homes. The potential is that anyone with access to a
personal computer could tap into a vast world of electronic information.

How will libraries, museums, archives, publishers, and authors take
advantage of this new resource? How can libraries, archives, museums,
publishers, and authors contribute to the success of this new resource? It is
important that the leaders in the information profession be committed to the
critical role standards play in ensuring interoperatibility of information
systems and be knowledgeable of how standards are developed and
implemented. This book gives that necessary background, and more.

The essays and bibliographies that follow provide an essential foundation and philosophical context to understanding why standards must be a crucial component of information planning and management. These writings also give a panoramic view of the extent of information resources that can be a part of this anticipated national information network. Also, they provide a retrospective look at the body of literature that has been created around standards.

The decade of the 1990s will be a challenging time for all standards developers, especially for those serving the information sciences. The value of standards is clearly appreciating. As a result, there is fiercer competition be a part of the standards-setting process. Librarians and other information professionals will be required to work aggressively to contribute their expertise. Specialists from other segments of the information arena may believe they have more to contribute to the standards setting process and attempt to dominate the process and design the standards for information products and services. Adding to the dynamics, the traditional players in standards development within the library profession are changing. No longer is the Library of Congress the only institutional viewpoint that demands recognition. With the emergence of networks at the local and regional levels and with the success of private-sector businesses offering automated services and systems, new voices are being heard.

This is clearly the time to be informed about standards, committed to standards, and willing to invest the energy and intelligence to build standards for tomorrow.

Acknowledgments

Several persons and organizations have contributed to the inspiration and the preparation of this book. The Standards Engineering Society (SES) has for years promoted the publishing of compendiums on standards information and education, whether through its auspices or through other organizations. The idea for this book germinated at SES and has its continued support. The American National Standards Institute (ANSI) and the American Society for Testing and Materials (ASTM), along with SES, early on graciously offered their permission to reprint articles and copyrighted material.

John Donaldson of the National Institute of Standards and Technology (NIST) reviewed the initial outline for our standards bibliography, encouraging us to structure it with both subject indexes and annotations for maximum usefulness. Collaboration on this bibliography eventually led us to compile this book. Robert Toth of R. B. Toth Associates was generous in providing many additional sources for the bibliography and encouragement for the book. Michael Spring of the University of Pittsburgh kindly shared preprinted materials of his work on information technology, which proved of assistance in the preparation of the glossary and other parts of the manuscript.

Keith Winsell wishes to recognize the following three individuals on the staff of the College of Library and Information Services (CLIS) program at the University of Maryland: Bill Wilson, director of the CLIS library; Frank Burke, a stimulating teacher and helpful consultant throughout the term of this project; and Paul Wasserman, whose directed reading – with an extensive international source list – provided the opportunity for exploration of library and archival standards sources.

We also express appreciation to the numerous contributors for both the original and revised material included here and to the copyright holders of reprinted material. Carol Cron and Alice O'Dea did most of the laborious word processing. The competent staff and editors at G. K. Hall have made the systematic work on the project a pleasant experience.

Finally, as recipient of the Slattery Award for Standards Information from the Washington section of SES, Steven Spivak dedicates this book's completion to the memory of William J. Slattery. Slattery's pioneering contributions in standards information while at NIST were cut short by his untimely death. We hope his goals are furthered by this sourcebook.

Introduction

STEVEN M. SPIVAK, UNIVERSITY OF MARYLAND
KEITH A. WINSELL, AMISTAD RESEARCH CENTER, TULANE UNIVERSITY

In any new and fast developing discipline like standardization, which owes its advancement, indeed, its very existence, to a handful of self-taught individuals of broad vision and keen foresight, the problem of education and training is bound to be full of many question marks.

Lal C. Verman
Standardization: A New Discipline, 1973

This volume is a collection of original articles, reprinted readings, an extensive glossary of standards-related terms, and a major new, annotated, and indexed bibliography of North American standardization. It is intended as an introduction to standards information issues and as a sourcebook for information specialists and standards professionals. It may also serve as a textbook for specialty courses in library science or information services and other fields.

The raison d'être for this book is to satisfy the expressed need for an exposition of the philosophy, principles, practices, and resources directed toward standards information and education. But it is also aimed at fostering greater levels of standards awareness and standards literacy, needs that were not otherwise being appreciated or met. As noted by James Pearse in his preface to the American National Standards Institute's collection, *Standards Management* (1990), ". . . the enlightened application of the principles of standardization demonstrate that, contrary to Toffler's proposition (that the end of standardization is already is sight), *standardization is the key to effective application of technology."* Albert L. Batik reiterated in *A Guide to Standards* (1989): "One general statement can be applied to all standards. Standards consolidate scientific and technical knowledge, making possible a mechanism that brings the benefits of scientific research into widespread application. Standards are mankind's best communication medium for broadcasting technical progress."

This book is the first of a kind in standards education. The American Society for Testing and Materials' (ASTM) "Standardization Basics" presents the thesis, "The making of standards is not a fundamentally entertaining subject, and we in the standards-developing business have not placed a great emphasis on education in the past. But suddenly . . . the word *standard* and the process of standards writing are being discussed in many new and significant circles."

Verman, in his seminal book written in 1973, devoted a full chapter to the current and future education and training of both professional standards users and standards developers. He emphasized, "This group has to be given the highest priority in helping to acquire familiarity with the significance of standardization and how and where to seek guidance from standards in the discharge of their normal functions."

Literature reviews and bibliographies are included in the present volume as a definitive source to the major reference works in North American, 20th-century standardization. Other references address the special needs of library, information services, and archival training. The major bibliography annotates and indexes, by subject, most of the important books, monographs, and reports written on North American and some international aspects of standardization during the 20th century. These sources are of particular utility to librarians charged with making selective acquisitions in the fields of information standards and standardization. A primary readership in education for information standards is thus the librarians and information specialists, for whom standards and standardization have become increasingly important. Computer literacy has become a sine qua non. It will become increasingly important in the field of records management. A secondary but equally important role for this book is to provide an introduction to standards education and standardization for other disciplines and standards practitioners.

Individuals affected may be educators in the information and systems sciences, other social scientists, business and standards professionals; faculty in engineering education, engineers and technologists, specification and technical writers; or archivists and library-information science specialists providing standardization, automation, electronic delivery of standards, and technical information. All of these diverse groups are users and benefactors of the U.S., Canadian, and international standards systems.

Part 1 of the book begins with an introduction to the importance of standardization in science and technology. It also introduces standards as the underpinning of advanced, democratic societies. Without standardization, our society and industrial organization would be mayhem. One particular emphasis of this book is the linkage between standards and the goals of libraries, archives, and information centers. This, too, is mirrored in the introductory essays. Part 2 sets out the rationale for considering standardization a subject worthy of academic and intellectual pursuit. The special needs and constraints of teaching standardization to social science students, to Librarians and information specialists, to physical science/engineering students, and to archivists are presented. Part 3 describes some of the basic information resources available to those seeking to use or purchase standards. The essays provide an overview of both public information centers and private sources for the purchase of standards and related technical documents. More detailed sources and descriptions are found in the appendix and bibliography. Part 4 is a "case study" of the complex factors that can affect the standard-making and enforcement process. Part 5 focuses attention on the importance and use of standards by librarians and information service personnel and especially on the need for standards education in the library sciences and information systems fields of specialization. Also addressed is the unique role of standards in archival and museum practices, which has been the subject of considerable efforts in recent years. Part 6 is a look at the past, present, and future trends in standardization work, encompassing problems, dangers, and indeed some promises fulfilled and others yet to be realized.

Of particular value is a comprehensive glossary of over 100 standards-related terms and definitions. These can be a ready reference to assist the reader in explaining the technical language that is descriptive of standardization in its many forms and uses. A standards-based annotated bibliography follows the glossary. It includes 16 separate categories of subject indexing to assist the reader in locating resources and published work specific to their interests. Historical works from the early 20th century are collected here and annotated for the first time.

The book represents a communal effort among library, museum, and archival experts; standards and information professionals; and academicians on the forefront of standards education. The bringing together of this diverse collection and the bibliography of resource works represents the culmination of three years' collaboration between the coeditors and their colleagues.

The integration of these works reflects the complementary backgrounds and experiences of the editors. Dr. Winsell is a historian, a librarian, and an archivist, with particular expertise in minority studies. His recent endeavors have also included research and the development of reference collections on standardization applied to architectural barriers for the disabled community in America. The special issues involved are presented in the article by Edward Steinfeld (part 4). It is an interesting example of the link between technological, social and economic issues in standardization. Dr. Spivak is among a small coterie of educators who have pioneered the teaching and study of standards information and education in colleges and universities.

Although trained as a textile engineer, he has also dedicated 15 years of academic work toward the promotion of education for standards information and the study of standardization policy issues.

The collected works, glossary, and bibliographies included herein attempt to create a network of standards *users* (information specialists, archivists, library science and museum professionals, standards and records managers, etc.) with standards developers and publishers (standards engineers, standards organizations, standards practitioners, and others). It is a unique and increasingly vital dialogue. We hope that this sourcebook contributes to a continuation of that process.

PART 1

Standardization, Technology, and Society

Democratic Forms: The Place of Scientific Standards in Advanced Societies

IRVING LOUIS HOROWITZ, RUTGERS UNIVERSITY

The purpose of these remarks is to discuss the multiplication of standards in advanced societies. I should say at the outset that this is not intended so much as a celebration, but more as a contribution to the social theory of advanced societies. As such, my aim is to situate standards between the two ends of modern industrial life: the democratic and the bureaucratic. For in truth, and as Max Weber long ago pointed out, the rationalization of norms that has become so commonplace in our lives is made possible by the extraordinary advances in the complexity of the formal modes and operations that drive an industrial-technological order. But Weber, and others since him, have also warned that this same set of formalization procedures carries the risk of a collapse and corruption of the industrial-technological system by inhibiting innovation and frustrating experimentation. In other words, the place of standards is subject to constant review, revision, and when necessary, termination.

In effect, the conduct of advanced civilization has a formal element and a content element. It is commonplace to consider that content comes first. That is to say, machinery, artifacts and goods of all sorts come into existence, and then, rules and regulations for the conduct of relationships in the production and consumption process follow. But while this may be the case in an earlier epoch, it would appear that content and form are far more intertwined as we approach the twenty-first century. For as Weber long ago anticipated, the very ability to manage, manipulate and master new processes, coupled with shorter life-spans for existing products, involves a settlement of forms; or, more precisely, an integration of standards into the life cycle of goods and services.[1]

Originally published in *Information Standards Quarterly* 2 (January 1990): 8-12. This text was delivered as the opening address for NISO's 50th anniversary, 18 September 1989. Reprinted with permission.

In its most rudimentary form, standards are driven by economic considerations. Specifically, they are a function of the social need to appeal to an established body of thought or conventions that can serve as a rule of measurement for quality, quantity, weight or change. One recent article has placed the subject of standards within the broad framework of information economics; by which is meant "the establishment of standards [that have] greatest significance when economic agents cannot assimilate without substantial costs all the relevant information about the commodities that may be exchanged with other agents, and the processes by means of which those goods and services can be produced."[2]

To give a simple illustration: many systems can drive a videocassette. There is the Beta format and the VHS format; there are three types of running time; there are multiple modes of reproduction; there are various hardware compatibilities; there is equipment available to translate one format into another and drive the system as a whole. And I beg to remind you that we are describing procedures and standards that by now are second nature to millions of people in the Western world. In this situation, the question of standards is not something which sits and awaits the implementation process. Rather, standards are intertwined with content and context from the onset of wide utilization. Corporate decisions on formats, say between Sony and RCA in the case of videocassettes, rest precisely on limits and advantages of one system over another – and standards are integral to such decision-making.

One reason why it has been so difficult to instill a broad consensus about the meaning of standards is that only in their absence are they perceived as critical. This is especially the case in a free market system, where innovations historically have been weakly, often indirectly, regulated. One analyst of information processing systems has put this issue succinctly: "There is currently no easy way to send electronic mail from one commercial network to another. MCI and CompuServe electronic mail networks, for example, are not interconnected. One has to subscribe separately to each system, with different system interfaces for each. Thus, almost unawares, we are moving in some areas back to the turn of the century, with its separate telephone systems. Ideally, there should be standards so that personal computers, fax machines, high quality printers, telexes, electronic mail services, and telephones could interconnect with one another. Major economic efficiencies could thus be attained."[3]

This fusion of utility and innovation in a brief time span is important if we are to understand the place of standardization in our post-industrial and multinational age. For an essential difference between the pre-industrial and post-industrial is precisely the rationalization of systems, the integration of form and content as a single unit – one that is disaggregated for the purpose of analysis, but linked in real time to global circumstances, that is, to the market processes of producing and consuming goods.

But standards of operations are different than norms of conduct as such. Norms are built into the social fabric over extended or long time waves. Standards are mandated artifacts, legislated steps and procedures that do not always take on the force of custom, but do have the force of law. For example, many standards are either publicly known, or if known, are not necessarily abided by. The provisions of the 1976 copyright legislation are an unfortunately good example of this distinction between custom and law. When these sociological elements are added to the economic costs and benefits of standards to selective groups, one can readily appreciate why so many standards are bitterly fought over. For what may seem to be an idiosyncrasy of the moment, or the clash of personalities involved, is in fact a reflection of very real social and economic forces at work in determining the character and conduct of human affairs.

Again, to take an illustration of the fiscal character of a standard: the struggle in the standard governing rules and regulations for professional indexing. The infusion of standards for machine-readable programs carries with it the implication that non-human processes may substitute for human labor. Artificial intelligence systems may, nonetheless, not sit well with a society of indexers. Similarly, questions of copyright procedures are matters of deep concern to publishers, librarians, authors, and editors. Not all of these sub-classes may share the same value framework or agree on what the law says. And hence, the struggle over standards is but one part of the struggle for control of substance and events – not only how things are to be done, but who is to do them and what is to be permitted.

The development of standards is joined to that of the struggle over democracy and bureaucracy. For standards reflect either a series of "bottom-up" or "top-down" considerations. There are limits to either bottom-up or top-down – in the sense that the standards of professional groups are not readily subject to a popular referendum. Indeed, standards are often not subject to a membership vote of relevant groups either. What does have a leavening effect is the integrity of the various elites that do come together in the formation of standards, and, no less, the carefully stitched consensus among different professional societies representing diverse interests.

Within the parameters of organizational life, the evolution of standards involves a constant struggle, a tension as it were, between experience and imposition – between calling forth the widest sample possible in generating standards, even if this means a clumsy set of procedures, a less elegant set of operations, or even a delay in uniform adherence. In contrast are standards that are a function of the union of technocracy and meritocracy – of a universe of expertise that does indeed generate utilitarian outcomes, without delays and often technically elegant – but often lacking inputs from end users and supposed beneficiaries.

There are dangers in the bureaucratization and routinization of standards, no less than in their absence. Too often standards for evaluation are stated in terms of proper processes rather than desired outcomes. In a clever recent book Martha Feldman points out that "emphasis on uniformity and impersonality in decision-making encourages bureaucrats to place more importance on the process of work than on the accomplishments. Following the rules and employing impersonal categories become more important than doing the work these routines were established to regularize."[4]

These caveats entered, and getting beyond how standards are derived, more or less bureaucratic or democratic, it remains inconceivable that a modern society could function without them. For standards are essentially constitutions of a specific event (how to order or manufacture a product) or a specific process (how to move a book from a factory warehouse to a library shelf); or what constitutes minimum levels of product acceptability (the quality and nature of paper, binding, and printing). I draw these examples from publishing because it is that industry with which I am most familiar. But in truth, standards must exist in every field for product reliability to exist – in the work of a producer and in the mind of a consumer.

I want then to turn from what happens when a breakdown in the production of standards takes place to a breakdown in the economic circulation of capital as such. For assuredly, if the above sort of analysis is on target, the absence of standards has, or would have, serious negative consequences on the conduct of advanced societies. I would like to illustrate this by reference to the current American trade deficit. In this, the singular and unique work of John R. Hayes deserves special accommodation. The case study that follows is in considerable measure drawn from his field efforts.[5]

In 1988, Westinghouse, General Electric, and Clorox found their products locked up and embargoed at the Saudi port of Dammann. There was nothing defective with their parts, but product standards had not been met. And why should this have been the case? Because the United States, as a result of a Commerce Department ruling on costs, decided not to dispatch a team, or a person, to Riyadh for the purpose of developing appropriate professional standards for Saudi Arabia, and hence were outmaneuvered by equivalent teams from Japan, the United Kingdom, Germany, and France who did advise the Saudi Arabian Standards Organization (SASO).

There are 42,000 standards for Saudi Arabia – covering everything from the shelf-life of lamb to the color of ground wires used in air conditioners. The failure to become involved is also consequential. United States trade with Saudi Arabia slipped from 21 percent in 1982 to 15 percent in 1989. And since the entire Middle East uses the Saudi standards, at risk are $1.5 billion of U.S. exports.

The same condition prevails elsewhere: in Brazil, which accounts for $17 billion worth of imported goods, the Germans have provided their Brazilian counterparts with a seventy-foot shelf of German product standards – in Portuguese. The United States countered feebly by reintroducing aged standards (five to twenty years old) of assorted trade association publications. A similar situation obtains in India, where equipment laboratories are being re-established using European standards. The thinking is that transponders, satellites, and computers can thus be plugged into European rather than American electronic standards.

The Japanese are going even further. The MITI (Ministry of International Trade and Industry) currently has technical experts working overseas on five nations' standards programs, and it has also brought personnel from twenty-eight developing nations back to Japan. The lack of private and public support for standards development has led to a huge gap in funding standards proposals, with a consequent loss of business. Clearly the slogan that "if it is good enough for the U.S. it is good enough to export," has gone the way of "my country right or wrong." In point of fact, while Japan and Germany, according to International Monetary Fund reports, have unusually high trade surpluses, the United States has dangerously high trade deficits.[6]

All of this indicates that if industrialization brought about rationalization, post-industrialization has brought about globalization. And hence, the magnitude of a standards gap is not simply a shortcoming in American industrial policy, but a risky situation in a highly competitive environment. In a sense, the "top-down" approach as represented by the assumption that American products are the norm or the standard as such has given way to a "bottom-up" approach in which the needs of a host country must be taken into account by more advanced sectors.

What we have then in this brief overview of standards is the movement from a specific industry to national and now international standards. But the magnitude of this evolution should not obscure the closing of the gap between the content of discovery, the context of usage, and standards for measuring size, materials, and performance.

We have moved far afield from the special work of the National Information Standards Organization. Thus, before closing, let me return to efforts of this group. Take the issue of acid-free paper as described in a recent issue of the NISO periodical, *Information Standards Quarterly*. First, there is the question of where such paper should be used. Second, there is the question of whether one should have a standard of what permanent paper should have in it, versus what it should not have in it. Third is the question of which available or proposed system for mass deacidification should be used. Fourth are issues about the chemical bonding, the tensile strength of a sheet of paper. In such a presumably simple and straightforward matter as acid-free paper we have contentious issues involving chemical manufacturers, paper mills, as well as other public and private interest groups, both in Canada and the United States.[7]

Advanced nations are clearly moving into a global pattern of standards – as societies themselves become intertwined and inter-networked. This will be no easy transition, since the political forces of nationalism and the economic demands for protectionism are also growing stronger. But the United States does have several advantages: (a) a tradition of exact standards of goods and services; (b) scientific methods for estimating and evaluating standards; (c) long experience with manufactured goods and services; and (d) the broad use of English as a lingua franca for international trade and research. Unlike the Germans in Brazil, the United States would not need to render standards in Portuguese, since English is the second language of the educated and commercial sectors of Latin America, the Middle East, and many parts of Asia and Africa.

How then does democracy enter into all of this? It does, I submit, in the very give and take between national entities, industrial sectors, and technological rivalries. Standards can also be changed, and frequently are, in the give and take of such competitive encounters. Democracy is not a thing but a process. At its best, standards development is a way of arriving, through non-violent means, at a consensus – a way of doing things by identifying or creating or constructing models of performance to which presumably rational persons can aspire.

The National Information Standards Organization fuses public sector interests, university research involvement, librarian and publishing inputs, and extensive connections with overseas groups aiming at similar tasks. It also works with a myriad of trade associations and organizations. Much of this work is done on a pro bono basis. For all of these reasons, NISO may be considered a model of how standards are developed in rapidly changing technological environments. In short, the consensual creation of standards is part of the long tradition of democracy that moves slowly but inexorably from a world of received wisdom and absolute authority to one of shared experience and exact knowledge. There are deep risks in this process of standardization. There are catastrophes in the failure to run such risks.

Notes

1. Max Weber, "Bureaucracy," in *From Max Weber: Essays in Sociology*, ed. H. H. Gerth and C. Wright Mills (New York: Oxford University Press, 1946), 196-266.

2. David A. Paul, "Some New Standards for the Economics of Standardization in the Information Age," in *Economic Policy and Technological Performance*, ed. Partha Dasgupta and Paul Stoneman (New York and Cambridge: Cambridge University Press, 1987), 206-239.

3. James E. Katz, "Pivotal Issues in Regulating Communication," 26, no. 5 (July/August 1989): 5-10.

4. Martha S. Feldman, *Order without Design: Information Production and Policy-Making* (Stanford: Stanford University Press, 1989), 108-114.

5. John R. Hayes, "Who Sets the Standards?" *Forbes* 143, no. 8 (April 17, 1989): 110-112.

6. Rich Thomas, "What You Won't Hear in Paris," *Newsweek* 114, no. 3 (July 17, 1989): 38-39.

7. Patricia Harris, "From the NISO Executive Director," *Information Standards Quarterly* 1, no. 2 (April 1989): 5-6.

Standards and Library Goals

PAUL EVAN PETERS, NEW YORK PUBLIC LIBRARY

I wish to explore the question of why standards are so important to libraries and librarians. I will approach this task by articulating my views on various aspects of this question and by drawing upon the experience of libraries and librarians to illustrate those views. I hope my argument may advance the general understanding of some of the values of libraries and librarians. Toward that end I will develop the theme that standards provide libraries and librarians with a key method of translating their values into actions. I also hope that this article will be informative and entertaining to those readers who are not librarians. Mostly I hope that the readers of this article will take from it an appreciation of the standards agenda of libraries and librarians, how that agenda has changed over time, and what form that agenda will assume in the years ahead.

THE STEREOTYPE

We all know exactly the stereotype of the librarian that I have in mind. It is a very familiar one, and it is not very complimentary to libraries or librarians. It subscribes to the view that librarians love order more than they love anything else in the world. It further subscribes to the view that libraries are conservative institutions in which new things are evaluated solely in terms of how well they fall within and advance certain long-standing traditions. This stereotypical view of libraries and librarians suspects that their devotion to standards arises from a desire for uniformity. It fears that there is no room for creativity and uniqueness in the worlds of libraries and librarians. It resents the fact that libraries and librarians play such a key role in the relationship between authors and readers. It also looks forward to that

Originally published as "General Library Standards" in *Book Research Quarterly* 4 (Fall 1988): 20-24. Reprinted with permission.

relationship being ended when technology renders libraries and librarians obsolete.

I concede that all stereotypes, like all myths, have some basis in fact. I will, that is, so long as it is acknowledged that such facts are overwhelmingly historical rather than contemporary in their origins. I also believe that a librarian without an inclination toward order or a library without an institutionalized respect for tradition is a librarian or a library without much of a future. I hasten to add, though, that such a concession and admission do not necessarily lead me to the stereotypical view of libraries and librarians. Neither the quest for order nor the conservation of tradition has been the sine qua non of any library or librarian I have ever known. Libraries and librarians rarely, if ever, reason for or against a proposed policy or practice on the basis of "order" or "tradition" as such. This stereotypical view of libraries and librarians suffers from a confusion of means and ends, mistaking a visible manifestation of effort by libraries and librarians for one of their goals or objectives.

THE MISSION

This confusion can be sorted out by reflecting upon the mission of libraries and librarians. At least in the United States, the textbook statement of this mission holds that libraries are institutions and librarians are professionals dedicated to the public's right to know and to the acquisition, organization, storage, preservation, and accessing of transmitted and recorded knowledge in support of that right. Looking from this perspective, it becomes understandable that libraries are built upon a foundation of tradition and that librarians strive to bring order to the vast scope of knowledge products and services that express that tradition. In short, this is precisely what we want from libraries and librarians. We want libraries to be ready to make our tradition available to us and our children upon demand. We also want librarians to have prepared themselves and their collections so that similar things can be brought together and so that we can get advice that saves us time and improves our results. The stereotypical view of libraries and librarians does justice to neither. It portrays their strengths as their faults and misses the point by confusing what libraries and librarians do for what they believe. If we are to understand why standards resonate so powerfully for libraries and librarians, we must look beyond this stereotypical view.

COLLECTIONS AND ACCESS

A good place to begin is with the concept of "access," something that is currently attracting a lot of attention in libraries and among librarians.

Libraries now build and coordinate their collections by painstakingly analyzing what sorts of materials need to be accessed by their clienteles, to what depth, and in what timeframe. Computer-based bibliographic information systems of all types make great quantities of data about specific materials and individual library collections accessible on a national and even international (as well as local) scale. New techniques and technologies of information dissemination and organization promise timely, comprehensive, and flexible access to a wide variety of information, and they are being evaluated and embraced by libraries and librarians at an impressive rate. A rallying cry has been sounded and heard concerning the crisis that has resulted from the acid residues left in paper from the way it has been manufactured for the last one hundred years, and a National Commission on Preservation and Access has joined other organizations to meet that challenge. A similar consensus is beginning to form concerning the need for a national effort to ensure the existence of a telecommunications infrastructure in the twenty-first century that can provide technologically sophisticated access to information across the entire spectrum of users in society.

These, and a host of other events I could cite, manifest a major change in how libraries and librarians conceive and approach their mission. In the past, libraries and librarians focused primarily on their collections and the materials contained in those collections; libraries and librarians now focus as well on their users and the interests and talents represented by those users. I give libraries and librarians a lot of credit for recognizing the need for and the opportunity presented by this reorientation of focus. This process is not complete, but it is at a very advanced stage. Nor can I imagine that the focus of libraries and librarians will ever again revert to its exclusive concentration on collections. No less formidable a force than the "information explosion" is driving this turn of events, and it shows no sign of abating. This explosion is affecting both sides of the information supply-and-demand question. It is well known that libraries and librarians strive to keep up with an information world that is experiencing explosive growth in numbers, diversity, and cost. What is less widely recognized is that they are also experiencing an explosive increase in user demand and expectations. This is why I believe that the relatively new focus of libraries and librarians on "access" as well as on "collection" is something that is here to stay.

BUSINESS PRACTICES

I hope that the preceding establishes my point that "access," along with "collection," is a paramount focus of a large, growing number of contemporary and future libraries and librarians. I still have to explain how this fact elucidates the devotion of libraries and librarians to standards.

Before I do, though, I want to introduce another pertinent consideration. Libraries and librarians are increasingly aware of and experienced with cost/benefit analysis, among other modern management and decision-making practices. The need for libraries and librarians to stretch scarce resources to cover an increasingly wide array of financial obligations functions as a major motivation in this regard. A second major motivation is the widespread restructuring of library budgets whereby hardware, software, and other capital expenses are increasing and personnel expenses are decreasing, in both absolute and relative terms. These two motivations define a situation in which libraries and librarians have become acutely aware of what things cost, what they get and do not get for the money they spend, and what the value of the things they buy can be said to be. The obvious result of these new realities is that libraries and librarians are continuing to become more informed and discriminating participants in the markets in which the products and services they care about are sold and bought.

Further, products and services in those markets have been evolving in concert with the changing business practices of libraries and librarians. Market segments form and mature through a sequence of at least three phases. The first phase begins with the arrival of an innovative and unique product or service. During this first phase the decision to acquire such a product or service is relatively simple, determined mostly, if not entirely, by the perceived need for the product or service and the resources available to the library or librarian in question. The market segment for most new products and services quickly progresses to a second phase characterized by the existence of two or more competing products or services. The decision to acquire one or the other such product or service is not a matter solely of identifying a need and allocating resources. It is also a matter of which product or service maximizes the degree to which the need is met while minimizing the resources that have to be allocated. The concern that most defines the third phase in the maturation of a market segment questions how well the products and services in that segment integrate with themselves as well as with the products and services found in other pertinent market segments. Procurement decisions made in this phase examine issues of cost and benefit in an organizational, and perhaps even a cross-organizational, context. The markets for quite a few of the products and services that concern libraries and librarians have entered the second and even third phases of their maturation. This has changed the nature of competition in those markets. Some market segments have begun to favor "open" rather than "proprietary" approaches. It also has become clearer exactly what features genuinely distinguish products and services in all market segments.

LIBRARY STANDARDS

I hope that the stage is now set well enough for me to offer a partial explanation of why libraries and librarians are so devoted to standards and why the stereotypical view of this question is so inadequate. One of the things that libraries and librarians have learned from their new focus on "access" and proficiency in business practices is that, at least in the short term, the information world of their users, like their own, is becoming increasingly complex and fragmented. Library users can no longer count upon each library to have a catalog organized according to roughly the same principles and containing cards that present roughly the same information. Library users are even being told that some reference resources are no longer the definitive tools they once were, especially when compared to new reference resources that were inconceivable as recently as five years ago. Libraries and librarians differ on whether and, if so, how soon this process will reverse, but optimists and pessimists agree that the short-term situation is worrisome. Libraries and librarians will be pleasantly surprised to learn that many library users are very willing and able to make as much, if not more, sense out of this new information world as they did of the old one. Libraries and librarians also have a tendency to overlook how complex and fragmented the old information world they now so fondly remember truly used to be. Regardless, I support and actively participate in the standards efforts of libraries and librarians which are motivated by the sincere desire to progress toward a future information world that is more coherent and comprehensible than the one we now face and will likely be facing for some time to come. This strikes me as a worthy goal and a productive way to invest institutional and professional resources.

CONCLUSION

Libraries and librarians have always been devoted to standards for two basic reasons: (1) standards help to reduce the time and effort that they and their users spend dealing with "packages" rather than with the things that come in those packages; and (2) standards allow economies of scale and other cost-controlling dynamics to shape the market segments in which they procure their products and services. It is important to be periodically reminded of this fact. I hope that an accurate understanding of the true and enduring motivations of libraries and librarians encourages the readers of this article, among other interested parties, to consider working with libraries and librarians on a common standards development agenda. I speak from personal experience when I say that libraries and librarians are eager to find a way for such a coordinated standards development enterprise to occur and are willing to work on those standards that bring all concerned parties together rather than to work on those that might move those parties apart. The best way to begin is with a sensitive appreciation for the needs and talents of the users and a realistic appraisal of the strengths and weaknesses of the markets that libraries and librarians share with other institutions and professionals in the information industry. The interests of all parties will be served by thinking of standards and standardization as powerful tools for addressing the needs and talents of these users and the strengths and weaknesses of these markets.

Standardization and Technology: The Impact on Libraries and Archives

FRANK G. BURKE, COLLEGE OF LIBRARY AND INFORMATION SERVICES, UNIVERSITY OF MARYLAND

Without standards there would be no technology–no telephones, railroads, or air navigation systems. Without standards there would, indeed, be no language. Only by adherence to rules do we understand each other, and we move from chaos to cohesion through the application of rules of standardization.

Standards exist in contexts. Meaning can be conveyed in many forms, but each form must adhere to the symbol set it represents, and within that symbol set must be standards. Thus, language consists of many symbol sets–Latin, Cyrillic, Greek, or one of many others. Information can also be communicated in transient symbol sets, such as sign language, or legible or audible sets consisting of short or long sounds, as in Morse code.

Even in nontraditional symbol sets, however, there are variants where nonconformance to one standard prevents comprehension. Someone using American sign language cannot easily communicate with someone using British or German sign language. The dots and dashes of American Morse code are not equivalent to international Morse and are quite distinct from telegraphic codes.

So it is with the modern technology of automation. C/PM systems are not compatible with DOS, and neither will function with the operating system employed by Apple. Even within compatible systems, coding formats differ–symbols representing one set of data are not necessarily the same as others representing the same set of data.

On the other hand, today there is a great desire for interconnectivity–the ability to transmit and receive information, or at least data, between many separate systems without any knowledge of their compatibility. While librarians have sought compatibility and transfer of information for many years in an attempt to share common information and reduce the redundancy of describing objects of research, archivists have found the question to be moot because *their* material was (and is) unique and offers no economic advantage to sharing with others the information about it.

This difference between libraries and archives – the multiplicity of copies in one and the uniqueness of copies in the other – has led to different approaches to communication and standardization. Librarians realize that the objects they handle in greatest bulk, commercially produced books and serials, are held in many other institutions. They realized long before the era of automation that if one authority were to describe those objects individually and prepare such a description according to professionally acceptable rules, then all would benefit by sharing that description and by applying it to their own objects of the same kind. Long before the Library of Congress began distributing copies of the catalog cards it had prepared for its accessions so that others could benefit from the work of the catalogers, other libraries and the American Library Association had already begun such a process.[1] Indeed, it was the appointment of Herbert Putnam, the director of the Boston Public Library, to Librarian of Congress that resulted in the technology transfer to the Library of Congress.[2]

The cataloging rules applied to the cards were standards agreed to by professional librarians and adhered to by most. The purpose for adopting such standards was at least threefold: First, if one library could simply copy what the national authority was doing, instead of each institution doing the work independently, it would be economical; second, full description of holdings in standardized terms would make identification of individual items more certain, leading to a reduction in inadvertent duplication of acquisitions; and third, descriptive standards would benefit researchers, who could move from library to library and be reasonably assured that the item to which they saw a reference was the same item they had seen elsewhere and not just something that seemed the same. Standards, therefore, are important for technical services, for purchasing, and for reader services.

The archivist has had no such imperative. Archives do not buy their holdings but receive them from the corporate body that creates them. Archives do not encounter redundancy in the holdings of other institutions because their holdings are unique to the creating corporate body. Researchers using archives do not wish to verify that what they are seeing is the same as they have seen elsewhere because the uniqueness rule applies once more except to media, such as filmed copies of original materials.

One may ask why, then, archivists are not only seeking the establishment of standards but also linking with librarians in that effort. It should be noted that since 1958 some standards have been applied to archives, but they have been external and passive and have not necessarily involved the custodial archivist or the archives' internal controls. The standards applied since 1958 have been those of the *National Union Catalog of Manuscript Collections*

(*NUCMC*), which has been distributing data sheets for archives and manuscript repositories to complete and return. The *NUCMC* data sheet has been requiring standardized answers to eleven questions, although its policy always has been to accept any information sent to it in almost any form, at which point the *NUCMC* staff standardizes it into their format. Thus, the *NUCMC* standards are passive, in that they do not require the institution to apply them internally but merely to respond to some standardized questions and have them externally converted to a standardized format. Such a process does not change the manner in which the institution itself describes its material. Indeed, if the *NUCMC* catalog cards produced from such a process are returned to the submitting institution and interfiled with its internally produced cards, the result is a bifurcated system, which is the antithesis of standardization.

In pursuit of such standards, the American Library Association reviews and comments on proposed revisions to the *Anglo-American Cataloguing Rules* (AACR) through its Committee on Cataloging: Description and Access, which has invited the Society of American Archivists (SAA) to appoint a liaison with the committee. The Library of Congress holds a primary role in establishing and maintaining library-based standards, some of which are now being applied to description of archives, beyond those of *NUCMC*. Primary for archivists is the USMARC (Machine-Readable Cataloging) format for the transmission of bibliographic and authority data, which, itself, is based on the ANSI Z39.2-1985 (Bibliographic Information Exchange) standard. The importance of this format for archivists became critical with the development of the USMARC AMC format, or Archives-Manuscript Control format, the maintenance of which is shared by the Library of Congress and the Society of American Archivists. Along with the movement to enter archival data into national databases through the standardized USMARC AMC format came the move to adopt the *Library of Congress Subject Headings* (*LCSH*) where possible when entering data in the subject-indexing fields of the USMARC format. To provide commonly recognizable information structures for archival data across systems, the interpretive manual *Archives, Personal Papers and Manuscripts* (*APPM*) has been prepared by Steven Hensen and adopted and published by the SAA so as to adapt the *AACR* 2 rules for cataloging to these forms of material.

What is driving the archivists to seek standardized approaches to description and to cooperate with librarians in the process is the advancement of technology in communications and information interchange. Archivists still do not feel that their holdings are directly related to those of other archives, at least to the extent that there is an economic advantage to sharing the descriptive processes applied to them. Nonetheless, the availability of local, regional, and national information networks has led archivists to consider exporting the information they have about their holdings so that it may be readily available elsewhere. Such an activity requires the application of standards to participate in information sharing.

To say that archivists are adopting descriptive standards does not imply that all archivists are doing so or that they are standardizing all of their descriptive processes. At present, it would be fair to say that the only archivists actively engaged in standardizing their descriptions for export are those who have access to national databases such as the Research Libraries Information Network (RLIN) or the On-Line Library Center (OCLC) or those who are applying internal, offline automation to their holdings through specialized software packages such as MicroMARC or MARCON. There is little indication that those untouched by networking or automation are using the newly promulgated descriptive processes. Archivists are, in fact, caught in a dilemma in many cases. When the archives is part of a larger institution such as a state government, a university special collections department, or a corporate library and when the archivist reports to the librarian as a superior, it is not uncommon for the archives to be required to adhere to whatever automated system the library is using. Although most libraries employ the USMARC format for description, not all libraries are willing to have their small archival units (compared to the size of the rest of the library) deviate from the standard and use the USMARC AMC format or to enter data into RLIN rather than into OCLC. Thus, when they are within a standardized system, many archives often find themselves nonstandard compared to the rest of their profession.

Even in those instances, which are still too few, when an archives is exporting data in the USMARC AMC format into RLIN or OCLC, the information coded is, for the most part, cataloging data and not descriptive information. Archivists describe their holdings in inventories or registers, which are essentially narrative, hierarchically structured analyses of the documents and their organization. Such *finding aids* may run to dozens of pages. The cataloging data created by archivists are abstracts of these finding aids, reducing the dozens of pages to a description that is structured to fit on a catalog card or two. While archivists have been concentrating their efforts on standardization of the catalog card format, they have done little work on standardizing the basic descriptive document, the finding aid. Some 15 years ago, recommendations were made to the profession through Society of American Archivists "manuals" to standardize at least the structure, if not the content, of finding aids,[3] but no attempt was made to achieve professional concurrence or conformance. Recent moves within the profession are aiming at providing standards for finding-aid description. The Working Group on Standards for Archival Description, funded by the National Historical Publications and Records Commission (NHPRC) and sponsored by Harvard

University, has recently issued a draft report that makes seventeen recommendations to the profession for the adoption of standards (see Appendix A). They are at the preliminary stage and will require considerable effort to bring into some general conformance the wide variety of descriptive procedures that have developed over the past ninety years of archival activity in the United States.

The USMARC AMC standards allow for standardized entry of information relating to donors and solicitations, accession activity, physical location of material within the stacks, and other administrative controls typical of archival management. Archivists, therefore, are enjoying the use of systems that permit them to assemble disparate data about their holdings into a single integrated database. Librarians have recently begun to look at their databases in much the same way, and the two fields are drawing closer together in their descriptive processes.

Archivists are now facing their greatest challenge, which is in the area of electronically created records. That problem is not as much one of description as it is a question of creating or converting electronic records in a standardized format. In a state or federal government system, many agencies apply a wide variety of software within a broad spectrum of equipment types. Rarely is there compatibility between agencies or within agencies between systems. The archives is destined to receive at least some of these electronically created records just as it now receives a portion of the agency's paper records. Bringing this diversity into one central location and attempting to preserve it and make it available for decades, if not for centuries, cause considerable difficulty for the archivist. The solutions being investigated involve either *creating* electronic records in a standard format through standard software – an impossible task – or *converting* those files that are deemed permanently valuable into a standardized structure that will be software and machine independent – in effect, the equivalent of ASCCII in word-processing systems. This problem is currently the most complex yet perhaps the most important, facing archivists. The National Archives and the NHPRC both have recognized the problem of standards in electronic record keeping as requiring attention for at least the next decade.[4]

The acceptance of some standards within the archival profession has created a philosophical shift in archival education. Until the adoption of USMARC AMC, the teaching of archives was theoretical and based to a large extent on common practices, which were not as common as many liked to believe. There could be no text because there were no agreed-upon rules. In a series of articles in the professional literature beginning almost with the first appearance of the professional journal *The American Archivist*, archival educators debated the value of the practicum if it meant sending students out to learn idiosyncratic processes of a variety of unrelated institutions.[5] Major archives found little standardization between or among their own units. Archival education, therefore, taught what the instructor knew or felt to be most important, not what the profession had agreed was necessary knowledge. The concept that archivists were historians with a practical bent was as valid as any other because the emphasis in archival hiring was placed on the applicant's understanding of historical processes, institutional history, or the ability to do research as a basis for providing reference service. Federal standards for employment of archivists stressed humanistic education and required no education or training in processes or information systems.[6] The advanced library degree (MLS) was abjured as irrelevant.

The expansion of the concept of archives as information systems, the move to computerization of individual institutional holdings, and then the desire to share such information through networking have considerably modified, if not revolutionarily changed, the philosophy of archives and archival education. Not surprisingly, the library and information studies programs and schools are moving into the area of archival education and are able to adopt such programs more easily as the archivists themselves adopt library-based rules and standards for the description of their materials. To date, only one standard has been accepted by the archival community—that is, the USMARC AMC format—but that now permits archival educators to teach the format in class and *then* to send the students out on a practicum or internship to hone their skills, using the knowledge learned in class. This is a first for archival education. One can hope that it is only the beginning.

Librarians and archivists, therefore, approach the end of the electronic century with a full agenda for the creation and implementation of standards. The process is driving the two professions together for the first time, but also it is encompassing the newer, hybrid professions of information resource management, information systems management, computer science, and a vast array of subprofessions that these have spawned. The pages that follow will attempt to reveal some of the questions being addressed and to give at least some hints to possible answers.

Notes

1. Edith Scott, "The Evolution of Bibliographic Systems in the United States, 1876-1945," *Library Trends* 25 (July 1976): 293-309, especially 302-303.

2. John Y. Cole, *For Congress and the Nation: A Chronological History of the Library of Congress* (Washington, D.C.: GPO, 1979), 71.

3. Committee on Finding Aids of the Society, *Inventories and Registers: A Handbook of Techniques and Examples*, (Chicago: Society of American Archivists, 1976). At the time of the preparation of the handbook, Frank G. Burke was chairing the committee. At the time of publication, David B. Gracy II was chair and went on to enlarge on the concept of the handbook in his *Archives and Manuscripts:*

Arrangement & Description, Basic Manual Series (Chicago: Society of American Archivists, 1977).

4. *Electronic Records Issues: A Report to the National Historical Publications and Records Commission*, Commission Reports and Papers, no. 4 (Washington, D.C.: The Commission, March 1990).

5. The first issue of the *American Archivist*, 1 (July 1938): 130-141, contained an article by Charles M. Gates, "The Administration of State Archives," which addressed the question of training. One year later, Collas G. Harris, a staff member of the five-year-old National Archives published "Personnel Administration at the National Archives," *Staff Information Circular* 7 (Washington, D.C.: The National Archives, 1939). More recent discussions of archival education, including the practicum, can be found in Francis X. Blouin, "The Relevance of Archival Theory and Practice for Library Education: An Argument for a Broader Vision," in *Archives and Library Administration: Divergent Traditions and Common Concerns*, Lawrence J. McCrank, ed. (New York: The Haworth Press, 1986), 155-166; Frank G. Burke, "Education," in *Archive-Library Relations*, Robert L. Clark (New York: R.R. Bowker Co., 1976), 51-68; Burke, "The Future of Course of Archival Theory in the United States," *American Archivist* 44 (1981): 40-46; John C. Colson, "On the Education of Archivists and Librarians," *American Archivist* 31 (April 1968): 167-174; Allen DuPont Breck, "New Dimensions in the Education of American Archivists," *American Archivist* 29 (April 1966): 173-186; Frank B. Evans, "Postappointment Archival Training: A Proposed Solution for a Basic Problem," *American Archivist* 40 (January 1977): 57-74; H. G. Jones, "Archival Training in American Universities," *American Archivist* 31 (April 1968): 135-154; Herman Kahn, "Some Comments on the Archival Vocation," *American Archivist* 34 (1970): 3-12; W. Kaye Lamb, "The Modern Archivist: Formally Trained or Self-Educated?" *American Archivist* 31 (April 1968): 175-177; William G. LeFurgy, "Practicum: A Repository View," *American Archivist* 44 (Spring 1981): 153-155; Theodore R. Schellenberg, "Archival Training in Library Schools," *American Archivist* 31 (April 1968): 155-165; Society of American Archivists, Committee on Educational and Professional Development, "Program Standard for Archival Education: The Practicum," *American Archivist* 43 (Summer 1980): 420-422; Robert M. Warner, "Archival Training in the United States and Canada," *American Archivist* 35 (July/October 1972): 347-358. A number of others from pre-1975 may be found in Frank B. Evans, *Modern Archives and Manuscripts: A Select Bibliography* (Chicago: SAA, 1975).

6. The requirements for the position of archivist (GM-1420) call for A. "A full 4 year course in an accredited college or university which has included or been supplemented by 18 semester hours in the history of the United States or in American political science or government or a combination of these, and 12 semester hours in any one or any combination of the following: history, American civilization, economics, political science, public administration, government; or B. Courses in an accredited college or university as described in A above, plus additional appropriate education or experience which, when combined, have provided the candidate with the substantial equivalent of A above." Note that there is no reference to information or library studies.

PART 2

Education for Technical Standards and Standards Information

Standards Education Today

STEVEN M. SPIVAK, UNIVERSITY OF MARYLAND

The need for standards was of sufficient importance, even in the very early economic history of our nation, to be included in the articles of the Constitution of the United States, article 1, section 8, which states: "The Congress shall have the power . . . to coin money, regulate the value thereof, and of foreign coin, and fix the standard of weights and measures."[1]

Another early reference, recognizing the importance of standards to the business, government and *educational* communities, is inscribed in the main entrance foyer of the National Institute of Standards and Technology (formerly the National Bureau of Standards NBS). "It is therefore the unanimous opinion of your committee that no more essential aid could be given to manufacturing, commerce, the makers of scientific apparatus, the scientific work of the government, of schools, colleges and universities, than by the establishment of the institution proposed by this bill."[2]

Why then, is there such confusion over standardization or standards engineering as a profession or function,[3] or as a teaching discipline?[4]

STANDARDIZATION: A NEW DISCIPLINE?

Those who are increasingly involved with the formal study or teaching of standardization at some point address the question of whether standardization is indeed a discipline, in the academic sense of the word; or is standardization a lesser subset of a basic or applied area; or is it simply a function or process, albeit important, but not worthy of scholarly research and teaching efforts? I do not accept the latter. Let us consider, therefore, that standardization can be taught in an academic milieu, and that this is a real need.

Originally published both in *ASTM Standardization News* 13 (May 1985): 42-45 and 15 (March 1987): 62-65 and in *Standards Engineering* 36 (November/December 1984): 124-126 and 38 (July/August 1986): 87-89, 94. Reprinted with permission of both periodicals.

A second and equally important question then arises, as to whether standardization would be classified as a branch of engineering. For example, "Standards Engineering" has its own publication, society and certification program. Are standards and standardization the eminent domain of the engineers? Consider if you will, that there were no "engineers" per se at the Continental Congress, nor were there any engineers that drafted the U.S. Constitution with its obvious reference to standards.

Some discussion of these issues can be found in the preface by Verman to his fine book *Standardization: A New Discipline*.[5] He concludes that standardization has indeed quietly but steadily developed into a bona fide discipline. But is it a discipline in the strictest sense?[6] Let us briefly explore the concept of teaching standardization, by analogy with similar questions and modality used by Brannigan[7] in analyzing the field of consumer science. Brannigan defines a "discipline" as a distinct field which can be separated into component parts for the purpose of analysis; and that there should be essential assumptions about theory and methodology that can be used to integrate these component parts. By contrast with this is a "field of study," comprising an aggregation of component parts, or disparate skills, which deal with essentially the same subject matter and thus can be organized together. A "profession," or professional study, differs from the above in that it is constituted of, or leads to, collective membership with a recognized body of experts, requiring specialized knowledge, extensive training and possibly licensing.

The question of standards engineering being profession or function was discussed by LaForte,[8] who demonstrated the problems and limitations with associating standards (or standards engineering) merely as a subset of engineering. There are many persons professionally engaged in standardization who would not classify themselves as standards engineers, nor as engineers, per se. A detailed discussion of what is a standards engineer, job description and duties, training requirements, educational courses for standards engineers, and the argument for a "standards engineer" versus the "engineer in standards" is available.[9] One could engage in lively and lengthy discussion as to the exact nature of standardization, or standards engineering, but that is not the primary purpose of this paper. It is sufficient for our purposes to consider standards information and education, standardization, and standards engineering, taken together or separately, to be a field of study worthy of academic pursuit. Like the earlier analogies to consumer science,[10] standardization should embody "... normative values, ... a professional orientation, ... an expansive construction and, as befits an interdisciplinary field, should beg, borrow, or steal concepts from any area." It is not the intent of this paper to detail the benefits of teaching and learning standardization, but rather to accept them as a given; and to accept standardization as one of many interdisciplinary fields of study. It is also the purpose to explore how standardization is taught (or learned), and how one can promote an increase in such activities and their recognition in the United States, Canada and throughout the world.

THE CHALLENGE: CAN STANDARDIZATION BE TAUGHT?

From the above discussion recognizing standardization as a field of study, where then does one learn the principles, the practices, the elements of standardization? The answer is primarily through professional development. This includes the entire gamut from on-the-job training, which is perhaps the most common, to seminars, attendance at professional meetings and conferences; in short courses and continuing education; as ancillary or minor elements of other subjects, or other courses of study in colleges and universities; and least likely in full (i.e., stand alone) courses on standardization, information systems, or standards engineering.

When first considering teaching a full university course on standardization, I was informed by standards practitioners that it was foolhardy to attempt to teach standardization, for it was a subject only to be *learned* (on the job), not to be *taught*. It was fortuitous that I had difficulty in understanding this simple distinction, for it could not be farther from the truth, in my opinion.

One sees an increasing number, and variety, of organized efforts in teaching various aspects of standardization. Most of these educational activities are aimed at supplementing on-the-job training. One- and two-day seminars are regularly held on varying topics such as managing standards information, software configuration management, parts numbering and dimensional tolerancing, engineering standards, company standards workshops, and putting standards to work. Major standards organizations hold one-day standards briefing seminars, to provide an overview on the workings of the standards community, and to initiate new members into standards writing activities. Conference and seminars on standardization are a regular occurrence throughout the year. Intensive short courses, of duration in weeks rather than days, are now becoming commonplace. The U.S. Department of Defense (DoD) regularly conducts a two-week course on defense standardization and specification management. In 1982 this author conducted a two-week short course on principles and practices of standardization in the People's Republic of China, as part of the cooperative exchange agreement between the American National Standards Institute (ANSI) and the China Association for Standardization (CAS). The Swedish Standards Institution (SIS) initiated a four-week international training program on standardization – management and techniques.

The above examples of standards training and education are not meant to be exhaustive, nor testimonials of their individual success. They simply highlight the diversity of professional, continuing education type programs available to the standards community.

The question of standards education in institutions of higher learning, i.e., colleges and universities, is the most complex to evaluate. Indeed, standards as a basic tenet of modern, industrialized society are knowingly and unknowingly an integral part of courses in many fields of study. Standards are used in physical science and engineering courses, especially laboratory sections; and standards are also discussed and used in courses involving information systems, business and management, human ecology, etc. The following section will emphasize how and where standards education is utilized in colleges and universities, and will discuss experiences in developing complete, university type courses involving standards and standardization.

THE CHALLENGE OF TEACHING STANDARDIZATION

Recognizing standardization as a field of study, it logically follows that it can and should be taught in our colleges and universities. In practice it is difficult to teach complete courses on the principles of standardization. This is in contrast to the "piecemeal" approach by which student engineers, information specialists, and others get exposed to standards, or learn how to use them. But very few are ever given any formal training in the fundamental principles of standardization.

Most of what is "learned" about standardization occurs through professional development and continuing education. These aspects will be briefly reviewed. Thereafter will follow a discussion of the pitfalls, pratfalls and occasional successes in teaching standardization as an integral part of higher education.

Professional Development

Most standards practitioners agree that the likeliest options in standards education lie in the realm of professional development seminars and continuing education. In addition to the traditional on-the-job training, it is the extramural educational seminars, short courses, conferences, technical meetings, which play the overwhelming role in educating new standards professionals; and in continuing the education of standardizers already engaged in important work in the sciences and engineering, information systems or management.

There are many successful activities in professional development. Permit me to highlight just a select few examples in different areas of continuing education in standardization. The list is not complete, nor an individual endorsement of any, but rather it is illustrative of a broad range of efforts by numerous individuals and organizations.

In short courses, there are the two-day, intensive offerings in "Engineering Standards," "Configuration Management," and "Company Standardization." These are designed for personnel engaged in standardization activities and/or company standards programs. The Department of Defense (DoD), in its two-week-long Defense Specification Management Course, covers DoD concepts and policies in the preparation, coordination and use of specifications, standards and commercial item descriptions.

Standards-related conference programs abound, sponsored by professional societies, standards developing and coordinating organizations, and users: the SES annual conference and recent SES/IFAN joint conference; the annual conference of the American National Standards Institute (ANSI); joint conferences by ANSI/GSA; American Society for Testing and Materials (ASTM), Society of Automotive Engineers (SAE) and DoD on defense standardization and non-government standards. Other information standards related programs of all kinds are key among the Special Libraries Association (SLA), American Libraries Association (ALA) and others.

Our Canadian colleagues have been active as well, with standards oriented professional education. Notable were activities of Phil Preston and the program on "Putting Standards to Work." More recent were the pioneering programs by the Education Department of the Standards Council of Canada, promoted by Dennis Coffey and Al Tunis.

Professional Education

A continuing program of professional education has been undertaken by the Standards Engineering Society (SES). These activities are expanding the overall base of knowledge, dialogue, resources and teaching/seminar activities for standards professionals.

An effort is being made to identify resource materials pertaining to many aspects of standards education. Recent offerings, for example, include IHS's "Information Sources"[11] seminar kit, with visuals, student workbook and study guide. Another study-seminar guide[12] is ASME's pressure vessel, codes and standards workbook for engineering students. SES's publication of the *Economics of Standardization*[13] is the first book in a continuing series on major issues of standardization.

As part of the expanding list of resources for use by standards professionals and educators, there are numerous standards bibliographies.[14,15] This book includes new bibliographies on (a) a comprehensive monograph-resource on general standardization in North America, and (b) library and information services.

The Fallacy in Standards Engineering Education

There is a common fallacy, in the author's opinion, when one first thinks of the more formal teaching of standardization in higher education. Based on the experiences of standards education professionals, the logical assumption is to expect a friendly reception to teaching standardization within the engineering curricula. As logical as that might appear in theory, regrettably it is far removed in practice. In general, within the four-year (or five-year "co-op") engineering programs, there is little or no interest in any *formal* teaching of standards or standardization per se. A 1984 article and survey of over 300 industries makes this point demonstrably.[16] They conclude: "that the end product of the university system – the engineer – is absorbed in general by industry that is code and standards oriented. Consequently, industry would prefer to employ a young engineer with more training in applicable codes and standards. Paradoxically, Kimbrell found in his study that there were no required courses devoted to codes and standards at any university. . . . Not only do the graduates not know the codes, they do not even know that codes and standards exist."

There are reasons for this apparent fallacy. Very few seminars or courses on standardization are offered in the engineering schools of our colleges and universities in the U.S. or Canada. There are numerous, competing demands for the limited available time and a heavy burden of coursework within existing engineering programs. A full course on the principles of standardization has to compete with other demands in systems analysis, computer-aided design, higher mathematics, computer programming, materials science, etc., and in an already tight degree program. It is my conclusion that the standardization field has not, and likely will not, be fully appreciated or promoted within existing engineering programs for the following reasons.

To quote Calvelli-Taylor again:[17] "the most outstanding deficiency in the new graduates is one that the universities will probably not take very seriously, i.e., there is little or no incentive for a young instructor . . . to devote time to develop a course centered on codes and standards. Such activity does not generally result in promotion, pay raises or tenure."

Industrial managers often complain that many of today's student engineering graduates cannot write short, concise, competent technical reports. Their public speaking skills are poor. They may not have learned design and drafting, or be competent in statistics and statistical quality control. Why then, given these *other* critical needs, does anyone assume that recent engineering graduates should also have learned about codes and standards, or standardization; or be taught its fundamentals, principles and practices, design and drafting, the "grunt" work of writing specifications, or applying standards to industrial design?

Putting Principles into Practice

The situation is more encouraging, however, when one moves away from traditional engineering schools. There is more flexibility in two-year programs of engineering technology. Programs such as these have shown interest in promoting applied standards engineering courses, and in the training of standards engineers with specific orientation and skills (telecommunications or software configuration management, for example).

But in conventional engineering programs, it is recognized that extensive use of standards may occur, although the emphasis as noted earlier was "piecemeal." Engineering students may use standards, but it is unlikely that they have any conception of where, how, or why such standards were developed. This author, while an engineering student, was regularly exposed to standards of the American Society for Testing and Materials (ASTM), and the American Association of Textile Chemists and Colorists (AATCC). But standards development in particular, and standardization in general, were seldom discussed, critiqued, or placed in any larger context of importance. Standards, specifications and codes are more often given to engineering students as the "gospel," or as a convenient cookbook approach to laboratory testing and test method development. This mere introduction is of some value to all students, but as a basis for understanding standards and standardization it is sorely lacking.

It is in the social sciences, information and library sciences and in applied science programs, that more novel and innovative approaches to standards education are occurring. Colleges of human ecology, and of library and information sciences/services, have shown considerable interest and indeed have ongoing courses in standardization. Schools of business and industrial management, as well as programs of finance and economics, are also examples where either standards education or research on standardization have been incorporated within their programs. Verman maintained that the recognition and value of standards education, especially by educators outside of the traditional engineering schools, is vital. He stated that it is just as logical to teach standardization as a management or applied science discipline as it is to teach standardization as a branch of engineering.

ASTM Faculty Interim Program

There are some important developments in the promotion of standards education in colleges and universities, which are worthy of note. A pioneering effort has been the Faculty Intern Program of the American Society for Testing and Materials. ASTM moved to bolster interest in standardization among academicians. A subcommittee on University Relations, acting on a recommendation from the ASTM Board of Directors, was charged with implementing an "internship program for selected professors." In 1976, the program began as a two-day comprehensive seminar on standardization which attracted fourteen faculty members from seven colleges and universities. Following the seminar, they attended committee meetings of their choice where they were exposed to the actual standards-writing process. All expenses were borne by ASTM, and the author assisted ASTM in its development.

Because of the enthusiastic response to this pilot program, it was repeated by ASTM from 1977 through 1983. Approximately 250 professors from the United States and Canada, representing over 100 colleges and universities and a wide variety of disciplines, participated in the program.

The objective of the program was to inform educators about standardization – what a standard is, how it is developed, the different types of standards, who writes them and how they are used. It is anticipated that once armed with this information these individuals will incorporate it into their courses, and perhaps develop seminar programs or other courses on standardization.

The beneficiaries of any academic affairs programs are innumerable. The instructor expands his expertise; the student gleans practical knowledge; future employers recruit better qualified personnel; and, lastly, standards developers, trade associations and other standards bodies will reap the dual benefit of a heightened general awareness of standardization and future members more accurately attuned to the standards development system.

There is now an increasing coterie of faculty members who are utilizing considerably more standards information within their existing courses. Standards-related courses have been introduced, with emphasis on a specific discipline, orientation, or educational-professional needs. As only one example among many, there follows a brief case study of the author's fifteen year experience in teaching a successful university credit course focused entirely on principles and practices of standards and standardization, and more recently with issues on international standardization and trade.

It is worth noting the first credit course on standardization in Canada. The 1981 course was called "Normes et Protocoles," a 29-session, two-credit course at the Ecole Polytechnique Engineering School affiliated with the

University of Montreal. The Canadian course is for credit toward a master's degree in engineering process control.

Two of the essays that follow in this part of this volume, one by Dean Toni Carbo Bearman and the other by Michael B. Spring and Martin B. Weiss, all of the University of Pittsburgh, relate their experiences in curriculum development and standards education for students of library and information science.

A Case Study

What began at the University of Maryland over fifteen years ago as an educational experiment, introducing a broad-based standardization course to all social science majors, has been very successful. A standards related course entitled "Product Standards" has been taught once each year since then. The university department offering the course has a consumer product performance, testing-marketing and applied economics orientation. One of their foci is on products (and services); thus "Product Standards," although the course is much broader in scope than its name. The product standards course spawned another course entitled "Product Safety," which is also taught each year. A third course in the sequence is "Products Liability and Government Regulation." In this latter effort, taught by an attorney, the course includes standardization as an important element in the development of modern tort law, and in products liability. The course also includes the development of government regulation under formal or informal rulemaking procedures. Recognizing that there are other college and university efforts in various aspects of standardization, the author merely wishes to highlight these University of Maryland activities as an illustrative case history of what can be done.

Approximately fifteen years ago, the department faculty decided that there was an identified need for a standards-related course. Based primarily on a prior engineering background and familiarity with technical standards, the author was the only faculty member willing to undertake this effort.

Advice and counsel was sought from other colleagues in standardization at that time, but I was given little hope or encouragement. Being sufficiently foolhardy to not believe my elders, I introduced the teaching of standardization with a new, "stand-alone" course at the University.

An average of twenty or more students completed both the standards course, and the safety course, each year. Both the standards and safety courses have been taught not only by the author, but also by other adjunct faculty. Student response in these courses has been excellent. The standards course is three credits, fifteen weeks long, with about forty total classroom hours. Several different books have been used as a text, the most successful being Verman,[18] which is now out-of-print. Due to the University's proximity to the Washington, D.C. metropolitan area, many standards professionals work in this area. Supplementing the professor's lectures, an additional eight or ten guest lecturers present their varied standards experiences within the course format. As a practical matter, I have also taught the entire course without any guest lecturers – both approaches work well. In some semesters, field trips to the National Institute of Standards and Technology, or to an actual standards committee meeting, have been included. Students enjoy the guest lecturers and/or field trips because these events demonstrate how the principles, aims and benefits of standardization are put into actual practice.

In addition, the standards organizations and their representatives have a wealth of supplementary written material (articles, reports, brochures, analyses). These materials are freely made available to each student. Permission to photocopy or reprint these materials, or other published standards articles, has always been granted.

A brief outline of the various topics covered within the Product Standards course follows. This outline is presented merely to demonstrate how it is done at the University of Maryland, and elsewhere in institutions such as the University of Pittsburgh.

Product Standards Course – Sample Outline and Topics

A. Introduction to standards and standardization.

B. A history of standardization – from biblical to modern times.

C. Standard terms and definitions, and the principles of standardization.

D. The various types, forms, uses of standards; including standards of measurement and the S.I. (metric) system.

E. The aims and benefits of standardization, including management objectives.

F. The standardization space, and a standards taxonomy; from company standards to national, regional and international standards. Review of the major standards organizations and their inter-relationships.

G. An overview and structure of the U.S. and world standards system – voluntary or non-government, mandatory, treaty and non-treaty standards development.

H. ANSI and coordination of the American National Standards System, international representation to ISO and IEC.

I. ASTM as a developer of voluntary, consensus standards.

J. Testing and safety certification – Underwriters Laboratories.

K. Information labeling, comparative testing on products.

L. Product certification, testing and laboratory accreditation.

M. The National Institute of Standards and Technology, and government standards coordination.

N. OMB Circular A-119, and the private sector-public sector standards interface. Federal use of non-government standards, and standards policy.

O. Voluntary (non-treaty) and treaty regional and international standards. The European Community and EC 1992 standards harmonization. National versus regional versus international standardization.

P. The GATT Code, standards and international trade, Uruguay Rounds. Agreement on technical barriers to trade, known as the "Standards Code."

Q. Economic analysis of standardization, value analysis, benefit: cost analysis. Class case study on the economics of standardization.

R. Legal implications of standardization. Antitrust, fairness considerations, principles of due process. Government intervention in the standards process.

S. Development of mandatory standards and regulations. Voluntary vs. mandatory standards. Standardization by federal regulatory agencies, state and local authorities.

Notes

1. Constitution of the United States, article 1, section 8, as discussed in "Weights and Measures Standards of the United States: A Brief History," *NBS Special Publication* 447 rev. (March 1976): 2-3.

2. Inscription in the entrance to the National Bureau of Standards, from the Committee report of the U.S. House of Representatives, on the bill to establish the National Bureau of Standards, May 14, 1900.

3. J. T. LaForte, "Standards Engineering-Profession or Function?" *Standards Engineering* 35 no. 3 (June 1983): 52-53.

4. "Discipline" defined as "a branch of knowledge or learning;" and "a subject that is taught: a field of study," (from various Webster's dictionaries.)

5. L. C. Verman, *Standardization: A New Discipline* (Hamden, CT: Archon Books, 1973). This comprehensive book on standardization is now out-of-print.

6. See note 4.

7. V. M. Brannigan, "Defining Consumer Science: A Legal Scholar's View," Proceedings of National Conference on Consumer Science in Institutions of Higher Education, Madison, WI, July 1982.

8. LaForte, "Standards Engineering."

9. R. Glie, ed. *Speaking of Standards* (Boston: Cahners Books, 1972), 73-108. See Part 2, The Standards Engineer.

10. Brannigan, "Defining Consumer Science."

11. T. E. Shoup, S. P. Goldstein and J. Woddell, "Information Sources: A Guide for the Engineer," Information Handling Services, (Inglewood, CO: Information Handling Services, 1984), 50 pages.

12. American Society of Mechanical Engineers, "An Introduction to ASME Codes and Standards for Mechanical Engineering Faculty and Students," American Society of Mechanical Engineers, (New York, NY: ASME, 1984), 35 pages.

13. R. B. Toth, ed, *The Economics of Standardization* (Minneapolis, MN: Standards Engineering Society, 1984), 112 pages. The Standards Engineering Society is now headquartered in Dayton, OH.

14. C. A. Chapman, "Bibliography on the Voluntary Standards System and Product Certification," in *NBSIR 79-1900* (Gaithersburg, MD: National Bureau of Standards, October 1979), 22 pages.

15. K. A. Winsell and S. M. Spivak, "Selective Readings in Standardization for Companies" in *Standards Management: A Handbook for Profits* (New York: American National Standards Institute, 1990): 453-493.

16. E. Calvelli-Gaylor, "Educational Needs," *Mechanical Engineering* (April 1984): 52-55.

17. Calvelli-Gaylor, "Educational Needs."

18. Verman, *Standardization: A New Discipline.*

Standards Engineering Education

THE AMERICAN SOCIETY FOR ENGINEERING EDUCATION AND THE
STANDARDS ENGINEERING SOCIETY, WITH THE AMERICAN NATIONAL
STANDARDS INSTITUTE, THE AMERICAN SOCIETY FOR TESTING AND
MATERIALS, THE U.S. DEPARTMENT OF DEFENSE, AND OTHERS

This report summarizes the results of discussions held during the Forum on Standards in Engineering Education in August 1988, co-sponsored by The Standards Engineering Society and The American Society for Engineering Education. The primary theme of the conference was the need to better educate personnel, both technical and non-technical, on the understanding and importance of standards to industry and government. This would not only promote product safety and quality, and design and manufacturing productivity, but would also serve to make America more competitive in a world market. It was agreed by the conference attendees that newly hired personnel, and particularly engineers, show a serious lack of education that would provide them with the understanding and expertise in the utilization of specifications, standards, and the standardization process. Further, it was agreed that appropriate actions needed to be taken by the four communities represented at the forum in order to correct this deficiency.

Among the underlying problems considered to be driving the need for better training in the development and use of engineering specifications and standards were:

1. *Government* – A need to eliminate an over-reliance on military standards and a greater use of readily available and relevant commercial standards. The purpose of this action is (a) the more rapid conversion of technology into usable military products and (b) essential cost reductions, i.e., affordability.

Originally summarized in *Standards Engineering* 40 (November/December 1988): 138, 144. Reprinted with permission.

2. *Industry* – A need to improve product quality and productivity factors. Central among industry's concerns was an enhanced ability to meet foreign competition through the greater use and adaptation of existing bodies of knowledge, including standardization.

3. *Academia* – A need to more appropriately relate engineering theory to practice by better instructing students in the use of existing and proven bodies of knowledge.

4. *Society* – An awareness of the deficiency in the training and accreditation of engineering programs, and the current lack of a "vehicle" for inducing these changes.

MAJOR FINDINGS

The major findings of the panels and working groups were as follows:

1. Recent graduates receive little, if any, practical education/training in the importance of specifications and standards in the commercial world. That is due to the lack of emphasis on these matters in engineering programs.

2. Despite their understanding of the need for this form of education, academia has not initiated actions to incorporate courses within existing curricula. The reasons for this include the lack of emphasis on these matters in our universities, particularly in the business schools and in schools of engineering; the lack of pressure from accrediting professional and employer groups insisting on this form of training; and the lack of national attention to the problem.

The root causes of these outcomes were discussed by each of the professional groups attending the meeting. It was agreed the problem areas noted above are the result of the fact that:

1. The impact on industrial efficiency and international competitiveness with the use of a fully articulated role of specifications and standards is not clearly understood or appreciated either by the employer or the engineer.

2. There is a lack of involvement and research by the academic community in standards and standardization as well as in the process itself used for development of standards and standardization programs.

3. Professional societies lack a coordinated, unified approach to assist both industry and academia in highlighting and resolving the problem.

4. There is an absence of a substantive role by the government in the subject matter. It does not function well in this regard either as the buyer of products or in its response to the growth of foreign competition in the United States and Canada.

5. In response to these problems, government and industry have training programs in specifications and standards. But these programs are tailored to their specific needs and requirements and are not broad enough to provide the more generalized knowledge needed by graduate engineers.

ACTION ITEMS

As part of the consensus that evolved during the forum, it was agreed that the following actions should be taken by the professional groups in attendance at the meeting.

All

1. Develop an awareness of the problem at the national level by initiating publications and meetings designed to make other professionals aware of the problem. Focus on top managers of industry and government, and professional and trade associations, and promote the benefits of standards and standardization activity based on return of investment and international competition.

2. Develop and implement a coordinated approach designed to convince the National Science Foundation (NSF) and the National Academy of Engineering (NAE) to fund and disseminate *research* on standards and specifications.

3. Develop and implement a coordinated approach designed to convince the NSF and NAE of the need to fund the *development and teaching* of undergraduate and graduate programs in specifications and standards.

4. Meet with academic and professional accrediting and licensing bureaus in order to (a) make them aware of the need for specifications and standards education and (b) to include this form of education in required qualification exams.

Individual action items assigned to each of the groups are as follows:

Academia

1. Address student needs.

a. Sensitize accreditation bodies to the need for "standards literacy" in professional education.
b. Offer standards-related lectures, seminars, and experiences.
c. Expand awards programs to recognize standards programs and courses.
d. Propose a new working group in specifications and standards at the National Academy of Engineering.

2. Educate the engineer further.
   a. Establish working groups to prepare sample module(s) for review by employers, engineering society, and academic groups.
   b. Expand upon existing programs.
   c. Develop new teaching and resource materials.
   d. Integrate several disciplines in order to further disseminate knowledge on the proper use of specifications and standards.

3. Coordinate the standards education process.

4. Expand continuing education programs.

Government and Industry (The Employers)

1. Inform industry and academia of the critical role played by standards and standardization programs in achieving product and process quality, cost reductions, and the ability to compete in a world market with conflicting national standards.

2. Inform industry and academia of the need to provide awareness and training both in business and technical schools with respect to standards and standardization programs, and the need for academic research and participation in these areas.

3. Work with various academic and professional accreditation and licensing bureaus in order to convince them to incorporate specifications and standards in their educational and licensing procedures.

4. Work with the National Academy of Science and National Academy of Engineering in order to (a) get them to recognize the problems and (b) to search for solutions.

5. Provide incentives to professional bodies and academic institutions to develop and implement training and educational programs in the field of specifications and standards.

6. Investigate the use of standards in foreign countries and adapt or adopt new procedures in the U.S. based on the "lessons learned" from this exposure.

7. Continue to develop and offer in-house training and education programs to its employees and specific contractors. Involve the academic communities in these training programs.

Professional Societies

1. Voluntary Standards Bodies (VSBs) should promote involvement of educators in all standards activities by:
   a. funding the development and publication of teaching materials for specific courses, and
   b. forming an Educators Advisory Council to advise boards of directors and staff.

2. The American Society for Engineering Education (ASEE) should encourage the Accreditation Board for Engineering and Technology (ABET) to include specifications and standards in undergraduate curriculum.

3. The Standards Engineering Society (SES) should develop:
   a. a catalog of available standards publications related to specifications and standards education, and
   b. a catalog of available standards courses and their times, places, and contents.

4. Professional societies should:
   a. promote literature explaining standards to the general public,
   b. promote advertising in popular magazines and on television explaining the value of conformance to standards,
   c. develop a program similar to a White House conference on U.S. Quality and Productivity,
   d. pursue support of the following alternatives:
      (1) integration of safety, quality, and productivity standards into existing college courses in engineering, and
      (2) develop specific standards courses on engineering design resources at the undergraduate, graduate and post graduate levels, including both academic based curricula and extension and correspondence courses.

Toward the Development of a Model Standards Curriculum for Library and Information Sciences

TONI CARBO BEARMAN, SCHOOL OF LIBRARY AND INFORMATION SCIENCE, UNIVERSITY OF PITTSBURGH

As technical standards become increasingly important for the information field, the question of how to educate professionals about standards has been raised repeatedly. The National Information Standards Organization (NISO) has grappled with this question and in 1987 asked the University of Pittsburgh's School of Library and Information Science (SLIS) whether it was willing to develop a model standards curriculum for use by the library/information science profession. Developing a model presents many difficulties, including those inherent in establishing anything that will be examined with all its flaws, scrutinized, criticized, and inevitably, found to be less than perfect. A second problem concerns the difficulty any one school has in providing a single curriculum for adaptation by many other very different schools, which vary greatly in size, faculty, student bodies, strengths, and so on. The University of Pittsburgh accepted the challenge because we had believed for some time that such a curriculum was needed.

CHALLENGES IN DEVELOPING A STANDARDS CURRICULUM

Also, this request has provided the opportunity to look more closely at the area of standards, to explore new courses, and to begin to identify how standards should be appropriately incorporated into other courses in the school's curriculum. The process of developing a standards curriculum has raised a number of challenges, and this paper highlights four of them.

This paper is based in part on a presentation made at the American Library Association (ALA) Library and Information Technology Association (LITA) Conference, 4 October 1988.

The first focuses on meeting the needs of a diverse student body and its future employers. SLIS is the largest library and information school in North America, with more than 600 students ranging in age from 19 to 60 and having varying backgrounds. There are two departments: information science and library science. Programs in information science include the bachelor of science in information science (BSIS), master of science in information science (MSIS), master of science in telecommunication (MST), and the Ph.D. degree. Library science programs include the master of library science (MLS), Ph.D., certification in the school library and agricultural information specialist programs, and a joint MLS/master of divinity. Both departments also award certificates of advanced study and provide continuing education programs.

Over a typical one-year period, the school hosts Hubert H. Humphrey fellows, Fulbright scholars, and a series of distinguished visiting scholars from several countries. At present nearly 10 percent of the graduate student population is from outside the United States, representing 19 countries.

Graduates work in a variety of settings: libraries of all types, many different corporations including information-on-demand companies, the information industry, universities, state and federal governments, international organizations like UNESCO, and even a robotics project proposed for the space station. Graduates must be prepared for many different, changing, and demanding careers.

The second challenge is to meet the needs of the faculty. The varying backgrounds of our faculty and staff make SLIS a unique educational environment. With 36 full-time faculty, 27 staff members, 12 adjuncts, and 5 teaching fellows in a typical term, the interest in and familiarity with standards and the standards-making process range widely.

The third challenge entails incorporating standards into a diverse curriculum. Courses offered during a typical fall term number over 60, plus 64 separate sections or independent studies. Courses include (to name but a few) interactive programming, human factors in system design, information storage and retrieval, artificial intelligence, network concepts, voice and data telecommunications, local area networks, collection development and management, oral history/oral tradition, library services for the underserved, world librarianship, resources for children, storytelling, library services to the aging, indexing and abstracting, history of books, printing and publishing, records management, legal issues in information handling, and information counseling.

The final challenge is to attempt to meet the needs of the nearly 60 other schools in the United States and Canada. According to the latest Association for Library and Information Science Education (ALISE) statistics, these schools have an average of nine faculty; no other has a telecommunications program, and few have an undergraduate program. Each school has its own focus and areas of strength and many are involved in the standards process.

STEPS TO DEVELOPING A STANDARDS CURRICULUM

The first step in developing a model standards curriculum was to decide whether a single introductory course was needed or whether we should include standards in most, if not all, of our courses. We decided to begin by developing an introductory course at the *master's level* to be offered to students in both departments. SLIS is very fortunate to have among its many distinguished faculty members Dr. Michael B. Spring, who is expert in the area of information technology standards. The introductory class has been taught twice and is cross-listed in both departments. A second course on the information technology standardization process is planned. (See the following article by Spring and Martin B. Weiss for a discussion of these two courses.)

Our next step was to examine all of our other courses and to suggest to members of the faculty which standards they might wish to consider including in their courses. We will be working very closely with NISO, ANSI-X3, and ALISE to encourage the incorporation of the latest information on standards and their development into curricula to meet the needs and interests of all the other library and information science schools. In addition, we feel that these recommendations for course development will be adaptable to other types of programs, such as computer science departments, business schools, and the engineering community. We have also received expressions of interest from the National Institute of Standards and Technology, the Standards Engineering Society, and the State Library of Pennsylvania.

We will continue to share information with the standards community and with other library and information science educators, and we welcome their ideas and suggestions. The model to be developed is intended as one possible curriculum for consideration, review, adaptation, and, one hopes, adoption (at least in part) by other schools. With the help and participation of the library and information community, a series of curricula can be developed to provide the best education possible for our future colleagues.

Education in Information Systems Standards

MICHAEL B. SPRING AND MARTIN B. WEISS, DEPARTMENT OF
INFORMATION SCIENCE, UNIVERSITY OF PITTSBURGH

Computer science, telecommunications, and information science are new fields of endeavor, both in industry and in academia.[1] Through the 1960s and into the 1970s, these growing fields were little concerned with standardization beyond their own internal standards allowing compatibility of new products. In the 1980s, as a result of the divestiture of AT&T, the widespread adoption of microcomputing based on the IBM PC platform and the growing anticipation of interconnectability based on the development of OSI standards and unix, standards have become a crucial issue for the U.S. information industries. As a result, standards have grown as a focus of academic interest. The Department of Information Science at the University of Pittsburgh has undertaken efforts over the last two years to develop both a research program and an educational program related to information technology standardization.

Education in information technology standardization has been an integral part of a number of courses offered by the department.[2] In the spring of 1989, a course dedicated exclusively to standards was offered on an experimental basis. It was predated by a course developed and temporarily offered by Dorothy Cerni for the telecommunication program at the University of Colorado at Boulder. The course differs from Cerni's, however, in its focus on higher-level information standards – interchange and application standards as opposed to interconnection standards – ISDN, and the lower-level ISO OSIRM standards.

The current situation in information science standards education is outlined below. Information technology standards are contrasted with other industrial standards, goals for standards research and education are outlined, and overviews of both current and planned efforts in the educational arena are provided.

BACKGROUND

As in any new field, there is little consistency in the use of terms or the classification of events in the standards arena. For this reason, we begin by briefly defining the scope of the activity. Standards can emerge by three principle mechanisms. They can be the result of the free interplay of market forces (*de facto* standards), they can be established by force of law (*de jure* standards), or they can emerge from formal standards-setting bodies (voluntary consensus standards). Much of the focus in information systems standards is on the development of voluntary consensus standards. It is important to note, however, that de facto and de jure standards exist as well. An example of a de facto standard is the IBM personal computer, and an example of a de jure standard is the electromagnetic radiation standards mandated by the Federal Communications Commission (FCC).

Paul David (1987) has proposed a taxonomy of standards that is fairly comprehensive. David separates standards into reference, minimum attribute, and compatibility standards, which can be applied to technical design as well as to behavior. For example, technical reference standards are the weights and measures that are maintained by the National Institute for Standards and Technology (NIST). A technical minimum attribute standard is the minimum strength of material such as steel. In contrast, the accreditation of a college or an institution can be considered a behavioral reference standard because it is compared to an absolute reference. In information systems, one of the key problems is the interoperability of systems, so the majority of standards are technical compatibility standards.

Information systems have some characteristics that are unique with respect to other standards. Spring and Bearman (1988) have suggested the need for a more appropriate model to guide information standards development. Cargill (1989) has noted that standards frequently precede products in the information technology marketplace. Weiss (1989) has considered the strategic product development aspects of this trend. If we are to educate adequately individuals who will be responsible for the development of products and services in the information systems profession, then we will have to consider actively these unique aspects of the information systems standards.

Information systems standards often include a high level of technical complexity that spans an enormous range of disciplines. For example, standards within the Open Systems Interconnection (OSI) Reference Model range from physical and electrical considerations (e. g., V.24) to high-level software constructs and structures (e. g., ODA/ODIF, X.400). This wide range requires a set of professionals with a wide variety of technical training. It is not unusual that these professionals do not always understand each other clearly or that they are unaware of work going on elsewhere. Thus, some standards overlap others in functionality and are incompatible with each other.[3] Furthermore, a standard at an application level of detail may take advantage of some function specified at a lower level of detail; changes to the lower level must be propagated through the dependency chain.

INFORMATION SYSTEMS STANDARDS EDUCATION

Rationale

A program of standards education should take into account and explore the fundamental rationale for standards. Standards exist primarily because they offer economic benefits to users or producers. These benefits are normally expressed in terms of lower product costs or lower operations costs. Standards promote lower product costs because manufacturers have a larger market available than they would have in a market that lacked standards or had multiple competing standards. Under a unified standard, manufacturers can take advantage of production economies of scale to reduce product costs. The reduction of operating costs normally arises because of variety reduction. Variety reduction implies that a firm must stock fewer types of parts or supplies that are used for a greater range of applications.

Scope

A program of standards education must take into account the diverse set of organizations involved in setting standards. Standards are developed in several international, regional and national organizations. Preeminent among these in the information systems industry are the CCITT,[4] ISO,[5] and ANSI.[6] The CCITT tends to focus on standards that are of greater interest to the telecommunications portion of the information systems industry, whereas ISO tends to concentrate on the computer and applications portions of the industry. These organizations work together to avoid duplicating their efforts whenever possible. With the divestiture of AT&T and the formation of the ANSI T3 committee on telecommunications, ANSI addresses both of these areas for the United States.

A program of standards education in the information science field needs to provide an introduction to important standards. We suggest that the following standards are most important to any education program in the field:

OSIRM is the basic reference model for open systems interconnection. It provides the conceptual framework within which particular standards for interconnection may be understood.

ISDN is the CCITT standard for integrated services digital networks and provides the underpinning for future development of common carrier networks for voice, data, and other digital transmissions.

Presentation, session, and transport are the three layers of OSI standards crucial to all OSI applications. Their operation and functionality determine the scope of any application layer standards that might be developed.

X.400/MOTIS and *X.500* represent current ISO standards for electronic mail and directory services.

FTAM and *VT* are important base application standards for interconnection and operation. Without virtual terminal service and file transfer, access, and management, few other higher-level applications can exist.

ODA/SGML are important examples of interchange standards for documents.

GKS/Facsimile are important standards for the interchange of graphics and images.

Postscript is emerging as a de facto page description language standard for – that is, communication of information between computer and printer.

EISA/MCA are standards for the microcomputer bus that provide a great deal of insight into the complex of factors that affect the selection of a given technology as a standard.

X Windows is a standard for interface management that is being widely implemented by the information technology industry.

Organization

No sound educational program can be carried forward at the graduate level without a corresponding research program. This section articulates the educational and related research structure in the area of information technology standards. King and Brownell (1966, 95) identify the following as among the characteristics of a discipline:

1.   A domain.

2. A conceptual structure.

3. Syntactic methodology-mode of inquiry.

4. A heritage of literature.

We reference the work of King and Brownell not to suggest that standardization is an academic discipline or even to suggest that we should make it one, but simply to lay groundwork for those aspects of the academic endeavor that must be present to allow serious research and scholarship. Within the domain of standards, three requirements must be met to allow research and educational activities in the area of information technology standardization:

1. A conceptual framework for theory development must be defined.

2. A literature must be developed, collected, and organized.

3. A methodology for inquiry compatible with the domain to be studied must be developed.

Each of these is discussed below.

CONCEPTUAL FRAMEWORK FOR INFORMATION SYSTEM STANDARDS

Traditionally, both de facto and voluntary consensus standards have been based on existing products. This model makes sense where prototypes based on existing products can be easily demonstrated. In the manufacturing industries, the leading candidates usually have a history of quality, and other manufacturers have already built devices compatible to these candidates. The standard would cause minimal change in the marketplace except to provide additional credibility to the successful product. Initially, the information systems industry followed this model (Weiss, 1989). In large part, this was acceptable because the marketplace wasn't as dynamic in the 1960s and 1970s as it is today.

The pace of technological change is increasing, however. This rapid technological change leads to some unique requirements. The information systems industry is currently in the process of developing an infrastructure of standards that will guide it for years to come. One can imagine that this industry is currently where the railroads were in the middle to late 19th century. At that time, railroad gauges varied widely, causing great inefficiencies. Railroad cars had to be unloaded and reloaded as they traversed the country. Furthermore, each city had its own time, based on the sun passing through the local meridian at noon (Stephens, 1989). As the industry evolved, standard times as well as standard railway gauges were established. This made the industry far more efficient.

The information systems industry is highly competitive. Firms are racing each other to bring out products based on new technologies to perform functions that were not possible previously; others are bringing out products that are more cost effective implementations of leading-edge products. Small firms are able to compete with large firms for the purchasing dollar of the users. Standards provide a number of features to the marketplace that have a significant impact on the competitive climate. Most manufacturers believe these impacts to be desirable; otherwise, they would not participate in the development of the standards. Conceptually, information system standards, particularly U.S. standards, have the following attributes:

They are mechanisms for technology transfer. If a manufacturer develops a technology and it is included, by their urging, in a standard, they must agree to license it uniformly and consistently to all who wish to use it. For the standard to be adopted, the firm must clearly and completely explain the nature of the technology to the members of the committee. This explanation must be in sufficient detail to convince the other committee members of its practicality and superiority.

If successful, they assure large markets to manufacturers. This enables low-cost manufacturers to make large investments in large-scale production facilities and to be assured of a reasonable return on their investment. It also reduces one aspect of product development risk a firm makes when developing a product.

The development process is conservative. Firms that do not feel they can bring a product conforming to a standard and containing an innovative or unique technology to market will not support that technology, so technologies that have not been proven are seldom adopted. Furthermore, firms may prevent any single firm participating in the standards process from gaining a competitive advantage through the adoption of their technology.

They create a more predictable marketplace. Because the standards process takes place in the public domain, firms are unlikely to be surprised by a competitor. Firms will continue to attempt to differentiate their products, but the basic functionality and compatibility will remain beyond competition. The scope of the competition is limited.[7]

They extend the life cycle of derived products. The existence of an established standard will encourage users to adopt that standard for their applications. Once adopted, users are generally reluctant to switch to a new standard (Farrell and Saloner, 1986). Thus, manufacturers will continue to supply products conforming to the old standard even though a new, perhaps superior standard exists.[8] This allows manufacturers to extract additional profits from a market, particularly if it exhibits rapid technological change.

The characteristics of the information systems industry combined with the features of the standards development process has lead to what Cargill (1989) has called "anticipatory standards." These standards, instead of lagging behind products by several years, as was described in the static model above, actually precede the products. That is, manufacturers develop the standard *before* they build products. Manufacturers no longer compete to have their product adopted as a standard. Weiss (1989) has concluded that they are, in effect, performing a significant portion of their product development in the public domain. This is a rather astounding development. Some firms literally place technologies in which they have invested significant sums of money into the public domain so that they may be adopted as a voluntary consensus standard.

This aspect of the information system industry—the existence of anticipatory standards—gives it a unique character. It is this character that must be reflected in the educational programs in standards and in research on information system standardization.

LITERATURE COLLECTION

One of the difficulties that many students face in coming to grips with information technology standards is the complexity of the standards-setting arena and the diversity and complexity of the standards with which they have to become conversant. The field of information science is complex and requires the practitioner to be familiar with the range of information entities and processes employed by the client. Similarly, the information scientist must be aware of standards that may be of importance to a diverse set of end users. This situation is compounded by the evolving merger of computing and telecommunications technologies. At the University of Pittsburgh, information science includes the study, not only of operating systems and data structures, but also of human factors and cognitive information processing. Two years ago, a new degree program was added in telecommunications, which expanded the telecommunications-related graduate courses in information science from 4 to 40. It is clear that information professionals are beginning to suffer a severe case of information overload. Nowhere is this clearer than in the area of standards, where as much as $500 million are being spent annually on the development of national and international standards in the information field. Within this context, it may be that effective standards education can take place only if we adopt new methods for the publication and distribution of standards for educational use. In this context, we are exploring the use of hypertextlike systems to supplement the instructional process. The literature includes:

1. Source standards.
   a. Draft.
   b. Final.
   c. Updates.

2. Secondary standards documents.
   a. Explanatory documents.
   b. Critiques.
   c. Cross-references to related standards.
   d. Subcommittee/working group minutes, notes, and correspondence.

3. Organizational documents.
   a. Bylaws and other formal organizational documents.
   b. Publicity and explanatory material.

4. General standards documents.
   a. Popular explanations of standards.
   b. Related economic literature.
   c. Related technical literature.
   d. Related general literature.

Simply collecting these documents will not make the literature in the standards arena more accessible. The documents need to be cross-referenced both internally and externally. Generally speaking, standards do not contain indexes. Simple KWIC (Key Word in Context) indexes would help to identify the various locations in a given standard in which an important term is used. These indexes could be categorized to indicate where terms occur in multiple standards. This work could serve as the foundation for, and the beginning of, a hypertext system that would allow researchers to begin to extensively cross-reference standards using hypertext links within and across standards.

METHODOLOGY

Research and education in standards must, by its very nature, draw on methodologies developed in a variety of academic disciplines. Because the motivation for standards is rooted in cost reduction and market expansion, economics is the key discipline. Indeed, the great majority of research in standardization can be found in economics literature. The focus of this has been on the relationship of standards to market dynamics and predation. In information systems, standards often have a great deal of technical content;

effective standards participants must be competent engineers and scientists. Thus, the technologies on which information systems standards are based are critical, and the variety of disciplines that support them, such as electrical engineering and computer science, play a role. Finally, because many information systems standards are developed in committee, political theory is important. The standards research performed thus far has tended to neglect this important avenue of inquiry.

A PROGRAM OF EDUCATION

Within the masters and doctoral programs in information science and telecommunications, students are exposed to a number of courses in the areas of foundations of information science, cognitive science, and systems and technology. Standards fall in the systems and technology area and accompany course offerings in areas such as operating systems, programing languages, software engineering, interactive system design, and so forth.

Course I: Introduction to Information System Standards

Introduction

The course is an introduction to technical standards for information processing. This course introduces the concept of standards as specifications to which agreeing parties adhere in the design or production of some product. It covers the recent trends among manufacturers of information processing and telecommunication equipment to develop anticipatory standards and the emergence of standard specifications based on existing standards used by large consumers of information-processing equipment.

It addresses the spectrum of information standards, focusing on electronic standards. Industry, de facto, de jure, consensus, and anticipatory standards are considered. The course explores the creation, modification, adoption, and maintenance of standards. The course reviews the composition and operation of the major information processing standards organizations. Key standards are reviewed and implementation issues explored.[9] Issues arising from the growing importance of standards are addressed. The textbook used for the course was *Information Technology Standardization* by Carl F. Cargill.[10]

Course Goals

The goals of the course are as follows:

1. To define the basic characteristics of standards.

2. To review the impact of standards on the development of information systems.

3. To explore the processes by which standards are developed.

4. To experience the process of designing/programming information systems in accordance with some standard.

5. To examine the implications of standards for the interpretation and analysis of document creation, conversion, and design.

Course Requirements

Course requirements were designed to provide the students with a diverse learning experience related to the goals of the course that immersed them in the problems and benefits of standards. Because this kind of work is considered an essential part of the learning experience in graduate education, the nature of the outside assignments are briefly reviewed below:

1. Prepare biographic data and personal course objectives and mail to the instructor. This assignment provided several challenges: Addressing electronic mail across systems opened up a discussion of message exchange and directory services (X.400 and X.500); copy-making the documents instigated a discussion of document markup (ODA and SGML). In addition, the assignment made clear the need for style, content, and presentation standards to supplement the electronic standards.

2. Research the origin/history of a standard, such as electric plugs, book sizes, map symbols and colors, the RS232-C serial, and Centronics parallel interfaces.

3. Describe and contrast the EISA and MCA architectures. Specify which you think will dominate the market and why.

4. Write a program that accepts 15 GKS commands and produces the appropriate output on an IBM PC screen or a program that accepts information from the user about a poster (information displayed on a surface at least 500 inches square) and generates the appropriate Postscript program to produce the poster. This assignment is a minimal programming assignment that caused the students to understand enough of a standard to be able to write a program in accordance with it. The rationale for choice here is that enough has been written about these standards from an implementation point of view to allow the student to reasonably engage the activity.[11]

Students could undertake any activity of their choosing beyond the initial required activities to make up the remainder of the points required for their grade. Below are a few of the projects recommended:

1. Compare and critique Postscript and Interpress as page description languages. Make a recommendation for one or the other as a standard, or suggest why a new standard would be needed.

2. Compare and critique the SGML and ODA standards. Make a recommendation for one or the other as a standard, or suggest why a new standard would be needed.

3. Compare and critique the X11, NeWS, and Display Postscript standards. Make a recommendation for one or the other as a standard, or suggest why a new standard would be needed.

4. Research the unification of Unix:
   a. Cite the major obstacles to unification.
   b. Identify the major players and current trends.

5. Write a program to parse an SGML prologue for correct syntax.

6. Propose a standard for iconic interfaces that accommodates:
   a. Required functionality.
   b. Appearance/function restrictions.

7. Write a program that produces an X.400 mail message.

8. Write a standard for an electronic catalog interface.

9. Write a program that produces a Postscript description of the Pitt logo and places it at various places on a page, in different rotations, and in different sizes.

In addition to these recommended projects, students were free to suggest projects on their own. In the first offering, some of the projects undertaken by students were:

1. A paper on models of the standards process based on Cargill's keynote lecture and the model presented in his book. The paper is currently being revised for submission to ANSI.

2. A paper on International Standardized Profiles (ISPs) based on a lecture to the class by Ms. Dorothy Cerni, author of *Standards in Process: Foundations and Profiles of ISDN and OSI Systems*.

3. A critique of the Department of Defense (DOD) standard for Computer-aided Acquisition and Logistics Support – CALS. DOD has

indicated that contractors must be prepared to comply with the standards specified under CALS. The analysis examined the standard and assessed the likelihood of meaningful compliance with it.

Course Outline

The preliminary outline of the course is presented below. Three notable modifications were made to this outline during the offering of the course. First, more than three hours of course lecture time, out of 45, were devoted to models for standards and the standards process. Second, three hours were devoted to the topic of ISPs which had not been anticipated in the initial outline except as an outgrowth of the MAP, TOP, and GOSIP efforts. Finally, a significant amount of class time was devoted to discussion, where appropriate, of research questions that might be addressed in the standards arena.

1. Introduction
   a. The purpose of standards.
   b. The history of standards development.
      i.   Nationally (in the U.S. and in other countries).
      ii. Internationally.
   c. Types of standards.
      i.   De facto standard.
      ii. De jure standard.
      iii. Formal consensus standards.
      iv. Informal consensus standards.
   d. The impact of standards on a typical information transaction.
   e. A description of the standards that come into play in a typical session at a terminal or microcomputer – such as, a session with an online database.
   f. Terminal design.
   g. Character sets.
   h. Escape sequences and control characters.
   i. The communications interface.
   j. LAN (local area network) cabling and protocols.
   k. Programming language.

2. Standards evolving from vendor and institutional success in a market.
   a. Examples of de facto and informal consensus standards.
   b. The construction industry – windows, studs, joists, stairs, escalators, etc.
   c. The electrical plug, wiring, and appliances.
   d. The role of Underwriters Laboratory (UL).

    e. A look at a few information-related de facto and informal consensus standards.

    f. Paper sizes, types, book sizes, cataloging.

    g. PC-DOS, IBM PC, SNA, Postscript.

    h. The evolution of selected standards.

    i. Costs and benefits of "natural selection" in standards evolution.

3. De jure and client determination standards.
   a. De jure standards.
      i. Safety standards – automobile standards.
      ii. National security standards – highway standards.
   b. The impact of major clients on the evolution of standards.
      i. Military standards – DIF, MIL-STD-188, TCP/IP.
      ii. Unix OS in education.
      iii. General Motors and Boeing – MAP/TOP.

4. Consensus standards: the standards bodies.
   a. International Standards Organization (ISO).
      i. Total of 83 national representatives.
      ii. American National Standards Institute (ANSI).
      iii. British Standards Institute (BSI).
      iv. Deutsche Institute fur Normung (DIN).
      v. Association Francais de Normalization (AFNOR).
   b. Consultative Committee on International Telegraph and Telephone (CCITT).
   c. European Computer Manufacturers Association (ECMA).
   d. American National Standards Institute (ANSI).
      i. Institute of Electrical and Electronics Engineers (IEEE).
      ii. Engineering Industries Association (EIA).
      iii. National Information Standards Organization (NISO) and others.

5. Consensus standards: the development process (ANSI, as an example).
   a. Accreditation of a developer.
   b. Planning and coordination of standards.
   c. Designation, publication, maintenance, and interpretation of standards.
   d. Procedures for committee standards development.
      i. Organization of the committee.
      ii. Responsibilities, officers, and membership.
      iii. Subgroups of the committee.
      iv. Meetings.
      v. Voting.

      vi. Submission.
      vii. Communications.
      viii. Termination of the committee.
      ix. Appeals.
      x. Maintenance.
   e. Role of associations.

6. The ISO-OSI model and its implications.
   a. The seven layer model.
   b. Standards suites, MAP, TOP, GOSIP/CALS.

7. Consensus standards: examples include EIA RS-232C, X.25, CCITT V.24, SGML, Z39.2, Z39.59.

8. Information display standards.
   a. Windowing system languages: Presentation Manager, X window system, NeWS.
   b. Page description languages: Postscript, Interpress.

9. Information encoding standards: Z39.2, DCA/RTF/Interscript, SGML/Z39.59, ODA/ODIF.

10. Mail and messaging standards: X.400, X.500.

11. Standards validation organizations – the new UL, the NBS lab, the Corporation for Open Systems (COS), SPAG, POSI.

12. Ethical and legal issues in standards.
    a. Ethical issues.
    b. Liability of the standards groups, validating organization, or the vendor.

13. Political issues in standards development.
    a. Vendor participation.
    b. Professional associations.
    c. Responsibilities to ensure vendors' adherence to standards.
    d. National governments and international organizations: UN/UNESCO, NATO, EEC.
    e. Disagreements within states and regional systems between national and international standards (e.g., CCL).

14. Economic issues in standards development.
    a. Impact on research and development.
    b. Impact on end-user purchases.
    c. Cost of the standards themselves.
    d. Impact of technological developments.

Course II: Simulation of the Standards Development Process

In contrast to the first course in standards, described above, this course is more hands-on. In this course, students are given the opportunity to develop a standard over the course of the semester in a simulated standards committee.

The purpose of this simulation is twofold: to provide students with experience in the standardization process and to provide a capability for in-depth observation of and experimentation in the standards development process. The first objective is intended to address the industry's need for trained and experienced personnel in standards development.

The second objective is intended as a research vehicle. Raiffa (1982) has had considerable success using such a simulation to develop an understanding of negotiation. This course follows Raiffa's model but extends it to a problem area where the solution domain is discrete.[12] The actual operation of standards committees is currently poorly understood in an objective, scientific sense. The formal structure of the process is well known, and many anecdotes about the process are available, but none of these comprise complete understanding of the actual processes. Such understanding may allow adjustments that could increase the efficiency and effectiveness of the developers. These adjustments can be tested in the simulated environment to measure improvements.

In this course, students will learn the nature of the standards process by developing a standard. To do this, however, it is necessary to duplicate as closely as possible the constraints and the motivations faced by the standards developers. This can be fairly complex because many constraints and motivations, sometimes conflicting, exist in the actual standards development process.

COURSE DESIGN ISSUES

Several key issues are necessary if such a course is to be successful. The resolution of these issues is critical to the development of a realistic simulation. While each of these will be discussed in some detail in subsequent sections, the overall background is outlined below.

Earlier in this paper, we characterized information systems standards as part of the competitive product development process between firms. To have a realistic and effective simulation, essential aspects of this (external) environment must be reproduced. In a competitive marketplace, one can assume that each firm has a different portfolio of technical strengths, product history, corporate culture, and corporate strategy. Each of these factors can affect the posture and behavior of a firm's representatives in a standards committee. Firms adopt positions through their representatives that they believe will give them the greatest advantage in the marketplace after the standard is complete. The objective of this game is market dominance.

SIMULATING THE MOTIVATION OF PARTICIPANTS

Participants in the committee are individuals, motivated by the desire to meet personal objectives and achievements. The employer of the participants – that is, the firm they represent – influences those personal objectives to the extent that the representative becomes a spokesperson for the firm in the standards committee. In general, a victory for the firm also is a victory for the committee participant.

In the context of the course, this motivation must be simulated through group processes. The groups must be given an identity, and a sense of group loyalty must be developed. In the actual standards development process, this group loyalty is often supplemented by economic motivation. It will not be possible to simulate this in a practical (i.e., cost effective) way in the course. Because the group loyalty is the principle binding mechanism, care must be taken so that loyalty of an individual to the (simulated) standards committee does not exceed loyalty to the original group. Limiting the frequency and duration of standards committee meetings is perhaps the most practical way of doing this.

TECHNICAL BACKGROUND

In a given standards debate, several different technical contexts, or product development objectives, exist. For example, a firm that produces CAD systems would probably have a very different technical context for digital facsimile transmission than would a firm that has historically produced mass-market facsimile machines. The nature of the research and development activities at each of these firms would probably be quite different, as would be the design objectives. The CAD manufacturer would make a different cost-performance tradeoff, for example, than the mass-market fax manufacturer. In all probability, this phenomenon would be true even though these firms would be targeting the same (new) market because their technical expertise and corporate tradition would be carried into the new market.

To simulate this divergence of technical background, students from different groups can be tutored on (different) specific technologies relating to the standard to be developed. Various recitation sections would gain expertise in a specific area and not in another. This technical training should not only cover the theoretical aspects of the applicable technologies but should also focus on applications using these technologies. Students should develop enough expertise in their technology to make them unwilling to accept the other(s) without considerable debate. When the simulated standards committee begins its deliberations, this divergent training should have an effect similar to the one that can be observed in actual standards committees.

SIMULATING THE STANDARDS SETTING PROCESS

The position of a firm is argued by the representative of that firm to the committee. This individual must have a background that is sufficiently technical to thoroughly understand the content of the contributions to the committee and the debate surrounding them. He or she must be able to adopt a position in the committee that best represents the interests of his or her firm. Second, but equally important from an overall committee participation point of view, the representative must be able to "sell" the firm's internal product designers on the committee decisions, particularly if they are contrary to the firm's initial strategy. A participant who is unable to do this will not be viewed as an effective participant by the rest of the committee because any committee decisions involving the participant may be considered tentative in the future.

There is often ambiguity between the overt and covert objectives of a firm and the position adopted by the committee. The keeper of the corporate strategy is not always there to make key decisions in a committee, so the welfare of the firm lies in the hands of a representative with personal preferences and perhaps imperfect understanding of the firm's objectives. This can be simulated in the course by having separate individuals responsible for committee participation and for the group's design decision making. It will be up to the chief designer to lay out a strategy that should be followed by the committee representative. If sufficient group identity exists, then the committee representative will make his or her best effort to represent the strategy of the group's chief designer.

COMMITTEE STRUCTURE

The formal and, to a lesser extent, the informal structure of standards committees has been fairly well documented (Cargill, 1989). From the point of view of the simulation course, it is a small matter to reproduce this structure. Note that this is one variable that we can manipulate as researchers into the standards development process.

ECONOMIC MOTIVATION

Firms incur the cost of participating in the standards process because they perceive an economic advantage to doing so. This economic advantage may take the form of competitive advantage in the specific product market covered by the standard, or it may take the form of developing good will to be used in other arenas. If the benefit is in the marketplace, then the firm has an incentive to develop a standard that is practical given their technological expertise. A standard that utilizes outdated technology or is difficult, costly, or impractical to implement is not worthwhile. Thus, the firm's representatives must ensure that the standard not only is consistent with the firm's strategy but also can be implemented cost-effectively.

Given this practicality constraint, it is important that the standard developed by the students in the simulated committee be developed into a working product by other individuals from each group. The committee participant should act only as an adviser in this capacity. To simulate the economic benefit to being the first firm to market a compatible product that works, the first group to develop a product could earn a trophy or a pizza dinner sponsored by the remaining members of the class. Bragging rights and public acknowledgment can also be a powerful motivation.

Notes

1. The Department of Information Science at the University of Pittsburgh, established in 1969, is generally credited as being the first department of information science in the United States.

2. This integration has occurred in telecommunications courses dealing with networking and protocols and in information science courses concerned with interchange and interface standards – for example, graphics and document processing.

3. For example, the V.22bis and V.26ter modem standards each define products that transmit data at 2400 bits per second over dialup telephone lines.

4. Consultative Committee for International Telephony and Telegraphy. The CCITT is a branch of the International Telecommunications Union (ITU), which, in turn, is an agency of the United Nations.

5. International Standards Organization. In contrast to the CCITT, ISO is a nontreaty organization.

6. The American National Standards Institute (ANSI) is the United States national standards organization.

7. This means that, in general, competing standards are avoided. Manufacturers can focus their competitive efforts at other aspects of the product.

8. For example, 1200bps modems are still sold widely even though modems operating at 2400bps are available for moderately higher cost.

9. Because hardware and data protocol standards are generally addressed in other courses in the curriculum, the course focuses on higher-level OSI standards and interchange and display standards.

10. Mr. Cargill, senior staff consultant to the manager of corporate standards, Digital Equipment Corporation, was gracious enough to visit and deliver a keynote lecture to the students during its inaugural term.

11. Students are encouraged to use the Unix operating system and the C language for programming work. While there is no single accepted or standard programming language or operating system, there is a growing trend to view the C language and the Unix operating system as a standard toward which we are moving for interactive system programming on multiuser/multitasking platforms.

12. In standards, the participants must often choose between two alternatives; intermediate or compromise choices are not always available. Raiffa's domain of negotiation consists of dollars, a continuous entity.

References

Berg, Sanford V. "Technical Standards as Public Goods: Demand Incentives for Cooperative Behavior." *Public Finance Quarterly* 17, no. 1 (January 1989): 29-54.

Cargill, Carl F. *Information Technology Standardization* (Bedford, Mass.: Digital Press, 1989).

Cerni, Dorothy M. *Standards in Process: Foundations and Profiles of ISDN and ISO Studies* NTIA 84-170 (December 1984): PB85-165041.

David, Paul A. "Some New Standards for the Economics of Standardization in the Information Age," In *Economic Policy and Technological Performance*, edited by P. Dasgupta and P. Stoneman (Cambridge: Cambridge University Press, 1987).

Farrell, Joseph and Garth Saloner, "Installed Base and Compatibility: Innovation, Product Preannouncements, and Predation." MIT Department of Economics, no. 411 (February 1986).

Folts, Harold C. *Data Communications Standards* (New York: McGraw-Hill, 1982).

Katz, Michael L. and Carl Shapiro, "Network Externalities, Competition, and Compatibility." *American Economic Review* 75, no. 3 (June 1985): 424-440.

King, A. R. and J. A. Brownwell, *The Curriculum and the Disciplines of Knowledge: A Theory of Curriculum Practice* (New York: John Wiley and Sons, Inc., 1966), 95.

Raiffa, H. *The Art and Science of Negotiation* (Cambridge, Mass.: Belknap Press, 1982).

Rutkowski, A. M. "An Overview of the Forums for Standards and Regulations for Digital Networks." *Telecommunications* 20, no. 10 (October 1986): 84-96.

Spring, Michael B. and Toni Bearman, "Information Standards: Models for Future Development." *Book Research Quarterly* 4, no. 3 (Fall 1988): 38-47.

Stephens, Carlene E. "The Impact of the Telegraph and Public Time in the United States, 1844-1893." *IEEE Technology and Society Magazine* 8, no. 1 (March 1989): 4-10.

Weiss, Martin B. H. "Compatibility Standards and Product Development Strategies: A Review of Data Modem Developments." University of Pittsburgh, Department of Information Science Working Paper LISO18/IS89002 (June 1989).

Weiss, Martin B. H. and Marvin Sirbu, "Technological Choice in Voluntary Standards Committees: An Empirical Analysis." *Economics of Innovation and New Technology* 1, no. 1 (1990): 111-33.

Educating Archivists for Automation

LISA B. WEBER, NATIONAL HISTORICAL PUBLICATIONS AND RECORDS COMMISSION

WHY AUTOMATION EDUCATION?

Although often chided for lack of concern about automation,[1] more and more archivists and manuscripts curators are welcoming the use of computers to obtain better control over the materials in their custody. This new level of automation activity has, in turn, fueled an equally eager pursuit of education and training opportunities. Archivists want to learn about automation in general, as well as about automated archival techniques in specific.

What may appear to be an abrupt about-face has actually been a gradual evolutionary process. Faced with the challenge of coping with the glut of documentation produced by our contemporary society,[2] some archivists have long viewed the use of automation as a logical way to handle this onslaught. Members of the profession have, in fact, been involved in the development and use of in-house computer systems since the 1960s. It is no coincidence that for the past quarter-century, those players in the "automation game" were the major, well-established institutions with staff and budgeting resources as well as access to data processing equipment and professionals; they were the only ones who could afford to invest in automation. Computer hardware, the development of customized software, and ongoing maintenance were all costly. Archivists in other institutions, could only look on from the sidelines and read in the archival literature about such systems as the Library of Congress' Master Record of Manuscript Collections; the National Archives and Records Administration's SPINDEX (Selective Permutation INDEXing) and NARSA-1; the University of Illinois' PARADIGM; and the Smithsonian Institution's SELGEM.[3]

Originally published in *Library Trends* 36 (Winter 1988): 501-518. Reprinted with permission. c. 1988 The Board of Trustees of the University of Illinois.

This scenario is, however, quite different today. A recent, and pioneering, survey conducted by the Society of American Archivists (SAA) show that over 265 archival repositories are involved in some kind of automation activity.[4] A second SAA survey, conducted to gather information for its newly formed Education Office, revealed that archivists chose automation as the *leading* management issue about which they wanted to learn more. In this survey, automation outranked such other topics as preservation, legal issues, planning, finance, and personnel.[5] Contrary to popular perception, it was evident that archivists strongly desire education and training in automation.

Why all this automation activity and such a strong interest to learn? The most important reason is that low-cost, powerful, and easy-to-use microcomputers make automation more accessible to archivists than previously. A second reason for the change is the advent and increasing acceptance of the USMARC (MAchine-Readable Cataloging) format for Archival and Manuscripts Control (AMC). These are not the only relevant parts of the archival automation education equation, however. The profession is also concurrently coming to grips with the broader spectrum of archival education. Recent approval by the SAA Council of a plan for individual certification demonstrates that the archival profession is, albeit laboriously, resolving some of its long-pondered questions about graduate archival education programs, preappointment *v.* postappointment training, and professional standards.

It is not surprising then that archivists have, to date, written very little about automation education.[6] However, as a result of these trends which are simultaneously gathering momentum (increased automation activity, education, and a clearer definition of professional archival education), educating archivists for automation has finally come to the fore.

WHAT KIND OF AUTOMATION EDUCATION?

What do archivists want to learn about "archival automation"? Unfortunately, the phrase itself can be misleading because it covers a vast spectrum of activities. Archival repositories, like every other organization entity, have a wide array of office automation tools from which to choose. Word processing, spreadsheets, and lists processing are capabilities that many "off-the-shelf," generic, commercial software packages offer to users. These tools enable archivists – and anyone else working in office environments – to perform more effectively the daily tasks of writing letters, memoranda, and narrative reports; producing mailing lists; and constructing and monitoring budgets. This paper will not focus on these kinds of general automation uses, nor will it address the concerns of machine-readable records created by automated processes, which eventually will be added to archival collections. It will, instead, concentrate on those applications of automation that are specific to the administration and use of archives.

In general, although archivists are curious about a wide range of automation activities, their interests fall into three broad categories: applications of automation in archives; the USMARC AMC format and the standards used in conjunction with it; and new and emerging computer technologies.

Applications of Automation in Archives

Archivists, by and large, have approached automation through individual archival functions rather than by developing an integrated archival automation system that would accommodate all archival functions. These functions range from collection development (solicitation files in manuscript repositories or records schedules in archives) to records administration (accessioning, processing, describing, preserving, and space management) to reference service. Building an integrated system is a complicated and sophisticated task that most archivists have neither the money nor the staff to undertake. Even though some archivists have access to mainframe and minicomputers, most archivists are microcomputer users.

The majority of archivists want to use commercial software packages to help them with a wide range of archival functions. The ease of editing and updating makes using word processing packages to produce registers, inventories, folder and box lists, catalog cards, and other sorts of finding aids extremely attractive. Archivists can also use database management software to produce inventories and indexes as well as to keep track of all kinds of administrative information, such as box location, patron registration, accessions, donor information, and collection-use statistics. Online searching of records descriptions, at any level, expands access to materials. Archivists, therefore, want to learn how to apply these automation capabilities to a variety of their activities.

USMARC AMC Format and Standards

Only six years ago, SAA's National Information Systems Task Force (NISTF) was defining its role away from examining how to approach the issue of national archival information systems (then embodied in the National Historic Publications and Records Commission's database project[7] and the *National Union Catalog of Manuscript Collections* [NUCMC] toward a new mission of establishing the "pre-conditions" for archival information exchange.[8]

When NISTF recognized the need for a common exchange format, it decided to work within existing national and international communications standards. This meant USMARC. The end product of this work was the USMARC AMC format. The AMC format provides a technical structure – a container – for exchanging data, and a framework for organizing it, but the content of the data elements is defined by standards "outside" of the format. Information-sharing works only if all those exchanging or integrating data use a common approach to describing materials. Moreover, because archivists are increasingly involved in the library community, it is imperative that they work within the broad library-standards framework. Archivists not only want to learn about the USMARC AMC format, but they also want to learn about the standards used in conjunction with the format.

Agreeing upon archival descriptive standards has been almost as elusive as the pot of gold at the end of the rainbow. NISTF, well aware of the situation, consciously decided to avoid the "depths of the descriptive standards problem"[9] when they were defining the format. Unlike the library community, which has developed and used standard rules to catalog duplicate materials for decades, the incentive of derivative cataloging never existed in the archival community because of the unique nature of the materials. Instead of a common standard, archivists developed a variety of descriptive methods.

The desire to use the AMC format, however, and to integrate descriptive information into larger library networks, is giving archivists the incentive they need to standardize description. Because the library community developed most of the standards archivists need to use with the AMC format, archivists need to learn these rules.

The Anglo-American Cataloguing Rules, 2d ed., (AACR2) and the *Library of Congress Subject Headings* (LCSH) are the most important library-created standards used in conjunction with the AMC format. Although most archivists are following Hensen's *Archives, Personal Papers and Manuscripts* (APPM), instead of Chapter 4 of AACR2,[10] AACR2 has not been entirely displaced. Archivists need to follow the rules outlined in the second part of AACR2 when constructing headings for access points to descriptions.[11] These rules and standards, however, are complex and sophisticated. Archivists need more training and education in applying them to archival description.

New Computer Technologies

As overwhelming as they appear at times, new computer technologies require archivists' attention. The whole array of laser disk technology, for instance, from videodiscs to digital optical disks and audio discs, threatens to confuse even the most technologically oriented. Nevertheless, this technology demands consideration because of its potential for storage, retrieval, and dissemination of images, data, and audio recordings, as well as for the preservation of the multiple types of media that archivists encounter. The promise of low-cost storage, repeated use without deterioration, rapid random access, interactive environments, and ease of reproduction, cannot be ignored by archivists. Other examples of technologies that archivists should monitor include the development of artificial intelligence systems and their potential archival applications,[12] high speed text search systems, and text conversion capabilities. Computer technology is evolving at a tremendously rapid rate and archivists need and want to keep informed of these recent technological advances.

WHERE ARE THE EDUCATIONAL OPPORTUNITIES?

Where are archivists finding the educational opportunities to learn about the various aspects of automation? Certainly, archivists look first within the profession itself; professional associations are providing a host of different kinds of educational opportunities.

Professional Associations and Meetings

The SAA is the principal national association for archivists and manuscript curators – it has over 4,200 individual and institutional members. One of its primary missions is to advance professional education. In response to archivists' demand for education about automation, the SAA developed its Automated Archival Information Program. Partially funded by the National Endowment for the Humanities (NEH), the primary purpose of this program is to provide education and information about automated archival activities in North America.

Two major activities of the program do this directly. The first is a workshop that introduces people to the USMARC AMC format. This two-day workshop, often given in conjunction with meetings of regional archival organizations, provides a basic understanding of the format and introduces the descriptive standards used in conjunction with it. The workshop teaches the "generic" structure (that is, the USMARC AMC format alone, not tied to a specific automated system such as the Online Computer Library Center [OCLC], the Research Libraries Information Network [RLIN], or Michigan State University's MicroMARC:amc) and gives participants a fundamental understanding of how to apply MARC AMC in their own repository settings.

A second focus of the program is the development of an automation "clearinghouse," or set of files that maintains information about the state of archival automation efforts across the United States and Canada. Specifically, SAA is creating a machine-readable database that contains information about the kinds of hardware, software, and applications which archival repositories are currently using. The purpose of the clearinghouse is information dissemination – it helps put archivists in contact with others who are using or thinking of using specific kinds of hardware and software for archival applications. Although not a structured educational activity, the clearinghouse offers multiple opportunities for archivists to interact and learn from each other. For example, archivists can share a wealth of information about software packages: applications, data element definitions, file structures, and problems encountered and solved. The possibilities are endless. Information gleaned from the clearinghouse files is periodically reported through the *SAA Newsletter*, and individual inquiries are directed to the SAA office.

SAA offers many other educational opportunities in addition to the Automated Archival Information Program. The society's Automated Records and Techniques Task Force (ARTTF) has developed a core curriculum to teach archivists and manuscripts curators the fundamentals of automated techniques. Their workshops, often held in conjunction with SAA's annual meetings, include such titles as "Basic Computer Concepts," "Automated Techniques in Archives," "Basic Data Bases and Planning Concepts," and "Integration of Data Between Commercial Software Packages in an Archival Setting." The SAA Education Office organizes and coordinates the entire array of education offerings.

In addition to these targeted opportunities that focus on automation education, SAA's annual meeting programs are filled with sessions that also grapple with archival automation issues. For example, the 1987 program included sessions entitled "Preparing for Automation: What To Do Before the Computer Comes," "Reference and the Age of Automation," "Archives Information Management: Plugging the Software Gap," and "The USMARC AMC Format: Applications for Academic Archivists." Given the demand for information about archival automation, it is not surprising that over the past five years annual meeting sessions about automation have consistently had the highest attendance.

Another SAA educational offering is a series of "Roundtables" – informal groups of archivists who come together at the annual meetings to discuss and exchange information about particular topics. Some of these roundtables have become de facto users' groups: two of them are focused on the OCLC and RLIN automated systems. SAA members have discussed forming several other roundtables, including one each for the microcomputer software packages MARCON and MicroMARC:amc. Archivists have also formed a group for MARC VM (Visual Materials) Users.

Finally, one of the most attractive educational opportunities at the annual meetings is the exhibit area. Each year, the SAA exhibit area is filled with more and more computer vendors eager to talk to archivists about their various automation products.

Another archival organization concerned about automation education is the National Association of Government Archives and Records Administrators (NAGARA). Although smaller than SAA, with approximately 300 individual and institutional members, NAGARA provides leadership for the management of government records in the United States. NAGARA's annual meeting programs consistently contain workshops and sessions about automation; the 1987 program theme, "Government Archives in an Information Age," included sessions on "Automating Records Information Systems" and the "Seven-States RLIN Project and the Future of Automation." The Research Libraries Group (RLG) project is of particular interest to government archivists because not only is it building a database of information on government records holdings, but it is developing a thesaurus of terms that describe state archives' functions, and is testing the feasibility and utility of sharing archival appraisal information online.

The Association of Canadian Archivists (ACA) is a third national archival organization that offers education about automation. Its 1987 meeting theme, "Archives and the Information Age," was similar, if not somewhat broader, than that of NAGARA. All ACA session papers and workshops were within the context of the "information age," addressing such topics as planning, automated access, designing archival databases, indexing and cataloging, and appraisal. Significantly, the NAGARA and ACA meetings marked the first time that any national North American archival organization (let alone two!) devoted an entire program to the theme of automation.

Regional archival organizations are another group within the profession, and these organizations provide a variety of educational opportunities. For such a small profession, archivists across the country have formed an astonishing number of regional alliances. The current *Directory of Regional Archival Organizations* lists thirty-six such groups.[13] These regional organizations range from large, multistate groups that have nearly 1,000 members who gather at formal biannual meetings. Examples include the Mid-Atlantic Regional Archives Conference (MARAC) and the Midwest Archives Conference (MAC), to small, local groups that congregate informally several times a year such as the Boston Archivists Group (BAG) and Twin Cities Archives Roundtable (TCART). Like the national associations, the regional groups offer a chance for archivists and manuscripts curators to learn about archival automation in a variety of ways.

For some archivists, the regional groups can be more convenient, affordable, and accessible than the national organizations.

Nearly every meeting program of the larger regional organizations includes sessions or workshops about archival automation. For instance, the Society of California Archivists' 1987 program contained a two-part session about decision-making for automation. In the spring of 1987, the Kansas City Area Archivists presented a one-day symposium entitled "History 'On Line,'" which discussed the topic of computers and historical collections. In 1986, the Midwest Archives Conference with grant funds from the National Historical Publications and Records Commission, offered a host of workshops, including three specific to automation: "Using Commercial Software in the Archives," "Introduction to MARCON and MicroMARC:amc," and "An Introduction to Using Microcomputers."

The National Archives and Records Administration is involved in several archival automation research and development projects, including optical disc technology, optical character recognition, conversion of paper-based findings aids, and artificial intelligence for reference applications. In December 1987, the National Archives held its first automation conference entitled "Automating the Archives," to describe and disseminate information about its activities.

Educational opportunities for learning about automation exist through associations and meetings outside the archival profession as well. Although many of these activities may not be directly focused on archival automation, archivists and manuscript curators have much to gain by exposure to sessions, workshops, and vendor exhibits that present innovative ideas and technology. It takes just a short leap of the imagination to see related archival applications.

The American Library Association and the Special Libraries Association offer archivists and manuscript curators a number of educational opportunities. The library community's interest, concern, and use of new computer technologies give archivists and manuscript curators the chance to see firsthand applications of automated techniques at conferences, workshops, and meetings. Those archivists who are interested in the cutting edge of research and evaluation in information science and technology should become acquainted with the American Society of Information Science (ASIS). This interdisciplinary group of librarians, computer scientists, information scientists, and vendors sees its role as promoting research and development information science. Many of the problems confronting archivists and manuscript curators are identical to those confronting other information professionals – for example, information storage and retrieval techniques and the use of artificial intelligence. ASIS provides a forum for all information professionals to come together and learn from one another.

Possibly not as well known in the library community are professional organizations such as the Association of Records Managers and Administrators (ARMA) and the Association for Information and Image Management (AIIM). These groups, both with annual meetings and regional chapters, also provide forums for learning more about automation in an information environment.

Publications

Perhaps the most accessible form of education is reading the literature concerning archival automation. As interest and activity in archival automation have increased, so have the available publications. Journal articles about specific applications, theoretical concepts and ideas, and software reviews are the most numerous. Archival journals that frequently carry these kinds of articles and reports include *The American Archivist* (SAA), the *Midwestern Archivists* (MAC), *Provenance* (Society of Georgia Archivists), and *Archivaria* (ACA). Most of the national and regional associations also publish newsletters that occasionally include archival automation news.

One of the most exciting recent events is the publication of a two-part journal entitled *Archival Informatics Newsletter and Technical Reports*. The newsletter prints updates on uses of automated techniques in archival repositories and museums, while the technical reports are assessments of particular technologies and the opportunities they present to archives and museum management. The first technical report assesses the implications of optical media.[14]

Thus far, book-length publications about archival automation are few. Two works that provide an over view of the structure and implementation of the USMARC AMC format are Nancy Sahli's *MARC for Archives and Manuscripts: The AMC Format*[15] and Max J. Evans and Lisa B. Weber's *MARC for Archives and Manuscripts: A Compendium of Practice*.[16] Richard M. Kesner's *Automation for Archivists and Records Managers: Planning and Implementation Strategies*[17] gives archivists and manuscript curators the basic principles and tools for planning and implementing automated systems. Kesner has also compiled *Information Management, Machine-Readable Records, and Administration: An Annotated Bibliography*.[18] In addition, the *American Archivist* publishes a yearly bibliography that includes an automation section.

The National Archives has published several reports summarizing research in various areas. These reports include *The MARC Format and Life Cycle Tracking at the National Archives*,[19] and *Technology Assessment Report: Speech Pattern Recognition, Optical Character Recognition, Digital Raster*

Scanning.[20] The importance of publishing and disseminating developments in archival automation cannot be overemphasized. These publications promote professional awareness and expertise and ultimately advance the entire profession.

Coursework

Taking college or university coursework is obviously the most formal approach to learning about archival automation. The 1986 SAA *Education Directory*[21] lists seventy-six multi- or single-course programs or institutes that teach archival administration. The vast majority of these programs are parts of the history and/or library and information science departments on college and university campuses. Of these, only eleven programs show courses covering archival automation.

However, most, if not all, library and information science departments offer courses in information science, computer technologies, and automated applications. In addition, many community colleges and adult education programs provide evening classes in different aspects of computer science and technologies.

Formal courses require a greater commitment of time and money than the other options mentioned earlier. On the other hand, coursework offers a depth of education and training that may not be possible in short workshops and institutes.

HOW DOES PROFESSIONAL ARCHIVAL EDUCATION FIT IN?

From the time of the presidential address at the first SAA annual meeting in 1936 up to the present, SAA membership has heard and considered numerous proposals for a structure and procedures that would establish standards for the archival profession. If archival standards are to be strengthened and extended it is imperative that archival education, both at the entry and continuing education levels, also be strengthened. Archival education is the key to professional standards.

The responsibility for archival education historically has been caught between two different academic traditions, history and library science. Early on, it was assumed that history departments would take the lead, but others saw the close parallels between library science and archival administration and so advocated placing archival education programs in schools of library science.[22] A plan to accredit archival education programs had its supporters but it did not seem feasible to the profession.

While considering how to proceed in the area of "standards," the profession concentrated on developing guidelines and models (that is, voluntary standards) in different areas of the profession. SAA's Committee on Education and Professional Development prepared guidelines for graduate education programs in 1977 and again ten years later. During the 1980s, SAA's Task Force on Institutional Evaluation developed principles and guidelines for the self-study of archival repositories. In 1986, the Society's Task Force and Goals and Priorities published a major planning document for the profession that provides a framework for archival planning and decision making.[23]

After several years of intense discussion, research, and debate, the SAA Council approved, during its January 1987 meeting, a plan to certify individual archivists. The purpose of certification is to establish the professional qualifications, knowledge, skills, and abilities of practicing archivists rather than those planning to enter the field.

Advocates for certification assert that it will create, raise, or make uniform the standards of archival practice, and that it will help to establish criteria for professional accomplishments. Opponents argue that educational standards should be strengthened first; that the program will absorb too many resources; that too few archivists will pursue certification; and that certification is philosophically wrong-headed or excessively technical in nature. Opinions for and against still run strong within the archival community, and much work remains before the concept is fully developed and workable.

How does the move toward more concrete (and enforceable) standards apply to archival automation education? The approved certification plan itself does not delineate any of the skills or experience required of a "certified" archivist. An appointed board is now beginning to wrestle with those thorny issues. The newly proposed "Guidelines for Graduate Archival Education Programs," on the other hand, does incorporate within its structure the need for archivists to be educated about automation.[24] The highly praised report of the Task Force on Goals and Priorities, *Planning for the Archival Profession*, also addresses many of the concerns about archival automation in this information age. Since "the real challenge of automation is to rethink almost everything learned about traditional archival operations and procedures,"[25] archival automation confronts the very core of archival education. It will be the profession's responsibility to see that the challenge is met.

FUTURE ARCHIVAL AUTOMATION EDUCATION: NEEDS AND DIRECTIONS

Considering the complexity, diversity, and possibilities of archival automation, an education agenda for the future is quite an exciting, if not daunting, task. Notwithstanding the current available opportunities outlined earlier in this article, there are several major areas that need to be addressed in the future.

Standards

Teaching the SAA workshops on the USMARC AMC format made the instructors keenly aware that the format itself, although initially intimidating, is relatively easy to learn. What tends to perplex archivists and manuscripts curators much more, even those who have taken cataloging courses in library school, are the standards used in conjunction with the format. For this reason, SAA, through its Automated Archival Information Program, has secured funding from NEH to develop a new workshop that will teach these standards.

The standards workshop will endeavor to familiarize archivists with the applications of AACR2, the Library of Congress Name Authority File, the *Library of Congress Subject Headings*, and other standards such as the list of function terms currently under development by the RLG Seven-States Project. The workshop will also acquaint participants with the fundamentals of the theory and practice of standards in general. Choosing and constructing personal and corporate names, subject headings, genre and form terms, and other access points are complex and difficult tasks. The standards workshop will help archivists and manuscript curators to approach this undertaking with greater understanding and confidence.

Related to the need for more education about standards is a need for expanded guidelines for archival description. With the publication of Hensen's APPM,[26] for the first time archivists and manuscript curators have a standard set of agreed-upon rules to follow to help them describe historical records. Although APPM is a successful and consistently used tool, it is not definitive in its coverage. SAA published an expanded version of APPM in the summer of 1989 as part of its NEH funding for archival standards. The revision of APPM gives archivists and manuscript curators a better, more complete set of standards to describe their materials and contributes to the development of uniform descriptive standards that can be integrated into library and other information systems.

Shared Access and Potential Uses

While archivists and manuscript curators need further education in order to create serviceable, shared databases of information about primary resource materials, they also need to exploit the applications of the existing national databases that are daily increasing in size. It is often assumed that the sole reason archivists are developing national union databases of archival descriptions is so that scholars, researchers, and other users of historical records will have more complete and timely access to archival materials. This is indeed one of the incentives for exchanging information, but archivists must go beyond just educating themselves and think about educating archival users as to how the databases can assist them in their research.

The archival profession has paid shamefully little attention to its user communities.[27] With the development of automated databases, the opportunity is ripe to do systematic, quantifiable studies of the users of archival materials. It is the perfect means of learning how people approach and get access to the information in historical records. The debates between subject access *v.* provenance as a means of retrieval,[28] and the recent assertion of the retrieval power of combining "form of material" with "function" of the creating organization, can be tested within the context of these databases.[29] Databases of descriptions of primary resource materials are new and exciting tools that have the potential for tremendous impact on the way archivists describe records. First, however, serious, rigorous research in user approaches and information retrieval strategies is required.

There are many more reasons to exchange or share information about archival records.[30] Librarians have been using bibliographic databases as a tool for collections development and archivists see similar possibilities. Many archives are interested in sharing appraisal information to help each other in making disposition decisions about the records that could potentially come into their custody.[31] In fact, the RLG Seven-States Archives Project is currently testing this concept.

Sharing authority data is another possible use of national archival databases. Although certainly not a new idea in the library community, the concept of authority control is a relatively recent arrival on the archival scene. As NISTF members defined the data elements for the dictionary, they began to see relationships or categories of information that archivists keep. One such category is authority – information about the individual or organizational creators of the materials. Biographical notes and administrative histories comprise archival authority information. Archivists are now discovering that by keeping authority records separate from but linked to records that describe the actual materials, a whole host of possibilities is becoming evident.[32]

Systems

Archivists must continue to develop and refine systems, or entice vendors to build new systems that meet the profession's needs. NISTF recognized that archivists tend to create separate automated systems for administrative control *v.* intellectual or descriptive control of the archival records. The Task

Force also recognized that these two functions were related, and it proceeded to define a standard format that would encompass both requirements. The revised USMARC AMC format contains data elements for descriptive purposes, but it also accommodates the concept of control over archival processes or actions that are performed upon the records themselves.

The format or standard structure is only half of the equation, however. Of equal importance is having software that performs the necessary functions. Being able to input action information into a MARC record does not necessarily mean one can "do" anything with it. What many archivists are looking forward to is an integrated system that can import and export USMARC AMC records; control archival and manuscript material throughout their entire life cycle; maintain more detailed levels of description; keep track of donor or scheduling data, patron use, and reference requests and other like data; and support linked authority files.[33]

Software packages with USMARC AMC record import-export capabilities currently exist that provide varying levels of control over archival materials, but further development is needed. Some members of the archival community are interested in the development of a local work-station application linked to larger networks that would maintain some data locally but would let other pieces of information migrate to the national database. Integrating more detailed finding aids, such as folder or box listings, registers, inventories, with more general levels of description within the AMC format is an additional development direction. For those who are not interested in an integrated system that can import and export MARC records, software development for a variety of archival functions is still needed.

New Technologies

The computer revolution is truly that. It has changed the shape of our lives in ways we are just beginning to recognize. Technological advancements take place at such a rapid rate that archivists constantly need to look ahead in an attempt to discern what is coming next and how the new developments will change what they are currently doing.

CONCLUSION

Automation challenges the basic assumptions underlying archival practice. More than one archival prognosticator has warned that the archival profession will be subsumed by other professions and disappear unless archivists confront the technological revolution head-on and abandon the familiar "passive role of recipient of documents to (take) a more active role in the creation, distribution, and preservation of information."[34] To do this, archivists must thoroughly educate themselves in archival automation. The opportunities are available now, and will continue to expand in the future. It may take a leap of faith to begin the educational process. New and unknown territory is always difficult at first. This education is, however, critical to the very existence of the profession. Automated techniques and applications are perhaps the most exciting area in the archival profession today, with both tremendous challenge and opportunity.

APPENDIX: ADDRESSES AND TELEPHONE NUMBERS OF THE NATIONAL ASSOCIATIONS

American Library Association (ALA)
50 East Huron Street
Chicago, IL 60611
312/944-6780

American Society for Information
Science (ASIS)
1424 16th Street, NW, Suite 404
Washington, D.C. 20036
202/462-1000

Association of Canadian Archivists (ACA)
P.O. Box 2596
Station D
Ottawa, ON
Canada KIP 5W6
613/232-3643

Association for Information and Image Management (AIIM)
1100 Wayne Avenue, Suite 1100
Silver Spring, MD 20910
301/587-8202

Association of Records Managers and Administrators (ARMA)
4200 Somerset, Suite 215
Prairie Village, KS 66208
913/341-3808

National Association of Government Archives and Records
Administrators (NAGARA)
Executive Secretariat
NYS Archives
10A75 Cultural Education Center

Albany, NY 12230
518/473-9037

Society of American Archivists (SAA)
600 South Federal, Suite 504
Chicago, IL 60605
312/922-0140

Special Libraries Association (SLA)
1700 18th Street, NW
Washington, D.C. 20009
202/234-4700

Notes

1. Lawrence J. McCrank, "The Status Quo," in *Automating the Archives: Issues and Problems in Computer Application*, ed. Lawrence J. McCrank (White Plains, N.Y.: Knowledge Industry Publications, 1981); David Bearman, *Towards National Information Systems for Archives and Manuscript Repositories: Problems, Policies, and Prospects* (Washington, D.C.: NISTF, 1983); and Richard M. Kesner, "Automated Information Management: Is There a Role for the Archivist in the Office of the Future?" *Archivaria* 19 (Winter 1984-85): 162-72.

2. Gerald F. Ham, "Archival Choices: Managing the Historical Record in the Age of Abundance," *American Archivist* 47 (Winter 1984): 11-22.

3. Thomas H. Hickerson, *Archives and Manuscripts: An Introduction to Automated Access* (Chicago: Society of American Archivists, 1981).

4. Administered by SAA's Automated Archival Information Program, this is the first time that SAA has conducted a comprehensive survey about automated archival activities in all archival institutions, regardless of repository type. Previously, SAA's Automated Records and Techniques Task Force conducted surveys about automation in various types of repositories. See Leon J. Stout and Donald A. Baird, "Automation in North American College and University Archives: A Survey," *American Archivist* 47 (Fall 1984): 394-404; Ben DeWhitt, "Archival Uses of Computers in the United States and Canada," *American Archivist* 42 (April 1979): 152-57; and Richard M. Kesner, "Automated Records and Techniques in Business Archives: A Survey Report," *American Archivist* 46 (Winter 1983): 92-95. The results of the most recent survey were still being tabulated at the time this article was being written.

5. Frederick J. Stielow, "Society of American Archivists 1986/87 Continuing Education Survey: A Preliminary Analysis" (Paper presented at the Society of American Archivists Continuing Education Conference, Savannah, Georgia, 12-14 Feb. 1987).

6. Frederick J. Stielow, "Continuing Education and Information Management: Or, the Monk's Dilemma," *Provenance* 3 (Spring 1985): 13-22; M. H. Fishbein, *A Model Curriculum for the Education and Training of Archivists in Automation: A RAMP Study* (Paris: Unesco, 1985); and Lawrence J. McCrank, "Prospects for

Integrating Historical and Information Studies in Archival Education," *American Archivist* 42 (October 1979): 443-55.

7. Larry J. Hackman et al., "The NHPRC and a Guide to Manuscript and Archival Materials in the United States," *American Archivist* 40 (April 1977): 201-06.

8. Richard H. Lytle, "An Analysis of the Work of the National Information Systems Task Force," *American Archivist* 47 (Fall 1984): 357-65.

9. Ibid., 360.

10. Chapter 4 of AACR2 is still valid and is used by some repositories.

11. Although outside the scope of this paper, it would be misleading to imply that archivists are entirely satisfied with these standards. Steve L. Hensen in "Squaring the Circle: The Reformation of Archival Description in AACR2," *Library Trends* 36 (Winter 1988): 539-42, details the problems archivists encounter using AACR2. Using LCSH presents problems for archivists as well. Problems include the inconsistencies within LCSH; the use of contemporary, not "historical" terms; chronological subdivisions that have been arbitrarily developed based on current book cataloging; form subdivisions; and geographic access. It is generally recognized, however, that in spite of all its problems it is necessary to work within the LCSH structure to ensure inter- and intra-institutional compatibility.

12. Daniel A. DeSalvo and Jay Liebowitz, "The Application of an Expert System for Information Retrieval at the National Archives," *Telematics and Informatics* 13, no. 1 (1986): 25-38.

13. Available from Society of American Archivists.

14. David Bearman, "Optical Media: Their Implications for Archives and Museums," *Archival Informatics Technical Report* 1 (Spring 1981).

15. Nancy Sahli, *MARC for Archives and Manuscripts: The AMC Format* (Chicago: Society of American Archivists, 1985).

16. Max J. Evans and Lisa B. Weber, *MARC for Archives and Manuscripts: A Compendium of Practice* (Madison: State Historical Society of Wisconsin, 1985).

17. Richard M. Kesner, *Automation for Archivists and Records Managers: Planning and Implementation Strategies* (Chicago: American Library Association, 1984).

18. Richard M. Kesner, *Information Management, Machine-Readable Records, and Administration: An Annotated Bibliography* (Chicago: Society of American Archivists, 1983).

19. National Archives and Records Administration, *The MARC Format and Life Cycle Tracking at the National Archives: A Study* (Washington, D.C.: NARA, 1986).

20. National Archives and Records Service, *Technology Assessment Report: Speech Pattern Recognition, Optical Character Recognition, Digital Raster Scanning* (Washington, D.C.: General Services Administration, 1984).

21. Available from Society of American Archivists.

22. Richard C. Berner, *Archival Theory and Practice in the United States: A Historical Analysis* (Seattle: University of Washington Press, 1983); Robert M. Warner, "Librarians and Archivists: Organizational Agenda for the Future," in *Archives and Library Administration: Divergent Traditions and Common Concerns*, ed. Lawrence J. McCrank (New York: Haworth Press, 1986), 61-98; and Jacqueline Goggin, "That We Shall Truly Deserve the Title of 'Profession': The Training and Education of Archivists, 1930-1960," *American Archivist* 47 (Summer 1984): 243-54.

23. Society of American Archivists Task Force on Goals and Priorities, *Planning for the Archival Profession* (Chicago: SAA, 1986).

24. Society of American Archivists Committee on Education and Professional Development, "Proposed Guidelines for Graduate Archival Education Programs," *SAA Newsletter* (May 1987): 10-11.

25. Lawrence J. McCrank, "The Impact of Automation: Integrating Archival and Bibliographic Systems," in *Archives and Library Administration*, p. 76.

26. Steven L. Hensen, comp., *Archives, Personal Papers and Manuscripts: A Cataloging Manual for Archival Repositories, Historical Societies and Manuscript Libraries* (Washington, D.C.: LC, 1983).

27. Elsie Freeman, "In the Eye of the Beholder: Archives Administration from the User's Point of View," *American Archivist* 47 (Spring 1984): 111-23.

28. Richard H. Lytle, "Intellectual Access to Archives: I. Provenance and Content Indexing Methods of Subject Retrieval," *American Archivist* 43 (Winter 1980): 64-75; and Richard H. Lytle, "Intellectual Access to Archives: II. Report of an Experiment Comparing Provenance and Content Indexing Methods of Subject Retrieval," *American Archivist* 43 (Spring 1980): 191-207.

29. David Bearman and Richard H. Lytle, "The Power of the Principle of Provenance," *Archivaria* 21 (Winter 1985-86): 14-27.

30. David Bearman, *Towards National Information Systems for Archives and Manuscript Repositories: Opportunities and Requirements* (Washington, D.C.: NISTF, 1982).

31. Max J. Evans, "The Invisible Hand: Creating a Practical Mechanism for Cooperative Appraisal," *Midwestern Archivist* 11, no. 1 (1986): 7-14.

32. David Bearman and Richard Szary, "Beyond Authorized Headings: Authorities as Reference Files in a Multi-disciplinary Setting," (Proceedings of ARLIS/NA Conference on Authority Control, 10 Feb. 1986); and Max J. Evans, "Authority Control: An Alternative to the Record Group Concept," *American Archivist* 49 (Summer 1986): 249-61.

33. Max J. Evans and Lisa B. Weber, "An Ideal Computer-based Information Management System for Archives and Manuscripts Repositories," 1984.

34. Kesner, "Automated Information Management," p. 164. and Bearman, *Towards National Information Systems for Archives and Manuscripts Repositories*, p. 8.

PART 3

Accessing Standards and Technical Information in North America

Accessing Standards Information in Canada

NORMAN A. HAGAN, CONSULTANT

Recent years have seen an ever increasing need to make standards information more accessible. Pressure to implement existing standards, and to develop new ones, amplifies this need. Whether the pressure comes from the public, industry or government, there is little question that health, welfare, and safety are high profile issues.

Increasing competition in international trade also emphasizes the need for industries to comply with foreign standards – if those industries wish to remain competitive.

These pressures have a pronounced effect on the necessity of finding information related to standards . . . quickly. Individuals and organizations are showing a greater interest in knowing more about standards, including how and where to obtain them. Standards organizations are responding by providing additional educational and promotional material.

This issue of *SYMPOSIUM* has been developed for use as an educational aid and practical reference guide. It will also serve as a handbook to those persons pursuing careers as Information Resource Specialists, as well as others who use standards.

Standards and related information are sometimes difficult to retrieve, particularly for those who are not familiar with the various organizations that make up the world of standards. This guide provides the reader with a logical approach to locating needed documents and information.

The guide does not duplicate the large volume of information already existing elsewhere. Rather, it will provide the reader with information on how to make use of those publications, and who to contact when additional help is

Originally published for Symposium Series, Standards Council of Canada, Ottawa. Reprinted with permission of the author and the Standards Council of Canada. The document was current as of March 1989; it has been updated for publication in this volume.

required. This guide will aid users in selecting and ordering additional standards and related reference material.

Developed primarily for the Canadian scene, the guide provides an insight into how Canada relates to the international standards community in information exchange. A section on how to gain access to foreign and international standards and standards-related information is also included.

Standards organizations are usually more than willing to provide both general and specific information on standards and standardization. Seminars are offered to groups on request, often at no charge.

STANDARDS

What Are They?

The Standards Council of Canada's *Glossary of Common Administrative Terms Used in Standardization Activities* defines a standard as "a published document which contains requirements, procedures or definitions for a specific activity."

The International Organization for Standardization's Guide 2 *General terms and their definitions concerning standardization and related activities* states that publishing a standard is usually the result of having established provisions for repetitive use, aimed at the resolution of actual or potential problems. In other words, having identified a recurring or potentially repetitive problem, an agreed upon solution for its resolution is developed and published as a standard.

Published standards are produced by a great number of organizations. Companies, industry associations, government and others develop various standards aimed at meeting their own particular requirements. But there are also a number of Canadian organizations that produce standards intended for the use of anyone and everyone. These standards are known as voluntary consensus standards.[1]

Who Produces Them?

In Canada there are five independent organizations that develop voluntary consensus standards within the National Standards System; the Standards Council of Canada (SCC) coordinates their work. Because these organizations meet the criteria established by the Council, they have become "accredited." They are:

Bureau de normalisation du Quebec (BNQ)

Canadian Gas Association (CGA)

Canadian General Standards Board (CGSB)

Canadian Standards Association (CSA)

Underwriters' Laboratories of Canada (ULC)

Standards published by the five accredited standards-writing organizations are developed by committees whose members represent those segments of society that may be affected by such standards. These standards represent a consensus of a group of experts on the best solution to a problem – taking into account all pertinent factors, at the time the standard is developed. Subject areas are divided among the five organizations to minimize or eliminate duplication of effort.

How Are They Classified and Identified?

Standards are usually categorized by *subject*. For example, PAINTS AND FINISHES are considered as one subject. The majority of standards-writing organizations use systems that permit the classification and identification of their documents by subject matter.

Although on a world-wide basis standards are published in various sizes and formats, in Canada the differences among documents produced by the accredited standards-writing organizations are minimal. These organizations use two different paper sizes for standards. They are 215 mm X 280 mm (8 1/2 x 11 inches), and 150 mm X 225 mm (6 x 9 inches). Nomenclature is essentially the same, consisting of:

- acronym for the standards-writing organization;

- series of numerics or alphanumerics indicating the classification/subject/type of standard;

- additional series of alphanumerics (or numerics only) indicating whether the standard is in metric measure, and its date-of-issue.

The nomenclature on some Canadian standards is preceded with the abbreviation CAN. This abbreviation for Canada indicates that the standard has been classified as a National Standard, by virtue of its development and publication meeting criteria prescribed by the SCC.[2] These criteria ensure that, among other considerations, such a standard responds to an identified national need. As an example, CAN/CGSB-2.19-M86 provides the following information:

- CAN indicates this is a National Standard of Canada;

- CGSB is the Canadian General Standards Board, the producer;

- 2.19 where 2 stands for the subject category of Soaps and Detergents, and 19 is the actual number of the standard for hand dish washing compound;

- M86 indicates that measurements are in metric; year of issue is 1986.

In the above example CAN/CGSB-2.19-M86, CGSB shows this standard was developed by the Canadian General Standards Board. The use of an acronym (i.e., CGSB) to indicate the producer of a standard is a fairly recent change. The previous method employed a code number which indicated the producing standards-writing organization. The codes assigned were as follows:

1. Canadian Gas Association

2. Canadian General Standards Board

3. Canadian Standards Association

4. Underwriters' Laboratories of Canada

5. Bureau de normalisation du Quebec

Many standards still use the previous numerical method of identification and will only be changed to the new system as they are reissued.

Who Uses Standards?

Everyone uses or is influenced by standards every day. Companies use standards to ensure their products meet a particular level of quality, and to reduce production costs. Purchasers use standards to obtain the level of quality in products their organization requires, and to ensure appropriate value is received for dollars spent. Businesses use standards to expedite financial and other transactions between institutions. Governments use standards to ensure the health, welfare and safety of the public in fields such as transportation, construction, environment, food and drugs. Engineers use standards to design facilities, equipment and systems. With such diverse interests making use of standards, information resource specialists are called upon to provide documentation on a wide range of subjects from many different sources.

One major benefit of using standards is the ability to reference them in other documents. Standards eliminate the necessity of developing and including detailed technical requirements in every shop order, purchase order, regulation, drawing, specification or other documentation. For example, a government regulation (law) will stipulate that seat belts in automobiles must meet a particular standard, to ensure the belts are safe.

This makes it unnecessary for legislators to develop their own technical requirements, when drafting regulations.[3]

Copyrights

Copyright protection applies to almost all standards. The reason is that standards-writing organizations derive a great deal of their income from the sale of their documents. Under certain written agreements this protection may be waived. However, as with other copyright protection, those who ignore it do so at their own peril. Several lawsuits have been initiated by standards organizations against those who have ignored copyright statements. For standards documents where no copyright statement is made, it is prudent and considerate to request permission if you wish to reproduce them.

International Standardization

The SCC and the accredited standards-writing organizations take part in international standardization activities through a number of bodies. Much of this activity is through the International Organization for Standardization (ISO), and the International Electrotechnical Commission (IEC).

ISO is a specialized international agency for standardization. Its members are the standards bodies of some 90 countries representing over 95 percent of the world's industrial production. Standards published by ISO encompass a great number of finished products and raw materials. However, their standards do not include the electrical and electronics fields. ISO is a non-governmental agency established for the purpose of developing world-wide standards, to improve international communication and collaboration, and to promote the smooth and equitable growth of international trade. The IEC has essentially the same structure and goals as ISO but specializes in the electrical and electronics fields. Several publications which describe these organizations in greater detail are available from SCC. See Reference 12.

CATALOGUES, DIRECTORIES AND DATABASES

Catalogues and Directories

The five Canadian accredited standards-writing organizations all produce a catalogue of their own standards. They also have available a number of other publications intended to keep users and others up-to-date on new developments in standardization and other related activities. Many of these publications are available at no charge.

An annual directory published by SCC, and available at nominal cost, is particularly useful. It is titled *Directory and Index of Standards*. Included are listings of all the standards by KWOC (keyword-out-of-context). Thus it is not necessary to know which organization produces a standard on a particular subject in order to locate it.

Catalogues also exist for the standards produced by many other non-accredited Canadian organizations. For example, Supply and Services Canada, in cooperation with various provincial, territorial and municipal governments, publishes a directory known as the *Index of Standards and Specification used in Procurement*. Standards and specifications referenced by participating jurisdictions in their purchasing activities are included in the *Index*.

Directories of standards published by accredited and non-accredited standards-writing organizations of foreign countries are also available. There are also directories of standards produced by international organizations such as the International Organization for Standardization (ISO), International Electrotechnical Commission (IEC) and the International Maritime Organization (IMO). It is beyond the scope of this guide to reproduce a list of these directories, which refer to upwards of 600,000 documents.

Recent initiatives have seen the development of directories which list standards referenced in legislation. These directories are useful because they indicate which standards are called up in government regulations. In 1986 the SCC implemented a database of standards referenced in Canadian federal legislation.

Databases

The information contained in many directories and catalogues is obtained from computerized databases. Some of these databases may be accessed by microcomputers or terminals, for a fee. Since it is relatively easy to update databases, the information they obtain is usually much more timely than printed media. The search for information and its retrieval is also more effective than manual methods when large volumes are concerned, because searches can be made as inclusive or exclusive as required, as determined by the database system design.

In Canada, a number of databases are available that are useful when researching standards, or products certified as meeting those standards. The following is a partial list of currently available databases.

Database name: STANDARDS AND DIRECTORIES
Producer: Canadian Standards Association
Document collection: Catalogue of CSA standards and certified product directories.
Host: Canadian Centre for Occupational Health and Safety (CCINFO).
Further information: References 03 and 08.

Database name: CERTIFIED PRODUCTS DATABASE
Producer: Canadian Standards Association
Document collection: Listing of products that have been certified as
meeting CSA standards.
Host: QL Systems Ltd.
Further information: References 08 and 10.

Database name: CANADIAN STANDARDS
Producer: Standards Council of Canada
Document collection: Bibliographic data of standards published by
accredited Canadian standards-writing organizations.
Host: Standards Council of Canada, CAN/OLE, iNet 2000.
Further information: References 07, 12 and 13.

Database name: GATT TBT/NOTIFICATIONS
Producer: Standards Council of Canada
Document collection: Information on notifications of proposed
regulations, mandatory standards or certification systems received from
countries that have signed the GATT Agreement on Technical Barriers
to Trade (Standards Code).
Host: Standards Council of Canada iNet 2000.
Further information: References 12 and 13.

Database name: INDUSTRY & INTERNATIONAL STANDARDS
Producer: Information Handling Services
Document collection: Bibliographic data of major United States
standards-writing organizations. Also includes Canadian (CGSB &
CSA), British (BSI), German (DIN), Japanese (JIS) standards and
military (MLSS) specifications.
Host: BRS Information Technologies.
Further information: Reference 09.

STANDARDS COLLECTIONS

Collection Formats

Standards documents exist in essentially four formats: *individual
standards* in hard copy, *handbooks of standards* covering specific subject
areas, *microform* and *magnetic media*. The choice of the most suitable media
to be used will vary from one collection to another. In extensive collections,
more than one type of format will probably be required.

Each format has its own advantages and disadvantages.

Individual standards require the most storage space and maintenance effort. Outdated standards may be easily replaced with new ones; if desirable, the outdated copy can be retained. Archival information may be an important feature in some organizations where a particular issue of a standard is of more concern than the latest issue.

Handbooks of standards, covering specific subject areas, are one of the least expensive formats. Handbooks may have to be supplemented with other individual standards which are referenced but not included. Individual standards within the handbook may be superceded following publication. It is therefore necessary to identify changes as they occur.

Microform is a very convenient method of handling documents. A large collection takes no more space than the average office work station. Both microfiche and microfilm formats are available from suppliers, usually on a subscription basis. With a subscription service, keeping a collection up-to-date probably takes less than six hours a year. Reader/copiers are available which provide hard copies. Although the number of organizations whose standards are available on microform is extensive, in most cases microform collections require supplemental hard-copy documents. The directories provided with microform collections are, in themselves, useful research tools.

One disadvantage of microform formats is that when newly updated microfiche or microfilm is received, old issues must be returned to the supplier. Later on, should a copy of an older edition of a standard be required, it will have to be ordered from the supplier or the standards-writing organization concerned. The Visual Search Microfilm File (VSMF), produced by Information Handling Services and distributed by IHS Canada, is an example of this format.

Whether an organization can justify the cost of microform collections depends to a great extent on the savings that will accrue from reduced maintenance and search time, as well as space requirements. These formats deserve more than a cursory consideration.

Magnetic media in one form or another is used by most standards-writing organizations in maintaining their documents on word-processing facilities. Such facilities are capable of handling graphics, which may form a part of the document. At present, there are no Canadian collections which may be acquired in this format.

Classification of Documents

The only occasion when there will be some choice in how to classify a standards collection is when individual standards documents are being maintained. All other formats will be classified automatically.

It is highly recommended that standards be classified in exactly the same sequence as they appear in the directory or catalogue of the producer. Use of a different system may eventually result in maintenance and retrieval problems. In some catalogues an organization may reference standards of another organization. It is best to classify the referenced standards according to the directory of the producer. A typical example is the American National Standards Institute (ANSI). ANSI may adopt the standard of another organization, without change. In such cases the nomenclature of the standard will be ANSI, followed by the number of the producing organization. For example: ANSI/UL 1438-1982.

Other Considerations

Some key points for establishing and maintaining standards collections include:

- In establishing a collection, not only the standards from a particular organization, but also the documents those standards reference within their text will be required. Use of a standard may require copies of the other documents to which it refers. When providing information or copies of standards, it is important to make the user aware of these other references.

- When answering enquiries regarding standards, it is important to understand exactly what is being requested. Often a particular issue or edition of a standard is needed. Identification is usually by date-of-issue. Be sure to know whether the latest issue, or a particular date-of-issue, is required.

- The method of advising users of revisions, cancellations, and new editions of documents varies from one standard-writing organization to the next. It is therefore important to know about these methods, and set up the appropriate system for maintaining the collection.

INFORMATION AND SOURCES

The Canadian Scene

The Canadian scene with respect to public standards information sources consists of: five standards-writing organizations; the Standards Council's Information and Sales Branch; and a number of municipal and provincial libraries.

On the one hand, the standards-writing organizations provide information or points-of-contact for national and international organizations.

The kind of information available includes, but is not limited to: standards, government regulations, technical trade requirements, certification and qualification programs.

The collections held by municipal and provincial libraries are far less comprehensive than those of the Standards Council. Nevertheless they are key elements in providing standards information.

Canadian Accredited Standards-Writing Organizations

The five organizations referred to earlier all have information centres of their own. These organizations are:

Bureau de normalization du Quebec (BNQ),

Canadian Gas Association (CGA),

Canadian General Standards Board (CGSB),

Canadian Standards Association (CSA),

Underwriters' Laboratories of Canada (ULC).

All five publish directories, booklets and brochures. These publications provide in-depth information on the activities, services and programs of each organization. Many of the publications are available at no charge. Some of these organizations also make available video tapes, films and other audio/visual material.

Collections of standards and other related reference material are maintained in the libraries of each organization. Public access to these collections is available. Collections are tailored to the requirements of each organization and therefore reflect the type of standards they publish. In the case of CGA and ULC, the collections are generally made up of their own standards and those of other organizations whose standards they reference. The collections of BNQ, CGSB and CSA are much broader in scope, and include the standards of many other organizations.

One of the largest holdings of foreign and international standards collections in the country is open to the public for consultation, at the Rexdale office of the Canadian Standards Association (CSA). Second largest of its kind in Canada, this collection includes complete sets of International Organization for Standardization (ISO) and International Electrotechnical Commission (IEC) standards, as well as collections of numerous national standards organizations.

To become familiar with the type of standards published by the different standards-writing organizations, obtain copies of their catalogues. The information centres of these organizations will answer enquiries related to their own standards and programs. For enquiries outside their scope of activities, callers will usually be referred to other sources. As well as providing general standards information, technical enquiries are answered by the appropriate technical personnel with the organization.

These standards-writing organizations are listed in References 02, 04, 05, 08 and 14.

Standards Council, Information and Sales Branch[4]

Through its Standards Sales Division, the Branch handles sales of foreign national standards for many countries. The Branch will provide information required to obtain standards from countries or organizations it does not service. The Branch also functions as a Canadian clearing-house for enquiries regarding national standards, international standards and related information, as well as enquiries from foreign countries.

The Branch maintains a collection of over 400,000 standards documents. Copies of the statutes and regulations of the federal and provincial governments of Canada are included in their library. Although not a lending library, it is open to the public for reference purposes.

Staff are proficient in several foreign languages, to assist in researching information from other countries. Except for the purchase of standards, the services of this Branch are free-of-charge.

ISONET

ISONET is the acronym for the International Organization for Standardization, Information Network. ISONET is made up of the national standards information centres of sixty countries. These centres exchange information with, and answer enquiries from, other ISONET members. An *ISONET Guide* and *Directory* have been published by ISO. These documents provide ISONET members with procedures and other information pertaining to the network's operation.

The Council's Information and Sales Branch is the Canadian ISONET member. Access to this network permits a rapid exchange of information when an enquiry is received. Canadians wishing to know about standards or regulations of another country may obtain information through the *Information Division* of the Branch. The service is particularly important to companies wishing to export Canadian goods and services. Likewise, access to information on Canadian technical requirements is important to Canadian importers.

General Agreement on Tariffs and Trade (GATT)

Canada, along with approximately ninety other countries, is signatory to a multilateral agreement intended to improve international trading relationships. A part of this agreement, known as the *Standards Code* and aimed at reducing technical barriers to trade, requires that member countries establish Enquiry Points. There are presently 39 signatories to the Code. The role of each Enquiry Point is to exchange information relative to changes in the country's technical regulations, where implementation may affect a trading partner. Under contract from the federal Department of External Affairs, the Council's Standards Information Division fulfills that role.

In support of this service, the Division receives from and disseminates to both public and private sectors proposed changes in technical regulations of GATT member countries. Comments or objections from these sectors are referred back to the country proposing the change. Subsequent action may involve the Department of External Affairs.

There are three types of notification services available to Canadians:

1. Recorded summaries of current proposed changes are available through a telephone service TELEGATT, in both English and French.

2. The publication INFORMATECH provides a brief summary of all current proposed changes.

3. The publication, *GATT/TBT Notification*, includes a separate sheet for each proposed change, and gives more details than INFORMATECH. GATT/TBT notifications are also available through an on-line database. The database provides bilingual information on GATT notifications received by the Canadian Enquiry Point. Users have the option of searching for information by subject, notification number, or by scanning a summary of recent notifications. To obtain additional information, foreign and domestic users should contact SCC.

These documents are useful to exporters in the manufacturing and service sectors, as well as government agencies interested in exports.

The Division can obtain from a specific country additional technical information that may be required. If necessary, staff will arrange for the translation of this information into English or French. This service is free-of-charge. See Reference 12.

Typical Enquiries

Typical enquiries received by SCC's Information Division are listed below. They provide an indication of the scope of information available.

"What are the chemical compositions and mechanical properties for the following steel types? Germany Designation TSt 37-2; Japan Designation SM 41 C."

"Can you identify North American types which have similar compositions and mechanical properties?"

"What are the standards, regulations and certification requirements that must be met in order to sell electrical appliances in the United Kingdom?"

"Are there any Canadian standards for industrial protective headwear?" "Is there a mandatory or voluntary certification program for this product?"

"What international standards exist for graphic symbols used to identify equipment in motor vehicles?"

Help for Exporters

The information and Sales Branch is a representative for Technical Help to Exporters (THE), a service of the British Standards Institution (BSI). This service provides exporters with essential information and advice on technical requirements in foreign countries. The four elements of this service are:

- enquiry service for day-to-day problems of exporters

- research and consulting service for problems of greater magnitude

- special updating services provide specific information on changing technical requirements, tailored to the requirements of particular industries

- technical translations of foreign standards, legislation and codes of practice.

A booklet published by THE entitled *Technical Barriers to Trade, an Introduction for Exporters* gives additional information on this service. Copies may be requested through the Branch. See Reference 12.

Le Bureau de normalisation du Quebec provides further information through a similar arrangement with **NOREX**, a division of Association française de normalisation (AFNOR) in France. This service is oriented towards French language clients. See Reference 02.

Regional Standards Collections

Both the Bureau de normalisation du Quebec (BNQ) and the Canadian General Standards Board (CGSB) provide complete collections of their standards to various regional public and educational institute libraries. The locations of these collections are shown in their respective standards directories or catalogues. New and revised editions of standards are provided in order to keep these collections current.

The Government of Alberta has developed a comprehensive directory of standards collections held by various public and private sector libraries throughout the province. This directory permits interlibrary loans or viewing privileges, depending on each library's policy. A major advantage is that users can review the content of many standards almost immediately. Reviewing standards helps eliminate delays when ordering documents from publishers by ensuring the correct document is ordered. Thus the entire standard can be reviewed, instead of simply making reference to a title which may not be comprehensive enough to ensure correct selection.

Other collections of standards exist in both private and public libraries. A number of these libraries are listed under "Reference to Sources of Additional Information and Documents."

OBTAINING DOCUMENTS

There are essentially four sources for obtaining standards and related documents. These sources are classified under the following headings: CANADIAN STANDARDS of accredited standards-writing organizations, FOREIGN NATIONAL STANDARDS, OTHER FOREIGN STANDARDS and OTHER CANADIAN STANDARDS.

Canadian Standards

Documents published by the five Canadian accredited standards-writing organizations should be ordered directly from them. The National Standards of Canada that they produce are available in both English and French.

Some organizations include a notification card as part of their standards. This notification card, when completed and returned to the producer, will ensure the user is advised of amendments or other changes to a standard. The organizations that use this system are CGA, CSA, and ULC. Some of the organizations also provide an automatic update service for all of their standards, making it unnecessary to return the notification cards. The procedures for ordering and payment differ from one organization to the next as follows:

Bureau de normalisation du Quebec:
While catalogues are available at nominal cost, standards are free of charge. Updating of standards is automatic when requested. Telephone orders are accepted for small quantities. Otherwise orders should be placed by using the form which is included in their catalogue. See Reference 02.

Canadian Gas Association:
Catalogues are free-of-charge. Orders with a value of $250.00, or less, must be made in writing and accompanied by a remittance. Orders with a value of more than $250.00 will be accepted by telephone, telex or facsimile, if a purchase order number is provided. See Reference 04.

Canadian General Standards Board:
Catalogues are free-of-charge. Mail orders require that remittance or credit card number be included. Phone orders are accepted using credit cards. Standing orders may be arranged. All documents are available in English or French. A subscription service for updating of documents on an automatic basis is available at nominal cost.

CGSB issues an *Update Bulletin* several times a year. This publication provides comprehensive information on new, revised and cancelled standards, as well as other pertinent information. A subscription to this bulletin is available at nominal cost. See Reference 05.

Canadian Standards Association:
Catalogues are free-of-charge. Orders may be placed by mail, telephone, telex or facsimile. Deposit accounts and standing orders can be arranged. Orders can be placed using a credit card. Documents may be ordered from CSA's Rexdale office or from any one of their regional offices, where limited quantities of copies are held. Orders under $175.00 must be prepaid by cheque or credit card. Each location has a sales counter for pickup orders.

CSA publishes *Information Update* with comprehensive information on CSA standards and programs. Subscription is available at a nominal cost. Also available at no charge is the publication *Focus*, which summarizes current CSA activities. See Reference 08.

Underwriters' Laboratories of Canada:
Catalogues are free-of-charge. Orders must be placed by mail. Orders with a value of $50.00, or less, must be accompanied by a remittance. See Reference 14.

Foreign National Standards

Foreign standards of some 90 foreign countries are handled through the Information and Sales Branch of the Council. These standards may be purchased from the Sales Division. A partial list of countries and organizations dealt with are listed below:

AUSTRIA (On-Osterreichisches Normungsinstitut)

BELGIUM (IBN-Institut belge de normalisation)

DENMARK (DS-Dansk Standardiseringsraad)

FINLAND (SFS-Suomen Standardisoimisliitto)

FRANCE (AFNOR-Association française de normalisation)

GERMANY (Fed. Rep.) (DIN-Deutches Institut fur Normung)

ITALY (UNI-Ente Nazionale Italiano di Unificazione)

NETHERLANDS (NNI-Nederlands Normalisatie-instituut)

NORWAY (NSF-Norges Standardiseringsforbund)

SWEDEN (SIS-Standardiseringskommissionen i Sverige)

SWITZERLAND (SNV-Swiss Association for Standardization)

UNITED KINGDOM (BSI-British Standards Institution)

UNITED STATES (ANSI-American National Standards Institute, ASTM-American Society for Testing and Materials)

USSR (GOST-USSR State Committee for Standards)

INTERNATIONAL ELECTROTECHNICAL COMMISSION (IEC) (all member countries)

INTERNATIONAL ORGANIZATION FOR STANDARDIZATION (ISO) (all member countries)

CANADIAN GENERAL STANDARDS BOARD (National Standards of Canada only)

Continuous efforts are being made to increase the number of countries and standards organizations represented. See Reference 12.

Other Foreign Standards

The purchase of other foreign documents is usually from the producer. Information on the source of these documents may be obtained from the Council's Information Division. See Reference 12.

Other Canadian Standards

The Standards of non-accredited organizations must be ordered directly from the organization concerned. Included in this category are: governments, industry associations, private companies, and others. The Council's Information Division will provide points of contact for enquiries regarding these documents.

Standards published by non-accredited standards-writing organizations are not always available to the public. Details concerning the maintenance or cancellation of such standards may be difficult to determine. But, in the absence of other sources, these standards are valuable as reference materials.

PLANNING FOR THE FUTURE

The Standards Council of Canada has a number of committees established to recommend policies and directions. One of these committees is concerned with information.

Advisory Committee on Standards Information Services (ACSIS)

This committee has a mandate to advise and make recommendations to the Council on:

- policy matters related to the role of the Council in standards information

- the development and operation of a comprehensive national standards information service

- relationships with other information services, nationally and internationally

- Canadian interests with the information committees of the International Organization for Standardization (ISO/INFCO).

The ACSIS committee consists of members from the resource information and standards communities across Canada. Work is carried out voluntarily, with out-of-pocket expenses for attendance at meetings funded by the Council.

The overall objective of the ACSIS committee is to improve the accessibility of standards and related documents to the Canadian public at large. Council document CAN-P-7, Standards Information System of Canada, outlines the terms of reference and procedures for the committee.

Current goals aimed at achieving this objective include:

- establishment of additional centres in Canada where standards will be available for public access

- identification of existing standards collections held by both private and public sector resource information centres

- simplification of the process and reduction of the lead time necessary to acquire standards documents. This may include limited extension of photocopy rights to designated regional centres, additional sales outlets, electronic ordering of documents and, in the long term, the possibility of computerized full on-line text.

National Standards Information System of Canada (CANSIS)

To carry out the mandate of ACSIS, the Council established the Standards Information System of Canada, or CANSIS. CANSIS is a network for standards information. The CANSIS network consists of the (five) accredited Canadian standards organizations, a number of other Canadian organizations which have related information services, and the Council. ACSIS gives advisory support to CANSIS. The Council's document CAN-P-7 also states the terms of reference and procedures for CANSIS.

The council's goal is to establish enough regional CANSIS outlets needed to serve Canadian needs. Resource information centres holding standards collections of any size are encouraged to participate in this network. Presently there are eleven such outlets in Canada.

Information regarding membership in ACSIS or CANSIS may be obtained through the Manager of the Council's Information Division 1-800-267-8220. In Ottawa, call 238-3222.

Alberta Public Works
Supply and Services
Standards and Technical Services
6950 - 113 Street, 3rd Floor
EDMONTON, Alberta T6H 5V7

Bureau de normalisation du Quebec
70, rue Dalhousie, 2è étage
QUEBEC, Quebec G1K 4B2

Canadian Gas Association
55 Scarsdale Road
DON MILLS, Ontario M3B 2R3

Canadian General Standards Board
OTTAWA, Ontario K1A 1G6

Canadian Standards Association
Information Centre
178 Rexdale Boulevard
REXDALE, Ontario M9W 1R3

Ecole Polytechnique
Campus de l'Université de Montreal
Case Postale 6079, Succursale A
MONTREAL, Quebec H3B 3A7

Ministry of Consumer and Commercial Relations
Technical Standards Division
3300 Bloor Street West
Shipp Centre - West Tower 4th Floor
TORONTO, Ontario M8X 2X4

Queen Elizabeth II Library
Memorial University of Newfoundland
ST. JOHN'S, Newfoundland A1B 3Y1

Research & Productivity Council
921 College Hill Road
Fredericton, N.B. E3B 6Z9

Standards Council of Canada
Information Division
350 Sparks Street, Suite 1200
OTTAWA, Ontario K1P 6N7

Underwriters' Laboratories of Canada
7 Crouse Road
SCARBOROUGH, Ontario M1R 3A9

Vancouver Public Library
750 Burrard Street
VANCOUVER, British Columbia V6Z 1X5

REFERENCE TO SOURCES OF ADDITIONAL INFORMATION AND DOCUMENTS

Reference	Organization

01   **Alberta Public Works, Supply & Services,**
Supply Management,
Operational Support Services Branch,
3rd Floor, 6950 113th Street,
Edmonton, AB T6H 5V7
Telephone: 403-427-8896
Facsimile: 403-422-1801

02   **Bureau de normalisation du Quebec,**
70, rue Dalhousie, 2è étage
Quebec, QC G1K 4B2
Standards Information, Telephone: 418-643-5114
Certification Information, Telephone: 418-643-5813

03   **Canadian Centre for Occupational Health & Safety,**
250 Main Street E.
Hamilton, ON L8N 1H6
Telephone: 416-572-2981
or 1-800-263-8276

04   **Canadian Gas Association,**
55 Scarsdale Road
Don Mills, ON M3B 2R3
Telex: 06-966824
Facsimile: 416-447-7067
Telephone: 416-447-6465

05   **Canadian General Standards Board,**
Ottawa, ON K1A 1G6
Telephone: 819-994-5373
for CGSB standards on microfiche
Micromedia Ltd.,
165 Hotel de Ville,
Hull, QC J8X 3X2
Telephone: 1-800-567-9669 or 819-994-5382
1-800-567-1914 (Nfld, W. Canada)

06   **Canadian Government Publishing Centre,**
Supply and Services Canada,
Ottawa, ON K1A 0S9
Telephone: 819-997-2560
Telex: 053-4296

07   **Canada Institute for Scientific and Technical Information,**
c/o National Research Council,
Ottawa, ON K1A 0S2
Telephone: 613-993-2013
ENVOY 100: CISTI.REF
CAN/OLE: OLE034DE

08   **Canadian Standards Association,**
178 Rexdale Blvd.,
Rexdale, ON M9W 1R3
Information Centre, Telephone: 416-747-4058
Standards Sales Service, Telephone: 416-747-4044
Telex: 06-989344
Facsimile: 416-747-4149

09   **Information Handling Services Canada Ltd.,**
111 Peter Street, Suite 411
Toronto, ON M5V 2W2
Telephone: 416-596-1624

10   **QL Systems Ltd.,**
1 Gore Street, P. O. Box 2080
Kingston, ON K7L 5J8
Telephone: 1-800-267-9470
or 613-549-4611

11   **Quality Management Institute,**
1420 Mississauga Executive Centre,
4 Robert Speck Parkway,
Mississauga, Ontario, L4Z 1S1
Telephone: 416-272-3920
Facsimile: 416-272-3942

12   **Standards Council of Canada,**
Information and Sales Branch,
350 Sparks St., Suite 1200,
Ottawa, ON K1P 6N7
Telephone: 1-800-267-8220 (in Ottawa: 238-3222)
Telex: 053-4403
Facsimile: 613-995-4564
TELEGATT (English): 613-238-1501
TELEGATT (French): 613-238-1450

13	**Telecom Canada,**
	iNet 2000
	410 Laurier Avenue, W.
	Ottawa, ON K1P 6H5
	Telephone: 1-800-267-8480

14	**Underwriters' Laboratories of Canada,**
	7 Crouse Road,
	Scarborough, ON M1R 3A9
	Telephone: 416-757-3611
	TELEX 06-963643
	Facsimile: 416-757-9540

15	**Vancouver Public Library,**
	Science and Technology Division,
	750 Burrard Street,
	Vancouver, BC V6Z 1X5
	Telephone: 604-665-3585
	Facsimile: 604-665-2265

APPENDIX: ACRONYMS

AHAM	Association of Home Appliance Manufacturers
ANSI	American National Standards Institute
ACSIS	Advisory Committee on Standards Information Services
BNQ	Bureau de normalisation du Quebec
BSI	British Standards Institution
CAN/OLE	Canadian Online Enquiry System
CANSIS	National Standards Information System of Canada
CCINFO	Canadian Centre for Occupational Health and Safety Information
CGA	Canadian Gas Association
CGSB	Canadian General Standards Board
CISTI	Canada Institute for Scientific and Technical Information
CSA	Canadian Standards Association
GATT	General Agreement on Tariffs and Trade

iNet 2000	The Intelligent Network, Telecom Canada
IMO	International Maritime Organization
ISO	International Organization for Standardization
ISO/INFCO	International Organization for Standardization, Information Committee
IEC	International Electrotechnical Commission
SCC	Standards Council of Canada
UL	Underwriters Laboratories (USA)
ULC	Underwriters' Laboratories of Canada

Notes

1. In Canadian standards terminology, *consensus* is defined as substantial agreement reached by concerned interests involved in the preparation of a standard.

2. SCC's publication CAN-P-2, entitled *Criteria and Procedures for the Preparation and Approval of National Standards of Canada*, outlines 15 criteria for National Standards. CAN-P-2 is available from SCC.

3. A government is said to reference standards in legislation when it adopts standards as the basis for specifying technical requirements in legislation.

4. The Information and Sales Branch comprises the Standards Sales Division, and Standards Information Division.

Accessing Standards Information in the United States: Verification, Identification, Acquisition, and Technical Assistance

LINDA R. MUSSER, THE PENNSYLVANIA STATE UNIVERSITY
JOANNE OVERMAN, OFFICE OF STANDARDS SERVICES, NATIONAL
INSTITUTE OF STANDARDS AND TECHNOLOGY

Standards pose particular problems when it comes to answering the question, "Does a standard for x exist and, if so, what is it?" While other sources of information such as books, journal articles, technical reports, and patents have been widely cataloged and indexed, standards remain a largely unindexed and underutilized source of technical information. This article describes some of the tools and resources available to assist in the verification and identification of standards.

SOURCES OF ASSISTANCE

A variety of organizations offer assistance in identifying standards. These include groups such as government agencies, societies, commercial vendors, and libraries. The major differences among these groups are the amount of assistance and scope of expertise they offer. While most groups offer some basic assistance free of charge, many either charge a fee for or do not offer assistance with more complicated queries. Basic assistance generally covers the identification of a standard's number, identification of the governing body, and so on.

Adapted and revised from Linda R. Musser, "Identifying Standards," *ASTM Standardization News* 17 (April 1989): 44-47, and JoAnne Overman, "Information Center Assists Users in Identifying Standards and Provides Technical Assistance," *ASTM Standardization News* 18 (June 1990): 28-31. Reprinted with permission.

The scope of expertise offered by a particular organization is a determining factor in how helpful that organization will be in a standards search. Very few organizations offer broad subject coverage of the world of standards. Most professional societies, for example, offer assistance in identifying only standards issued by that society. Government agencies, commercial vendors, and libraries generally cover a broader range of subjects, but the scope of expertise of each organization varies. One group may cover only U.S. industry standards, while another may offer assistance in identifying military and federal standards as well. More details on the following sources can be found in Appendix B, under "Standards Information Centers."

One of the best providers of assistance and expertise is the National Center for Standards and Certification Information (NCSCI). The center is part of the National Institute of Standards and Technology, formerly known as the National Bureau of Standards. NCSCI offers free assistance in identifying standards and government regulations developed by the United States, other nations, and regional and international organizations. The center maintains a large library of U.S., foreign, regional, and international standards and related materials as well as a variety of catalogs and indexes. A typical request to the center obtains a list of standards and regulations as well as contact points for obtaining more information. Sources for obtaining copies of the standards are also identified. NCSCI does not sell copies of standards, but the reference collection of standards is open to the public. Generally, requests for information are filled within five working days, although many requests for help are easily answered in minutes. The center is open to the public and services are free of charge.

Information Handling Services (IHS) is a commercial vendor of standards and standards information services. The resources of IHS are quite large and similar to the NCSCI in scope. Assistance is readily available from the IHS Extension 99TM service, which assists in identifying and locating sources of standards around the world. Use of the Extension 99TM service is generally free of charge except in cases of difficult or complicated standards searches. IHS offers collections of standards for purchase, with individual standards available for purchase from its affiliate, Global Engineering Documents. IHS may be contacted at 15 Inverness Way East, Englewood, CO 80150 (800-241-7824).

The National Standards Association, Inc. (NSA) is a vendor of a broad range of U.S. government information, including standards and specifications developed or used by industry, the military, or the federal government. NSA's Techinfo department offers assistance in identifying U.S. standards of interest. While basic assistance is generally provided free of charge, there may be a fee for more complex standards searches. NSA can be reached at 1200 Quince Orchard Boulevard, Gaithersburg, MD 20878 (800-638-8094).

The American National Standards Institute (ANSI) is the coordinator of the U.S. voluntary standards system and provides representation for the U.S. to international standards organizations such as the International Organization for Standardization (ISO) and the International Electrotechnical Commission (IEC). ANSI makes available all approved[1] American national standards and international standards of the ISO and IEC. Foreign standards are available from ANSI as well. The main functions of the organization are in the areas of coordination of standards creation, representation, and sales of standards. The sales staff of ANSI will provide some assistance to purchasers, but help is limited. ANSI is located at 11 West 42nd Street, 13th floor, New York, NY 10036 (212-354-3300).

Most professional societies involved in standards development offer some assistance in identifying the standards that they produce. Good examples of the kind of assistance available are illustrated by the following two societies, both heavily involved in the standards development process.

The American Society for Testing and Materials (ASTM) is a scientific and technical organization formed for the development of standards on characteristics and performance of materials, products, systems, and services. It is the world's largest source of voluntary consensus standards.[2] The ASTM offers free assistance via its information center. The center attempts to identify appropriate standards produced by the ASTM and refers inquiries to committees or working groups, if appropriate. ASTM standards are available for purchase directly from the society. ASTM is located at 1916 Race St., Philadelphia, PA 19103 (215-299-5400).

The Institute of Electrical and Electronics Engineers, Inc. (IEEE) offers assistance to those needing information on standards in the field of electronics and electrical engineering. (Note: The IEEE does not cover all areas dealing with standards in the aforementioned fields. Areas such as electronic packaging, for example, are handled by other related societies. IEEE assists in identifying standards that they produce.) Personnel in the IEEE Standards Office try to identify appropriate standards or provide referrals to the chairperson of a standards committee or working group. Assistance is free, and standards may be purchased directly from the society. The IEEE Standards Office is located at 445 Hoes Lane, P.O. Box 1331, Piscataway, NJ 08855-1331 (201-562-3800).

One other source of assistance is libraries. Libraries are traditional providers of free assistance in locating information in all fields of knowledge. Many large public and academic libraries maintain collections of standards and offer assistance in their use. Standards are generally available for loan or in-house use.

PRINTED SOURCES

For those who must do repeated standards searches or who are simply interested in having convenient access to lists of standards, a variety of sources is available to assist in the verification and identification process. Indexes to standards are available in printed and electronic formats; however, there are no truly comprehensive indexes to standards of all countries and organizations. Most indexes are limited to the standards of one nation or organization.

The closest example of a comprehensive index to standards is the *Index and Directory of Industry Standards*. This index provides coverage of U.S., international, and selected regional and foreign industry standards and is searchable by subject and standard number. The four-volume set is updated annually and is available from Global Engineering Documents at 2805 McGraw Avenue, P.O. Box 19539, Irvine, CA 92714 (800-854-7179).

United States, Industry Standards

Several fairly comprehensive indexes of U.S. industry standards are available. The National Center for Standards and Certification Information has produced a *Key-Word-In-Context*[3] *(KWIC) Index of U.S. Voluntary Industry Standards*. The *KWIC* index provides coverage of U.S. industry standards and is searchable by key word. The index is available in either paper or microfiche (48X) from the National Technical Information Service, 5285 Port Royal Road, Springfield, VA 22161 (703-487-4600). Last produced in 1989, the NTIS report number for the *KWIC* index is PB89-154322. No further *KWIC* indexes are anticipated.

The *Catalog of American National Standards* is an annual publication that provides access to all current, approved American national standards by subject and standard number. This catalog, as well as catalogs of foreign and international standards organizations, is available from the American National Standards Institute.

Finally, two volumes of the *Index and Directory of Industry Standards* (described previously) may be purchased separately and used as an independent index to U.S. industry standards.

While comprehensive indexes to U.S. standards are relatively uncommon, many fairly specific indexes are available. These indexes are generally produced by a particular society, organization, or agency and cover only those standards produced by that organization. A description of several of these indexes follows.

The *Annual Book of ASTM Standards* includes an index that provides access by subject and standard number to formally approved ASTM standards, practices, specifications, guides, test methods, terminology, and related materials such as proposals. The index is published annually and is available for purchase from ASTM. ASTM also produces an annual standards catalog, which is available free of charge. The catalog describes the contents of volumes in the *Annual Book of ASTM Standards* series, compilations of standards on specific topics, and a service for custom designing a volume of standards tailored to the customer's needs.

The IEEE produces an index entitled *Quick Reference to IEEE Standards (QRIS)*. The index provides access by key word and standard number to IEEE standards and ANSI standards published by the IEEE. An added feature of this index is that it includes the table of contents of each standard listed in the index. The *QRIS* is available for purchase from the IEEE. The IEEE also produces a biannual standards catalog, which is available free of charge. The catalog gives a subject listing of all IEEE standards and ANSI standards published by the IEEE.

The Society of Automotive Engineers (SAE) is involved with standards in the areas of materials, safety, and fuels as well as automotive engineering. SAE has a variety of tools available to identify standards produced by the society. Several indexes are available including the *Aerospace Index*, the *Ground Vehicle Standards Index*, and the *AMS (Aerospace Materials Specifications) Index*. The SAE produces an annual standards catalog, which is available free of charge. The catalog lists collections of standards, indexes, and other services available from the SAE. It does not list individual standards. All these products are available from the SAE at 400 Commonwealth Drive, Warrendale, PA 15096 (412-776-4970).

Underwriters Laboratories produces a catalog entitled *UL Standards for Safety*. It contains a listing of published and proposed standards indexed by key word and standard number. The catalog is available free of charge from Underwriters Laboratories Inc., 333 Pfingsten Road, Northbrook, IL 60062-2096 (708-272-8800).

United States, Government Standards

A variety of indexes of military and federal standards and specifications is available. The *Department of Defense Index of Specifications and Standards (DODISS)* indexes unclassified federal, military, and departmental specifications, standards, and related standardization documents and industry documents approved for use by the Department of Defense. Departmental documents include those used by the Army, Navy, and Air Force. The *DODISS* is indexed alphabetically by the title of the document and numerically within each document type. The *DODISS* may be found in many depository libraries or can be purchased from the U.S. Government Printing Office, Washington, D.C. 20402 (202-783-3238).

The *Federal Supply Classification Listing of DOD Standardization Documents* is a companion publication to the *DODISS*. It covers the same material as the *DODISS* but is indexed alphabetically within each federal supply classification code. This publication is also a depository item or is available from the U.S. Government Printing Office.

The *Index of Federal Specifications, Standards and Commercial Item Descriptions* contains a listing of federal specifications, standards, qualified products lists, commercial item descriptions, and USDA institutional meat purchase specifications. It is indexed alphabetically, numerically, and by federal supply classification listing. A depository item, it can be located at depository libraries or is available from the U.S. Government Printing Office.

Foreign, Regional, and International Standards

The types of printed tools available for identifying foreign, regional, or international standards are for the most part limited to catalogs of publications of each country or organization. The only exception to this rule is the *Index and Directory of Industry Standards* (described previously). Two of its four volumes cover international and selected regional and foreign standards. These volumes may be purchased separately and used as an independent index to non-U.S. industry standards.

The International Organization for Standardization produces a catalog of its publications that indexes by subject and standard number ISO standardization documents in all fields except electrical and electronic engineering, which are the responsibility of the IEC. The IEC has its own catalog of publications. These catalogs, as well as catalogs of various national standards organizations, are available either from ANSI or directly from the standards organization in question. For a listing of foreign, regional, and international standards organizations, the *Scientific and Technical Organizations and Agencies Directory* (Detroit, MI: Gale Research Co., 1987) is a good source.

ELECTRONIC SOURCES

Computer databases provide the most comprehensive coverage of standards of many nations and organizations. Although many databases contain information concerning standards, only the largest and most comprehensive of those dealing specifically with standards will be mentioned here. These databases are accessible via commercial database vendors such as Dialog, BRS, and ORBIT. Online searching of these databases offers several advantages over the more traditional search using printed tools. The databases are more comprehensive, and a search can be performed quickly and efficiently. Searching can be done by key word, organization, and standard number, to name just a few of the searching options. The main drawback is that a charge is assessed for each online search performed. With the proper equipment and training, online searching can be done from the home or office. For those lacking the training or equipment, however, an online search can be done on demand by many libraries or by a commercial standards vendor.

Dialog has two fairly comprehensive standards databases available for searching. The Standards and Specifications database (File 113) is produced by the National Standards Association, Inc. and contains titles and descriptive information on U.S. industry, military, and federal standards and specifications. The other database is IHS International Standards and Specifications (File 92). This database is produced by IHS and contains information on U.S., foreign, and international standards and specifications. For information on how to search databases on Dialog, contact Dialog Information Services, Inc., 3460 Hillview Ave., Palo Alto, CA 94304 (800-334-2564).

The Standards Search database is provided by Pergamon ORBIT Infoline. This database contains descriptive information on all standards developed by the ASTM and SAE. For information on using the Standards SearchTM database, contact ORBIT Search Service, Pergamon ORBIT Infoline, Inc., 8000 Westpark Dr., McLean, VA 22102 (800-456-7248).

INFORMATION CENTER PROVIDES ACCESS TO STANDARDS INFORMATION

A U.S. exporter is interested in selling a product in Europe and needs to know about relevant French, German, and British standards and regulations. The company, aware of the EC 1992 Single Internal Market developments, wonders how they will affect its business. A lawyer, representing an injured client, needs to know if any federal government regulations or U.S. industry standards relate to a specific product. An individual wants information about proposed foreign technical regulations that have been reported by signatories to the General Agreement on Tariffs and Trade (GATT) Agreement on Technical Barriers to Trade (Standards Code) concerning telecommunications equipment. Where can this information be found? It is at the National Center for Standards and Certification Information (NCSCI).

Located at the Department of Commerce's National Institute of Standards and Technology (NIST) in Gaithersburg, Maryland, NCSCI was established in 1965 and provides information on:

- Approximately 42,000 U.S. voluntary standards developed by more than 400 standards-developing organizations.

- Foreign and international voluntary standards and regulations.

- Government regulations, including procurement specifications and mandatory codes, rules, and regulations containing standards developed and adopted at the federal, state and local levels.

- Rules of certification.

The center, part of the Standards Code and Information (SCI) program, acts as a referral service and focal point in the United States for information about standards and standards-related activities.

Information Services

Center staff respond to requests by identifying relevant standards, regulations, or both using various indexes, contacting professional and standards-developing organizations, and communicating directly with foreign standards bodies. The requester is referred to the appropriate standards-developing organization for additional (technical) information and copies of the documents. NCSCI does not provide copies of standards.

The NCSCI reference collection of standards and standards-related documents includes:

- Microfilm files of military and federal specifications, selected U.S. industry and national standards, and international and selected foreign national standards.

- Reference books, including directories, technical and scientific dictionaries, encyclopedias, and handbooks.

- Articles, pamphlets, reports, and handbooks on standardization and certification.

- Standards-related periodicals and newsletters.

Standards Code Inquiry Point

On January 1, 1980, the Trade Agreements Act of 1979 implemented the U.S. response to the GATT Agreement on Technical Barriers to Trade (Standards Code). The Department of Commerce designated NCSCI to serve as the U.S. inquiry point for information on standards, regulations, and rules of certification. In addition, NCSCI staff must report proposed U.S. federal government regulations to the GATT secretariat; receive, disseminate, and maintain copies of all notifications of proposed foreign regulations; respond to inquiries regarding the Standards Code and notifications; maintain a GATT hotline of current foreign notifications; and publish reports on Standards Code activities.

One of the major requirements of the Standards Code is for signatories to notify other signatories through the GATT secretariat in Geneva, Switzerland, of proposed governmental technical regulations that may affect trade. These notification procedures allow U.S. exporters to obtain and review copies of proposed foreign regulations and comment on them if they feel the regulation will impact their product. NCSCI provides, free of charge, the full text of all notified proposed foreign regulations. Because many of these regulations are not in English, NCSCI has arranged a translation service; the costs of translations are paid by the requester.

Notifications of proposed foreign technical regulations are published in several government and private sector journals and newsletters. The GATT Hotline (301-975-4041) provides this information on a 24-hour recorded message, which is updated weekly.

NCSCI staff prepare a newsletter, *tbt News*, to inform readers of government services available to industry in support of the Standards Code and to report on current activities of the Committee on Technical Barriers to Trade. The committee, made up of representatives of the 40 signatory countries,[4] meets regularly to discuss the implementation and status of the code and make suggestions for improvements where needed.

International Network

NCSCI serves as the U.S. representative to the International Organization for Standardization (ISO) Information Network (ISONET). NCSCI, with other foreign national inquiry points, forms a network that regularly exchanges standards-related information. The network also provides NCSCI with access to foreign trade-related technical standards, regulations, and rules of certification. In some instances, the requester may be referred directly to the appropriate foreign inquiry point to obtain information.

Single European Market (EC 1992)

NCSCI recognizes the importance to U.S. exporters of the European Community (EC) single European market effort. Companies must have information on new and existing standards and product acceptance procedures to maintain market positions and to develop opportunities for increased export sales. The European commitment to adopt international standards as new regional standards, where these are available, makes it critical for U.S. firms to have access to information on standards activities at both the international and European levels.

Center staff use the following documents, which are available in the reference collection, to assist U.S. exporters in identifying internal market-related product standards and regulations:

- Standards catalogs for most of the EC member countries.

- *Official Journal of the European Communities*, which contains proposed and final directives.

- Catalogs and mementos of the European Committee for Standardization (CEN) and European Committee for Electrotechnical Standardization (CENELEC).

- Microfilm files of relevant documents related to the harmonized standards and legislation for the single European market and EC directives.

Center staff work closely with other U.S. government agencies, such as the International Trade Administration's Office of European Community Affairs, to provide current and accurate information on the EC 1992 effort. NCSCI staff serve on the Interagency Task Force on EC 1992 and the Working Group on Standards, Testing, and Certification as part of broader activities related to standards and trade.

Technical Assistance

NCSCI also includes a technical office and an assistance program for developing countries. NCSCI's technical office staff assist U.S. manufacturers, exporters, and government agencies with respect to specific technically-based, standards-related trade issues; develop technical positions for U.S. negotiators in bilateral and multilateral discussions; monitor the adequacy of U.S. participation in international standardization efforts; handle complaints from representatives of U.S. industry concerning foreign standards and certification practices that might be considered technical barriers to trade; and review and transmit U.S. comments on proposed foreign regulations through U.S. embassies to the appropriate foreign government organizations.

Office staff publish various reports on certification programs, U.S. participation in international standards activities, and technical trade barriers encountered by U.S. telecommunications equipment exporters.

When resources permit, NCSCI staff assist developing countries in developing their standards and work with U.S. standards-developing organizations to make their standards available to other countries. In March

1990, under an arrangement with the U.S. private sector, NCSCI implemented an activity under which a technical representative works with the Saudi Arabia Standards Organization in Riyadh in its standards developments.

Conclusion

NCSCI continues to work closely with the standards-developing community, U.S. manufacturers, foreign standards bodies, other government agencies, and certification and testing bodies to provide the most current and accurate standards information possible. For additional information on NCSCI activities, please contact:

National Center for Standards and Certification Information
National Institute of Standards and Technology
Administration Building, Room A629
Gaithersburg, MD 20899
Telephone: NCSCI 301-975-4036, -4038, or -4040
GATT Hotline (recorded message) 301-975-4041
Technical Assistance 301-975-4033
Telefax: 301-963-2871

SUMMARY

With over 200,000 standards in existence today and more constantly being developed, verification and identification of standards will pose an increasing challenge in the years to come. Given the wealth of information that standards contain and the vital role that they play in our lives, it is essential that their use be encouraged and facilitated. The resources in this article represent a few of the contributions being made toward achieving that goal.

Notes

1. Many voluntary U.S. standards are not ANSI approved. Only *approved* American National Standards are available from ANSI.

2. *1988 Annual Book of ASTM Standards* (Philadelphia, Pa.: ASTM, 1988), iii.

3. This type of index is similar to a subject index but uses significant or key words from the title for indexing rather than formal subject headings.

4. Argentina, Austria, Belgium, Brazil, Canada, Chile, Czechoslovakia, Denmark, Egypt, European Economic Community, Federal Republic of Germany, Finland, France, Greece, Hong Kong, Hungary, India, Ireland, Israel, Italy, Japan, Korea, Luxembourg, Mexico, Netherlands, New Zealand, Norway, Pakistan, Philippines, Portugal, Romania, Rwanda, Singapore, Spain, Sweden, Switzerland, Tunisia, United Kingdom, United States, and Yugoslavia.

Documentation and Information Exchange in the World of Standards

ALBERT A. TUNIS, EDUCATION AND INFORMATION, STANDARDS COUNCIL OF CANADA

TECHNICAL REQUIREMENTS

Today, the successful marketing of products is dependent upon a manufacturer's ability to comply with recognized national and international technical requirements. Each country, to a greater or less extent, has established distinctive technical requirements, whether these be based upon regulations, national or international standards. In order to be successful in the world market, a manufacturer must ensure that the product complies with the relevant technical requirements of the proposed trading partner and must be able to demonstrate conclusively to the relevant authorities that the product meets these requirements. Consistent compliance can be demonstrated through the use of quality assurance systems and nationally accepted certification systems.

Generally, technical requirements fall into four main categories:

- Technical regulations (health, consumer protection, safety, environmental, etc.);

- National and international standards;

Originally published in E.V. Smith and S. Keenan, eds., *Information, Communications and Technology Transfer* (New York and Amsterdam: Elsevier Science Publishers [North Holland], 1987). See also Albert A. Tunis, "ISONET: Ten Years of Experience," *ASTM Standardization News* 18 (June 1990): 44-48, or in ISO *Consensus* 17, no. 1. Reprinted with permission. Albert A. Tunis, consultant, is the former director of Education and Information, Standards Council of Canada. The author would like to thank Mr. E. J. French, ISO Central Secretariat, Secretary of INFCO, who allowed several of his works to be used in the preparation of this paper.

- Certification systems;

- Customer requirements.

Conservative estimates put the number of standards available worldwide at about 1,000,000 documents. If you add to this the laws of the various countries as well as company standards, you are dealing with a tremendous volume of information. Manufacturers must be aware of the technical requirements that apply to their own products so that they can consider them early enough to ensure that the finished product will be acceptable when it reaches the market place. Failure to consider these technical requirements can result in time-consuming delays, loss of sales, loss of revenue and lost opportunity for future business.

Many countries have accepted that government has a role to play in ensuring that the information is available to help suppliers compete in world markets. In this paper, I would like to describe the approach taken at national levels, and at the international level, by the International Organization for Standardization (ISO). But first it may be helpful to provide some definitions.

STANDARDIZATION DEFINITIONS

A special kind of relationship exists between standards and technical regulations. These are overlapping classes of documents and various attempts have been made to distinguish them. The following versions approved by ISO are now widely accepted internationally.[1]

Technical Specification: A document which lays down characteristics of a product or a service such as levels of quality, performance, safety, dimensions. It may include terminology, symbols, testing and test methods, packaging, marking or labeling requirements. A technical specification may also take the form of a code of practice. These documents are issued by companies and by governments, generally when specifying requirements for the procurement of products.

Standard: A technical specification or other document available to the public, drawn up with the cooperation and consensus or general approval of all interests affected by it based on the consolidated results of science, technology and experience, aimed at the promotion of optimum community benefits and approved by a body recognized on the national, regional or international level.

Regulation: A binding document which contains legislative, regulatory, or administrative rules, and which is adopted and published by an authority legally vested with the necessary power. This type of document is produced and published by all levels of government.

Technical regulation: A regulation containing or referring to a standard or a technical specification. As for regulations, these are issued by legislative authorities.

Standards and technical regulations are frequently amended and updated. Once included in an information system, they need constant attention to ensure that the information is correct, complete and up to date; otherwise the user may be dangerously misled. Each standards-writing organization has established procedures so that standards are reviewed at least once every five years. These procedures ensure that standards reflect changes in the state-of-the-art technology.

A product standard may include a requirement for a test method, a material or component which is specified in another standard. If one of these standards is amended or withdrawn, it may affect a number of others, or at least their application, and information services need to be aware of this.

Standards are copyrighted. Each standards-writing organization to a greater or lesser extent relies upon revenue from the sale of these documents for their continued operation. Therefore, it is most important that standards should not be photocopied. This practice is, however, very common – particularly when collections are held in libraries and where the user has access to a photocopying machine. It is a practice which must be discouraged, because of the financial implications for those organizations in the business of developing standards.

STANDARDS AND TECHNICAL REGULATIONS

The distinction between standards and technical regulations is not always clear and various types of relationships can exist between the two classes of documents. This will now be considered in more detail.

There are three important ways in which standards and technical regulations can relate to each other. First, a document can be simultaneously a standard and a technical regulation; secondly, a standard can be referred to in a technical regulation (this is what we call, in the trade, reference to standards); finally, and probably most important, standards and technical regulations should knit together to form a coherent system.

A standard is also a technical regulation when the provisions it includes are mandatory. This is the case for all standards in a number of countries, including most countries in Eastern Europe. The documents issued by the national standards bodies of these countries are called standards, but they have the force of technical regulations. Even where it exists the concept of the voluntary standard may sometimes be rather academic. A voluntary standard becomes mandatory in practice, if insisted upon by an important purchaser or by an authority who may refuse facilities for the use of a product which does not conform. For example, a gas board may refuse to allow an appliance to be connected to the mains if it does not comply with certain standards. In Canada, each province and territory has made it mandatory that all electrical household appliances meet the relevant standards of the Canadian Standards Association (CSA). The documents issued by the CSA are called standards, but once mandated, they have the force of technical regulations.

The second important relationship concerns technical regulations which do not include in themselves the complete technical details necessary for their application but, instead, make reference to a standard which does include such details. This procedure helps international and national governmental agencies to simplify and accelerate legislative work; it is described in a publication issued jointly by ISO and by the International Electrotechnical Commission (IEC).[2]

The principle of reference to standards also helps to secure a harmonious, compatible system of standards and technical regulations, taken together. The extent to which standards and technical regulations complement and do not contradict each other is of prime importance in securing an optimum degree of order.

THE ORGANIZATION OF STANDARDIZATION

Standardization takes place at national, regional and international levels. At each of these levels there are bodies whose principal function is standardization, and other bodies with broader functions including certain activities concerned with standardization. The former are referred to as standards bodies. These terms have been formally defined and the distinction is mentioned here since the standards bodies, apart from being the main publishers of standards, generally also have a coordinating role.

National Standardization

In some countries standardization is almost completely centralized and based on a single organization. This is the case for most countries of Eastern Europe where the national standards body is a governmental agency, dealing with standardization for all fields including electrotechnology. The standards bodies have the additional responsibility of enforcing the implementation of standards.

At the other end of the scale there are countries in which standardization work is spread over several standardizing bodies. An extreme case is the United States of America where standards are issued by more than 400 organizations operating in various branches of trade and industry. In such countries it is usual to find an organization with a coordinating role for international purposes, and often a separate governmental agency keeping an eye on public interests.

In between these two extremes there are many countries where standardization is nominally the concern of a single national standards body, but in which certain fields of standardization have become the responsibility of other bodies. This is the situation in Canada, where responsibility has been assigned to the Standards Council of Canada, a crown corporation created in 1970 by an Act of Parliament. Its object – "to foster and promote voluntary standardization in the health, safety and welfare of the public, assisting and protecting consumers, and, not least, facilitating domestic and international trade, and furthering international cooperation in the field of standards."

The Standards Council does not write standards. Instead, it acts as the coordinating body of the National Standards System (NSS). The System is made up of organizations concerned with voluntary standardization in Canada. Voluntary standardization includes such activities as standards-writing, certification, testing and the operation of quality assessment schemes. The System was designed to provide a comprehensive Canadian standardization capability to meet both national and international requirements and responsibilities.

Regional Standardization

Regional standards organizations have been established in several geographic areas. Their members are the national standards bodies of the countries in their regions and their objectives include the promotion and harmonization of standardization activities. Most of them publish standards intended for adoption by their members as national standards.

In Europe, the regional standards organizations are the European Committee for Standardization (CEN) which deals with standardization for all areas of technology not within the scope of the European Committee for Electrotechnical Standardization (CENELEC). These organizations link the national European Communities (EC) and the European Free Trade Association (EFTA).

Other standardizing bodies exist at the regional level in Europe and elsewhere. Some of them are governmental, and responsible for a great deal of activity leading to the publication of standards and technical regulations.

International Standardization

ISO is one of two specialized international agencies for standardization. ISO works in virtually every subject area of technology with the exception of electrical and electronics, which are the responsibility of the IEC. Both organizations publish international standards.

Apart from these two international standards organizations, many governmental and nongovernmental international organizations are involved in some way with standardization and more than 300 are listed as being in liaison with ISO technical bodies.[3] Information on some 40 international standardizing bodies has been prepared in the form of a directory.[4]

ISO membership, at present, comprises a single member body or correspondent member from each of 90 countries. These bodies are the recognized standards institutes, chosen as being most representative of standardization in their respective countries; the ISO member body for Canada is the SCC.

The technical work of ISO is carried out by technical committees, sub-committees, working groups and study groups. The secretariats of these technical bodies are distributed among the ISO member bodies. Other international organizations make an invaluable contribution to the work of ISO through their liaisons with the technical committees and sub-committees.

The technical work is coordinated by the ISO Central Secretariat in Geneva. So far it has resulted in the publication of more than 7,000 international standards.[5]

ISONET

In 1969 ISO Council formally recognized the importance of ensuring the universal availability of information about standards and related matters by establishing an Information Committee known as INFCO. This committee has two main tasks: to advise Council on matters concerning scientific and technical information and to link the standards information centers of the member bodies more closely to form a network, now known as ISONET.

The second initiative taken by Council in 1969 was to set up an ISO Information Center at the Central Secretariat in Geneva. The main tasks of the Center are to meet the needs of ISO members for information on international standards and similar documents, to provide information on standardization when required by other international organizations and to serve local needs in the Central Secretariat. The ISO Information Center is a member of ISONET and also has a coordinating role.

Even before the formal establishment of ISONET there had been exchanges of information between the standards bodies. Every member body of ISO receives copies of all ISO standards and there is an agreement for the mutual exchange of national standards and standards catalogues. The result is that in nearly every country there is a library of standards available for consultation. Most member bodies have sets of international standards and of nearly all foreign standards and of the related catalogues. Most of the standards bodies have a further arrangement to act as each other's sales agents for documents in their respective countries.

ISONET therefore had a good start, but more was needed. The levels of information activity in the various countries differed widely. Also some member bodies preferred to delegate the information activity, in whole or in part, to another body. The need to associate technical regulations with any comprehensive standards information system was becoming obvious. To take account of these various factors, it was decided to draw up a constitution for ISONET and to define the conditions for participation in its activities. The Third Edition of the Constitution was published in 1985, incorporating in the same booklet the conditions for participation.[6]

The aims of ISONET were stated as:

- to promote closer cooperation among its members on questions of information;

- to aid the transfer of technology for development;

- to reduce technical barriers to trade;

- to encourage coordination on standardization and implementation of standards, by promoting the flow of information on standards, technical regulations and related matters.

The basic idea behind ISONET is that each national member shall accept responsibility for providing information about standardizing activities in its own country, with the ISO Information Center playing a similar role internationally. Each should aim to become the focal point for information about all kinds of technical requirements operative in the country concerned. Members agree to make this information available to each other as required and to respond to all reasonable inquiries.

INFCO has become the general assembly of ISONET which now has 72 national members and five international affiliates. INFCO has formed an ISONET Management Board with a chairman and members from nine countries to act as an executive committee. Working groups established by INFCO have prepared second editions of the ISONET Thesaurus[7] and of the

Indexing Manual.[8] A guide[9] has been prepared to help ISONET members with the more routine aspects of operating a standards information center.

While ISONET cannot yet offer worldwide online access to information on standards and technical regulations, it can offer assistance in most countries by way of the national ISONET member.

ISONET is fortunate in that most of its members are also publishers of standards; with the agreements mentioned above, it should be possible to obtain almost any national or international standard by applying to the national ISONET member. Technical regulations may sometimes prove more difficult but the national ISONET member should be able to identify the supplier in most cases, by way of international contacts through ISONET.

THE AGREEMENT ON TECHNICAL BARRIERS TO TRADE (STANDARDS CODE)

The Agreement on Technical Barriers to Trade[10] is one of the multilateral agreements, or codes, within the General Agreement on Tariffs and Trade (GATT); it is also referred to as the GATT Standards Code. It aims to ensure that when governments or other bodies adopt technical regulations or standards, for reasons of safety, health, consumer or environmental protection, or other purposes, these should not create unnecessary obstacles to trade. It also provides for measures of assistance to developing countries in the application of technical regulations or standards.

One of the important provisions of the Standards Code is that signatories agree to take account of international standards in their own national technical regulations or standards. Whenever a relevant international standard does not exist or the technical content of a proposed technical regulation or national standard is not substantially the same as the technical content of relevant international standards, and if the technical regulation or standard may have a significant effect on the trade of other signatories, the signatory is obliged to publish a notice and to notify other parties through the GATT Secretariat. Another provision is that signatories shall ensure that inquiry points exist in their countries to answer inquiries from other signatories about standards, technical regulations and certification systems adopted or proposed in the country concerned.

The Agreement on Technical Barriers to Trade which entered into force on 1 January 1980 has so far been signed on behalf of 39 countries and the European Communities, making the total number of signatories 40.

ISONET AND THE GATT STANDARDS – COOPERATION

With the large measure of common objectives, it is natural that those responsible for the implementation of ISONET and of the Standards Code should work closely together. The cooperation starts with the secretariats. The GATT Secretariat and the ISO Central Secretariat are both in Geneva. There are frequent consultations and exchanges of information between the two secretariats. A GATT Secretariat representative is invited to all meetings of INFCO and ISO is invited by the GATT to send an observer to meetings of the GATT Committee on Technical Barriers to Trade.

Equally close liaison is essential at the national level. Many countries have recognized the advantages of locating the information center of the national member of ISO and the GATT Inquiry Point together in the same place. Nineteen of the signatories of the code have located a GATT Inquiry Point with the national ISONET member and in 15 of these cases this is the only inquiry point with complete responsibility for all information activities concerning technical regulations, standards and certification systems in the framework of both ISONET and the GATT Standards Code.

The fact that the GATT Agreement involves governments, while the national ISO member body may be either governmental or non-governmental, has had different effects in different countries. In some countries the government has delegated responsibility for the GATT Inquiry Point to the ISO member body which is also the ISONET member. This is the case, for example, in Canada, the FRG, France, and Norway amongst others. In contrast, the ISO member body for the USA which is a private organization (the American National Standards Institute – ANSI) has nominated the National Institute of Standards and Technology (NIST) as the national member of ISONET. The NIST is also responsible for the GATT Inquiry Point. Both these methods have the same satisfactory result of bringing the two information activities together with a consequent economy of effort and greater efficiency.

Unfortunately, in a number of countries obstacles have arisen to prevent the merging of the two activities. In such cases it is very important that the two centers, usually one for voluntary standards and the other for technical regulations, should maintain close contact with each other.

INFORMATION SYSTEMS AND SERVICES

All national standards bodies receive inquiries about their standards from the public that they serve. The growth in international trade has meant that they also receive inquiries about international and foreign standards. The consequence has been that almost every standards body has set up some sort of information service.

In general, these national standards information services are responsible for providing to their own national public, and to those in other countries, information on national, international and foreign standards, specifications, codes, standards-related information, certification systems, and standardization activities.

STANDARDS IN INFORMATION TRANSFER

An international standard is the result of a study of the technical, economic, and social aspects of its subject, taking into account both producer and user considerations. It is a technical digest and represents an advanced form of information analysis and presentation, tailored to a particular purpose. Hence the standard itself is the result of an information exercise and is a powerful instrument for the transfer of technology. These remarks apply also to national standards which are, to an increasing degree, based upon the international standards. National and international standards represent an important bank of information affecting almost every aspect of human activity.

While all standards are carriers of information, some are of double interest to the information profession since they are designed to aid the various aspects of information transfer. The standards prepared by the following three ISO technical committees are of particular importance in this connection:

ISO/TC 37: Terminology. Scope: standardization of methods for setting up and for coordinating national and international standardized terminologies.

ISO/TC 46: Documentation. Scope: standardization of practices relating to libraries, documentation and information centers, indexing and abstracting services, archives, information science and publishing.

ISO/TC 97: Computer and information processing. Scope: standardization in the area of computers and associated information processing systems and peripheral equipment, devices and media relating thereto.

CONCLUSION

An attempt has been made in this paper to provide an overview of standards and technical regulations and their importance to trade. The paper has also provided a brief overview of the worldwide network of information centers which can provide the user with access to sources of this specialized information. As a first step in accessing this information, the user should contact his national member of ISONET and/or GATT.

Notes

1. ISO Guide 2: General terms and their definitions concerning standardization and certification. 3rd ed. (Geneva: ISO, 1980) Addendum 1 - 1981.

2. ISO/IEC Guide 15: ISO/IEC code of principles on "reference to standards". (Geneva: ISO, 1977).

3. ISO Liaisons, (Geneva: ISO, 1985).

4. Directory of International Standardizing Bodies. 3rd ed. ISBN 92-67-01026-3. (Geneva: ISO, 1982).

5. ISO Catalogue, (Geneva: ISO, 1990).

6. ISONET Constitution, 3rd ed. ISBN 92-67-02011-0. (Geneva: ISO, 1985).

7. The International Technical Thesaurus (Le Thesaurus International Technique) (TIT). (Paris: AFNOR, 1981).

8. ISONET Manual, 2nd ed. (Geneva: ISO, 1984).

9. ISONET Guide, 1st ed. ISBN 92-67-20042-9. (Geneva: ISO, 1980).

10. Agreement on Technical Barriers to Trade. (Geneva: Agreement on Tariffs and Trade, 1979).

Electronic Access to Standards and Technical Documents

JACK L. MASSAU AND JAMES L. TEAL, E.I. DU PONT DE NEMOURS & COMPANY

ELECTRONIC STANDARDS – THE REALITY AND THE DREAM

Rummaging through stacks and volumes of paper for a single mathematical equation is no one's idea of a good time. Retrieval from hard copy is difficult, time-consuming, costly, and tedious. The worst part is that many standards users run out of time or patience before they even find the information they need.

Further complicating matters is the fact that today's standards users must deal with standards developers on an individual basis. With more than 270 active standards developers in the U.S. alone, users must spend untold hours managing their standards – receiving and assimilating the revisions, updates, and new standards. As an added frustration, the format of the standards they receive often varies greatly from one developer to another.

Most standards users know enough about computers to believe that an electronic delivery system could make better use of their time, effort, and budget dollars. The ideal system, they feel, would be one where users view and address standards developers as a single entity; in other words, they want one-stop shopping for all standards and related technical information. They also want that information to pass quickly and easily from developer to user.

This material was prepared in a larger report by the technical subcommittee of the ANSI Standards and Data Services Committee. It was also presented in part as "Issues in Electronic Publishing" at the 82nd Annual Meeting of the American Association of Law Libraries, Reno, Nev., 21 June 1989. For related information, see also Jack L. Massau, ed., "A Standard Approach for Electronic Access to Standards and Technical Documents," *Standards Engineering* 42 (January/February 1990) 9-10.

The electronic transmission would consist of text, graphics, hot (i.e., instant) links to references and other standards, formulas, and eventually even video and audio components. Of course, it would be user friendly with one set of keystrokes and one way to locate the needed information. Lastly, because the standards developers would be cooperating with one another, this ideal system would surely lead to greater format consistency.

IN SEARCH OF AN ELECTRONIC DELIVERY SYSTEM

As one such standards user, Du Pont has been well aware of the potential benefits to be derived from electronic distribution of standards and technical information. A user of national standards and a developer of internal engineering standards, Du Pont spends roughly $5 million per year developing, revising, and reaffirming its set of three thousand engineering standards.

In 1985, Du Pont estimated that it could save $2 million per year by distributing standards electronically but only if it could receive compatible national and international standards electronically via a common delivery system with a common user interface.

Venturing into the electronic publishing arena, Du Pont quickly learned that individual standards developers and publishers were looking at electronic delivery and that some were even beginning to implement systems. However, as suspected, there was very little, if any, cooperative effort on behalf of users.

Du Pont was unwilling to accept a host of different user interfaces and different hardware and software systems and so delayed computerizing its standards. It instead channeled its energy into encouraging a cooperative effort among standards developers. As a logical first step, Du Pont contacted the American National Standards Institute (ANSI), the organization that coordinates voluntary standards activities in the United States and serves as the U.S. member of the International Standards Organization (ISO) and the International Electrotechnical Commission (IEC).

Responding to the stated needs of Du Pont and others in the standards community, ANSI's board of directors established a Standards and Data Services Committee (SDSC) in September 1988 to explore the possibility of a cooperative electronic publishing and delivery effort among standards developers and publishers.

In early 1989, the Standards and Data Services Committee surveyed ANSI company members to determine user interest in electronic delivery. As expected, the survey results showed users of standards and technical information to be keenly interested in electronic delivery and access. A clear majority (74 percent) of the respondents expressed interest in receiving copies of standards in electronic form today, with 77 percent desiring that capability within five years. In fact, 66 percent of the respondents already distribute documents electronically within their companies. As experienced computer users, most of those surveyed want to access standards from a desktop workstation, preferably a personal computer. Fully half of the respondents are now looking for electronic search capabilities. A common concern is the cost factor.

PUTTING THE EXPERTS TO WORK

Hearing the resounding call for a state-of-the-art, yet cost-effective electronic delivery system, the SDSC formed a technical subcommittee to assess current technology and to recommend a strategy for a cooperative effort.

In August 1989, this subcommittee, consisting of ANSI company member representatives from both industry and government, submitted its findings to the ANSI board of directors. Edited by Jack L. Massau and entitled "A Standard Approach for Electronic Access to Standards and Technical Documents," the subcommittee report begins by recognizing that, without a cooperative development effort, standards organizations will likely take independent and dissimilar approaches to electronic distribution of standards. Besides greatly reducing efficiency and productivity, the cost of such an approach would keep many standards users in hard-copy mode indefinitely.

To avert that dismal forecast, the technical subcommittee experts began by reviewing the needs of standards users and those of the standards developers and publishers; they then envisioned the type of system that could meet those needs. In addition, their report considered the impact–both positive and negative–of such a system on the standards community. Finally, the experts surveyed the status of their vision (illustrated in Figure 1).

WHO NEEDS WHAT?

Beginning with the group that stands to benefit the most from an electronic delivery system, the technical subcommittee described the needs of the user. To meet user needs, the envisioned system must be able to:

- Access the document libraries and databases of different publishers from a personal computer (workstation) through a standard user interface.

- Present an interface that is functionally the same among different publishers on the same workstation (e.g., uses the same keystrokes and uses a windowing environment, such as the Apple MacIntosh).

FIGURE 1. AN ILLUSTRATION OF A STANDARDIZED APPROACH TO THE ELECTRONIC ACCESS AND DELIVERY OF STANDARDS AND TECHNICAL DOCUMENTS

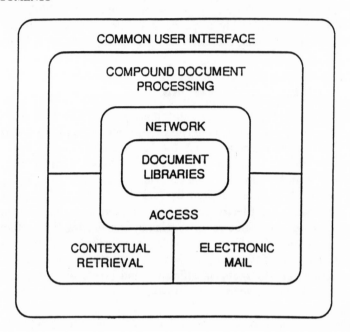

- Use a standard query language to find documents of interest by key words abstracted from the text or title, by author or version, or by full-text search.

- Obtain a copy of a desired compound document and display, print, save, or transmit through electronic mail all content types included in the document.

- Edit text and tables in the document and resize or crop other content types.

- Operate independently of the hardware vendor's computer and workstation hardware, operating system, and communications technology (vendor transparency and application portability).

- Perform all of these functions quickly and easily in the user's normal desktop computing environment (e.g., DEC ALL-IN-1).

From the standpoint of standards developers and publishers, the envisioned system must be able to:

- Use the same content capture and editing systems in preparing material for both hard-copy and electronic distribution.

- Capture and store all material in editable form in an electronic database to allow more efficient and reliable retention and faster, more efficient retrieval and use.

- Electronically process all of the content types required for normal technical publishing (e.g., text, tables, drawings, images).

- Electronically disseminate manuscript drafts for review and electronic comments.

- Perform all of these functions in a totally integrated manner.

THE VISION

It sounds like a tall order, but the technical subcommittee believes it is possible to develop an electronic delivery system that (1) meets user needs and (2) fits into existing technical publishing activities, allowing publishers to create both electronic and hard-copy versions of standards without a lot of extra effort. The committee even believes that it is well within the realm of technical capability to achieve this vision by 1992.

The integrated system the subcommittee has envisioned is based on the creation, storage, and distribution of compound documents. For standards and technical data, a compound document can contain many different content types, including text, graphics, images, tables, mathematical equations, graphs, and artwork. The system would capture information in a format useful to commercial technical publishers and standards users alike. In the future, with the introduction of affordable technology, the content types in electronic compound documents would likely include sound, animation, and full-motion video.

The components required to make the envisioned system a reality fall into the following areas of technology:

- Electronic equipment (computers, image scanners, workstations) and software (word processors, drawing packages, image processors) that can capture the various types of information (equations, photographs, drawings) in an electronically processible form.

- Software that can format compound documents for printing or display in the required format (newspaper, technical journal, monograph).

- Hardware and software that can actually present the material on the desired medium (paper, display, microfiche).

- Software that can be used to classify the contents of a document so that it can be easily retrieved.

- Software that can be used to search through a library of documents to find those that satisfy a user's search criteria.

- Hardware, including large volume transportable media (CD-ROM), that stores large libraries of compound documents for rapid and convenient access.

- Communications hardware and software that allow electronic transport of documents between central libraries and users.

- Software running on a user's personal workstation that will allow him or her to search, retrieve, view, edit, print, save, and mail documents.

OPPORTUNITIES AND COSTS

An electronic delivery system will have a major impact on everyone involved in the creation, publication, distribution, and use of standards and technical information as well as on the suppliers of the hardware, software, and communications technology.

The Vendor

Hardware and software vendors will discover a rich market for products that support the vision – specifically, hardware and software products that allow the author to prepare an electronic manuscript directly usable by the publisher.

However, some of these products must first be developed and brought to market. Communication suppliers, for example, must supply much higher bandwidth to the end user for transmission of compound documents. While development of these products will demand an initial investment, the technical subcommittee believes that the broad-based market for such products probably justifies vendor development at no cost to the standards user community.

The Author

Authors will benefit from guidelines and instructions specifically geared to the type of manuscript (newspaper article, technical paper, etc.) they need to create. Equipped with required file formats and style sheets for the manuscript as a whole and for each different content type, authors should find it easier to outline and structure their work.

To successfully interface with the publisher, authors will need to use document processing software that conforms to the selected international standards and that supports the required compound document features. This will require the purchase of new software not currently available and, for many, the purchase of more powerful personal computers.

The Standards Developer, Publisher, and Distributor

The standards developer will begin receiving electronic manuscript drafts that conform more closely to the appropriate standards – drafts that require much less editing. The use of electronic transmission will enable the publisher to quickly mail the draft to a reviewer distribution list. By giving a broad audience access to the draft, the envisioned document library will set up an ongoing and informal means of capturing comments. Overall, such a means of receiving and disseminating drafts and capturing comments will greatly speed the standards development process while reducing manpower requirements. Furthermore, the envisioned system gives standards developers, publishers, and distributors the opportunity to provide superior service and value to their customers, which should increase their customer base.

First, however, standards developers, publishers, and distributors must agree collectively to support the selected standards. They must also install hardware and software and implement practices and procedures that support the vision. A major change will be the conversion of existing systems to new, fully electronic versions. There will be added costs to make this transition. However, once the transition is accomplished, costs should be lowered through improved efficiency and offset by greater revenues from increased market opportunities.

The User

Electronic standards users will receive all of the benefits associated with a single method for faster, easier search of and access to an impressive collection of information. They will need only one set of hardware and software to access, search for, retrieve, process, retain, and share information from many different sources.

To achieve these benefits, users will also need to make an initial investment. They must have access to a personal computer equipped with hardware and software that are able to electronically access remote libraries and handle compound documents locally. In addition, they will need subscriptions to the information sources they want to access.

WHERE DO WE GO FROM HERE?

The first step is to communicate the vision to key organizations involved in the development, publishing, and distribution of standards to achieve alignment and cooperation. This effort thus far has been driven by the user community and not by the standards organizations. The users, including agencies of the United States government, are well aligned on the need for the vision. Agreement among standards developers, publishers, and distributors is now required.

Reaching the level of agreement required will depend in large part on how successfully these groups can navigate key marketing issues. Many standards developers generate 50 percent or more of their income from sale of standards, and they must know that their income will be protected in the electronic world before they will continue down this path.

Once alignment and cooperation have been achieved, the current high-level vision must be converted into a detailed plan. We must develop functional specifications based on the appropriate standards and review them with sponsors, users, and potential vendors. While a number of technical obstacles are currently impeding our progress, technology is expected to evolve rapidly in the next few years, and we must be prepared to go forward the moment those problems are resolved.

Technological factors currently limiting the electronic distribution and sharing of standards and technical information fall generally into five categories.

- Adequate handling of compound documents requires larger, higher-resolution displays than those currently available at a suitable cost.

- Transmission of compound documents between a central host and a local workstation requires higher communication bandwidth than that currently being installed.

- Although individual software products are available to perform all of the individual tasks within the envisioned system operation, an integrated solution is not available.

- Workstations capable of performing the tasks required to support electronic compound documents are currently too costly (about $10,000) for many users.

- Large-volume optical storage required to support large document libraries is not in widespread use, although cost, availability, and capacity are improving rapidly.

Finally, it should surprise no one that full realization of the envisioned system will rest on the standards governing its creation and development. The success of a common approach that can be implemented with different vendor hardware and software products will require adherence to standards. At present, a suitable base of international standards exists for document functionality. However, additional standards development is required to cover more advanced capabilities now supported for hard-copy presentation but not for electronic display.

For those who share in the dream of electronic standards, the vision put forth by the technical subcommittee is an honest yet motivating map to the future. In challenging the standards community to unite on this issue, the subcommittee members remind us that, separately or together, we influence the face of American creativity and innovation.

PART 4

Developing Standards for Accessibility

A Case Study in the Development of a Research-Based Building Accessibility Standard: ANSI A-117.1 (1980)

EDWARD STEINFELD, SCHOOL OF ARCHITECTURE AND ENVIRONMENTAL DESIGN, STATE UNIVERSITY OF NEW YORK AT BUFFALO

The Federal government, every state in the United States and many municipalities issue regulations for making outdoor environments and buildings accessible and usable by people with disabilities. Most of these regulations are based in whole or in part on a consensus standard, ANSI A117.1 (1961, R1971), *Specifications for Making Buildings and Facilities Accessible to and Usable by the Physically Handicapped*. A consensus standard includes criteria that are supported by representatives of consumer, industry, official and professional interests. It is believed that a consensus standard reduces the proliferation of varied and conflicting regulations by serving as an authoritative source. To be truly authoritative, the standards must be acceptable to *all* interest groups affected by the regulations. For several reasons, ANSI A117.1 (1961, R1971) did not achieve this end. Thus, over the years, regulations issued by many authorities departed significantly from the basic ANSI standard. Its credibility eventually became questionable and the proliferation of different criteria caused confusion. This situation promoted a major revision of the original ANSI standard which was adopted in 1980.[1] A further revision is now underway.

In the development and revision of a standard for accessibility, certain pivotal issues must be raised and resolved. How this is accomplished will determine the success of the standard as an authoritative and generally acceptable document. Its adoption by government agencies as regulations will be based on political positions taken on these issues.

Originally published in *The Cost of Not Knowing*, proceedings of the 17th annual conference of the Environmental Design Research Association. Oklahoma City: EDRA, 1986, 323-27. Reprinted with permission.

A standard represents codified social norms. Revisions to such a document over time reflect changes in political power, attitudes and values and technical knowledge. From a researcher's point of view, they also reflect the extent to which empirical knowledge has been accepted by authorities as a basis for "good design."

ISSUE 1: TARGET POPULATION

ANSI A117.1 (1961, R1971) was explicitly developed to provide accessibility for: (1) the non-ambulatory, (2) the semi-ambulatory, (3) those with hearing impairments, (4) those with incoordination, and (5) the elderly. The actual criteria, however, implicitly omitted consideration of people who were very severely disabled and those with sensor disabilities. For example, the minimum toilet stall design requirements satisfied the needs of people who use wheelchairs only if they had full use of their upper body and limbs or some use of legs in addition to sufficient strength to lift and pivot themselves from a frontal position. Likewise, only a few statements in the standard focused on features related to the needs of people with sensory disabilities. The features were not sufficient for full and convenient use of facilities by totally blind people and those with partial sight. For example, no requirements were included to ensure that blind people would know at which floor an elevator had stopped. There were several reasons for these omissions: (1) the state-of-the-art of research rehabilitation medicine at the time, (2) the demographics of disability, and (3) the expediency of developing a standard that would be accepted on a nationwide basis. During the 1970s, there developed an increased public consciousness of accessibility concerns and an increase in the number of disabled people who could live independently. Thus, an extension of scope to a wider target population became timely.

By its very name, ANSI A117.1 addresses the needs of disabled people. Thus, the standard identifies things that should be done to improve their quality of life. This approach reinforces their "special" status in society. However, all people may benefit from an environment that is more convenient to use. One might ask why the standard did not treat disabled people as simply a subset of the general population and deal with broader issues of access and usability. In fact, it can be demonstrated that those who are disabled are not a finite group of people. Inevitably, most able-bodied people will experience disability and those who are disabled in youth will become more disabled in old age. The developers of the successive versions of ANSI A117.1 believed that the goal of the standard was primarily to obtain accessibility for those to whom it had been denied. If that goal was not explicitly identified, opponents could question the need for a standard to promote accessibility of buildings for all people, most of whom can obviously use them reasonably well already. Thus, the standard has retained a title that focuses on this specific goal.

Identifying the target population for an accessibility standard, nevertheless, raises two important additional issues: (1) Which disabilities should be considered? (2) What levels of environmental competence should be assumed for people with each disability?

The 1980 revisions gave attention to all types of physical and sensory disabilities but not to equal degrees. The non-ambulant person was used in much of the standard as the "lowest common denominator." With regard to the second issue, it was decided to focus on people who would be able to live independently. Thus, for example, the standard did not address the needs of residents of group homes for the developmentally disabled. The current revisions have not extended the target population any further.

ISSUE 2: SCOPE OF APPLICATION

ANSI A117.1 (1961, R1971) focused on providing basic principles for accessibility and usability of publicly used buildings in general. As it was adopted into regulations, however, its application for the most part was limited to such buildings constructed in whole or in part with public funds. This approach was certainly the most feasible politically, given that accessibility had never been mandated before. However, access to community facilities such as stores and restaurants is necessary for normal independent living. ANSI A117.1 (1980) was extended in scope to address a full range of building types. That scope has been retained in the current revisions.

As the civil rights movement for racial minorities moved from concern with public accommodations to concern with housing and employment, so did the movement for barrier-free design. Making housing accessible became a major goal of the revisions to the original ANSI standard. Two major questions that had to be resolved were: (1) should accessibility be built in from the start or should units be made adaptable so that modifications that are needed can be made with minimum cost and effort and? (2) should only some units be made accessible, or should they all be accessible? The developers of ANSI A117.1 (1980) opted for adaptability because it would be less costly per unit, more flexible for users and promote wider application. The number of units to be made accessible was deemed to be a subject for regulations rather than a standard. The revisions now in progress have taken the approach that either adaptability or fixed accessibility are acceptable. However, the number of units to be accessible has not been specified in the latest draft.

A similar issue arises when considering places of employment. Many employment settings are typically inaccessible to people with certain disabilities. Yet, accessibility of a building is not always a prerequisite for the full solution to equal opportunity in employment. In developing ANSI A117.1 (1980), it was decided that full access to places of employment was another topic that should be a concern of regulations, and not a standard. This approach has remained in the current revisions.

Accessibility to *new* buildings alone is not sufficient to normalize life for people with disabilities. A very real part of achieving full accessibility in the community is changing that part of the built environment that already exists and is not accessible. This effort could be unfeasible if renovations must meet the same criteria as new construction. These issues were addressed in the 1980 standard by specifying only a minimum threshold of acceptability and leaving it up to administrative authorities to determine which buildings had to comply and to what extent. The current revisions utilize the same approach.

ISSUE 3: USABILITY OF STANDARDS AND REGULATIONS

The use of the document presents another set of issues. The 1961-71 ANSI standard stated technical criteria as minimum requirements. Because the minima, when applied, became the maximum provided, the 1980 and the current revisions encouraged designers to go beyond minimum levels.

A related issue is the use of performance or prescriptive criteria. The 1980 ANSI standard was much more performance-oriented than the original. Ideally, standards and regulations should specify objectives rather than the means of achieving them; yet this "performance approach" can be a two-edged sword. If standards and regulations are overly prescriptive, they become unwieldy and inflexible for use in design. For example, specifying only one acceptable bathroom layout would be too prescriptive. On the other hand, performance objectives that do not provide specific criteria against which designs can be evaluated often promote lack of enforcement. Thus, ANSI (1980) incorporated the performance approach in quantitative form, wherever possible. The form of criteria has remained essentially unchanged in the current revisions.

Standards for accessibility are only one of the many sets of standards that are used in the building industry. Adopted as regulations, they have not only been issued by government agencies but also incorporated in building codes. Building codes are usually organized into sections dealing with general provisions and specific provisions for building types. Other standards used by the industry are trade or component specific, such as those of the electrical industry or elevator manufacturers. Compatibility with the form of the existing regulatory system can have a great impact on implementation of accessibility standards. Neither the 1961 or 1980 versions nor the current revisions followed the building type, trade, or component format. It was felt that this approach would keep the standard concise and well focused on its goal.

ISSUE 4: THE ROLE OF RESEARCH

A key issue in the development of standards is the source of knowledge on which technical criteria and scope will be based. At the time that ANSI A117.1 (1961, R1971) was written, there was little empirical research on accessibility. This knowledge gap became apparent over the years. The gap resulted in lack of confidence in the standard. Many modifications of technical criteria in the standard were made through local, state and federal regulations. By 1980, a considerable body of research had been completed that improved the state of knowledge. This research, however, was not comprehensive. Many issues still needed attention or further work. The 1980 revisions were based on an empirical knowledge base as much as possible in contrast to relying solely on anecdotes and expert opinion as in the original version. Even though enough research had not been completed on certain topics, it was felt that "something was better than nothing" so that some criteria were based on a heavier "dose" of professional opinion than empirical knowledge. In still others, professional opinion alone was used.

This mix of approaches raises problems but it also stimulates further research and development. For example, over the last several years, one Federal agency, the U.S. Architectural and Transportation Barriers Compliance Board (ATBCB) has generated its research agenda primarily by focusing on the "soft" areas of the ANSI standard in order to improve the knowledge base.[2]

IMPLICATIONS

The issues discussed above are fundamentally policy issues. If they are not resolved adequately, standards may have serious flaws in use. The most critical flaw for ANSI A117.1 would be restrictions on accessibility for people with disabilities. What good are accessibility standards if they don't measurably improve accessibility? Another serious flaw would be major cost implications. If the cost of accessibility detracts from marketability, there will be serious objections to implementing the accessibility requirements. Another flaw would be "red tape." If the new standards and regulations are difficult to use as an evaluation tool or if unreasonable means must be used to satisfy them, delays in obtaining code approval can severely impact construction projects. Given the profusion of such problems in the building industry already, a new difficult regulation is not greeted warmly.

IMPACT OF THE 1980 VERSION

In general, the 1980 versions were well received by disabled consumers, with resignation by architects, with mixed feelings by code officials, and with some resistance by building owners. Much of the positive reaction could be attributed to the increased attention given to the full range of disabilities, the expanded scope, the greater flexibility and the great increase in technical information. On the negative side, the 1980 version required a major reorientation for those familiar with the old version. There were several areas in the standard that needed editorial clarification and there were some requirements that were felt by building owners to be too costly or stringent. The latter dealt primarily with the idea of adaptability in housing. Much of the negative reaction was related to the applications of the standard rather than the technical criteria and was a direct response to the decision made by the ANSI A117.1 Committee to relegate the scope of application to individual administrative agencies.

The 1980 version seems to be very well accepted now that its newness has been overcome through familiarity and use. Thus, the current revisions have focused primarily on improving text and illustrations from an editorial point of view and increasing flexibility in some areas. One measure of the standards's impact is its use by federal agencies. The U.S. ATBCB's *Minimum Guidelines and Requirements for Accessible Design* follow the ANSI A117.1 (1980) criteria closely. The technical criteria of Uniform Federal Accessibility Standard (UFAS), promulgated by the four Federal standard-setting agencies is practically identical to ANSI A117.1 (1980). However, both of these documents had to augment the ANSI technical criteria with "scoping" requirements since the standard purposely did not address the extent of application beyond minimum levels. Moreover, UFAS added several sections that addressed specific building types and spaces found in Federal construction.

There has been considerable variation in the scoping provisions from state-to-state and agency-to-agency. This had led to discussion about developing a second model document to focus on this issue but the ANSI A117.1 Committee regards this as the province of building code officials. Moreover, no agency has sought to clarify these issues by sponsoring empirical research on the extent of accessibility that is needed or desirable.

IMPLICATIONS FOR RESEARCH

The issues described here cannot and should not be resolved by one interest group alone. They are issues of political significance that require input from a wide spectrum of interest groups. That is why ANSI committees that approve standards must include broad representation.

Research in human factors and on the social impacts of the standard can be a valuable means toward resolving many of the pivotal issues. However, in order to have a major impact, research results must be received positively and objectively by those involved in standards development. Professionals may not accept findings that imply design solutions different than established practices. Consumers may not accept findings that differ from their own personal experiences. Code officials may resist information that makes design review more difficult and industry may not accept findings that create problems for their business. Changing attitudes may require an educational effort on the part of researchers to convince the various interest groups that an empirical knowledge base is valuable. This can best be accomplished by focusing research on the specific information needs of those groups. For example, one should study whether existing design approaches are usable as well as developing criteria for completely innovative approaches.

Research results will be received more positively if they are based on high quality research methods and/or can be validated by replicating. Sample size and selection, research protocol and analytical methods all play a role in convincing the standards developers that empirical findings are better than professional judgement. Unfortunately, few research sponsors are willing to pay for the highest level of research quality. They generally want more questions answered than can be reasonably handled within the budgets and time limits provided. Researchers, therefore, must help sponsors to establish acceptable cost/benefit trade-offs. The alternative – inconclusive studies or those which have major technical deficiencies – may create even more negative attitudes toward research.

In the end, the development of an authoritative and acceptable standard for accessibility is based on who is involved in the process, how they work together, and what their attitudes are, as well as the quality of information they have to use.

The environmental design research community should take an active role in the development of standards like ANSI A117.1 because they are the most familiar with empirical knowledge bases. Yet, only two research organizations, the National Institute of Standards and Technology and the Gerontological Society, are represented on the Committee which has more than fifty members. To be effective in improving standards, researchers must be willing to enter into the debate on issues for which they often do not have hard data. They must be willing to defer to professional opinion on issues where data is "soft" while being strong advocates of the empirical perspective on others where data is "hard." Such dialogue will not only bring them into the arena as valuable members of the standards community but also help them create research agendas that are grounded in a real "need to know" rather than an individual's intellectual curiosity alone. Practicing professionals and consumers must be taught the value of empirical knowledge in improving standards as well as how to evaluate research and how to make good inferences from it.

During the current review and revisions of the 1980 version, practically no attention has been given to the developing empirical database in the area of barrier-free design, particularly the studies sponsored by the U.S. ATBCB. Perhaps this is justified because the 1980 revision was such a major change. However, it certainly cannot be justified over the long term or for topics where the earlier knowledge base was more limited than it is now.

Given that standards development is an on-going optimizing process, the need for an improved database for ANSI A117.1 is obvious. One could argue today that widening the scope to disabled people in group residential occupancies, providing greater variation in criteria based on building type, establishing guidelines for application of the standard through codes and other regulations, inclusion of more technical information of an advisory nature and other changes in content would improve the standard considerably. Research is needed on all these topics. Information on the most appropriate form for communicating the intent of the standard and insuring its enforcement would be valuable as well.

Notes

1. The author served as Secretary of the ANSI A117.1 Committee during this revision process as well as director of the research project that supported the development of the revisions.

2. The Board has supported, through its research program, the development of a series of state-of-the-art reviews on these "soft" areas and several empirical studies focusing on wayfinding, signage, and hand anthropometrics/mechanics.

PART 5

Information Exchange and the Utility of Standards

An Introduction to Library and Information Services Technical Standards Literature

KEITH A. WINSELL, AMISTAD RESEARCH CENTER, TULANE UNIVERSITY

The purpose of this section is to provide readers with a general introduction to the literature of technical standards as it applies to the field of library and information services. Included is a reprint of the thirty-eight item bibliography prepared by the Library and Information Technology Association of the American Library Association. It covers only material from 1974 to 1984. At the time of this writing (September 1990) there are no immediate plans to update it. However, the organization of that bibliography, as well as the annotations, still provides a useful introduction to the subject.

A good overview of the subject is found in special issues of *Library Trends* published in 1972, 1982, and 1988. Two of the articles reprinted in this volume (Lisa Weber's in part 2 and H. Thomas Hickerson's in part 5) come from the winter 1988 edition. Articles of particular value in the earlier issues are Jerrold Orne's "Standards in Library Technology," *Library Trends* 21 (October 1972): 286-97 and those by Robert W. Frase, Sandra K. Paul, and James L. Wood, *Library Trends* 31 (Fall 1982), cited in the LITA bibliography.

Book Research Quarterly 4, no. 3 (Fall 1988), is a special issue titled "Technical Standards for Books and Journals." It includes the Paul Evan Peters and Walt Crawford ("Future Directions in Standardization") essays included in this volume.

Annotated bibliography issued in *Information Reports and Bibliographies* 15 (1986): 21-24. Reprinted with permission of the American Library Association.

Although some updating is clearly needed, a historical view of aspects of technical standards can be obtained in the following articles that appeared in the *Encyclopedia of Library and Information Sciences* (New York: Marcel Dekker, Inc.): Henriette D. Avram, "Machine-Readable Cataloging (MARC) Program," 16 (1975): 380-413; K. Subramanyan, "Technical Literature," 30 (1980): 176-208; Robert W. Frase, "Technical Standards in the Fields of Library and Information Sciences and Related Publishing Practices: American National Standards Committee Z39," 37, supplement 2 (1984): 361-366; James L. Wood, "The National Information Standards Organization (Z39)," 39 supplement 4 (1985): 291-332.

In his 1982 *Library Trends* article, Robert Frase lamented the fact that "evidence on the use of standards relating to libraries, information services and publishing has not been collected in any systematic way." One method of tracing the random development is through a systematic review of the *Bowker Annual of Library and Book Trade Information* (New York: Bowker), starting with the 1970 volume. This annual provides authoritative essays on the entire scope of library-related issues. Many aspects of standardization, including bibliographic control of nonprint media (1972), are reviewed. Prominent contributors to this annual during the past two decades have included Henriette D. Avram, Patricia W. Berger, Ann T. Curran, Robert W. Frase, Patricia Harris, Sally H. McCallum, Sandra L. Paul, and James L. Wood.

The annual also reports the activities of the National Commission on Libraries and Information Science, the permanent independent agency established in the executive branch in 1970. The commission actively interrelated with the Z39 Committee and issued a sixty-three page report on its effectiveness in 1978. In 1984 Z39 became the National Information Standards Organization. In January 1989, the newsletter title was changed from the *Voice of Z39* to the *Information Standards Quarterly*. The new publication is edited by Walt Crawford. Other periodicals that report related developments are *Information Technology and Libraries* and *Advanced Technology Libraries* (Boston: G.K. Hall).

The *Bowker Annual* also presents an international perspective, with a review of the activities of IFLA (International Federation of Library Associations), which was founded in 1927.

The major monograph on the subject remains Walt Crawford's *Technical Standards: An Introduction for Librarians* (Boston: G.K. Hall). A new edition was published in 1991. The 1986 edition includes a partially annotated bibliography (pp. 279-284).

Another helpful source is the quarterly column "The Standards Connection," written by Lois Upham in the *Journal of Education for Library and Information Science*. Since the spring 1988 issue, she has been offering "general news items" on the subject of library technical standards. She has agreed to utilize that outlet of information to coauthor a more comprehensive literature review in the future. It will include an evaluation of historical sources as well as post-1984 sources and databases.

Following is the 1974-84 annotated bibliography prepared by the Library and Information Technology Association of the American Library Association.

LITA ANNOTATED BIBLIOGRAPHY, 1974-1984

Scope

The LITA Education Committee has prepared this selected bibliography of readings about technical standards for libraries. There are many standards for libraries. There are many standards applicable to libraries. Examples are cataloging standards, the MARC formats, standards developed by bibliographic utilities such as OCLC, collection standards, the library keyboard for typewriters, standards related to services provided by libraries, and standards for materials used by libraries such as the 3 x 5 card. However, the emphasis of this bibliography is on technical standards, i.e., standards related to library automation.

Level and Range

The bibliography is meant to provide citations to articles of an introductory level although in some cases, those of a more advanced nature are included. Citations range from general articles about standards and standard making activity to those dealing with specific areas in which there has been significant technical standards activity. Selections were made for their availability as well as content. Emphasis is on U.S. publications and U.S. and international activity. Lists of standards are not included in this bibliography. They are available from the various standards organizations.

Organization

The bibliography has six sections: (1) *general*, which has citations to articles giving general, introductory information; (2) *current activities*, which cites sources that provide current and updated information; (3) *micrographics*, for which there has been significant activity; (4) *networking*, an area in which standards activity is increasing; (5) *serials*, which has seen recent activity as a holdings standard has been developed; and (6) *other standards or needs*, which cites articles dealing with several other standards or areas in which standards are needed.

Some articles are cited in more than one section. An issue of *Library Trends*, devoted to technical library standards, is cited as well as individual articles of particular interest from that issue.

Updating

The LITA Education Committee plans periodically to review and update the bibliography.

General

Library Trends 31 (Fall 1982).
> Entire issue devoted to technical library standards. Highly recommended.

ALA Standards Manual. Chicago: Committee on Standards, American Library Association, 1983.
> Discusses the purpose of standards, sources, how standards come into being, and procedures for developing ALA standards. Examples of ALA standards are provided.

"ANSI Opposes Enactment of Standards Act." *Journal of Library Automation* 9 (December 1976): 351-52.
> Discusses the reasons for opposition to the Voluntary Standards and Certification Act of 1977, S. 3555. Gives an historical perspective to the concept of the voluntary standards system that has existed in the United States for over 60 years.

Avram, Henriette K., Sally H. McCallum, and Mary S. Price. "Organizations Contributing to Development of Library Standards." *Library Trends* 31 (Fall 1982): 197-223.
> Excellent overview of organizations which develop standards or which have an impact on or affect the development of standards related to library and information technology. Includes information about activities and organizations which are national, international, library-professional, and library-related.

Frase, Robert W. "Procedures for Development and Access to Published Standards." *Library Trends* 31 (Fall 1982): 225-36.
> Summarizes information about the major organizations developing technical standards related to library and information science. Brief histories of the organizations, their structures, and how standards are approved and disseminated are described.

Henderson, M. M. "Standards: Developments & Impacts." *Special Libraries* 72 (April 1981): 142-8.

Provides general information about standards, as well as specific examples of successes (AACR) and failures (variant reduction ratios for microforms). It also provides specific examples of parallel standardization efforts and discusses the mechanisms and motivations for them. Trends and projections discussed are relevant. The final section "Cautions" is a very useful presentation of the problems and pitfalls in standards development and implementation.

Heynen, Jeffrey. "International Micrographics Standards: Report of the 1979 Paris Meeting of ISO/TC 171." *Library Resources & Technical Services* 24 (Winter 1980): 58-63.

Provides a summary of the function of the International Organization for Standardization (ISO), and how a standard is proposed to and approved by this organization. The work of ISO's Technical Committee 171, Micrographics is discussed in the context of the role libraries play in creating and applying standards concerning reproduction of materials.

Orne, J. "Standards in the World of Information Science." In *Information Age: Its Development, Its Impact,* edited by Donald P. Hammer, 145-65. Metuchen, N.J.: Scarecrow Press, 1976.

Readable overview of library and information science standards. Includes brief histories and lists of accomplishments of the various agencies involved in standards; an account of the problems which cause development in this area to be glacial; and an explanation of the standards setting process. Also covers the importance and need for awareness of standards, as well as requirements for the future.

Paul, Sandra K., and Johnnie E. Givens. "Standards Viewed from the Applications Perspective." *Library Trends* 31 (Fall 1982): 325-41.

Discusses a wide range of common standards applications in book publishing and librarianship. User participation and contributions are emphasized (included is a list of Z39 member organizations as of April 1982). Economic impacts are forthrightly presented and future needs are outlined.

Rush, James E. "A Proposed Model for the Development of an Integrated Set of Standards for Bibliographic and Related Data." *Library Trends* 31 (Fall 1982): 237-49.

Proposes a coherent model for standards. The model describes data and messages with the use of seven levels (0 through 6), each level being decreasingly concerned with formal content and structure, and increasingly concerned with human-sensible aspects. Describes how this model relates to already existing standards, and discusses significance of levels in this model missing from other models.

Setting Standards for Libraries: Papers Presented at the ALA Standards Committee Program, June 29, 1981, Sheraton Palace, San Francisco, California. Chicago: American Library Association, 1982.

Topics include determining the need for standards and identifying what the standards should contain; selecting a committee to develop standards; research as the foundation for standards; writing standards from start to finish; implementation and promotion of standards; testing, validating, and revision of standards.

Silberstein, Stephen M. "Standards in a National Bibliographic Network." *Journal of Library Automation* 10 (June 1977): 142-53.

Provides an historical perspective of the field in the late 1970s. Explains the advantages of standards and pressure to adopt standards as a replacement for expensive "custom-fitting," but identifies several issues the library world must fact in adopting standards. Discusses the current standards-setting process and the author's perceived lack of democracy in the process. Calls for more concern with technical standards rather than so much emphasis on standards for intellectual content of records, which can be easily manipulated by computer indexes.

Current Activities

"American National Standards Committee Z39: Library and Information Science and Related Publishing Practices and International Organization for Standardization Technical Committee (TC) 46–Documentation." In *Bowker Annual of Library and Book Trade Information*. 29th ed., 170-73. New York: Bowker, 1984.

Brief description and review of the year's activities of these two organizations. NOTE: each edition of the *Bowker Annual* has an update on these organizations.

McCallum, Sally, "Standards," *RTSD Newsletter* (1984).

Column which updates standards activity related to libraries.

"Standard Fare," *LITA Newsletter*.

Regular column covering standards and the activities of the LITA Committee, Technical Standards for Library Automation (TESLA).

"Standards." In *ALA Yearbook: A Review of Library Events*, 1982, 261-64. Chicago: American Library Association, 1983.

Description of the activities of various organizations involved with standards related to library and information technology. Included are

Z39, X3, ISO's TC46, ALA, and SLA. Information includes a brief description of the group and an overview of the year's activities. NOTE: each edition of the *ALA Yearbook* has an update on standards activity.

Voice of Z39 (now *Information Standards Quarterly*).

Newsletter published by NISO and available at $40 per year from the National Information Standards Organization, P.O. Box 1056, Bethesda, MD 20827.

Micrographics

Avedon, Don M. "Standards," *Journal of Micrographics*.

Written by the technical director of the National Micrographics Association, this frequent feature appeared from 1974 to 1977. The brief articles are very readable and discuss many subjects related to technical standards concerning photographic reproduction of documents. Topics range from descriptions of specific standards, to summary reports of committees working on standards, to explanations of what standards are and who the organizations are that develop them.

Heynen, Jeffrey. "International Micrographics Standards: Report of the 1979 Paris Meeting of ISO/TC 171." *Library Resources & Technical Services* 24 (Winter 1980): 58-63.

Provides a summary of the function of the International Organization for Standardization (ISO), and how a standard is proposed to and approved by this organization. The work of ISO's Technical Committee 171, Micrographics is discussed in the context of the role libraries play in creating and applying standards concerning reproduction of materials.

Networking

Avram, Henriette K., and Sally H. McCallum. "Directions in Library Networking." *Journal of the American Society for Information Science* 31 (November 1980): 438-44.

Discusses the need for standards in today's society where networking has greatly increased our dependence on external, centralized agencies, while at the same time, increasing our need for decentralized automated systems. Standards are cited as very important in order to avoid "fragmentation, which reduces services."

Brown, Thomas P. "Communication Standards for Online Interchange of Library Information." *Library Trends* 31 (Fall 1982): 251-63.

Gives an explanation of ISO's Open Systems Interconnection model which is being developed for the purpose of computerized information interchange within the library community. The model is then used to explain the development of the CLR-funded Linked Systems Project being undertaken by the Library of Congress, RLG, and WLN. The article is technical in nature and requires some prior knowledge of telecommunications terminology in order to understand much of the content.

McCallum, Sally H. "Role of Standards in Networking." *Catholic Library World* 51 (April 1980): 376-9.

Discusses the relationship of cataloging standards to the development of shared cataloging and the evolution of online systems and bibliographic utilities. Extends this development to the next step of increased sharing through national and international databases and the need for communication standards to accomplish such standards.

Pope, Nolan F. "Library Planning for Future Networks." *Resource Sharing Library Networks* 1 (Fall 1981): 11-18.

Emphasizes the necessity of standards so that cooperative activity and resource sharing can be achieved.

Reid, R.S. "Data Communication Protocols: Data Link Controls." *LASIE* 11 (July/August): 12-20.

Excellent presentation of standards applicable to data transmission. Includes an explanation of the layered hierarchies concept of communications protocols – required reading for all who would understand the basics of developments in cooperation between diverse systems and technologies. Beginning with the physical protocol level and ending with the application level protocol, the author explains the specific function-related tasks and the role of standards in each.

Silberstein, Stephen M. "Standards in a National Bibliographic Network." *Journal of Library Automation* 10 (June 1977): 142-53.

Provides an historical perspective of the field in the late 1970s. Explains the advantages of standards and pressure to adopt standards as a replacement for expensive "custom-fitting," but identifies several issues the library world must face in adopting standards. Discusses the current standards-setting process and the author's perceived lack of democracy in the process. Calls for more concern with technical standards rather than so much emphasis on standards for intellectual content of records, which can be easily manipulated by computer indexes.

Wood, James L. "Factors Influencing the Use of Technical Standards in a Nationwide Library and Information Service Network." *Library Trends* 31 (Fall 1982): 343-58.

Explores the history, current use, and issues of standardization in relation to the development of a national information network. The value of a national information network and the importance of technical standards to achieving this goal are continually reaffirmed. However, political, economic, and motivational factors influence progress. Although his analysis of the problems national networking faces is thorough, Mr. Wood's tone and conclusion are optimistic.

Serials

Bales, Kathleen. "The ANSI Standard for Summary Holdings Statements for Serials: The RLIN Implementation." *Serials Review* 6 (October/November 1980): 71-73.

Discusses the practical considerations related to the development and implementation of a national standard for machine-readable summary holdings statements for serials. Standardization of the display, manipulation and transfer of serials holdings information affects the potential of library resource sharing.

Bloss, Marjorie E. "The Standard Unfurled: ANSI Z39 SC42: Holdings Statements at the Summary Level." *Serials Review* 9 (Spring 1983): 79-873.

Discusses the practical considerations related to the development and implementation of a national standard for machine-readable summary holdings statements for serials.

Hirshon, Arnold. "Considerations in the Creation of a Holdings Record Structure for an Online Catalog." *Library Resources & Technical Services* 28 (January/March 1984): 25-40.

Discusses the practical considerations related to the development and implementation of a national standard for machine-readable summary holdings statements for serials.

Wittorf, Robert. "ANSI Z39.42 and OCLC: OCLC's Implementation of the American National Standard Institute's Serial Holdings Statements at the Summary Level." *Serials Review* 9 (Spring 1983): 79-83.

Discusses the practical considerations related to the development and implementation of a national standard for machine-readable summary holdings statements for serials.

Other Standards or Needs

Atherton, Pauline. "Standards for a User-System Interface Language in On-line Retrieval Systems." *Online Review* 2, no. 1 (1978): 57-61.

Deals specifically with the need for standardization in the language or terms used for searching on-line systems. Also gives good general definition of standards.

Ayres, F. H., *et al.*, "The USBC and Control of the Bibliographic Database." *Information Technology and Libraries* 1 (March 1982): 44-48.

Describes the Universal Standard Book Code (USBC) as an alternative to the ISBN; explains the problems inherent in the ISBN; delineates the USBC structure and function. The problem of duplication in databases is discussed from the point of view of how the USBC can operate to uncover duplicates that result from variations in catalogers; interpretations of data.

Bell, Colin, and Kevin P. Jones. "Towards Everyday Language Information Retrieval Systems via Minicomputer." *American Society for Information Science Journal* 30 (November 1979): 334-39.

Describes MORPHS (Minicomputer Operated Retrieval [Partly Heuristic] System), a retrieval system using Boolean logic and a minimum of special control characters.

Crawford, Walt. "Library Standards for Data Structures and Element Identification: U.S. MARC in Theory and Practice." *Library Trends* 31 (Fall 1982): 265-81.

Somewhat technical discussion of MARC formats and the relation to ANSI standards. Recommended for those interested in information about standards beyond the general introductory level.

Hickey, Thomas B., and Phyllis B. Spies. "Standards for Information Display." *Library Trends* 31 (Fall 1982): 315-24.

Discusses the standards issues in applying effective presentation of data in information services and products to the end user. Trends, such as increased attention to the human factors by designers, are emerging, and the authors urge the development of practical guidelines.

Tannehill, Robert S., Jr., and Charles W. Husbands. "Standards and Bibliographic Data Representation." *Library Trends* 31 (Fall 1982): 283-305.

Begins with a brief discussion of the philosophy, background and reasons for data representation. A general introduction to the different types, techniques and characteristics of coding systems is followed by more detailed descriptions of specific kinds of codes. This section includes descriptions of:

1.   identifiers of bibliographic entries such as ISBN, ISSN and LCCN;

2. codes for geographical, political and corporate entries such as the ISO 3166-1981 (for countries), the NUC symbols (for libraries), the OCLC codes (for libraries), and the SAN (an I.D. code for the book industry);
3. binary codes and character sets for Information Exchange such as ASCII and EBCDIC; and,
4. script conversion codes such as ISO and ANSI standards for romanization.

The article concludes with a discussion of problems associated with standardization, including the amount of time that it takes to develop and approve a standard, difficulties in getting people to use standards, and difficulties in getting people to understand standards.

UNISIST Guide to Standards for Information Handling, prepared by UNISIST Working Group on Bibliographic Data Interchange, compiled by Erik Vajda. Paris: UNESCO, 1980.

Provides information about standards, rules, guidelines, directives, and other documents relating to system interchange. Part one deals with an analytic study of the different potential users and the functional processes performed by each category of user. Part two gives references to standards and other materials related to information handling processes.

Williams, M. E. and L. Lannom. "Lack of Standardization of the Journal Title Data Element in Databases." *Journal of the American Society for Information Science* 32 (May 1981): 229-33.

Discusses the problem of changes in journal titles and differences in journal representation within different databases. Analyzes eight databases and determines that there are many differences between journal representations. Recommends that a dictionary search be done before an online search to locate all journal forms and that online vendors develop conversion tables with cross database representations to allow for multi-database searches of the same journal.

Libraries and Access to Information in an Open Systems Environment

CYNTHIA J. DURANCE, NATIONAL ARCHIVES OF CANADA
NEIL MCLEAN, MCQUARRIE UNIVERSITY LIBRARY, AUSTRALIA

ELECTRONIC RESOURCE SHARING AND IFLA

We in the library profession have devoted our careers to finding ways to improve society's access to and use of information. We are equally concerned with organizing and preserving information. Resource sharing is a method by which librarians can provide their clientele with access to information resources beyond the scope or means of their own library. Among librarians it is a time-honored tradition. IFLA (International Federation of Library Association) and its member organizations are dedicated to facilitating resource sharing for the simple reason that no library, however large, can have all of the information required by its clients all of the time. Librarians have always spent significant time and effort looking for new or improved mechanisms to increase their ability to share data and to permit other libraries access to the documents in their collections.

The need for resource sharing has largely influenced the priorities and programmers of IFLA and the library sector. In the manual environment of decades past, this meant the development of international standards for recording data. In most recent years, in recognizing the benefits to be derived from automation of library processes, IFLA has also fostered the creation of standards for machine-readable data formats and dissemination. This programme has been accelerated by the rapid development of library automation and the recognition of the economies to be achieved by sharing bibliographic data in machine-readable form.

Originally published in *IFLA Journal* 14 (1988) 2. Reprinted with permission of the International Federation of Library Association.

Over the past five years we have seen a growing maturity in both systems and services associated with library automation. All major applications in libraries have been addressed and there is a multiplicity of commercial and in-house systems available for use. But it is equally true that the tremendous diversity of systems, and the very different means of approaching what are fundamentally the same tasks, present considerable problems and barriers to resource sharing between libraries, both nationally and internationally. A complex array of library networks has developed in response to particular needs at the local, regional, national and international levels and it is extremely difficult to identify the important linkages between these networks.

Enlightened self-interest has fostered continuing cooperation on an international as well as national scale. However, IFLA, in its efforts to promote effective electronic resource sharing, has been hampered to date by the inability of the existing technology to interconnect, effectively and economically, the many diverse electronic library and information databases which exist worldwide, and thereby provide the mechanisms to reduce the existing fragmentation of information resources and to improve access to information and service delivery. This, then, is the major hurdle which must be overcome if electronic resource sharing is to be both economical and effective either nationally or internationally.

OPEN SYSTEMS INTERCONNECTION

At the beginning of this decade, international standards bodies (le Comité consultatif de téléphonique et télégraphique) [CCITT] and the International Organization for Standardization (ISO) approved the Open System Interconnection (OSI) Reference Model. The fundamental objective of the Reference Model is "to provide a globally agreed framework for the design of systems required to interoperate and to provide a common basis for the coordination of standards development for the purpose of systems interconnection while allowing existing standards to be placed into perspective within the overall reference model."[1]

Selected libraries have, over the past seven years, conducted research and cooperative pilot implementations and studies to gain a clearer understanding of the opportunities and constraints of OSI technology for the library and information community.

These research and development projects had proceeded successfully to the point that in August 1987, the IFLA Section on Information Technology, and the IFLA core programme for Universal Dataflow and Telecommunications (UDT) organized in London, UK, the first international seminar on OSI specifically for the library and information community entitled "Open Systems Interconnection: The Communications Technology of the 1990's." The purpose of the seminar was to assess the potential of OSI for the improvement of resource sharing on an international scale, and IFLA's role in realizing that potential.

OSI has aroused high expectations within the international library and information community. The four core programmes of IFLA are each dedicated to improving resource sharing on an international scale, and hence are potential vehicles for furthering OSI development for library and information needs.

IFLA CORE PROGRAMMES AND POTENTIAL REDUCTION OF RESOURCE SHARING BARRIERS

The first of IFLA's core programmes, Universal Bibliographic Control International MARC (UBCIM) promotes the production and use of an internationally compatible bibliographic record for each publication, thus eliminating duplication of effort in bibliographic data creation. The programme also promotes the exchange of these records in machine-readable form, and works to ensure that such exchange is based on internationally accepted standards.

As we all know, cataloguing a library's collection is a labour-intensive and costly task, and library collections have great overlap in titles held. Hence, for many decades librarians have sought ways to share their cataloguing records. For years, many national libraries provided cataloguing of their national imprints in book or printed-card form for the use of other libraries.

In the 1960s, with the advent of automated library systems, the demand grew for delivery of cataloguing data in machine-readable form. The Library of Congress (LC) led in developing the MARC format and distributing data on magnetic tape as well as on cards. LC was followed by national libraries in other countries who began creating the cataloguing data for their national imprints in machine-readable form. Exchange agreements were negotiated between national libraries which allowed redistribution of tapes of foreign imprints in each country.

At about the same time, IFLA created working groups to develop an International Standard Bibliographic Description and UNIMARC to improve both the standards for data being exchanged and the format in which they were exchanged. IFLA also initiated a working group to reach agreement on standards for the data and the format for electronically recording name and subject access points to the records (authority files). While all of these developments have profoundly improved the sharing of bibliographic data, barriers still exist.

Machine-readable tapes are issued on a weekly or monthly basis and are sent internationally through the mail, resulting in a delay of days to weeks. When received, usually by a national agency, they must be loaded or copied, and often converted to the national format as well: a time-consuming task. Tapes are then distributed (usually also by mail) to other libraries within the country, incurring further delays. The most up-to-date data are only available through remote online search access and such data must, in most cases, be re-keyed for use at the client site. Therefore, while the advent of the optical disk may greatly improve local availability of source cataloguing data, it would seem that both the ability to transfer data files online, system to system, and improved and faster data conversion mechanisms are also desirable developments.

The enormous interest in OSI worldwide has increased the realization in other sectors besides libraries of the need for data and format as well as telecommunication standards. It is apparent that these sectors will become increasingly active in developing data and format standards for their industrial applications. Many of these standards potentially will overlap with existing approved library standards, and also may need to be accommodated or incorporated by libraries. Therefore, it behooves the library community in general, and within IFLA, the UBCIM core programme, to take an active interest in ISO committees working on such standards, even if they appear to be beyond its core concerns. Examples would be office automation standards (including invoicing standards), and those for the publishing industry. Yet another example is the work now underway to standardize electronic mail directory entries. While librarians have a great deal of expertise and experience in the creation of unique data strings for personal and corporate names in machine-readable form, that expertise has not to date been fully appreciated by those who are working on data standards for electronic mail directories. There may be an important role for the UBCIM in ensuring that appropriate expertise from the library and information community is available to many of these ISO committees.

The second aspect of the UBCIM programme is that of promoting effective exchange of bibliographic records. It is important for improved resource sharing in an electronic environment that the UBCIM Office investigate and promote OSI as a tool for more effective electronic transfer of bibliographic records.

The Universal Availability of Publications (UAP) programme promotes access to and availability of published materials to all categories of users by encouraging and improving policies and procedures for the production and distribution, acquisition, retention and interlibrary supply of publications within and among countries.

Interlibrary loan is a major resource sharing function for libraries. The interlibrary loan function, while invaluable to researchers, has traditionally been labour-intensive, costly and slow. There have been many efforts over the years to improve and speed the processes involved in interlibrary loan (citation verification, searching, locating the item, requesting the item for loan, and delivering the item), most notably the development of large centralized lending collections, such as the Document Supply Centre of the British Library (BLDSC), or the Centre for Research Libraries (CRL) in Chicago, as well as others, all of which have a world-wide clientele and are dedicated to the timely supply of documents.

In spite of efforts to make interlibrary loan more efficient, barriers to achieving that efficiency still exist in all of the processes that comprise the interlibrary loan function. First, the citation/verification and the location process. As electronic abstracting and indexing databases and bibliographic union files proliferate, one's ability to search multiple databases is restricted by several things: different proprietary terminals are sometimes required and if so, there are costs associated with maintaining these separate terminals; there are difficulties of unconnected telecommunications networks; there are separate log-on procedures to the databases; there are separate billing mechanisms for each; and finally, different search arguments and language must be used to search different databases to find either the desired citation or location, or both.

Having located the desired item, the second barrier is encountered: the multiple methods of messaging the request for the item are often slow and require separate procedures. Processing of unformatted requests and of the status reports that are needed to control interlibrary loan transaction at the target institution are often manual, resulting in further delays.

Finally, there are barriers to effective document delivery. The delivery of photocopies has speeded the process, but often at the expense of risking infringement of copyright laws. However, be it a book or a photocopy, the item is still usually transmitted by mail which is slow. So, present methods of delivery remain a detriment to providing client services effectively. All of these barriers have the potential of being overcome or reduced by technological means.

Libraries and publishers have always had a symbiotic relationship. From the library point of view, the acquisition of material is a labour-intensive operation. The discovery and selection of available published material, be it new or antiquarian, unavoidably requires knowledge, time and perseverance. However, having made a selection, considerable mechanical barriers exist to acquiring the item. Orders are usually typed on multiple part forms and sent by mail to the publisher. Subsequent status reporting, such as out of stock, can't locate, etc., is also predominantly transacted by mail. In addition to the built-in delay of the mail, the processing at each end is often a totally manual operation.

In recent years, some of the book and periodical wholesalers and publishers have automated their inventories and some libraries have automated their acquisition function. These developments have hastened the process of acquisition and of status reporting, but the problem remains, of incompatibility of systems amongst wholesalers, libraries and publishers who each have, of necessity, different internal functional requirements. The development of a standard means of electronically creating, transmitting and receiving book orders and associated status reports would enable the acquisition process to become more efficient and cost-effective for all parties in the book order chain. These efficiencies would, in turn, reduce barriers which librarians, publishers and wholesalers all face in providing timely client services.

OSI would seem to be a tool applicable to improving production of published materials through use of office automation technology, allowing manuscripts to be transferred automatically from author to publisher to printer. Equally, it holds potential for the acquisition process through improved electronic book order messaging and status reporting on orders, both between libraries and publishers and between publishers and their distribution agents worldwide. OSI also has great potential for interlibrary supply through electronic messaging for ILL requests and status reporting, and through the use of telefacsimile for document delivery.

The recently created Universal Dataflow and Telecommunications (UDT) core programme aims to support the recognized need for the electronic transfer of data between libraries and related information sectors and between libraries and their suppliers and users, and aims to reduce telecommunications barriers to effective transfer of data. The UDT programme is conceived somewhat differently from the other core programmes in that it is a programme to support the service delivery mandates of the other IFLA core programmes and hence plays a facilitating role to IFLA as a whole. The following is an example of the need for support to several service delivery programmes.

A generalized obstacle to electronic resource sharing and access to information which is becoming more and more acute as electronic information databases proliferate, is that of knowing which databases are available and how they can be accessed. A great deal of information about a database is needed before it can be used: the subject content and coverage of the database; the condition of use; the services it provides; and the costs. In addition, knowledge of access paths and procedures are essential, that is, the telecommunications carrier used, the type of terminal required, the database address, the log-on procedure and search query procedure, and the hours of availability. This latter item is complicated by different time zones. Currently, most documentation on the use of a database is available only in printed form, and is often out of date or incomplete. Electronic directory databases providing users with information needed for access to multiple databases would provide an invaluable service to many aspects of library activities.

In addition, many of the technological solutions to electronic service delivery are applicable to more than one service and should be coordinated by IFLA for the mutual benefit of multiple services.

It would seem, then that the UDT programme has an important coordinating role to play in the development of the infrastructure necessary for IFLA core programme and Sections to realize the potential of OSI for service delivery.

The Preservation and Conservation (PAC) programme promotes programmes to overcome the serious problems of physical deterioration of published and manuscript material, and investigates media other than print for purposes of preservation, thus helping to preserve and conserve publications of the past, present and future.

Although, because of the nature of this programme, it will have limited use for OSI technology, it is possible that the use of electronic databases pertaining to preservation and conservation could be made more widely available by having OSI technology in place.

OSI: ISSUES AND CHALLENGES

During the past eight years, the increased activity worldwide to develop and implement OSI standards across many industrial sectors has impressed upon all those involved the complexity of the endeavour, but not dampened their conviction of its utility. Moreover, all groups involved–the standards organizations, the telecommunications and computer industries, and user groups like ourselves–now have a more realistic understanding than we had in the beginning of the time and effort that will be required before OSI is fully implemented. From the current perspective, it would appear that it is a technology whose impact will be widely felt in the 1990s, but its exploitation by the library and information community requires active planning. OSI "embraces several aspects: a conceptual model, a family of specific standards that specify protocols, plus the actual implementation of these protocols."[2] In other words it aims to facilitate the inter-working of computer systems both within an organization and between organizations.

With the seven layers of the OSI Reference Model: physical, data link, network, transport, session, presentation and application, it is the top four, and especially the top two, that are of primary concern to those wishing to provide specific services through OSI. A variety of standards and protocols have been developed for each layer. However, "to achieve compatible implementations of these standards it is imperative to have strict interpretation of the specifications and strict conformity to a basic kernel (core specifications) and agreed set of options for each layer."[3] It is this problem that provides the greatest challenge and requires standards bodies, industry and government-driven groups to cooperate to define functional profiles for OSI.

Some of the characteristics of OSI development which are most relevant to the developments of IFLA strategies are as follows:

- OSI is an evolutionary development and it never has been, nor ever will be, in a static state.

- OSI is a communications facility and managers have to identify the services they expect to receive or provide using OSI interconnectivity with remote systems.

- Not all services require OSI interconnectivity, but systems planning is better done within a broad OSI architecture.

- Most developments are being carried out in a national context which poses problems for international cooperation.

It should be noted however that many governments and large multinational computer companies are providing the catalyst and the financial support for international developments in OSI: developments which we ignore at our peril.

- The rate of development varies enormously between different service areas, between groups within service areas, and between countries. (Within the library community at the present time Canada, the Netherlands, Norway and the USA are most active.)

- There are considerable problems with migration strategies which are very complex but both the theory and practice are evolving rapidly. In some cases OSI can be implemented as add-on software but increasingly it will affect the heart of operating systems offered by major commercial suppliers.

The primary requirements in developing OSI-based library applications are: standards applications definitions, data definitions, character set repertoire and information retrieval models.

The development of standards is a complex matter. There is a bewildering array both at the national and international level and the large number of players complicates the monumental task facing librarians in monitoring, influencing and drafting, where appropriate, the relevant standards. The complexities of developing an applications protocol for information systems in this environment are not to be underestimated. Based on experience to date, it would appear that the creation and approval of each protocol standard takes five to seven years. In the interests of successful inter-working and for economy of effort the library community needs to take advantage wherever possible of standards developed by other sectors. The primary body for the development of library applications protocols is ISO and within ISO the TC46/SC4/WG4 Working Group on Documentation is developing OSI protocols for library and information products when they are unique to that sector. ISO/TC97 is responsible for generic OSI protocols.

Furthermore, the challenges to bibliographic management in an OSI environment are considerable. The central points of the analysis are that in an OSI environment the systems multiply, hence producing intrinsic differences in the rates of change of data and in the different sets of databases. The need for a complex set of enhancements for the distribution and management of bibliographic data is apparent. In order to achieve these objectives the following steps are needed:

- An agreed-upon formal specification language for bibliographic syntax and semantics;

- A higher level of abstraction to encompass record structure, database structure and data distribution;

- Reliable identity of the bibliographic entity;

- Associated but distinguished versions of the same logical record in terms of origins and processing history;

- Recognition of linkages between record headings and authority records in multiple authority frameworks.[4]

Nine countries are presently developing a plan to develop and/or implement OSI-based services. There is a great deal to be learned from studying these different approaches because an international programme is unlikely to be successful without forging links with existing national activities. While the nature of the organization of national initiatives and the resources devoted to them varies considerably, certain common objectives appear to be emerging in the formulation of national programmes. The main thrust of these objectives is:

- To share information about international, national and industry standards;

- To share information about and to participate in the drafting of standards for library systems applications;

- To advise libraries on the implications of standards or options within standards for their particular applications;

- To encourage the use of recommended standards by libraries and related organizations.[5]

Most national initiatives are at present concentrating on three primary goals: the transfer of bibliographic data, information retrieval and inter-lending. The need for international coordination of these initiatives in the library and information sector is urgent if the goal of inter-operability between systems is to be achieved in practice.

PRACTICAL ISSUES FOR IFLA

The fact that the seminar held by IFLA in August 1987 represents the first international attempt in the library and information community at pooling knowledge on OSI is indicative of the present lack of formal communication channels. Information is required on standards development in the respective national and international contexts, on service objectives of national libraries and library networks in each country and on working papers for implementation, together with a forum for the debate of theoretical and practical issues.

One of the first tasks in developing services in an OSI environment is to define and develop services criteria and objectives. That is no easy task because it is necessary to have some prior knowledge of OSI capabilities in order to set realistic service objectives. Almost certainly such a system would provide standard facilities for transferring bibliographic data records, for processing interlibrary loan requests, for managing book purchase orders, and for querying databases. However, the ways in which existing systems operate both within and between countries and the degree of commonality required to operate these services in an open systems environment is a matter requiring extensive debate. At the highest level this requires a complete rethink of the principles and practice of bibliographic management to ensure cost-effective, reliable services on a local or national level and subsequently improved services to the international community. All these service objectives have to make use of OSI standards. It is necessary to have a statement or set of international library services objectives with common elements specified in terms of these relevant standards.

Because OSI comprises many standards, each with a series of options, it is necessary to agree on a subset of possible standards and options which will achieve a particular task. This can only be done in the light of defined service objectives; however, the range of technical options makes agreement difficult, and the time-consuming nature of such deliberations imposes a constraint on international collaboration. There is no agreement as yet on how this task should be tackled, but it would seem essential in the initial phase that there be a coordinating body to facilitate a critical examination of the existing functional profile standards being developed.

Every effort should be made to conform where possible to these functional profiles/standards which are likely to have industrial acceptance. Where they fail to meet specific library requirements, representation should be made at the appropriate national and international levels while they are still being developed.

Considerable progress has been made over the years in developing machine-readable files which conform to USMARC standards. It is evident, however, that there are still considerable problems in exchanging records on an international basis because of the different formats used at national levels. Many of these issues are managerial problems which have little, or nothing, to do with OSI. But, as with all computer applications, it is necessary to have some agreement on objectives prior to creating a technological solution. There appear to be major difficulties in adapting OSI relational database models to the transfer of bibliographic records but this is secondary to the primary task of agreeing on standard formats.

The constraints operating within each country compound this problem. It will be important to choose relatively simple applications in the initial phase of international collaboration, because:

- the intrinsic benefits to be derived from the interconnections need to be practically demonstrated before more complex applications are attempted;

- such demonstrations would help to establish the efficacy of the reference model;

- such demonstrations would introduce standards based on the OSI Reference Model before proprietary protocols become sufficiently entrenched as *de facto* standards.

At the moment no international forum exists to further such an objective and IFLA may well be able to provide an appropriate vehicle for promoting such initiatives. Associated with such a strategy would be questions of choice of applications, choice of libraries to be participants and assessment of resources required to facilitate the development.

The importance of protocols and applications which are being developed for electronic publishing is becoming increasingly obvious and "the AAP (Association of American Publishers) standard for electronic manuscripts may eventually make possible the automation of laborious cataloguing and indexing routines."[6] Retrieval systems are being developed, particularly in relation to CD-ROM, which will have a major effect on library users. Mechanisms are required to ensure that there is a strong representation of the library community in these separate but closely related fields.

There are a multiplicity of interrelated standards in the OSI Reference Model, particularly at the application level.

Mechanisms are required by which appropriate representations are to be made to OSI protocol development and promotional organizations. The most important, but by no means the only of these, is ISO. It has been noted that the library community is not represented on the Corporation of Open Systems (COS) or Standards Promotion and Application Group (SPAG), both of which will have considerable influence on the content of functional profile standards. There needs to be close liaison between those involved in making national representations to ensure optimal compatibility prior to consideration by ISO.

There are now many commercial products being made available by various hardware vendors and third party software houses. At the present time questions of OSI system performance are frequently raised and for the most part remain unanswered. The ability of the various vendors' products to inter-work with one another remains to be demonstrated. However, a great deal of caution is required in tackling this problem because it is unrealistic, at least in the short term, to expect vendors to demonstrate such compatibility and at the same time for users to expect large discounts on hardware and software. For the majority of inter-working testing the library community will have to rely on the industry itself, or other bodies such as the National Institute of Standards and Technology in the USA, COS and SPAG.

It is imperative that there be collaboration between libraries, technical experts, users and commercial vendors in developing new systems. There are barriers to such collaboration because commercial vendors, in particular, are often reluctant to forego perceived advantages in maintaining their own systems, although this is a trend that appears to be changing rather rapidly. It is in the interests of all user communities, including the library community, for as many commercial vendors as possible to embrace open systems architecture both for functional reasons and for reducing the cost to the user. There are several such organizations in existence such as the Information Technology Users Standards Association (ITUSA) in the United Kingdom which attempt to achieve such objectives. IFLA needs to consider mechanisms by which they can involve all interested parties in achieving what are ultimately common goals.

It is clearly not within the capability of IFLA or its organizations to resource practical initiatives. Such initiatives will require funding by national bodies either directly through national libraries, or through acquiring foundation or special government funding. IFLA could however play an important role in providing extensive promotion and, where feasible, access to sources of funding through inter-governmental agencies and multinational companies in the information industry.

Given that there are already four core programmes within IFLA it would seem unwise to create yet another programme because of the resource constraints and the effort of coordinating programmes. Each programme will have the important task of contributing to the development of service criteria and objectives but it would seem most appropriate for the Universal Dataflow and Telecommunications (UDT) programme to coordinate the various initiatives on behalf of IFLA.

RECOMMENDATIONS

The following recommendations were endorsed by the 146 participants from 30 countries at the IFLA OSI Seminar in 12-14 August 1987, London, UK, entitled "Open Systems Interconnection." They were further endorsed during the Brighton Conference by the Section on Information Technology and the Advisory Committees of the four core programmes. It was recommended that IFLA:

1. Define and specify the service criteria and objectives of its programmes in terms of present and future inter-working requirements, taking into account the ever increasing potential of OSI as a facilitator of improved services;

2. Identify the relevant communications support and capabilities that exist within, and between, the constituent member countries;

3. Critically examine existing functional profiles/standards being promoted by national and international agencies to assess their suitability in meeting the requirements of the national and international library and information communities;

4. Contribute wherever possible to the development of application level protocols for library and information needs;

5. Promote specific initiatives to develop common library applications between two or more countries;

6. Create appropriate mechanisms to ensure that there is adequate representation to OSI protocol development and promotion agencies;

7. Consider the mechanism for involving users, library systems' vendors, national libraries and those offering related services in the formulation of both service objectives and the means of delivering services;

8. Ensure that there is close liaison between the Universal Dataflow and Telecommunications core programme, which has a specific responsibility for promoting OSI standards, and the other three core IFLA programmes;

9. Gather and disseminate relevant information on all aspects of OSI affecting the international library and information community.

Further, the Section on Information Technology submitted a resolution which was approved by the IFLA Professional Board in Brighton which reads as follows: "In order to promote the ability to share resources through electronic means for improved service to library users, in order to facilitate communication for the interchange of information and resources, and in order to reduce the effort and cost of implementing and using computerized library systems, IFLA endorse(s) the further development of ISO and CCITT standards for Open Systems Interconnection and their adoption by the IFLA membership. Further that the Professional Board take the appropriate steps to fulfil these objectives."[7]

At the direction of the Professional Board, the appropriate core programmes and Sections are currently evaluating their respective roles in carrying out these resolutions.

CONCLUSION

Access to information through resource sharing in an electronic environment is both more challenging and more exciting than in a manual environment. More challenging in the sense that the complexities to be overcome are enormous and will require the concerted effort of many committed and highly dedicated professionals in many sectors. More exciting because if these complexities can be resolved and the resulting standards implemented, the resulting service and economic benefits could change the shape and scope of library service worldwide and place libraries firmly as essential players in the worldwide information community. If the IFLA membership is to be in a position by the end of the century to benefit from electronic data interchange, planning and experimentation must begin now.

Notes

1. McCrum, William A., "What Is OSI?" (Paper delivered at the IFLA Pre-Conference Seminar: "Open Systems Interconnection: The Communications Technology of the 1990's," London UK, 12-14 August 1987), 5.

2. Thomas, Keith A., "OSI and the Evolution of Library Systems: Prospects and Challenges for the 1990's" (Paper delivered at the IFLA Pre-Conference Seminar:

"Open Systems Interconnection: The Communications Technology of the 1990's," London, UK, 12-14 August 1987), 8.

3. McCrum, William A., op. cit., 8.

4. Thomas, Keith A., op. cit., 23.

5. Webb, Kerry, "OSI Implementation in Australian Libraries" (Paper delivered at the IFLA Pre-Conference Seminar: "Open Systems Interconnection: The Communications Technology of the 1990's," London, UK, 12-14 August 1987), 2.

6. Martin J. Sperling, "Electronic Document Interchange" (Paper delivered at the IFLA Pre-Conference Seminar: "Open Systems Interconnection: The Communications Technology of the 1990's," London UK, 12-14 August 1987), 14.

7. *IFLA Express*, Brighton, No. 5.21, August 1987, pp. 5-6.

Archival Administration, Records Management, and Computer Data Exchange Standards: An Intersection of Practices

CHARLES M. DOLLAR AND THOMAS E. WEIR, JR., NATIONAL ARCHIVES AND RECORDS ADMINISTRATION

In the 1990s, knowledgeable managers of organizations (private and public) recognize the importance of understanding managing the flow of information. Information–the what, why, where, who, and how of daily decisions–has a major impact on an organization's success in meeting its goals and fulfilling its missions.

Existing practice in records management emphasizes paper-based information; consequently archivists and records managers have developed procedures to manage the creation, flow, and storage of paper. Underlying paper-oriented records management programs is the concept of managing the life cycle of records. The new emphasis on the flow and use of information without regard to medium of recordation has created the new discipline of information resources management (IRM). IRM is closely, but not necessarily exclusively, affiliated with the management of computer created, stored, and presented information.

The objective of this paper, therefore, is twofold: first, to integrate the existing disciplines of information resource management and records management and consequently to integrate the management of paper and computer-based information into the same framework; and second, to relate computer data exchange standards to the integrated model.

This paper is an exploratory document representing the opinions of the authors and not the policy of the U.S. National Archives and Records Administration.

Within the field of computers, particularly computer communication, there is a growing movement to increase the interoperability of computer hardware and software manufactured by various companies. This overall endeavor is called the *open systems environment*. A major aspect of this environment is transparent data exchange in a heterogeneous computer environment. The emphasis, so far, has been on overcoming the technical problems of immediate transfer. Attention now needs to be paid to the long-term storage and effective and efficient use and reuse of data transferred by these standards. Such practices fall into the domain of information resources management.

THE LIFE CYCLE OF RECORDS IN RECORDS MANAGEMENT

The concept of life cycle of records encompasses the management of records[1] from creation to disposition – that is, from the time information is recorded until its ultimate disposition is carried out, either through destruction because there is no residual value or through archival storage because there is residual value. Basic life-cycle stages are:

Creation and identification: To create a new document, record, or file and provide unique identifying information.

Appraisal: To determine the ultimate disposition of documentary material and schedule it for destruction or archival retention.

Control and use: To store and retrieve information for use by the creator.

Disposition: To convey recorded information to others as part of the administrative use of information or to convey such information to others for secondary reuse. This concept includes transfer to an archival repository.

Life-cycle management developed as the growing volume of records retained required costly storage in multiple locations: office space, holding areas or records centers, and archives. Because the destruction of unneeded records or the removal of little used records from office space to a less costly holding area was a cost reduction benefit, it became useful to schedule orderly destruction or transfers to maximize the savings. Once the material was transferred, a systematic method of further reduction or destruction could be implemented, depending upon the usefulness of the information. Another benefit of life-cycle management for organizations with archives was the identification of permanent records as early in the life cycle as possible. Permanent records series could then be created in a manner to reduce the inclusion of nonpermanent materials and to provide special treatment (e.g., secure storage and preservation planning) as early as possible.

In implementing life-cycle management for paper-based information, records managers developed tools (forms management, correspondence management, and the like) to control the flow of paper rather than the flow of information. Records management tools, therefore, focused upon reductions in the volume of paper records and their efficient storage and retrieval.

Because these records management *tools* were implemented to control paper-based information systems, they are only partially useful in managing electronic records. For example, concepts from forms management, design, and control may be used to assist in the design and control of input and display screens in a computer system. Managing the underlying information may, however, require a radically different approach. In a paper system, there is a one-to-one relationship between a paper form and the information on it. In an electronic database, information displayed on a form may be spread over different files, databases, or, in a truly distributed application, over several organizations and dispersed locations. Yet, to the viewer, the disparate information appears to be a single document.

The point is that the tools that have been developed in records management generally tend to reflect a paper framework or mind-set. The notions of processibility of information, rapid searching of voluminous information, and use of a volatile medium as storage for miniaturized information are products of an electronic environment, not a paper one. Even more important is the nature of electronic information that "resides" in different parts of different databases. This information may simply be a "view" of a database or a portion of one at an ephemeral point in time. "Views" of a database along with other developments such as hypertext undermine the notion of "original records" or even the model of a discrete entity that is a record. Therefore, the tools developed in paper-based records management need substantial rethinking and extensions if they are to be effective in electronic records management.

In contrast, the basic stages of the life cycle of information may be transferred by analogy more easily to an electronic information handling environment. This is because the stages of the life cycle relate to processes of information handling (e.g., creation) rather than to specific physical manifestations (e.g., a report).

The modern management of electronic records must incorporate the concept of the life cycle of information into the broader concept of information management. In paper-oriented records management, records are seen as an overhead cost that must be reduced. In information management, on the other hand, information is viewed as a corporate asset that must be exploited. There are, of course, cost reduction components of an information management program that are analogous to records management, but they are part of a larger view of information as a resource. The change in emphasis from cost reduction to resource exploitation can be applied to paper records as well as to electronic records. Consequently, records managers who work with electronic documents have the opportunity to merge records management and information management.

DATA EXCHANGE ISSUES

The growing issue of computers to create, file, retrieve, transmit, and display information in electronic form is a mixed blessing. Although the potential easy reuse of information in electronic form adds significant value to records, reuse faces a "system-specific technology dependence" that can militate against dissemination and archival preservation. Technological dependence occurs when noncompatible systems are used or when systems become obsolete, with no suitable migration path for data to the next generation. Hardware and software vendors traditionally have sought to protect competitive advantages by developing their own methods of transferring data between their products, thus making it difficult for different computer systems to communicate. The increasing complexity of most computer systems along with the mushrooming of different systems are creating such incoherence that, in comparison, the Tower of Babel would seem monolingual.

Of course, simple text and databases can be transferred through rudimentary formats such as ASCII text or delimited ASCII sequential files. Data transfer, however, becomes much more formidable for complex databases, for text documents in which the original presentation must be preserved, or for compound documents comprising tests, pictures, graphs, and tables.

The document you are now reading can be used to illustrate some of the problems that can occur when using ASCII for document transfer. ASCII is primarily a character coding standard that has very few layout codes and no logical relationships. It does contain carriage returns and line feeds that are used to delimit lines and mark paragraphs. This document, however, has additional typographical features that are not supported in ASCII. For example, the document is printed in 10-point Times Roman type. The title and the footnote numbers are the same typeface but a different type size. Although the characters can be transferred, information about the typeface and type size cannot be transmitted in ASCII. Parts of the document are in bold or italics. These enhanced print options also cannot be supported in an ASCII transfer.

The word processor used to create this document handles footnoting as a logical relationship between a section of text and the footnote itself. It does not provide layout information about where the footnote should actually be placed except when displaying or printing out. ASCII cannot transfer the logical relationship, and footnotes are lost when an ASCII dump is used to transfer documents from this word processor to another. Most obviously, this paper is a compound document containing drawings as well as text. Images cannot be transferred in a character oriented standard like ASCII.

Other common layout options such as columns, tables, and graphs frequently cannot be transferred in ASCII because they usually depend on logical as well as layout relationships that are supported differently in each word processor. This document would still be intelligible if transferred in ASCII, but that would not be the case for documents that rely heavily on illustrations, complex tables, or typeface differences to convey information.

Databases are even more complex. They consist of data, definitions of the data, and relationships between parts of the data. All three are needed to transfer a working database from one system to another. The transfer of complex databases with hierarchal, network, or relational structures requires substantial information to clarify relationships between parts of the data so that the recipient system can use the data. To use a simple example, suppose this paper were a hierarchical database rather than a sequential text file and were divided and subdivided as follows: the paper, the sections, the paragraphs, the sentences, and the illustrations. In addition to the pieces of data, the hierarchical level and other relationships between information in this "database" are noted (i.e., a piece of data is the third sentence within a specific paragraph within a specific section). These raw data (sentences and so forth) themselves, however, are stored sequentially in order of creation, not sequentially in order of presentation or viewing by a reader. The relationship information is needed to restore the database file into a usable text file. Obviously, transfer and reconstruction of even this simple example of a hierarchical database is not easily done. Transferring databases with complex relationships in an automated manner requires standards more complex than those that currently predominate.

Figure 1 is a schematic representation of incompatibility and system-specific technology dependence when transferring complex databases with simple standards.

FIGURE 1.   SIMPLE AND COMPLEX DATA TRANSFERS WITH SIMPLE TRANSFER STANDARDS

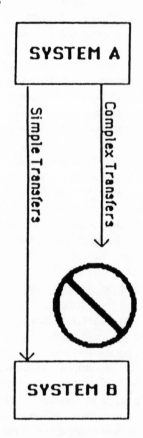

OPEN SYSTEM INTERCONNECTION (OSI)

Beginning in the 1970s, a number of computer users and vendors recognized the magnitude of the interoperability/data exchange problem. Their general solution was to work toward an *open system environment,* a computer environment in which those parts of computer processing that needed to be shared would be standardized. Working together, they developed a reference model for open systems communication (i.e., not system dependent) to which most computers could conform. The reference model, which provides the overall framework for the development of specific standards, became an international standard in 1979 (ISO 7498). In addition to the Open Systems Interconnection (OSI) model and the standards developed to fill out the model, other standards for open computer systems developed concurrently.

These standards may collectively be referred to as the open systems environment. The operative word here is *standard* because information communicated through a widely used standard is no longer system dependent. Advocates believe that, as the open systems environment continues to mature and more conforming products become available, information managers will be able to select computer systems on the basis of conformance to publicly defined standards rather than on the basis of what conforms to the proprietary facilities an existing system provides.[2]

OSI consists of a set of mutually agreed upon rules for exchanging information between computers. The basic reference model for OSI divides the rules into seven layers of protocols,[3] which are used in system communication. These layers, from bottom to top, are physical, data link, network, transport, session, presentation, and application. On top of the stacked layers are the actual user applications. Underlying the stack is the actual physical device. (Figure 2 briefly explains the seven layers.) The bottom four layers collectively transmit electronic encodings end-to-end through the communication system. The top three layers ensure the transmission of coherent information through the system.

Each layer uses services provided by lower layers and provides services to the next higher layer. Each layer also communicates with its equivalent layer in the other system through the lower layers and the physical connection. As information passes from one user to another, it first passes down the seven-layer stack on the sender's system. Each layer in the sender's stack provides protocol information that the equivalent layer in the recipient's stack will need to decode the transmission. The receiving stack then passes the message up the stack, with each layer using the information provided by its peer layer to further decode the message. The top layer – the application layer – then provides services to the user's application programs. (See figure 2.)

Most data exchange standards concerned with the presentation and content of information work either in the top two layers (presentation and application) or as extensions to OSI in user applications. Hardware and software developers whose products conform to these standards, therefore, provide the basic infrastructure that can help reduce and control information interchange incompatibility problems.

This OSI infrastructure provides neutral data interchange services between heterogeneous computers. Broadly, the service works as follows: The sending system translates data from its proprietary format into an OSI-compliant format, and the receiving system translates the data from the OSI compliant format to its proprietary format where it can be used as if it had been created on the receiving system. Several OSI services and formats are now available; others will be available in the future. Figure 3 displays the process of using an OSI-compliant neutral format for data exchange.

FIGURE 2. BACKGROUND: OPEN SYSTEMS INTERCONNECT (OSI) REFERENCE MODEL

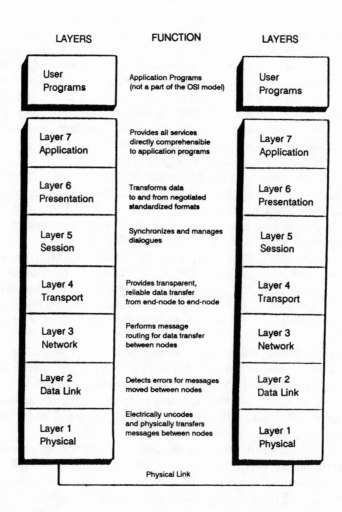

FIGURE 3. DATA TRANSFERS WITH ROBUST NEUTRAL TRANSFER STANDARDS

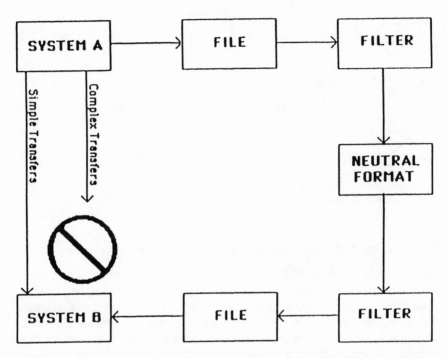

Archivists, records managers, and others concerned with the long-term transfer, preservation, and dissemination of electronic information can capitalize on system-independent data exchange standards to provide system-independent, long-term storage standards. After all, archival storage and reuse are simply data exchange over time. (See figure 4.)

EXCHANGE STANDARDS

A preliminary review of standards has identified several that are part of the open systems environment and that are relevant to the concerns of records management and archives.[4] This same review has also identified several older standards that were developed outside the open systems environment and the OSI seven layers but that can be implemented in user applications. Records managers and archivists should know about these standards as well.

Recorded information conforming to non-OSI standards can be transmitted through an OSI environment as long as sender and recipient use the same standard.

FIGURE 4. DATA TRANSFERS OVER TIME WITH ROBUST NEUTRAL
TRANSFER STANDARDS

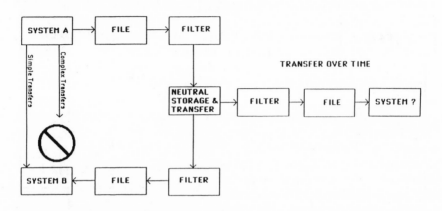

OSI Standards for Records Management and Archives

ASN.1 (Abstract Syntax Notation One) is a standard "language" for defining data structures (ISO 8824). It is also associated with a set of basic encoding rules that specify a standard binary encoding for values in a defined data structure (ISO 8825). The bifurcated standard allows information to be exchanged in two parts: a statement formed from the ASN.1 language that defines a data structure and a string of bytes that encodes the values defined in the data structure.

ASN.1 is based on the principle that all data types can be defined from a limited number of elementary data types. Because the basic data types are defined in the ASN.1 language, a programmer can combine them in an ASN.1 statement to further define the very complex data structures that are actually being transferred.

The basic encoding rules for the conversion of data for transmission are used at the presentation layer for all data passed through an OSI-compliant network. Because ASN.1 assumes less about the underlying database structure than older transfer standards assume, it is a more flexible and consequently a more complex standard.

MHS (Message Handling System) is a message handling system (electronic mail service) in OSI that works at the highest level, the application level. It originated as a recommendation (i.e., a standard) of the International Telegraph and Telephone Consultative Committee (CCITT) and was revised in 1988.

Messages transferred by X.400 consist of two parts, the envelope and the body or message. X.400 defines and standardizes the envelope and the transfer methodology. Additional standards are required to standardize and make a message intelligible. For each message transferred, X.400 supports a group of basic services including delivery and nondelivery notification, submission and delivery time stamp, multidestination delivery, grade of delivery selection (i.e., urgent, normal, nonurgent), deferred delivery, content conversion (e.g., ASCII to EBCDIC), disclosure of other recipients, and hold for delivery.

Building upon the basic message transfer services described above, the InterPersonal Message (IPM) service provides, as part of the body of the message, a standardized message header similar to a header in a memorandum. The header includes message identification, originator identification, primary and copy recipients identification, blind copy recipients indication, subject indication, cross-reference indication, obsoleting indication, sensitivity indication, expiry data indication, reply request indication, typed body indication (i.e., identifies the form of the content), and other functions.

Currently IPM and "undefined"[5] are the only specified types of transmissions that can be conveyed by MHS. Additional services beyond IPM service will be defined in the future. For example, Electronic Data Interchange (EDI) messages may become a standardized message type like the Interpersonal Message. EDI messages are electronic versions of accounting and billing documents such as orders, invoices, and price lists that conform to a standard. Other information that might be transferred in the future within an MHS system includes facsimiles and even digitized voice. For each of these additional message types, a header similar to the IMP header must be defined for use with the standardized MHS envelope.

X.400 systems will underlie much future communication within the OSI world. Because of their importance in communicating documents and because of the standard fielded envelope and header information that can be used for records management purposes, this is a particularly important standard.

IRDS (Information Resource Dictionary System) (ANSI X3.138-1988; FIPS PUB 156; ISO TC97/SC21/WG3 N166R1)[6] will standardize the organization of data stored in information resource dictionaries. Information in an IRDS may include data such as field definitions, field length, validation information, data formats, and relationships between different parts of the database. An IRDS can also be designed to contain data about the hardware and software of the system as well as about related data stored in nonelectronic forms such as paper. Other functions that an IRDS can support are data entry, information retrieval, and database administration.

An addendum to the current standard that will provide a dictionary-to-dictionary transfer mechanism is under development. Archivists and records managers may be able to use this mechanism to capture in electronic form the documentation about a database with the electronic records themselves that are transferred for preservation. The transferred dictionary might include field types and constraints, field definitions, and relationships.

ODA/ODIF (Office Document Architecture/Office Document Interchange Format) is a standard (ISO 8613)[7] to facilitate the exchange of office documents such as reports, letters, and memorandums. The standard supports compound documents (those containing text and images) by incorporating existing standards. ODA/ODIF supports both logical and layout relationships in documents. Logical relationships identify the intellectual relationships of parts of a document. For example, a footnote is associated with a specific piece of text. Layout relationships identify the way text should appear when it is displayed or printed out. For example, footnote 15 belongs at the bottom of page 32.

ODA currently supports three content types: character, raster, and picture. Character data may be transferred as formatted, processible, or formatted/processible files. Formatted files retain the layout of the document and ensure a similar physical layout form system to system. Processible files are intended to retain the logical relationship of the parts of a document for editing. Formatted/processible files retain both layout and logical relationships in a document. Raster content is transmitted in group three or group four FAX standards (CCITTT.4 and T.6 See p. 191). Raster data may be either formatted or formatted/processible. Pictures are transmitted in Computer Graphic Metafile (See p. 204). Picture data are formatted/processible only. The ODA/ODIF standard will be extended to support the exchange of computable data (spreadsheets), digitized voice, and color.

In addition to documents, ODA also supports document profiles. Document profiles are a collection of document attributes that support the management and retrieval of documents. The profiles may be retrieved and transmitted with the document they describe or may be retrieved and transmitted separately. Attributes in the document profile include ODA version data, content character sets, title, subject, keywords, abstract, creation data and time, filing data and time, preparers, owners, authors, copyright information, and number of pages.

ODIF defines the encoding of the bit stream for transfer from one system to another either by data communications or by a storage medium.

FTAM (File Transfer, Access, Management) (ISO 8571) is a service provided in the OSI environment. In OSI, FTAM works at the highest level, the application level.

FTAM allows heterogeneous systems operating in an OSI environment to access files on other systems in the OSI environment and perform (if permitted) basic file management functions such as file transfers, selection of parts of a file for transfer, and changing attribute names. FTAM supports the manipulation of hierarchical files. Flat files are supported as a single node hierarchical file.

Files on heterogeneous systems are accessed through a virtual file store. A virtual file store is a non-system-specific, generic file store that represents existing real file stores. Each system conforming to FTAM must have a mapping or filter function that will convert its internal file structure to the virtual file store structure. Once converted to the virtual file store, a file and its properties will appear the same to all users accessing it through FTAM.

DFR (Document Filing and Retrieval) is in the early stages of standardization (ISO TC97/SC 18 N1264). DFR is part of the application layer in the OSI reference model that enables a user to communicate with a remote document filing and retrieval server to access a remote document store. The standard provides the capability for multiple users in a distributed office system to access a large, nonvolatile document store such as disks on a mainframe.

In DFR, documents have assigned attributes that support management and retrieval. The basic attribute set includes document type, group membership criteria, unique permanent identifier, previous version, next version, root version, owner, and title. The current extension attribute set includes subject, keywords, creation date and time, purge date and time, author, status, and languages. Additional sets of extensions may be defined in the future. Documents may be grouped and groups may be nested. Grouping supports hierarchical relationships between documents. A DFR user with the appropriate authority can create and delete documents, copy or move documents, create and manipulate references to documents, create and manipulate groups of documents, create and manipulate attributes types and attribute values, and find, retrieve, and store documents.

DTAM (Document Transfer, Access, and Manipulation) is in the early stages of standardization by CCITT (T.431, T.432, T.433). DTAM is part of the application layer in the OSI reference model and supports the retrieval and manipulation of ODA documents in a distributed database. The basic services provided are the bulk document transfer, document manipulation, and bulk document transfer and manipulation. Manipulation includes create, delete, modify, call, and rebuild.

CGM (Computer Graphics Metafile) is a standard (ISO 8632; ANSI X3.122-1986; FIPS PUB 128) for the transfer of picture information between systems. The file consists of delimiter elements, descriptor elements, picture descriptor elements, control elements, graphical primitive elements, attribute elements, and external elements. CGM graphical primitive elements used to transfer descriptions of parts of pictures include polylines, text, polygons, poly sets, cell arrays, circles, rectangles, ellipses, circular arcs, and elliptical arcs. These elements can be combined to describe pictures in a way that is compatible between systems of different architectures and devices of differing capabilities and design.

Standards Developed Outside the Open Systems Environment

As noted earlier, this review has identified several standards developed outside the OSI model of which archivists and records managers should be aware. These standards were developed in response to specific application needs that generally are concerned with how to make files intelligible between users rather than with how to transfer files between systems. For example, MARC and DDF more or less assume that, because it is relatively easy to exchange computer tapes, the real problem is intelligibility of the information on the tapes.

SGML (Standard Generalized Markup Language) (ISO 8879; FIPS PUB 152) is a standard for defining tags to mark parts of documents and to record the logical relationship of those parts. Documents may include reports, articles, books, journals, and other text entities. The parts are marked by tags indicating data type (title, chapter title, paragraph, etc.). Specific tag sets are developed for various applications. SGML also supports a hierarchical relationship between document parts. For example, tags can be defined so that a paragraph cannot contain a chapter.

The tags do not include procedural or presentation instructions such as center, boldface, or begin Times Roman. Printing or display format decisions are made by the final user. SGML ensures the transfer of the content of documents and the relationship between document parts. It does not attempt to ensure the final appearance.

SGML specifies a Document Type Declaration (DTD). The DTD is a header that identifies an agreed-upon document type such as "article" and includes additional information needed to process the specific document. The tags in a document are interpreted in terms of the DTD.

By using tags to identify parts of documents, SGML text created on one computer system can be transferred and processed on another. Although SGML does not transfer images, graphs, or other noncharacter data, SGML documents can include pointers to indicate the existence of other files that are relevant to the document at hand. These other files may be stored in a non-SGML standard format such as the Computer Graphics Metafile. During processing, the external file can be incorporated into the finished document if the processing software supports the additional standard.

Currently, SGML is used primarily to support the electronic submission of text to publishers. Publishers add value by providing layout information to the logical documents submitted by authors.

DSSSL (Document Style Semantics and Specification Language) (ISO/IEC JTC1/SC18/WG8 N606) is in the very early stages of standardization. It provides a means to define the desired appearance of an SGML document. Such a standard is necessary because SGML provides only the logical relationship of documents, not the layout or appearance of documents.

SPDL (Standard Page Description Language) (ISO/IEC JTC1/SC 18/WG8 N561) is in the early stages of standardization. When completed, the language will be used to provide a device-independent description of the image of a document. The image will be nonrevisable. SPDL will be similar to page description languages used in desktop publishing applications.

When a document with SPDL coding is sent to a conforming printer or other display device, the image should be identical without regard to the system producing the display. This is accomplished by sending detailed instructions in a standard language that a conforming printer can use to create an image displaying the document in original form. The language can include information such as physical location on a sheet of paper of specific pieces of information, the typeface and size to use, print enhancements to use, and instructions for drawing a graphic.

When the standard is completed, it will have the ability to represent documents produced using SGML or ODA. The layout of an SGML document will need to have been described using DSSSL before being encoded with SPDL. Because of the nearly exact representation of compound documents as seen by the creator and the difficulty of revising the documents, NIST believes that SPDL should be the preferred form for accessioning permanent documents.

Format for Bibliographic Interchange on Magnetic Tape (ISO 2709; ANSI Z39.2) is a standard for the creation of formats for the exchange of bibliographic information. ISO 2709 provides a framework for forming specific bibliographic exchange standards. Two such formats are of special interest to archivists and records managers in the international arena: the Common Communications Format (CCF) and the Machine-Readable Catalog for Archival and Manuscript Control (MARC AMC) format.

The CCF is a format for the transfer of bibliographic cataloging and abstracting information. CCF was created and is used by the UNESCO General Information Program to provide a means of transferring data between computer systems in the United Nations system. Data fields include Language and Script of Item, Physical Medium, International Standard Book Number (ISBN), National Bibliography Number, Title and Associated

Statement(s) of Responsibility, Name of Person (responsible for the work), Name of Corporate Body (responsible for the work), and Place of Publication and Publisher. CCF has not been extended to support archival and records management needs. Such extensions could be made.

MARC is a standard for data exchange used by libraries and bibliographic networks in the United States. USMARC AMC is one of the family of MARC formats created under the more general American National Standard, Z39.2, parallel to the international standard ISO 2709. MARC formats in general began in the library community. USMARC AMC is an extension of the library format to better support archival and records management needs.

MARC AMC transfers descriptive and processing information about archival material. In addition to a technical exposition of descriptive material in electronic form to facilitate computer processing, MARC AMC provides defined fields that may contain traditional archival descriptive information. These fields include Title, Bibliographic/Historical Note, Scope Note, and Subject Added Entries. Standards such as the Anglo-American Cataloguing Rules (2d ed.), outside the MARC AMC format, are generally used to control the use of some fields in the format.

DDF (Data Descriptive Format) is a standard (ANSI/ISO 8211; FIPS PUB 123) for the exchange of computer-generated information. The data may be character, vector, binary, or most other forms of data. Although text files could be transferred through DDF, DDF is most generally applicable to database files.

DDF consists of two parts, the Data Record (DR) and the Data File (DF). The DR is a header record that identifies the type of data (character, binary, etc.), the type of fields (variable or fixed length), the field name associated with a tag, and other defining information for the records found in the DF.

The DF consists of as many records as needed to represent the data. Each record has a leader that identifies characteristics of the record, a directory that associates tags with specific pieces of data in the record, and the data itself. DFs comprising fixed length records with fixed occurrence fields require only one leader for the entire file.

DDF provides a standard means of transferring data and limited portions of the database schema and documentation between systems with DDF filters. Although this standard has been available for many years and could meet many of the needs of archivists and records managers concerned with the long-term storage of electronic information, it has not been implemented.

FAX (CCITT Group 3 and Group 4 FAX) facsimile transmission standards (T.4 and T.6) originated in the telecommunications arena of standards making. They provide a means of transmitting facsimiles of images based on the raster scanning of a document. The image is usually text but may contain graphics or anything that can be represented by bits. The standards include compression routines to reduce the transmission costs and, if used as a storage standard, the costs of storing facsimiles. Group 3 facsimile is used for analog transmission over telephone services. Group 4 facsimile is used primarily for digital transmission over public data networks.

The Document/Image Processing and Information Handling Technologies Standards Matrix in figure 5 summarizes the salient features of the standards reviewed above and provides a framework for relating them to life-cycle information management stages. This matrix, therefore, is suggestive rather than definitive and is subject to revision as the data exchange environment changes.

CONCLUSION AND RECOMMENDATIONS

To exploit the possibility of using and influencing standards to the fullest, archivists and records managers must be active both within and outside their organizations. Several courses of action need to be followed:

- Apply the life-cycle approach to new automated records systems as well to older paper-based systems. This requires a conscious decision to include appropriate information, particularly scheduling information, in electronic document and database systems.

- Adopt the broad view of information resource management and focus on the underlying data that electronic systems store rather than on the finished products only.

- Seek appropriate training to manage electronic information effectively. This does not mean that each person needs to be an automation expert but that sufficient knowledge of computer systems be gained to understand the implications of electronic information creation, manipulation, and storage and to discuss with the automation staff the needs of archivists and records managers.

FIGURE 5. DOCUMENT/IMAGE PROCESSING AND INFORMATION HANDLING TECHNOLOGIES STANDARDS MATRIX

Life Cycle Stages

Schedule	Creation and Identification	Schedule	Use	Transfer
Abstract Syntax	-	-		+
MHS	+	-	+	+
ODA/ODIF	+	-	+	+
FTAM				+
DTAM*				+
DFR*				+
DIF				+
DDF	-			+
SGML	+	+	+	+
CGM	+			+
IRDS	+	+	+	-
BIB		**		+
FAX				+

+	The standard explicitly supports this activity.
-	Support is not currently available but could be implemented in the future.
	No entry means this activity does not apply.
*	Not yet a standard.
**	+ for MARC; - for CCF.

- Based on the knowledge gained in computer training, work with automation staff to make archival and records management needs known and to understand the implications of the specific system used in an organization.

- Help define institutional information architecture and strategies based on cooperative work with the automation staff.

- Examine organizational structure and policy for appropriate allocation of information management tasks and define the goals of the archival and records management function in the electronic information arena.

- Alert senior management to long-term issues involved in data exchange and storage. The long-term success of an archival and records management program depends on support from senior staff. A program developed from the bottom up may define ideal plans, but, unsupported, the plans will not ripple through the organization to become effective procedures.

- Work with other archival and records management organizations to define generic needs that can be brought to the attention of the appropriate standards organizations and thereby gain a voice in standards making. Generally, standards such as ODA and MHS need to be expanded to explicitly support the life-cycle management of the information they are transferring. In MHS, for example, this can be done by expanding the document header to include scheduling information so that message transfer and destruction can be handled automatically. The appropriate method of working on standards will vary with each standards organization and each country.

Archivists and records managers need to be aware of these data exchange standards both to prepare to use them and to influence their future development. The developing need for interoperability within heterogeneous computer environments provides an unrivaled and unique opportunity for archivists and records managers to influence the development of data exchange.

Notes

1. Traditionally, records managers and archivists have defined an organization's records as recorded information created or received in the course of business. This definition is so broad that it could conceivably encompass every note scribbled down on a scrap of paper; a variety of limitations have been placed on it. The limitations usually take the form of a list of exceptions to the general rule. Examples of such exclusions by exception are drafts or extra copies of documents kept for reference only.

In David Bearman's recommendations to the United Nation's Technical Panel on Electronic Records Management (TP/REM), he proposes a different general rule to define records that reduces or avoids the need to enumerate exceptions. His suggested definition of a record is based on the concept of an information transaction. Any information that is recorded and transferred to another person (including a memorandum for the record that is not immediately transferred to a specific person) constitutes a record. Because materials received by an organization must involve a transaction, Bearman's proposal affects only internally created documents. As an example of the effect of Bearman's proposal, drafts that are circulated for comment are a record while successive drafts that the creator reviews personally are not records. See David Bearman, "Electronic Records Management Guidelines: A Manual for Policy Development and Implementation," chapter 2 of *Management of Electronic Records: Issues and Guidelines* (New York: UN, 1990), 17-67. For further definitions of other records management terms in this paper, see the TP/REM (from same publication) "Glossary for Electronic Archives and Records Management" (pages 135-87).

2. In this paper, the term *standards* refers to standards approved by a standards organization. Standards organizations at the international level are the International Standards Organization (ISO) and the International Consultative Committee on Telephony and Telegraphy (ICCTT). National organizations are the American National Standards Institute (ANSI), the British Standards Institute (BSI), and the German Industrial Standards Organization (GISO). Other specialized bodies serve distinctive groups. An example is the National Institute for Standards and Technology (NIST) in the United States, which serves the federal government. This paper does not discuss so-called industry standards that result when one vendor dominates a market and determines format issues. It also does not discuss ad hoc groups formed by vendors outside the standards bodies to work on a specific issue.

3. A *protocol* is a formally and precisely defined set of conventions governing the format and control of exchanges between two communicating systems. Adapted from Richard Hipgrave, *Computing Terms and Acronyms: A Dictionary* (London: Library Association Publishing Limited, 1985).

4. The Archival Research and Evaluation Staff of the United States National Archives and Records Administration has recently received a report and demonstration software produced under an interagency agreement by the National Institute of Standards and Technology (NIST). The report identifies exchange standards and makes policy recommendations for archival data exchange where standards exist or are developing.

5. An undefined message is simply handled as a bit stream. Any interpretation of the bit stream and translation into a usable message requires private agreement between the transmitting parties.

6. The American National Standard is a fully approved standard. The international standard is in an earlier stage but currently is not fully compatible with the ANSI standard. The compatibility problems will likely be resolved as the standard progresses.

7. ODA/ODIF will become a federal government standard.

COMP: Following is accurate list of captions for figures. --IK.

FIGURE 1. SIMPLE AND COMPLEX DATA TRANSFERS WITH
SIMPLE TRANSFER STANDARDS

FIGURE 2. BACKGROUND: OPEN SYSTEMS INTERCONNECT REFERENCE
MODEL

FIGURE 3. DATA TRANSFERS WITH ROBUST NEUTRAL TRANSFER
STANDARDS

FIGURE 4. DATA TRANSFERS OVER TIME WITH ROBUST NEUTRAL
TRANSFER SYSTEMS

FIGURE 5. DOCUMENT/IMAGE PROCESSING AND INFORMATION HANDLING
TECHNOLOGIES STANDARDS MATRIX

Archival Information Exchange and the Role of Bibliographic Networks

H. THOMAS HICKERSON, CORNELL UNIVERSITY

More than 70,000 bibliographic records describing archives and manuscript holdings had been entered into the Research Libraries Information Network (RLIN) by 1 August 1986.[1] These catalog records were contributed by forty-seven archival programs, including special libraries, art museums, state archives, and the National Archives, as well as university repositories. This database, inaugurated in January 1984, is already the largest compilation of archival data accumulated and is currently growing at a rate of 900 records per week. In 1988, the Library of Congress' *National Union Catalog of Manuscript Collections* (NUCMC) began using RLIN to compile descriptive data for its annual volumes.[2] The OCLC (Online Computer Library Center) database includes about 50,000 Archival and Manuscripts Control (AMC) records.[3] In addition, the University of Toronto Library Automation Systems (UTLAS) has announced implementation of the USMARC AMC format, and the Washington Library Network (WLN) has begun planning for format implementation. The evidence suggests that participation in library bibliographic networks is becoming integral to the management of archival information.

At this point, the adoption of library bibliographic networks as viable means of managing archival information seems a natural development. Archivists and librarians share the same goal of information control and dissemination. Library networks use the MARC (MAchine-Readable Cataloging) format, the most widely adopted implementation of the American National Standards Institute's (ANSI) standard for exchange of bibliographic information, and access to the bibliographic networks is available in thousands of libraries across the country.

Original published in *Library Trends* 36 (Winter 1988): 553-571. Reprinted with permission. c. 1988 The Board of Trustees at the University of Illinois.

213

The concept of integrated access to the variety of library holdings is becoming increasingly attractive; however, the Society of American Archivists (SAA) had not anticipated this outcome a decade ago when it formed the National Information Systems Task Force (NISTF) to examine current national programs for the development of a national information system.[4]

There are basic differences between common archival practice and standard library procedures. That technical compatibility and a community of interest have developed is the result of a cooperative process. In continuing this process, it is necessary to understand the issues that have been central to cooperation and which will be important in determining the role that bibliographic networks will play in the future. This article reviews past developments, describes current activities, and examines basic issues for the next decade.

IDENTIFYING STANDARD ELEMENTS FOR ARCHIVAL DESCRIPTION

The task initially assigned to NISTF by the SAA council was the resolution of a conflict generated by a request from the staff of the National Historical Publications and Records Commission (NHPRC)–the staff requested SAA endorsement of their effort to develop a national database of archival information. This request seemed to conflict with the profession's traditional support of NUCMC. By authorizing a comparative evaluation, SAA sought a technical solution to a largely political question. Chaired by Richard Lytle of the Smithsonian Institution, the task force avoided the choice between two highly charged options by broadening its focus from a consideration of "current national programs" to an exploration of ways to construct the best possible national informational system for archives and manuscript control.

Fundamental to NISTF planning was the assumption that archives (institutional or governmental records) and manuscript collections (personal papers) were sufficiently similar to be well served by the same system. Traditionally, distinctions have been made between methods appropriate for the management of archives and methods for the management of manuscript collections. Representative of this division was NUCMC's exclusion of institutional or governmental archives maintained by the originating agency, which effectively excluded the vast majority of such records.[5] In order to address the issue of similarity, NISTF commissioned a study to examine current archival descriptive practices.

With the support of the National Endowment for the Humanities (NEH), Elaine Engst of Cornell University conducted an analysis of the descriptive practices of a broad variety of repositories and of the various national and specialized databases. Based on this study, a report, "Standard

Elements for the Description of Archives and Manuscript Collections," was submitted to the task force in September 1980. The study found that various types of repositories have similar needs and responsibilities to provide physical and intellectual control of and access to their holdings, and that commonly accepted methods of archival description are used to carry out these functions.[6] Because of these similarities, common standards for bibliographic description, encompassing the needs of both archives and manuscript repositories, could be developed; however, the development of viable information-sharing mechanisms would be obstructed by the lack of a common nomenclature for recording information. It was increasingly apparent to the members of NISTF that the role of SAA was to develop and maintain standards to facilitate the interinstitutional exchange of information, rather than to build or operate an information system. Therefore, development of a data element dictionary and an exchange format was begun in early 1981.[7]

In order to prepare a data element dictionary, NISTF established a working group, chaired by David Bearman, NISTF project director, and composed of representatives of the National Archives and Records Service (NARS), the Library of Congress (LC), the Research Libraries Group (RLG), and the NHPRC Data Base participants. The dictionary was intended to provide standard definitions for all information elements employed in any and all archives, records centers, and manuscript repositories; it included administrative data as well as bibliographic information. A draft was prepared by the working group and was issued for professional review in February 1982.[8]

DEVELOPING COMPATIBILITY BETWEEN LIBRARY STANDARDS AND ARCHIVAL PRACTICE

The task force next embarked on the creation of an exchange format. While the data element standard was intended for manual as well as automated systems, the exchange of data in machine-readable form was always a primary concern.[9]

The exchange format needed to include designated fields for recording all information elements defined in the dictionary, and it needed to conform to national and international standards for exchange of bibliographic information in machine-readable form. In addition, the format had to accommodate the collective approach to bibliographic description and include fields for recording the activities involved in the acquisition and maintenance of archival materials. While a manuscript collection may be composed of a single document, most collections include thousands of items which are treated as a single bibliographic entity. Documents in a collection may have several personal or corporate authors, address a broad range of topics, and include correspondence, diaries, account books, and other types of documents. It was essential to include fields for recording collection management data in order to reflect the integration of bibliographic description with other processes – such as acquisition, arrangement, storage, and preservation – in the control, maintenance, and use of archival holdings.

The most commonly used and widely accepted standard for bibliographic exchange is the MARC format. Unfortunately, the MARC format for manuscripts published in 1973 was primarily designed for individual item cataloging and poorly suited for archival use.[10] In early 1981, however, LC indicated its willingness to make substantial changes and allowed SAA to conduct the revision process.

The revised format, USMARC Format for Archival and Manuscripts Control (AMC), was accepted by the SAA Council in the fall of 1981, approved by the American Library Association (ALA) Committee on the Representation in Machine-Readable Form of Bibliographic Information (MARBI) in January 1983, and published by LC in late 1984.[11] The format incorporates the collection approach to cataloging and includes all data elements defined in the dictionary; an "Actions" field (MARC field 583) can be used for recording information about administrative and reference actions.[12] In response to discussions with the Standard Elements Committee of the ALA Division on Rare Books and Manuscripts, the format also includes fields for cataloging publications handwritten before the advent of printing. The preexisting fields – for single item cataloging and for other bibliographic systems – were retained. These inclusions broadened the acceptability and usability of the format. Future modifications require approval by both LC and the SAA Committee on Archival Information Exchange, which succeeded NISTF in 1983.

The development of MARC AMC was essential to the current level of archives/library integration, but the degree of its success would not have been possible without the completion, almost simultaneously, of two other projects. One of these was the substantial revision of the Anglo-American Cataloging Rules for manuscripts, compiled by Steven Hensen at the Library of Congress.[13] This revision was part of an LC project (sponsored by NEH and carried out in conjunction with the Council of National Library and Information Associations) to prepare a series of manuals to treat special format materials not adequately covered in the second edition of the *Anglo-American Cataloguing Rules* (AACR2).[14] The resulting manual, *Archives, Personal Papers, and Manuscripts: A Cataloging Manual for Archival Repositories, Historical Societies, and Manuscript Libraries* (1983), has not been accepted as an "official" revision of AACR2 but has been accepted as a standard for AMC cataloging by both OCLC and RLG.[15] The other significant project was the development of enhancements to RLIN that supported the functions and design of the new format.

LIBRARY BIBLIOGRAPHIC NETWORKS AND ARCHIVAL MANAGEMENT GOALS

Providing effective access to the wealth of historical documentation housed in archives and manuscript repositories is a fundamental goal of archival practice. In attempting to meet this goal, the creation of a national database long has been seen as a critical objective. In 1949, a Joint Committee on Historical Manuscripts was formed by SAA and the American Association for State and Local History to study the development of a national union catalog. After deciding that such a catalog could be established through the voluntary cooperation of libraries and other repositories, the committee began to search for a host institution.[16] The offer in the fall of 1951 by LC to house and administer this catalog eventually led to the establishment of NUCMC. The potential benefits of automation in providing nationwide access to archival resources led to the creation of the NHPRC Data Base Project in 1976 and the establishment of NISTF the next year and is a significant element in the continuing growth of network participation.[17]

Library bibliographic networks have become major databases of information concerning the nation's published resources. However, this significant development has come as a by-product of the effort to derive the maximum benefits inherent in shared cataloging. While the networks have, to varying degrees, developed other programs and services, shared cataloging remains the primary motive for library participation. Shared cataloging also remains critical to the financial well-being of the networks, and their fiscal management is largely predicted on this factor.

Archival participation falls almost entirely outside of this fiscal structure. Since their collections are unique, archivists contribute original records at minimal cost and seldom "derive" bibliographic records. Therefore, they do not benefit from the economics of shared cataloging, nor do they contribute substantially to network income. The number of AMC records in any bibliographic database is unlikely to exceed 1,000,000, so archival participation is not a substantial drain on the system resources in gross terms. However, the need for greater record lengths, special processing functions, and the capacity to use numerous name, form, and topical headings to facilitate access means that AMC use cannot be ignored in estimating development and operating costs.

In addition to economic considerations, there are other differences between library and archive network participation. In the realm of published materials, as a network matures, the value of each new membership by a similar institution tends to decrease. With archival participation, the potential value of each new member's contribution remains constant. Conventional borders of membership also differ. Membership by state, federal, and corporate repositories, which may have little interest in other network programs and services, are critical to the enrichment of the database. Additionally, archivists have more to lose from the traditional competitiveness and division between the bibliographic networks. For archivists and users of historical documentation, divided access is limited access.

All of these differences serve to complicate issues of both governance and mission. It seems apparent that in order to satisfy archival goals and expectations and to rationalize their management, networks must acknowledge their role as scholarly and public resources and develop the mechanisms necessary to support that role.

PROCESSING AND DISSEMINATING ARCHIVAL INFORMATION

Archivists first began to use computers in the mid-1960s, primarily in order to provide detailed access to the contents of a specific collection or small groups of related collections.[18] These printed indexes and inventories, commonly referred to as archival finding aids, were generated by mainframe computers in the 1960s and 1970s; today they are usually produced by microcomputers. But whether manually created or computer generated, archival finding aids are central to the control and use of collections and are the chief source of information in compiling an archival cataloging record.[19] It is unlikely that the AMC format will be widely used in the compilation of finding aids, but there is considerable interest in developing online interfaces between cataloging databases and finding-aid databases maintained locally. This would allow a system user to go directly from a catalog record of interest to a finding aid describing the collection in detail. This interface parallels the natural progression of the research process and will be a focus of future development. Currently, there are three major areas of AMC-related development: broadening access to archival information; developing mechanisms for recording and tracking collection management functions; and integrating access to published and unpublished sources. In all three of these areas, some of the issues are technical, but many are matters of policy, practice, and politics.

Broadening Access to Archival Information

The implementation of RLIN AMC in early 1984 established the viability of the new MARC format. This crucial development resulted from a cooperative project of Yale, Cornell, and Stanford University Libraries, the Hoover Institution, and RLG, with funding from the U.S. Office of Education's Title II-C (Research Libraries) Program.[20] The system was designed to meet the needs of a broad range of repositories, and RLG has maintained its commitment to build a database of national scope. In addition, in the summer of 1986 RLG tape-loaded 12,507 records describing the holdings of 594 New York State repositories. These records were originally produced using SPINDEX (Selective Permutation INDEXing), a batch-processing system developed by the National Archives, and were compiled by the Historical Documents Inventory, a statewide survey conducted by the New York Historical Resources Center at Cornell University. In 1985, the Historical Resources Center began entering survey records directly into RLIN has now (1990) added the holdings of some 400 additional repositories. When NUCMC began to use RLIN in 1988, it offered an avenue through which any repository can contribute data to the RLIN database. The Center for the History of Physics is planning to serve as a similar avenue for collections documenting the history of physics. These and other special projects, as well as member contributions, will continue to enrich the database. RLG has also assiduously encouraged "special membership" by archival programs and has given archivists a formal voice in governance through the establishment in 1983 of a Task Force on Archives, Manuscripts, and Special Collections.

To this point, RLG has played a predominant role in integrating archives management and access with network activities and services. This is due to a combination of factors – the initiative taken by certain RLG member libraries; the availability of funding from the Title II-C Program, NEH, and the NHPRC; and support by the RLG Board of Directors and staff. Additionally, RLG's mission statement explicitly acknowledges its role as a scholarly information resource. Nonetheless, the process of integration has not been without its difficulties. Questions regarding consistent application of system-wide standards have concerned both archivists and librarians. Allocation of staff to support archival projects will never be timely or sufficient. Clarification of the roles various archives and special collections should play in the shared resources programs is only now beginning. Developing mechanisms to facilitate shared access to RLIN and to holdings in other networks is also a concern. These and other practical and political issues must be addressed. Fortunately, it does appear that a forum for constructive discussion is in place.

OCLC implemented the original MARC manuscript format in the mid-1970s, but few repositories adopted it. In addition to constraints in the format's design, the limited length of OCLC's bibliographic records and the absence of subject searching further discouraged interest. However, OCLC added AMC in November 1984. With expanded record size and subject searching capabilities, it could become a more viable system. It continues to be used selectively by archivists.

Many archival programs are divisions of OCLC libraries, and an increasing number will use OCLC AMC to catalog their holdings. OCLC will not use the type of special archival management features which RLG developed, but repositories will use the system to provide multi-institutional access, to produce catalog cards, and to generate machine-readable tapes for loading into local online catalogs. OCLC now has begun to actively solicit archival participation, and the potential exists for OCLC to play a major role in expanding access to archival holdings. However, in order to limit possible frustrations, OCLC must be aware of archival requirements and objectives, be willing to make technical enhancements to support these requirements, and to adopt "political" strategies that foster these objectives.

The role of any one network in broadening access is vital but limited; cooperation between networks is essential. Whether through the regular exchange of data between networks or through the implementation of telecommunication protocols allowing mutual access to the various databases, information-sharing is necessary to meet archival access goals.

Tracking Collection Management Functions

While considerable attention has been focused on expanding access to archival information, substantial effort has been devoted as well to the development of information processing and management capabilities. In the RLG database, an RLIN AMC record is composed of two parts, a "bibliographic" segment for recording bibliographic information, and an "archival control" segment for recording management information. The archival control segment, which is based on MARC fields 541 (Immediate Source of Acquisition) and 583 (Actions), is itself divided into two parts, a processing control screen which includes accessioning, donor, and location information, and an action screen where specific management functions can be specified. Multiple processing control screens can be included in a single AMC record to record additional accessions to existing collections, and multiple action screens may also be recorded for any particular accession. Access to archival control screens can be restricted to the creating repository, and access to donor information is always restricted.

The use of management data in RLIN AMC is facilitated by the RLIN Reports System (RRS), a generalized reporting package which can be used to produce a variety of printed reports, including accessions lists and donor lists. RRS can also generate time-triggered alerting reports on the status of materials in process, on access restrictions due to expire, on the scheduled transfer of documents from an office to the archives, or on any other designated functions. Particularly valuable to government archivists is its ability to link access to all of the records from the various divisions of a large state or federal agency. The "related title" search in the online system, based on data in field 773 (Host Item Entry), allows the retrieval of bibliographic records for materials that are component parts or subunits of a particular "host" or "parent" collection. Additionally, local indexes allow one to search one's own holdings by any local control number or by donor name or originating agency.[21]

Government archivists are quite interested in investigating the use of AMC for recording and tracking management functions and for decision-making. The seven state archives that are RLG "special members" (a membership category available to nonresearch libraries) are participants in an NHPRC-funded project. The project supports both integrating access to government records with access to other historical materials, and evaluating RLIN AMC as a mechanism for sharing management information; the project's purpose is to share data regarding archival appraisal.[22] Appraisal does not mean monetary value but indicates, rather, the process of determining the value of records based upon their current administrative, legal, and fiscal use; their evidential and informational or research value; their arrangement; and their relationship to other records.[23] Based on this appraisal, records are selected for archival preservation or designed for destruction.

Appraisal is a major function of government archival programs. While the statutes and agencies of the various states differ, increasingly, the same functions of government are conducted in all states, and records containing comparable data are generated. This project seeks to determine whether mutual access to appraisal decisions – and the grounds for those decisions – will improve and simplify the appraisal process in these repositories. If successful, the project could broaden the basis for archival participation in bibliographic networks.

Between July 1984 and January 1986, the staff of the National Archives and Records Administration (NARA) conducted a study which examined the capacity of the USMARC AMC format to carry information for both the control of, and access to, federal records throughout their "life cycle." (The "life cycle" of a body of records dates from their creation through their active use, occasional use, and ultimate disposition – either archival preservation or destruction.) RLIN AMC was selected as the "test" vehicle, allowing a comprehensive evaluation of RLIN. Seven terminals were installed, and archivists responsible for appraisal, arrangement and description, reference, and record center activities entered information that their units generated or used.[24]

Testing was completed in the fall of 1985, and a final report was submitted in February 1986.[25] The format is capable of holding descriptive information across the entire range of life cycle stages and the AMC fields are compatible with most data elements inherent in NARA and agency-produced descriptions. However, NARA staff found that the process control functions were not sufficiently sophisticated to handle easily the needs of a repository as large as the National Archives. Nonetheless, the project staff recommended developing automated systems with data elements compatible with MARC fields that will also support the creation of MARC records for exchange purposes. The project staff also recommended continued use of RLIN as a means to disseminate descriptive information about their holdings and to provide NARA staff with access to this valuable source of archival data.[26]

NARA's decision to process management information locally and to generate bibliographic data in MARC format for loading into national networks is an approach that may be adopted by many repositories. This approach, in fact, is integral to the design of MicroMARC:amc, microcomputer system software developed at Michigan State University; it will support local cataloging, reference, and report generation, and will also create a USMARC AMC data file for transfer to other systems. OCLC advocates a local-processing approach, which is consistent with their decision not to incorporate special features for processing AMC data. However, local-processing assumes a willingness by networks to load locally-produced magnetic tapes or to develop the necessary links for electronic transmission. (This process may require special costs to support the loading of relatively few bibliographic records.) It is essential that appropriate agreements and protocols be established early in order to avoid unrealistic expectations.

The AMC format was designed to provide integrated access to bibliographic and process management data. Devising effective, cost-efficient means to support this integration is a current priority; local integrated library systems will play a major role in this area.

Integrating Access to Library Holdings

Traditionally, access to unpublished library holdings was isolated from the listings of published materials. If an archival department maintained a card catalog, it was often maintained as a separate entity, both intellectually and physically separate from the "general" catalog. Library of Congress Subject Headings (LCSH) were considered too broad for archival use, and AACR conventions deemed inappropriate. Often these methodological differences were accompanied by administrative separation – collections existed as libraries within libraries. While few would suggest that this situation has benefited the user, library administrators have often allowed this situation to continue, concentrating instead on "mainstream concerns." Archivists and other special collection curators, too, have guarded their independence and opposed efforts to increase conformity. Library networks have mirrored the situation in their member libraries, concentrating on monographic and serial control. This situation is changing however. New or revised formats for visual materials, archives, and manuscripts, and machine-readable data files have been recently developed as library administrators increasingly expect that networks should support the control of all forms of library holdings.[27]

The cooperative project by Yale, Cornell, Stanford, and RLG, which developed RLIN AMC, sought to integrate library records. The participants chose to adopt conventions supporting the use of LC Name Authorities, AACR2 forms of headings, and LCSH. While these sources often have been criticized by archivists, they were necessary; common standards and access terms are essential to providing multi-institutional access to archival holdings and integrated access to the various materials within each library.[28] These practices have been widely followed, in government archives as well as in library repositories.[29]

Increasingly, integrated access will be provided via online public access catalogs. RLIN AMC records have been loaded into online catalogs at Stanford and New York University (NYU). These transfers have led to some difficulties; at NYU, over 90 percent of the AMC records were too long for the full public display, and restricted management data appeared in the public displays. With the installation of the next generation of Geac hardware and software, it is expected that these problems will be resolved. In addition, the Geac system will provide a linked authorities subsystem which will be of considerable value to the archivists at NYU.[30] At the Ohio Historical Society, OCLC cataloging will be used to generate AMC records for loading into a local online catalog, which in turn will provide the kind of subject searching capabilities not yet available in OCLC.[31] The growing number of online public access catalogs and the development of local processing capabilities make it essential that archivists get involved in planning and formulating local library systems' requirements; the traditional methodological and administrative isolation of special collections must become a thing of the past.

The creation of the AMC format led to new ways of processing and disseminating archival information. National bibliographic networks offer capabilities long needed by archivists and researchers. Network participation will open new opportunities, affecting acquisition, preservation, and use of documentary materials. And new mechanisms for communication and cooperation will develop. In conclusion, this article describes some of these developments and their impact.

THE IMPACT OF BIBLIOGRAPHIC NETWORKS ON ARCHIVAL PRACTICE AND THE ARCHIVAL PROFESSION

During the next decade, archival practice will be significantly influenced by widespread participation in national bibliographic networks. Some changes will be directly attributable to this participation; other changes will be more subtle, resulting from the interaction of various factors. In surveying these developments, five general areas will be examined: standards, professional relationships, cooperative arrangements, collection use, education and training. These categories are not exclusive; developments in one area clearly will affect other areas. The examination is only cursory and is intended to present issues facing archivists and to suggest the effects they may have on the profession.

Standards

Standards are common to both the archive and library environments. There are specification standards, designed for simplification and interchangeability. Other standards are guidelines: sets of definitions and rules that will produce improved results if applied, but that are not designed for mechanical uniformity or interchangeability.[32] While a standard may be derived from the policies of a single individual or institution, the creation and maintenance of a consensus standard is often a complex and demanding process. It was a significant step for the archival profession when, in 1980, NISTF decided to develop a standard for the exchange of descriptive information.[33]

Although archivists have traditionally cited the virtues of standardization and criticized the profession for its lack of descriptive standards, little progress was made until the 1980s.[34] Impetus for recent progress came primarily from three closely related areas: use of automation, interest in multi-institutional data exchange, and participation in bibliographic networks. When archivists first began using automated techniques, it was quickly apparent that increased standardization was necessary in order to derive any benefits from computerization. It was equally clear that standards were essential for multi-institutional sharing of descriptive information.[35] Bibliographic networks are playing an important role in the development of descriptive standards for several reasons. Network participation requires conformity to certain standards through the networks' incorporation of enforcement mechanisms that support standardization. Networks provide an effective working environment for the creation and maintenance of standards, and networks can represent archival concerns in the development of national and international standards. Networks will continue to play an important part in standardizing descriptive practice, but it is important that their role not become confused with the role of SAA in the standards process.

Professional Relationships

Many different forces are changing the professional relationships of archivists, including the "information explosion," the use of new technology, and the rapid deterioration of printed and other information sources. However, it appears that network participation will be the most influential in affecting relationships between the archival and library professions, between the different types of archival programs, and among the various departments in libraries.

A little over a decade ago, when SAA was offered an opportunity to play a consultative role in the revision of the *Anglo-American Cataloging Rules*, the matter was not considered sufficiently germane to the primary interests of archivists to be pursued actively. Now, the SAA bibliographic exchange standard is also a library standard, and it is being jointly maintained by SAA and LC. In 1986, an RLIN Users Roundtable was established by SAA, followed by an OCLC Roundtable. These changes are indicative of trends to expect in the future. SAA has broadened its perspective and expanded its role; it must now be willing to devote the resources necessary to fulfill this role and to adequately represent the widening interests of its members.

Institutional divisions have always characterized the archival profession. Now a diversity of documentary holdings is represented in a single database, and integrated access to this information is available across the country. University repositories and governmental archives can belong to the same network, share an electronic mail system, and use the same conventions in describing and providing access to their holdings. Network participation may serve to bridge long-standing institutional and methodological differences.

Librarians, archivists, and curators will feel a greater sense of common cause. This should produce a general strengthening of library resources. For archivists, there may be increased automated systems support. Awareness of archival holdings and methods will increase. It is possible that the collective approach to cataloging may be adopted for control of various printed and microform materials. Additionally, improved communication and cooperation among special collections staff may enhance the role of special collections in overall library management.

Cooperative Arrangements

Most archivists share a rather holistic view of the universe of documentation and a sense of common purpose in the continuing effort to document the nature of human existence. While there is occasional competition for a few select collections, most archivists now agree that there are many more collections deserving preservation than there are archival resources with which to preserve them. As a result, institutional cooperation has been viewed as a means to expand archival capabilities. In the 1960s and 1970s cooperative archival networks were established in several states, primarily in the Midwest. The goals of these statewide networks were to increase the preservation of historical materials and to expand the accessibility and use of archival sources. While the organizational structure of the networks varied, they were all based on the leadership (or generosity) of a central state agency. Although these networks made progress in meeting their primary goals, the budgetary constrictions of the late 1970s and early 1980s reduced funding overall and placed constraints on the program support role of central agencies. These cutbacks made it apparent that the breadth of cooperative support and services was, in some states, inadequate to maintain a viable level of network activity.[36]

While the success of these statewide networks has been limited, there are demonstrable benefits to sharing bibliographic information and broadening access to archival sources. Although in some states, such as Missouri, a comprehensive catalog of the holdings of network repositories is available at all sites, the advantages offered by an online bibliographic network are substantial. In addition to being an effective tool for sharing access, bibliographic networks could greatly facilitate the centralized cataloging functions provided in some states. Electronic mail and interlibrary loan systems will also support cooperative programs. In a state like New York, where the holdings of most repositories will be in RLIN and most research universities belong to RLG, the potential is considerable. However, the vitality of statewide archival networks is dependent on the development of organizational structures with adequate resources, effective governance, and essential services.

Collection Use

Bibliographic networks could have a considerable effect on the use of archival holdings. Within a given repository, access will be improved as a result of more consistent cataloging procedures. In those systems offering sophisticated searching capabilities, the user can search the holdings using various combinations of personal, corporate, topical, chronological, geographical, and form and genre headings. Researchers will be able to use just one search strategy to identify relevant published and unpublished sources; and they will be able to do national searches to find related collections housed in repositories across the country. Although the effects will be gradual, the expanded availability of bibliographic information will lead to an increase in both the volume and diversity of collection use.

Reference services also will be substantially affected. Researchers will have the ability to access data regarding archival holdings at sites other than the reading rooms of archives and manuscript repositories. In some cases, access will be located in the library's general reference area, necessitating a broadened knowledge by reference librarians of the nature and usage of archival materials. In other cases, researchers will use a public access catalog terminal, although it is not yet clear what kinds of online displays will be best for AMC catalog data. Network participants will have to develop cooperative protocols for reference and interlibrary services. The RLG Task Force on Archives, Manuscripts, and Special Collections has recently prepared guidelines regarding the loan, photocopying, and microfilming of special collections materials for scholarly research. These developments will alter traditional archival reference functions and existing patterns of interaction among librarians, archivists, and researchers.

Education and Training

In recent decades, a graduate degree in either history or library science met the educational criteria for admission into the archival profession. According to a study done by David Bearman, of the 140 job advertisements that appeared in the SAA Newsletter between September 1985 and August 1986, more advertisements requested either an MA or MLS than cited either alone.[37] Evidence suggests, however, that the prominence of the MLS is now gradually increasing. Bearman's study reports that, of those advertisements requesting one degree or the other, more than two-thirds cited an MLS. However, the rate of change is not great. Much more striking is the rapidly increasing frequency of requests for "knowledge of the USMARC AMC format" or, more specifically, "knowledge of RLIN/AMC." SAA workshops teaching the fundamentals of USMARC AMC cataloging are being heavily attended across the country. Familiarity with these new descriptive practices and standards and with their application will become an important element in the education and training of archivists.

Bibliographic networks are playing an important role in this educational process by providing basic training and serving as a tool for developing and refining new techniques. Network participation will contribute to a homogeneity of experience, making it possible for a trained archivist to move from one repository to another without extensive retraining. Having this base of common experience will contribute to increased professionalism and a sense of common mission.

CONCLUSION

In summary, then, bibliographic networks can play an important role in the management and dissemination of archival information. They can improve access to archival holdings and integrate access to both published and unpublished resources. Networks can also serve as a link for communication and cooperation between the various professions and institutions engaged in preserving historical documentation. Bringing these opportunities to fruition will require innovative policies, programs, and governance.

Notes

1. As of 6 Aug. 1986, 71,024 bibliographic records had been entered into the RLIN AMC files. Research Libraries Group, "Growth of the AMC File." (Unpublished report to the Society of American Archivists RLIN Users Roundtable, Chicago, 27 August 1986.)

2. With the publication of its twenty-second issue in 1986, the *National Union Catalog of Manuscript Collections* has published descriptions of approximately 54,799 collections located in 1,297 different repositories. Library of Congress, Processing Services, *National Union Catalog of Manuscript Collections, Catalog, 1984* (Washington, D.C.: LC, 1986), iii.

3. Of the estimated 50,000 records in the OCLC database as of August 1986, approximately 40,000 were originally entered in the MARC Manuscript format prior to the implementation of the MARC Archival and Manuscript Control format in November 1984. (Glenn Patton, Senior Support and Training Specialist, OCLC, to H. Thomas Hickerson, personal communication, 27 August 1986.)

4. "Minutes of the Meeting of the Council of the Society of American Archivists, 6 October 1977," *American Archivist* 41 (January 1978): 119-20.

5. Library of Congress, *National Union Catalog of Manuscript Collections, 1959-1961* (Ann Arbor, Mich.: J. W. Edwards, 1962), v-vi.

6. Elaine D. Engst, "Standard Elements for the Description of Archives and Manuscript Collections" (Unpublished report to the Society of American Archivists Task Force on National Information Systems, 1980).

7. David Bearman, "Toward National Information Systems for Archives and Manuscript Repositories," *American Archivist* 45 (Winter 1982): 53-56.

8. H. Thomas Hickerson, "Archival Information Exchange: Developing Compatibility," in *Academic Libraries: Myths and Realities* (Proceedings of the Third National Conference of the Association of College and Research Libraries), ed. Suzanne C. Dodson and Gary L. Menges (Chicago: ACRL, 1984), 62-65.

9. Richard H. Lytle, "An Analysis of the Work of the National Information Systems Task Force," *American Archivist* 47 (Fall 1984): 362-63.

10. Library of Congress, MARC Development Office, *Manuscripts: A MARC Format* (Washington, D.C.: LC, 1973).

11. Library of Congress, Automated Systems Office, MARC *Formats for Bibliographic Data, Update No. 10* (Washington, D.C.: LC, 1984).

12. Nancy Sahli, *MARC for Archives and Manuscripts: The AMC Format* (Chicago: Society of American Archivists, 1985).

13. Steven L. Hensen, comp., *Archives, Personal Papers, and Manuscripts: A Cataloging Manual for Archival Repositories, Historical Societies, and Manuscript Libraries* (Washington, D.C.: LC, 1983).

14. Michael Gorman and Paul W. Winkler, eds., *Anglo-American Cataloguing Rules*, 2d ed. (Chicago: ALA, 1978).

15. OCLC Online Computer Library Center, Inc. *Online Systems, Archives and Manuscript Control Format* (Dublin, Ohio: OCLC, 1984). Research Libraries Group, Inc., *RLG Standard for Archives and Manuscripts in RLIN* (Stanford, Calif.: RLG, 1984). A new edition (1989) of the Hensen manual, now published by the Society of American Archivists, was adopted as the standard for archival cataloging by the Council of the SAA in 1990.

16. "Report of the Joint Committee on Historical Manuscripts," *American Archivist* 17 (April 1952): 176-80.

17. H. Thomas Hickerson, "Expand Access to Archival Sources," *Reference Librarian* 13 (Fall 1985/Winter 1985-86): 195-99.

18. H. Thomas Hickerson, *Archives and Manuscripts: An Introduction to Automated Access (Society of American Archivists Basic Manual Series)*, (Chicago: SAA, 1981), 22-29.

19. Henson, *Archives, Personal Papers, and Manuscripts*, 2d ed. (Chicago: SAA, 1989), 9.

20. Lofton Abrams, "Yale, Cornell, and Stanford Awarded Grant for Development of RLG Automated Bibliographic System for Manuscripts and Archives," *American Archivist* 46 (Fall 1983): 477-80.

21. Elaine D. Engst, "Nationwide Access to Archival Information," *Documentation Newsletter* 10 (Spring 1984): 4-6.

22. "Project Creating National Public Records Database Using MARC AMC Format," *SAA Newsletter* (November 1986): 3.

23. Frank B. Evans et al., "A Basic Glossary for Archivists, Manuscript Curators, and Record Managers," *American Archivist* 37 (July 1974): 417.

24. William M. Holmes et al., "MARC and Life Cycle Tracking at the National Archives: Project Final Report," *American Archivist* 49 (Summer 1986): 305-06.

25. National Archives and Records Administration, Archival Research and Evaluation Staff, *The MARC Format and Life Cycle Tracking at the National Archives: A Study* (Washington, D.C.: NARA, 1986).

26. Holmes et al., "MARC and Life Cycle Tracking," pp. 307-09.

27. Lawrence Dowler, "Integrating Archival Management with Library Networks: Implications for the Future," in *Academic Libraries: Myths and Realities* (Proceedings of the Third National Conference of the Association of College and Research Libraries), eds., Suzanne C. Dodson and Gary L. Menges (Chicago: ACRL, 1984), 80-84.

28. Steven L. Hensen, "The Use of Standards in the Application of the AMC Format," *American Archivist* 49 (Winter 1986): 36-40 (article included in this section of book).

29. Holmes et al., "MARC and Life Cycle Tracking," p. 308.

30. Thomas J. Frusciano, "Integrating the Archivist: AMC, Local Systems, and Archival Management in Research Libraries" (Paper delivered at the annual meeting of the Society of American Archivists, Chicago, 29 August 1986) Np: nd.

31. Marjorie J. Haberman, Resource Sharing Group Manager, Ohio Historical Society, to H. Thomas Hickerson, personal communication, 19 November 1986.

32. Walt Crawford, *Technical Standards: An Introduction for Librarians* (White Plains, N.Y.: Knowledge Industry Publications, 1986), 34-43.

33. Lytle, "An Analysis of the Work of the National Information Systems Task Force," pp. 360-64.

34. Edward C. Papenfuse, "The Retreat from Standardization: A Comment on the Recent History of Finding Aids," *American Archivist* 26(October 1973): 537-42. Working Group on Archival Descriptive Standards of the Bureau of Canadian Archivists, *Toward Descriptive Standards: Report of the Canadian Working Group on Archival Descriptive Standards* (Ottawa: Bureau of Canadian Archivists, 1985), 8-18.

35. H. Thomas Hickerson et al., *SPINDEX II at Cornell University and a Review of Archival Automation in the United States* (Ithaca, N.Y.: Cornell University Libraries, Department of Manuscripts and University Archives, 1976), 31-48.

36. Richard A. Cameron et al., "Archival Cooperation: A Critical Look at Statewide Archival Networks," *American Archivist* 46 (Fall 1983): 414-32.

37. "Recruitment of Archivists: 1985-1986," *SAA Newsletter* (November 1986): 9.

Data and Document Interchange Standards: A View from the National Archives of Canada

JOHN MCDONALD, GOVERNMENT RECORDS BRANCH, NATIONAL ARCHIVES OF CANADA

In reviewing the title that was originally suggested for this paper "Data and Document Interchange Standards – A Canadian Perspective," I realized that it might lead to the impression that I will be presenting an official Canadian position. Aside from the enormity of such a task, I certainly do not have the authority to announce at this meeting a formal Canadian position. Perhaps it might have been more appropriate if it had been retitled to read something like "Data and Document Interchange Standards – The Perspective of a Canadian." At least this title would have placed me on somewhat safer ground and would have more neatly complemented my next statement, which is that the opinions that I am about to express do not necessarily reflect those of the Canadian government as a whole or, certainly, the Canadian National Standards System.

My objectives in this paper are, firstly, to provide you with my views concerning why, in Canada, we are interested in standards (as you will appreciate, the reasons are not unique to Canada); secondly, to provide you with an overview of the standards development process in Canada generally and in the Canadian federal government specifically; thirdly, to describe the path that the National Archives is planning to pursue based on a recently completed study; and fourthly, to identify a number of challenges that, it seems to me, will have to be addressed before the National Archives or, I would suggest, any archival repository can begin to reap the benefits that are inherent through participation in the standards development process.

Paper Presented to The Society of American Archivists; New York, New York; October, 1987.

For over 10 years, the National Archives has supported a machine-readable archives program. This program has been primarily concerned with the appraisal and acquisition of, in general, simply structured data files generated as a result of survey research activity. These files are usually small in size (i.e., a few thousand cases stored on a single tape) and normally contain information derived from questionnaires or survey data collection instruments. They are usually structured in a form that can be used by statistical software packages such as SPSS and SAS.

The standard practice for acquiring such data has been to convert the data to a simply structured rectangular format for storage on high-quality magnetic tapes. The conversion of the data to such a format is intended to ensure that the data are not dependent upon software that could change over time. The data are recorded in EBCDID and are recopied every five years to ensure that they are not lost because of deterioration of the media. The data are also converted to a single standard recording density (6250 BPI), and standard IBM labels are affixed as headers to each data file. As you will have gathered, our standard with respect to a hardware environment is IBM. Any data files acquired from another hardware environment are converted to storage and reuse within the context of this "standard." The tapes themselves are rewound every year to ensure that data are not lost as a result of the stretching that can occur if the data are not accessed over a long period of time. A standard practice is to check the documentation to ensure that the data can be interpreted and that any errors in the data can be accounted for. A complete documentation package includes not only a record layout but also a complete history of how and why the data were collected or created, of how the data were used, and of how the data were managed within what technological environment.

This set of technical and procedural standards has been designed to ensure that future researchers can gain both physical access and intellectual control over the data stored in the National Archives. By adhering to these standards, the National Archives has ensured that, at least for the data files it has acquired, it will not have to support a museum of computer technology to ensure the future retrievability of data.

Until recently, this set of technical and procedural standards has been sufficient with respect to the acquisition of data files that can be easily converted to a simply structured software-independent format. It will likely serve the needs of the National Archives as it continues to acquire this type of data. On the other hand, it has become clear that such an approach may not be adequate with respect to the large volume of highly significant data stored in the complex data processing environments that have emerged in many government institutions.

At the National Archives, we have only begun to scratch the surface with respect to our understanding of the nature and extent of the vast data holdings that are currently being maintained in the federal government, a substantial proportion of which has potential archival value. For instance, we have yet to acquire data from complex systems such as those that support large sociodemographic databases (e.g., immigration systems, tax systems, income security systems, etc.) or remote sensing applications or applications that use cartographic or graphics software or applications that are supported within so-called office automation systems.

In reviewing the complex federal government landscape within which these data holdings are managed, we have discovered a wide variety of technological environments supporting a diverse array of hardware and software. We have discovered the dynamic manner in which these technological environments have evolved as government departments change and upgrade old software and hardware to accommodate new technologies and to meet new needs. In particular, we have also discovered the extent to which the data holdings generated by these technologies have been neglected and the degree to which a significant percentage of the government's electronic corporate memory has already been lost.

It has become clear that a need exists to expand the data archives program of the National Archives to a truly comprehensive data archive fully capable of addressing the diversity of data processing environments that exist across the government. If this is to occur, however, then the existing standards for acquiring, preserving, and making available machine-readable data will have to be enhanced. In recognizing that a successful data archive program can flourish only if archival considerations are built into the design of systems, we must ensure that any new standards can be easily adopted by systems designers (those who will be responsible for incorporating archival storage and transfer standards into the design specifications of systems).

With this in mind, we turned to the international standards world for possible solutions. In March 1987 the National Archives commissioned a study to describe the standards landscape particularly as it relates to the potential applicability of various data and document interchange standards to the needs of the National Archives. The timing of this study was fortuitous. The Treasury Board (the Canadian equivalent to the U.S. Office of Management and Budget) has just approved a policy that contained statements requiring government departments to respect the interests of the National Archives. Among these was the following: "Data management principles and procedures will be used to ensure that information holdings are inventoried, sharing occurs, duplication is avoided, burden and costs are minimized, information no longer required is discarded and that data with archival value are made available in suitable form to the Public Archives."

The same policy also provided the Treasury Board with the responsibility to manage the development of information technology standards. This new responsibility has already been reflected in the issuance of a policy statement that confirms the adoption of Open Systems Interconnection (OSI) as a federal government standard. The strength behind a standard such as OSI rests with the ability of the Treasury Board to require government departments to reflect approved standards in their procurement requests. In the case of OSI, for instance, government policy requires that all procurement requests state a clear preference for OSI-based systems and products. This is expected to become a mandatory requirement in the early 1990s.

The role of the Treasury Board in managing the government-wide standards development process has major implications for the National Archives. Through the board, the National Archives is in a unique position to assemble interdepartmental working groups to assess archival needs and considerations within a government-wide context. Various standards that might be applicable in addressing these needs would be assessed and, based on the Treasury Board approval process, would be considered for adoption either with or without modifications. Once approved as a Treasury Board information technology standard, the National Archives could also be confident that Treasury Board authority and influence over the procurement process and over the manner in which government departments manage their information holdings would ensure compliance.

The study itself, however, not only described the Treasury Board's role but also explained where this role was situated within the broader context of the National Standards System. In Canada this system is coordinated and supported by the Standards Council of Canada, an independent nongovernment agency that also supports Canada's participation in international standards work. The National Standards System is a federation of all of the accredited organizations concerned with voluntary standards. It includes the Standards Council itself as well as advisory committees, which have been established to provide the council with advice and recommendations on some of its current and future programs. There are currently four advisory committees in operation: the Advisory Committee on Standards for the Consumer, the Advisory Committee on a Standard Information Service, the Advisory Committee on International Standardization, and the Advisory Committee on Certification and Testing. The National Standards System also embraces the Standards Writing Organizations (SWOs) and those organizations accredited for certification, testing, quality assessment, and promotion of cooperation to meet national and international requirements. Currently there are five SWOs:

The Canadian Gas Association

The Canadian General Standards Board

The Canadian Standards Association

The Underwriters Laboratories of Canada

Le Bureau de Normalisation du Quebec

Each of these SWOs has been assigned specific areas of responsibility in an attempt to prevent overlap and duplication of effort. Each SWO publishes standards prepared by technical committees composed of experts from industry, government, and academia and of consumers, who provide representatives concerned with the subject area. The standards are arrived at by consensus and are approved by several levels of balloting. Once a standard has been published, its incorporation into product design is voluntary unless made mandatory through reference in a law, policy, or regulation (e.g., approved Treasury Board Information Technology Standard). Naturally, in developing a standard, these technical committees will study relevant international or foreign standards. For instance, the Canadian Standards Association is the SWO to which the subject of Open Systems Interconnection has been assigned and upon whose behalf these technical committees are functioning.

At the international level, the study suggested that within the International Standards Organization (ISO), there are four Technical Committees (TCs) that should be of continuing interest to the National Archives. These are as follows:

TC 46	Documentation
TC 97	Information Processing
TC 154	Documents and Data Elements in Administration, Commerce, and Industry
TC 184	Industrial Automation Systems

Technical Committees are divided into subcommittees, a number of which are further divided into working groups. The study suggested that the National Archives focus on TC97 and, in particular, on the following sub-committees:

SC 2	Character Sets and Information Coding
SC 6	Telecommunication and Information Exchange Between Systems

SC 15	Labeling and File Structure
SC 18	Text and Office Systems
SC 20	Data Cryptographic Techniques
SC 21	Information Retrieval, Transfer, and Management for OSI

In addition to ISO, the study suggested that the work of the International Telephone and Telegraph Consultative Committee (CCITT) should also be monitored. Headquartered in Switzerland, the CCITT is responsible for developing telecommunication standards related to the use of telegraph, telephone, and data networks. The membership of CCITT consists almost exclusively of common carriers that provide telecommunication services to the public (AT&T, Bell Canada, British Telecom, etc.).

Although the study suggested that ISO would be of much greater interest to the National Archives, it recommended that the work of the following Study Groups (SGs) of the CCITT continue to be monitored:

SG 11	Operational Aspects of Telematic Services
SG VII	Public Data Networks
SG VIII	Terminal Equipment
SG X	Languages and Methods for Telecommunications Applications
SG XII	SDN and Telephone Network Switching and Signalling
SG XVIII	Digital Networks (including ISDN)

Of these, the study suggested that SG VII and SG VIII should be of particular interest to the National Archives. SG VII has produced recommendations such as X.25, the X.400 series (message handling system), and other X-series standards for the transport and session layers of the OSI model. SG VIII is responsible for recommendations in the area of telematic services (e.g., teletex, videotex, and facsimile). One of SG VIII's current projects concerns the T.400 series of recommendations, entitled Document Transfer and Manipulation, which deals with document architecture and the interchange of documents.

In reviewing the roles of ISO and CCITT, we learned that both organizations cooperate extensively. For instance, all of the new OSI standards were developed through the joint efforts of both organizations.

Based on an understanding of the standards landscape, the study suggested that the National Archives focus its efforts in a number of specific areas. It highlighted the significance of OSI and the OSI-related standards and suggested that the National Archives pay special attention to the following standards:

OSA/ODIF	Office Document Architecture/Office Document Interchange Format
MACDIF	Map and Chart Digital Interchange Format
ISO 8211	Data Descriptive File for Information Exchange
FTAM	File Transfer and Access Method
TOP	Technical and Office Protocols

In presenting its recommendations, the study stressed the importance of the Treasury Board as the lead agency responsible for the establishment of federal government positions (i.e., user requirements), the approval of new information technology standards (as derived from international and national standards development activities), and the development of implementation guidelines to assist government departments in applying these standards.

Above all the study concluded that the recently approved policy on federal government standards activities, coupled with the growing recognition by the Treasury Board of the role of the National Archives, presented the National Archives with the unique opportunity to assume a lead role in federal government standards activities, particularly as these relate to data and document interchange.

In assuming this role, however, the Archives will be required to ensure that its work fits within the mainstream of national and international standards development activities. For instance, in the United States, the National Archives and Records Administration is embarking on an important new standards development project in collaboration with the National Institute of Standards and Technology. This landmark two-year effort will result in a comprehensive policy framework and standards development strategy that will be of direct benefit to all archival institutions. As a result and within the context of the Canadian federal government, the National Archives of Canada will ensure that its efforts are complementary to this important initiative.

At a more specific level, we will continue to exchange information with NARA and to work closely on a joint research project to determine the applicability of IOS 8211 to archival considerations. Based on the recommendations of the study, we have also invested resources to assess the applicability of the cartographic exchange standard MACDIF. This is being accomplished as part of a joint venture with the federal Department of

Fisheries and Oceans. Based on our involvement with a federally funded research institute, the Canadian Workplace Automation Research Centre (CWARC), we have also begun to explore the applicability of IDA/ODIF. CWARC is currently involved in developing a conformance testing framework for ODA/ODIF and has welcomed the involvement of the National Archives.

As we become more involved in the standards area, the issues and challenges become formidable. To begin with, data and document interchange standards are not very helpful if there are no data or documents to exchange. The standards that I have just discussed address problems related to interconnectivity. They do not address problems related to information management. In local area networks, for instance, how can ODA/ODIF be applied as an archival transfer standard if the retention and disposition of valuable electronic documents are scattered among the various users of the LAN? How will a data interchange format such as ISO 8211 be effective if the data are poorly documented or cared for? The development and implementation of standard operating practices (i.e., the application of sound information management principles) are just as important as the development and implementation of standards.

In addition to information management issues, archives must also consider the degree to which government agencies (and industry) are prepared to adopt various data and document interchange standards. What if the government agency has no need to exchange data? Who will pay the costs of converting the data to an archival interchange format for transfer to the Archives? When considered governmentwide, should standards be mandatory or discretionary? How should they be implemented, particularly if effective data scheduling procedures have yet to be developed and if the archivist is not around to advise on the matter, particularly when the system is being designed? And what about the National Archives itself? Is the department equipped to acquire, preserve, and make available data that have been transferred in accordance with approved data and document interchange strategies and standards? Will our involvement in standards force the department to rethink its approach to the archival management of machine-readable data?

How will appraisal be affected by policies that require the storage and eventual transfer of data in accordance with approved data and document interchange standards? Will traditional archival principles such as "provenance," "respect des fonds," "information value," and "evidential value" be affected by these standards?

Once the data have been transferred to the archives in a standard interchange format, how will they be conserved? How will they be described? Will another conversion be required to ensure that the data are properly maintained? Will the archives be required to develop dynamic conservation programs that will ensure that it can accommodate changes that may occur to the portfolio of standards it has adopted? With respect to future research use, do we really understand the impact that these standards could have on the ability of our research communities to make effective use of archival data? Will the ease of use be the same, less than, or greater than the use made of the data in its original format and technological environment? Should we consider providing an active service that would permit the conversion of data from the standard formats adopted by the archives to the specific formats desired by increasingly sophisticated researchers? What will be the costs?

Although these challenges may seem formidable, there is room for optimism. On an increasing scale, the vendors and users of information technology are recognizing the importance of interconnectivity–that is, the capacity to communicate information across technological environments. The standards that emerge from this recognition, while serving the needs of a variety of users, should also serve the needs of archives.

Archives are a part of the marketplace. Just as other elements of the marketplace influence industry to develop standards that meet their common user requirements, the Archives should also influence the standards development process through the expression of its own requirements. The initiative of the National Archives and Records Administration was an important step in this direction. For its part and in an effort to build a comprehensive approach to the development of an archival user position and the standards that should emerge to address this position, the National Archives of Canada looks forward to aligning its own contributions with this initiative. As stakeholders in this effort, the archival profession as a whole is encouraged to join us.

References

Data and Document Interchange Standards and the National Archives of Canada, Bureau of Management Consulting and Protocols Communications Inc., Ottawa, June 1987.

Federal Information Policy and Initiative Regarding OSI, Treasury Board Canada, Ottawa, 1987.

Information Management Policy Overview–A Framework for Information Technology Management, Treasury Board Canada, 1987.

Information Technology Standards (policy), Treasury Board Canada, Ottawa, 1987.

The Use of Standards in the Application of the AMC Format

STEVEN L. HENSEN, DUKE UNIVERSITY

The MARC Archival and Manuscripts Control (AMC) format has the potential to change the lives of archivists forever. The format provides a structure for description that is not only fully consistent with archival principles but also compatible with modern bibliographic description. Contemplating the possibilities for information sharing, automated union catalogs, network building, and computerized management is enough to make most archivists positively giddy. Not since the development of the acid-free folder has news this good broken upon the archival horizon.

With this new freedom, however, there are new responsibilities. As archivists join the great game of library automation, they will discover that there are a number of new rules, most of them previously unheard of in archival precincts. These include such things as cataloging codes, Library of Congress subject headings, and name authorities. This article addresses some of the problems and questions raised by these rules, or standards, and explores their implications for archivists.

It is part of the collective folklore of archivists that there is a certain idiosyncratic (some would even say eccentric) approach to certain aspects of the practice of the archival craft. This has certainly been true in the case of descriptive standards. As Alan Tucker of the Research Libraries Group, Inc., has pointed out, "The same historical factors which explain the emergence of . . . library-oriented standards . . . also explain the absence of a similar level of standardization among archivists. The repetitive cataloging of thousands of copies of the same item in thousands of institutions generated needs and solutions which have none of the same impact in an environment in which virtually all of the materials being described are unique."[1]

Originally published in *American Archivist* 49, no. 1 (Winter 1986): 31-40. Reprinted with permission.

Furthermore, until recently the theories and practices of the archival profession were not sufficiently well defined to allow any one person or institution to claim a monopoly on authority or to impose any given set of standards. Over the past few years, however, it has become increasingly clear that, in spite of certain institutional differences, archivists, manuscript curators, records managers, and all the others who look after the nation's documentary heritage do, in fact, have much in common with each other. It is also becoming clear that there is a vital stake in defining and articulating those areas of common terminology, methodology, philosophy, and mission that shape their profession. A large part of this task is the acceptance and use of certain standardized ways of communicating information about archival holdings.

A more immediate and compelling reason for archivists to abandon some of their more individualistic ways is the low tolerance that automated systems have for idiosyncrasy and individualism. Beyond this, however, and perhaps more to the point, the requirements of integrating automated systems demand that even more stringent standards be followed. As Alan Tucker noted in reference to the Research Libraries Information Network (RLIN) implementation of AMC, "If records for archival materials are to be included in the main . . . database and if they are to be retrieved by the same searches that retrieve books and serials, maps and sound recordings, then they have to be created in accordance with the same rules or standards that apply to the other files."[2]

The very existence of the AMC format owes much to a kind of sea change in archival thinking that occurred prior to its development. In the summer of 1980, working under the direction of the Society of American Archivists's National Information Systems Task Force (NISTF), Elaine Engst of Cornell University conducted a study of description practices in a broad variety of repositories. Her unpublished report, "Standard Elements for the Description of Archives and Manuscript Collections," clearly demonstrated, in the words of Tom Hickerson, "that there are common methods of archival description which could be integrated into a broadly applicable set of standards."[3] This study showed archivists and manuscript curators that they had more in common with each other than was popularly believed. More importantly, though, it helped lay an essential foundation for the subsequent development of a format to carry the various elements of description. It also helped facilitate archivists' understanding that there was an area of common ground between archival description and library cataloging.

Coincidental to the process of defining descriptive elements and developing a format, another project was underway that attempted to "reconcile manuscript and archival cataloging and description with the conventions of AACR 2" (the *Anglo-American Cataloguing Rules*, 2nd edition). A rationale for this work was based on the idea that if the "burgeoning national systems for automated bibliographic description . . . are to ever accommodate manuscripts and archives a compatible format must be established . . . (and that) with appropriate modifications, library-based descriptive techniques can be applied in developing this format."[4] The result of this task was recently published by the Library of Congress under the title *Archives, Personal Papers, and Manuscripts: A Cataloging Manual for Archival Repositories, Historical Societies, and Manuscript Libraries.*[5]

Thus, with NISTF's work in defining data elements and developing the AMC format, and the concurrent appearance of a cataloging manual based on archival realities, pieces of a puzzle, the contours of which had heretofore been only dimly perceived and understood, were starting to fall into place. While speculation on the forces of coincidence or archival serendipity may be risky, it is difficult to deny that, regardless of any other implications, these developments represent a quantum leap forward in the way that archivists perceive and use standards. It is gradually being understood that for the price of small losses in procedural autonomy, there may be much to be gained in terms of standardizing the way archivists communicate, both with each other and the world at large, about their collections and their procedures.

On the broadest level the AMC format itself represents a kind of standard. It has been designed to accommodate any kind of information or data about collections that archivists care to record. All that is required is that certain technical and structural standards be followed in using the format (particularly in such areas as fixed-field coding, record and field delimiters, and subfield coding), and that the various elements of description be entered into the specific fields that have been designated for them. Leaving aside for the moment the present uncertainty regarding exactly which fields are appropriate for which data, questions arise regarding the specific form of some of the information elements. This form can be determined through the application of bibliographic standards, specifically in the areas of cataloging and description and in name and subject authorities.

The archival world has had a long and uneasy relationship with the idea of cataloging. It is still seen by many archivists as the one area that is most susceptible to conflict between library science and archival practice. After all, when most librarians talk about processing, they usually mean some kind of cataloging; to archivists processing implies a whole spectrum of arrangement and description functions. Past attempts to "process" archival materials according to library practices – ignoring provenance to impose some exterior classification scheme – offer, even today, the most appalling examples of archival malpractice and "disrespect des fonds." Consequently, the inclusion of special provisions for cataloging manuscript materials in the ALA Cataloging Rules and in the first and second editions of the *Anglo-American*

Cataloguing Rules was never well received by archivists.[6] By and large, these rules continued to treat manuscripts as a curious species of book (or, more offensively, as nonbooks) that had only to be twisted ever so slightly to conform to standard library cataloging. Because of this, in addition to a general lack of understanding in the rules of some of the most fundamental archival truths, most archivists usually consigned these rules to an oblivion perhaps befitting their presumption. The resulting vacuum left the field wide open for individual practice to run amok – which it did.

Archives, Personal Papers, and Manuscripts (or APPM, as it has since come to be known) represents an attempt to fill that breach and to offer to archivists and manuscript curators a set of standards for the description of archival and manuscript materials that is faithful to archival principles while remaining within the general approach and structure of library cataloging as embodied in AACR2. As in all such endeavors, however, some compromises were necessary. In general, archivists who are unused to dealing with the seemingly painful precision of cataloging rules may find some of the details, such as the rules on punctuation, to be excessive and even obfuscating. On the other hand, librarians, perhaps not fully understanding the archival principles involved and what was necessary to accommodate them, may think the fabric of AACR2 has been shredded beyond recognition. Neither of these reactions are entirely valid. Subsequent wide use and acceptance of these rules have shown them to be a practical, useful, and much needed guide to the catalog description of all sorts and levels of archival and manuscript material, either in a manual or automated mode.[7]

One of the principal features of these rules is an overall emphasis on collection-level cataloging (although there are provisions for the item-level approach, as well as description at the series, subgroup, and subseries level). Previous attempts to provide cataloging rules for manuscripts and archives invariably made the mistake of assuming that, for cataloging purposes, the analog to the book was the individual manuscript, often treasured if for nothing more than its autograph value. (This mistake is based, no doubt, on the habits of the rare book community in cataloging codices and other ancient manuscripts.) The size of most modern manuscript collections and archival record groups has, at the very least, demonstrated the utter futility and impracticality of item-level cataloging, and, at most, made many archivists cynical about autograph value. Furthermore, archivists are beginning to understand that aggregate or collection-level description is the "approach most likely to observe the principle of archival unity which recognizes that, in organically-generated collections, at least, it is collective whole as the sum of the interrelationships of its components that has significance and that the individual item or subseries within a collection usually derives its importance from its context."[8]

Secondly, the rules recognize the relative role of cataloging in the description apparatus of most institutions. In general, library cataloging is derived directly from explicit identifying publication information usually taken from the title page of the item being cataloged. Manuscripts and archives, on the other hand, are, almost by definition, unpublished and original and obviously lack these explicit sources of information, as they are called. Furthermore, "unlike book cataloging, in which the catalog record is the primary (and often only) form of access to the material cataloged, manuscript and archival catalogs are usually only one part of an institution's total array of descriptive and finding aids."[9] In short, the approach of this cataloging manual is based on the understanding that, in most cases, cataloging is dependent on, and derived directly from, preexisting registers, inventories, calendars, and indexes.

Perhaps the chief advantage of these cataloging rules is that they are consistent with the style and standards of the *National Union Catalog of Manuscript Collections* (NUCMC),[10] the context in which most archivists and manuscript curators learned to appreciate and understand cataloging. The principal elements of description in NUCMC are still included: title, span, and bulk dares, physical description, notes on scope and content source, finding aids, and restrictions. To be sure, these elements are now more tightly defined and in some cases carry what some may consider to be odd-looking punctuation, but a catalog entry constructed using these rules still looks familiar. More important though is that these rules, by adhering to the general structure of AACR2, provide catalog records for manuscripts that are consistent with the records for books, maps, serials, and other library materials, thus allowing the full integration of archival and manuscript holdings into most existing bibliographic systems and networks.

Beyond the structural standards represented by formats and cataloging rules, the content and form of certain fields or elements of information in AMC is governed by more specific authority standards.

Through the Library of Congress's Name Authority Cooperative, headings for personal and corporate names are created by many institutions throughout the United States according to AACR2 and Library of Congress practice and are then submitted to the library's authority files. These files are subsequently distributed for use by the cooperating libraries, becoming a *de facto* national authority data base that is used by most of the bibliographic utilities in choosing headings both for main and added entries. For the very reasons of uniformity argued above, cataloging records for manuscript and archival materials integrated into such systems will also be required to follow these authorities insofar as possible.

It was not simply an oversight that the cataloging manual did not deal substantively with rules for determining choice of access points or headings.

Other than providing simple guidelines for coping with chapters 21-24 in AACR2, this whole area was seen as a potential mine field for archivists and thought to be best avoided. Unfortunately, while it is still a mine field, it can no longer be avoided and must now be gingerly negotiated.

Most archivists know that main entries are something more than the front door, although in the past main entries and titles were often confused. Put simply main entry for both library and archival cataloging is defined as the entity (i.e., person, family, corporate body) that is chiefly responsible for the creation of a work. The determination of the form of these entries is governed by very specific rules in AACR2 that apply not only to the use of these names in main entries but also to their application in any access point or heading.

These rules in AACR2 for the form of access points pose complex problems for archivists. When the rules state that personal names are to be entered under the "name by which he or she is commonly known"[11] and that a corporate name is entered "directly under the name by which it is predominantly identified,"[12] immediate questions arise. Under these rules, for example, the papers of Samuel Langhorne Clemens must be entered under Mark Twain, one of the pseudonyms he used as an author, because librarians have determined that he is better known by that name. Similarly, we may presume from two recent biographies of Hilda Doolittle that this imagist poet and lost-generation poseur must have left some archival legacy; however, under the rules her papers (or for that matter, any reference to her in the papers of others) would be entered under the name H.D. for that is the name under which she published her poetry. Indeed the archivist who becomes custodian of the papers of one of the two gentlemen who write under the name Ellery Queen shall face a real dilemma.

The rules for corporate headings are equally troublesome for archivists. For example, under the rules for direct entry, the use of full administrative hierarchy is virtually precluded, often making it impossible to determine whether or not a given heading represents a government body – usually a critical question to archivists. To a librarian cataloging publications from the Bureau of Insular Affairs, it is not particularly important that this bureau is an arm of the Department of the Interior; to an archivist establishing record groups and series, it is crucial.

Quite beyond the difficulties presented by the rules themselves, however, are various library practices and interpretations in using those rules. Chief among these is the reliance, in establishing an authoritative form of a name for the first time, on a title page manifestation of that name. If there is no conflict in the authority records with a proposed entry, the form found in the work being cataloged is used. Thus the heading for *United Nations, Educational, Scientific, and Cultural Organization* is simply *Unesco* because, presumably, that was either the form used on the title page of the work being cataloged when the heading was established or it was determined that that was the more familiar form.

This practice presents a greater problem for personal names. Librarians formerly provided on their catalog cards as full a form of a person's name as research could discover, complete with maiden name and birth and death dates. This is no longer the case. If there is no catalog conflict, a name is established as it is given in the work being cataloged and any subsequent discoveries about that person's name or vital dates must be ignored. In any event, extensive research is now discouraged. This occasionally can be awkward. For example, the heading for Princess Grace was established before her untimely death as *Grace, Princess of Monaco, 1929-*. Under current library practice and policy it will stay that way forever, even though most people are keenly aware of her demise. Such practice conflicts with the archival notion that finding aids, of which the catalog record is a part, are more than simply bibliographic surrogates. They provide information and assist research by putting individuals and their documentary remains in a meaningful context. It is sometimes difficult to comprehend why this information should be subject to artificial limitations.

To be fair, it is easy to understand, given today's publishing explosion, why library catalogers can no longer take the time to research fully the personal and corporate names that make up their headings. After all, most users of library catalogs are simply trying to find a book and the added detail of fuller name headings does not necessarily make that task any easier. It is perhaps harder for archivists to understand what these principles have to do with archival practice. As noted at the outset, however, the adherence to name authority standards is but one of the prices that must be paid so that the benefits of automation through AMC can be fully enjoyed. An obvious goal in embracing these standards is to make the price as small and painless as possible.

While there are certainly no easy answers to the problems posed for archivists by AACR2-based name authorities, all is not lost. For persons not known primarily as authors – and this includes perhaps the larger portion of persons represented in most nonliterary and archival collections – the rules provide for determination of forms of names from reference sources such as standard biographical and genealogical sources.[13] In many cases, the papers themselves will serve as the ultimate and most authoritative source. Thus, by using and staying within the rules, archivists still have the freedom to establish many personal names according to the habits and principles that have long been followed. Moreover, by participating in name authority work, archivists fill the authority files with names established under archival principles. This information is then available to fellow archivists using the files, and there is no longer the possibility of having the names entered elsewhere in a less than complete and useful form.

The Manuscript Division of the Library of Congress and the staff of the Manuscripts Section of the Special Materials Cataloging Division (which produces NUCMC) have recently concluded an agreement with the library's Processing Services Department whereby name authority records will be added to the library's outline authority file for names established in the course of cataloging manuscript collections. This agreement permits certain modifications to the library's normal procedures, which, in effect, allow most manuscript headings to be made in a way that archivists should find unobjectionable. They are established under the fullest name possible and with qualifying designations ("of Chicago," "blacksmith") added where necessary. The large number of historical persons added to the file through this project should make it considerably more useful to archivists using it for AMC cataloging.

Another method of coping with objectionable name authorities is through the use of the biographical/historical note in the AMC format. Although this was originally designed to "record any significant information on the creator/author of the manuscript(s) or records required to make the nature or scope of the materials clear,"[14] it is certainly appropriate and within the scope of the note to use it to clear up any possible confusion created by a somewhat opaque main entry. For example, under the rules, the papers of the first Archivist of the United States must be entered under *Connor, R. D. W., 1878-1950*, that being the name by which he was most commonly known. The biographical/historical note can then be used to record some salient facts of his career and to inform the reader that his full name was Robert Digges Wimberly Connor. For corporate headings, this note can be used not only to explain the functions of the body but also to delineate its full administrative hierarchy if the name is not fully given in the heading. Unfortunately, this technique works only for names used as main entries; there is currently no such amplification available in added entries except through notes added to authority records.

Even though the topic of subject cataloging of archival materials is of intense and increasing interest to archivists, it seems to have never been adequately addressed. This may be because this is the area in which local practices and idiosyncrasy are most firmly entrenched. Also, it seems that, as uneasy as archivists have been with library approaches to descriptive cataloging, they have been even less comfortable with traditional subject cataloging. Some have even dispensed with subject cataloging altogether, theorizing that "subject matter is implied by the instruments of action (people and their organizations), and that name control provides a means of subject access that is not dependent on content analysis."[15] For those who feel that some measure of content analysis is a vital part of being an archivist, this is not a very satisfactory approach either.

As with the descriptive aspects of cataloging, the question of standards in subject cataloging can no longer be ignored but must now be considered by archivists as part of the larger questions raised by bibliographic integrating. One of the problems in using book-oriented subject headings is that manuscript collections and especially archival records are not *about* things in the way books are. Books often have a fairly narrow topical focus that can be summarized in two or three well-chosen subject headings. A modern manuscript collection, on the other hand, may deal substantively with dozens of different subjects. Past attempts to apply library subject cataloging to archival materials were generally unsatisfactory; the headings used were simply too general to be useful. Witness the great proliferation in the first volume of the *National Union Catalog of Manuscript Collections* of the headings *United States – Political and government* and *United States – History – Sources*. Furthermore, the general library approach artificially limiting the number of headings is inappropriate for archival practice.

Beyond questions of general approach, however, archivists have genuine problems using standard library subject headings. The *Library of Congress Subject Headings* (LCSH), now in its eleventh edition, was originally offered as nothing more than a list of subject headings used by the Library of Congress in cataloging its collection of books; no particular claims of universality were made for it.[16] With the successful system of distributed Library of Congress cataloging, however, these headings (and indeed nearly all of the other cataloging practices of the library) have become a kind of *de facto* national standard. The success of the bibliographic networks and the distribution of MARC tapes have solidified this acceptance.

Although LCSH is now the standard for subject cataloging, there are still no claims of universality made for it. As new subjects are identified during cataloging and as old headings become outdated, obsolete, or even embarrassing, changes are formulated, debated, and ultimately published. For archivists and manuscript curators the problem is not that the lists in LCSH are not universal, or that the mechanism for change is awkward and slow. The problem is simply that the headings were designed for books. Headings that are perfectly adequate for books may be inappropriate for manuscripts and archives. One example is the practice of choosing a particular form of a family name as the official heading and relegating all variant forms to cross-references. Most archivists would find it very difficult to explain to their genealogical patrons why a reference to the *Kiley family* must be entered under *Kelley family* simply because the latter is the only acceptable form to LCSH. Other examples can be found in the period subdivisions under the *History* and *Politics and government* subheadings under names of countries; many of these subdivisions are entirely too general for archival use and in some cases are historically arbitrary or unsound.

These criticisms aside, it should be said that the majority of subject headings in LCSH are in fact perfectly useful for archival cataloging. Most subjects encountered in manuscript collections or archival records will be found in the lists of headings and their various subdivisions. For alternatives to LCSH, the MARC structure of AMC has allowed for endless variation and idiosyncrasy by offering a series of parallel fields for local subject headings. The RLIN manuscript record, for example, requires only one or two LCSH headings, allowing the rest to fall in local headings fields. Of course, the extensive use of local headings is counter-productive from the viewpoint of full bibliographic integration; subject searches across all formats will bear full fruit only when the subject indexing is standard.

There are other standards involved in AMC that deserve brief mention. These include the genre/form list prepared by Tom Hickerson and other archivists at Cornell University for use in the RLIN implementation. Although this list still needs some refinement, it is a fairly complete listing of the physical forms of material likely to be encountered in archival records and manuscript collections. There are also the various code lists appended to the *MARC Formats for Bibliographic Data*.[17] These include geographic area codes, language codes, country of publication codes, and relator codes, although few of these are pertinent to manuscript cataloging and they are seldom required.

Some of the standards that archivists must face as they use the AMC format should pose few real problems for them and may, in fact, offer a welcome rigor in areas where formerly only chaos reigned. Others will create problems and almost certainly provoke some archival soul-searching. On one point, however, there can be little argument: the AMC format has given the archival community the opportunity to become a full partner in the broader information community of which it was always an obvious and natural (albeit unwitting) part. The answer to the question of whether archivists are ready for the challenge and responsibility of this role will almost certainly be framed in their acceptance or rejection of the various standards required for the proper use of the format.

It is not required, however, that archivists meekly and supinely accept all rules relating to their use of these standards. Where these standards are flatly inappropriate for archival use, changes should be made. For the first time, archivists have a real stake in matters that were previously the sole province of librarians; cataloging rules, name authorities, and subject headings are now firmly part of the archival lexicon. Archivists will make their voices heard in the councils that decide on such things or they will almost certainly regret it.

For those who consider this unlikely, consider the fact that the Society of American Archivists is actively involved with the American Library Association's Committee on the Representation in Machine-Readable Form of Bibliographic Information (MARBI) and the Library of Congress as part of a cooperative effort to maintain and improve the AMC format. An alliance such as this (incredible at the beginning of the 1980s) is a measure of how far archivists have come in dealing maturely and realistically with the problems of automation. Momentum of this sort must not be lost. Having grappled with and successfully resolved larger questions relating to the MARC format, is there any reason archivists cannot have a similar role in and impact on the formulation and maintenance of AMC format-related standards? Surely the eventual resolution of these questions relating to the use of standards will determine the success or failure of AMC as a component of archival automation and more universal bibliographic integration.

Notes

1. Alan M. Tucker, "The RLIN Implementation of the MARC Archives and Manuscript Control Format" (Paper presented at "Academic Libraries: Myths and Realities," Proceedings of the Third National Conference of the Association of College and Research Libraries, Seattle, Washington, 4-7 April 1984).

2. Ibid.

3. H. Thomas Hickerson, "Archival Information Exchange: Developing Compatibility" (Paper presented at "Academic Libraries: Myths and Realities," Proceedings of the Third National Conference of the Association of College and Research Libraries, Seattle, Washington, 4-7 April 1984).

4. Steven L. Hensen, *Archives, Personal Papers, and Manuscripts: A Cataloging Manual of Archival Repositories, Historical Societies, and Manuscript Libraries* (Washington, D.C.: Library of Congress, 1983), 1.

5. This publication is one of a series of manuals interpreting AACR2 for special materials; others have been done for graphic materials, motion pictures and video recordings, rare books, and maps and cartographic materials.

6. *A.L.A. Cataloging Rules for Author and Title Entries* (Chicago: American Library Association, 1949), 21-26; *Anglo-American Cataloguing Rules* (Chicago: American Library Association, 1967), 259-271; and *Anglo-American Cataloguing Rules*, 2d ed. (Chicago: American Library Association, 1978), 110-124. This second edition is known as AACR2.

7. *Archives, Personal Papers, and Manuscripts*, 2d ed. (Chicago, SAA, 1989), has been mandated as the standard for descriptive cataloging of manuscript and archival material in the online cataloging systems of the Research Libraries Group, Inc. (RLIN) the Online Computer Library Center, Inc. (OCLC), the Library of Congress

(LC), and the Society of American Archivists (SAA). (See also recommendation 9 of the Working Group on Standards for Archival Description, Appendix A.)

8. Hensen, *Archives, Personal Papers, and Manuscripts*, p. 2.

9. Ibid.

10. *National Union Catalog of Manuscript Collections* (Washington, D.C.: Library of Congress, 1959-).

11. AACR2, Rule 22.1A.

12. Ibid., Rule 24.1.

13. Ibid., Rule 22.1B.

14. Hensen, *Archives, Personal Papers, and Manuscripts*, p. 22.

15. Richard C. Berner, *Archival Theory and Practice in the United States: A Historical Analysis* (Seattle, Washington: University of Washington Press, 1983), 33.

16. *Library of Congress Subject Heading*, 11th ed. (Washington, D.C.: Library of Congress, 1988).

17. *MARC Formats for Bibliographic Data* (Washington, D.C.: Library of Congress, 1980).

Museum Information Standards: Progress and Prospects

DAVID BEARMAN, ARCHIVES AND MUSEUM INFORMATICS

INFORMATION STANDARDS: WHAT ARE THEY?

Standards, or rules of behavior, are of growing importance within the museum profession as they are in all other areas of our society. In the past year alone, standards for museum educators, museum exhibit designers, museum couriers, museum accounting practices, and museum security systems issued by a variety of professional organizations within the larger orbit of museums, have crossed my desk.[1] Such process standards guide our practice directly and indirectly and deserve to be studied, but they are not the focus of this article which examines only a very specific kind of product standard: museum information standards. Product standards are quite central to many professions and businesses but they have played a lesser role in museums.

Information product standards are frameworks within which information is captured, stored or communicated. The term is used to refer to a very large number of different types of frameworks, with different purposes and effects. In order to speak about the role of information standards in museums, it is useful to distinguish between a variety of standards and their applicability. A similar analysis, just completed for archives, identified three degrees of standardization – guidelines, conventions, and technical standards – and four levels of information to which they could apply – systems, data structures, data contents, and data values.[2] These distinctions, which will be used throughout this paper, can be illustrated by examples from the history of standards development for and by museums and the history of the adoption of industry standards within museums. A third dimension of standardization identified by the archives study group was whether it was "internal" or "external"; this dimension also has considerable importance to museums as the recent crisis over the adoption of new standards for valuation of collections by the Federal Accounting Standards Board is demonstrating.

Guidelines are instructions that reflect accepted practice. When they were originally issued, they might even have defined a new practice for the first time, but since have become the accepted way of doing it. It is a tautology to note that a profession has guidelines for all those tasks that make it a profession, since the critical distinguishing characteristic of a profession is that it embodies a special knowledge of the tasks with which it is charged. Museums are the province of a large number of professionals, ranging from registrars and conservators to educators and accountants, each of which can point to seminal texts and basic manuals in their fields that provide guidelines. In spite of guidelines that are widely acknowledged, actual practice differs between museums, because guidelines are either not explicit about all aspects of practice, or because there is no reason for an institution to adhered to them rigidly. For example, the guidelines embodied in Dorothy Dudley's classic *Museum Registration Practices*, include an information standard for formulating an accession number that is widely accepted: an accession number has the year of accession as a prefix, followed by the sequence of the accession within the year, followed by a suffix indicating the part or item number of a multi-part or item accession.[3] However, in practice, individual museums diverge widely in the accession numbering conventions they use (although less widely that they did before a guideline was available). In addition, as guidelines they lack a mechanism for revision unless the authors decide to put out a new edition. Also there is no formal method for validating guidelines or subjecting them to professional review.

Conventions are more formal than guidelines in that they are adopted by a body with a degree of professional authority. Until relatively recently, professional associations of museums have shied away from adopting such conventions, but the standards applied in the museum accreditation process are certainly an example of this kind of convention.[4] Like other conventions, they are validated by a professional body, but they are sufficiently vague that several organizations that meet the standards could be producing different products.

Technical standards are also adopted by consensus of stakeholders and endorsed by a standards setting and standards maintaining organization. Technical standards are characterized by their explicity. They are formulated in such a way that objective tests can be defined for them; whether one is following a technical standard leaves no room for interpretation. Museums employ thousands of technical standards as participants in a broader culture that enforces such standards; some of these have little programmatic impact, others exercise an influence we are barely aware of. For example, using the standard wattage and amperage set for electricity in our countries doesn't constrain us significantly, but employing the standard television signal used in our countries impacts of the quality of the images we receive as well as the portability of visual information products from other museums. Professionals need to become aware of when such technical standards can provide opportunities and when they merely serve as constraints.

HISTORY OF MUSEUM INFORMATION STANDARDS

The primary strategy followed by those interested in establishing museum information standards since the late 1960s has been to dominate a market, establishing a de facto information system standard and imposing data structure and data content dictated by that system. In the United States this has failed consistently, but in the United Kingdom and Canada it appears to be working for quite different reasons. Even when it appears to succeed in promoting institutional automation, this strategy results in creation of data that is not inter-changeable from one system to another, thereby failing to achieve a major rationale for standardization.

In England, the Information Research Group of the Museum Association (IRGMA) received funds from the British Library to examine the standardization of museum documentation practices.[5] In the early 1970s, this effort led to the establishment of the Museum Documentation Association which issued inexpensive museum registration cards that ultimately proved very popular, especially with smaller museums, and defined what became accepted as the standard manual card system data for UK museums. Ultimately this data dictionary, or data content standard, became a de facto standard. In the past several years, the MDA data standard has demonstrated its power as a standard by appearing as the basis of automated systems, including some systems seeking to enter the UK market that are not sold by the MDA itself. The MDA has developed several systems that incorporate its data standard, but these systems are not designed to communicate with each other in any format other than simple delimited ASCII. The MDA has informally accepted the advice of its large constituency but it hasn't empowered its constituents as a standards body or even published its standards in such a way that they could be regularly updated. If they had, the influence of the MDA standard would doubtless be worldwide by now.

In Canada, a central and government funded database project of the early 1970s eventually became established as a national network (the Canadian Heritage Information Network). CHIN had a false start as the "National Inventory Programme" which tried to dictate a standard for a central database, but with the aid of growing annual governmental support it was able to recover as a service bureau to distributed museums.[6] During its early years, CHIN defined data standards that were inclusive, incorporating all the different practices of its individual members; in more recent years it has been able to guide its members towards consensual standards. However, while its members are the largest museums in Canada, they do not represent a majority of Canadian museums. Recently micro-computer systems intended to interface with the national network have followed the standard, but most Canadian museums are still not following it in their largely manual systems. Nevertheless, it is clear that as the CHIN network expands and as the micro-computer systems vended in Canada begin to be purchased by smaller museums not yet members of CHIN but hoping someday to participate, the CHIN data content standards will become standard within Canada.

The experience in the United States has contained elements of both the Canadian and UK experience.[7] The Museum Computer Network, formed in 1970, sought but never received adequate support. Its members tried to create an automated system that would become a de facto standard, but the software became obsolete rapidly. The absence of a compelling reason to exchange collection data between a diverse group of institutions (a problem that nearly resulted in the collapse of the Canadian network, but was overcome by a change in direction and continued funding) befell the MCN but it lacked the governmental funds to rise from its ashes. As a consequence, the MCN became a professional society rather than a true computer network. Because it now serves all the vendors and users, it is no longer trying to advance a de facto standard. Instead it has just launched a standards effort that depends on community consensus, and which will be discussed at length later in this article.

Other efforts in the United States to establish a de facto standard met the same fate. The Smithsonian Institution distributed the SELGEM software for a decade in an effort to make it a de facto system standard, but SELGEM was a general purpose DBMS and the Smithsonian specifically eschewed a role in creating a national data content standard for museum information.[8] The American Association of Art Museums formed a consortium in the mid-1980s to create software suited to its members and establish a de facto standard within the art museum community, but the product was unsatisfactory for reasons unrelated to the aim.[9] Nevertheless, the standards effort would almost certainly have proved a failure even if the software had been a success because the Art Museum Association was not in a position to advance guidelines and conventions for information handling within museums other than in the art museum community, and the target constituency was neither large enough to support an independent standard, nor discrete enough to have it really work. After all, much important art is held by museums other than art museums.

While the data content and structure standards efforts have been more flagrant, efforts to establish data value standards have also largely sought to dominate the market rather than build consensus. As became evident at the

Museum Documentation Association Conference on Terminology Control in Museums in 1988, a plethora of competing vocabularies and classification systems are vying for primacy and none has yet been endorsed by a body representing the profession.[10] In the world of art imagery, ICONCLASS, Garnier and others such as the Index of Christian Art, compete for iconographic description and classification.[11] In cultural history museums the United States is dominated by Nomenclature (recently reissued by the American Association for the Study of State and Local History [AASLH], but not actually endorsed by that organization), but the same concepts are being described in England using the Social History and Industrial Classification, or SHIC, system.[12] Museums haven't even accepted use of such generally accepted vocabularies as that of the Census Bureau for occupations, or of the International Standards Organization for country names, thereby missing opportunities to link their databases with outside sources.[13] A recent effort to establish a data content standard for architecture cataloging even employed a completely non-standard convention for recording dates, one of the few pieces of information that is elsewhere recorded in an internationally standard format.[14]

An important exception to the pattern has been a major vocabulary development effort, the Art and Architecture Thesaurus, which has consistently consulted the broadest possible community.[15] As a result it stands a good chance of being adopted as a vocabulary standard by many users, but it has not yet been endorsed by any professional organization or standards body.

Also, the American Association of Museums Registrars Committee has recently begun to take a somewhat different approach to information standards by developing consensual standard for a Facilities Report. The Standard Facilities Report, which defines the data content of this important instrument of museum practice at the level of data elements, has been well received since its publication in 1989.[16] Although adopted by the AAM, this convention is too new to have yet been broadly adopted; nevertheless, the approach seems to be working. A set of standards for loans is being discussed and a committee is in the process of developing standards for packing and shipping information using the same model.

POTENTIAL BENEFITS

Recognition of the benefits of information standards is not widespread in the museum community. The two arguments advanced by those who favor standards could be characterized as "altruistic" and "self-preservation," and it is the "altruistic" argument that is most frequently heard and which has to date been relatively ineffective.

The altruists argue for the creation of scholarly databases, for the benefit of museum researchers and the greater good of society. These scholarly databases, they have always assumed, contain descriptions of the artifacts and specimens in museums, and are available on-line, from a central source. Unfortunately, the construction of scholarly databases is largely an overhead for museums. Even basic inventory of objects in the care of the museum is rarely complete, and replication records made years ago require re-researching the items at tremendous staff expense. The experience of CHIN demonstrates that such national cultural databases must be by-products of services required by museums in-house or they won't occur.[17] The experience of many purely scholarly projects shows further that cooperation in description of museum holdings is at odds with continuing scholarly debate.[18]

Arguments from self-preservation could potentially turn museums to information standards. The most convincing of such arguments derives from the management imperative to secure the information holdings of the museum and add value to them over time. Without data content standards, the danger is that today's data will be captured in the automated system currently installed, and that the costs of migrating every several years to new software environments will be prohibitive.[19] The consequence will be that by making the decision for the short term to make information more accessible, management only succeeds in making data inaccessible within twenty or so years, which in the time frames generally employed in archives and museums is unacceptable.

Other arguments from self-preservation focus on the potential benefits of information sharing in museums, ranging from the obvious advantages of exchanging basic loan and exhibit data with other museums and with shippers, insurers, and other agents, to the hypothetical advantage to consortias of museums sharing information about members moving out of town. The range of information services that could be attractive or beneficial to museums is just now being explored: among those suggested are the possibility of a national exhibitions calendar, a regional museum services database, and a host of authority files on artists, manufacturers, archaeological sites, geographical locales, objects and other persons, places and things that occur in more than one institution's databases.[20]

BARRIERS

There are, however, numerous significant barriers to establishing effective information interchanges. Those that are most frequently cited include the size and diversity of the museum market, the complexity of museum applications, the independence of museum professionals who prefer to "adapt" standards rather than "adopting" them, and the absence, until very recently, of a plausible framework within which information might be exchanged.

The museum community is in fact extremely diverse. It is divided between institutions with very different collecting foci and therefore very different audiences. It includes institutions that have budgets exceeding $10M, but is very largely composed of tiny organizations, many without any full-time, professional staff. While almost all museums collect and lend, museums differ widely in their internal practices. More importantly, the museum market for automated systems is relatively small, so museum specific applications are very few and quite fragile. The very concept of museum specific hardware or software standards is preposterous. If museums are to succeed in standardization they will need to adopt standard hardware and software and implement museum specific but standardized applications and data contents.

The diversity of the museum community has major implications for museum data contents and application standards efforts. To succeed, standardization efforts must draw on experiences of museums of different types, and reflect the needs of more than one type of museum. They must also secure a broad political base. Finally, they need to deliver concrete results, in real implementations, and become of importance to at least an identifiable group of institutions.

The complexity of museum applications ought not be a real barrier to information standards. The standards that will have the greatest potential impact are those that enable applications to exchange information, and it is possible to develop such standards independently of the actual functions supported by different software systems. The "willfulness" of museum professionals with respect to standards, is a reflection of the fact that most of the standards which have been proposed for museums to date have prescribed data values. Without an implementation that supports shared museum functions, data value standards deliver no more benefits if they are adhered to strictly than if they are followed loosely. Until information is exchanged between institutions or used to build common databases, museums will not see the benefits of adhering rigidly to a standard.

Fortunately, a framework for international museum information interchange standards has been adopted by the International Council on Museums Committee on Documentation (ICOM/CIDOC). This framework endorses the International Standards Organization standard ISO-2709 as the basis for all museum data interchange.[21] ISO-2709 is an extremely flexible vehicle for such exchanges and is already used as the basis for interchange in the library and archives communities, which makes it attractive as the carrier for cultural information about objects and specimens. Museum professionals do not wish to be limited by the content designation accepted by libraries and archives but museums hold archival materials and publications just as many libraries and archives hold artifacts, so the benefits of operating within the same umbrella is obvious.

PRESENT SITUATION

For over twenty years, libraries world-wide have adhered to standards for documenting books and periodicals.[22] For more than a decade, zoos have engaged successfully in the exchange of information about their holdings. Archives in the United States began to follow a common standard for information exchange purposes seven years ago, and visual resources collections are still gaining acceptance for a standard adopted several years ago.[23] The potential for information interchange in the business practices of museums, whether ordering supplies or fulfilling photographic orders, contracting for shipping services or contracting to provide space for a reception, have been demonstrated by Electronic Data Interchange (EDI) in banking, insurance and transportation.[24]

Museums in other countries have also succeeded in establishing national information networks providing services specific to museums. In Canada most major museums participate in a national computer network funded by the Canadian government. In England the national network is grounded in 15 years of using standard data cards for recording of museum information, prior to the introduction of a now widespread automated cataloging system only a few years ago. In France, the Netherlands, Denmark and Sweden, the story is different, but the trend is towards a national database built on nationally accepted (or at least adopted) standards for information.[25] Unfortunately, none of the competing de facto national standards is accepted outside of its own domain.

This clearly provides an opportunity for ISO-2709, but it too is an empty container that has not been used yet for actual data interchanges in museums. It remains to be defined before it can be exploited. There have been some attempts to define a structure, but they have lacked the political legitimacy to succeed and were undertaken without plans for defining implementations that would assure their survival.[26]

If the technical problems of defining adequate content designation for museums to use ISO-2709 can be resolved, there will remain the problem of implementing solutions within the framework. Without implementable systems, the community will not be able to insist on using ISO-2709, and its future as a museum interchange format will be bleak. Existing networks (such as the Canadian Heritage Information Network and the Conservation Information Network) and existing commercial computer applications for museums need to be convinced to employ it as a communications protocol.

FUTURE PROSPECTS

The Museum Computer Network, a U.S. professional organization of museum automation professionals, recognizes the value of the ISO framework and is pursuing its definition and implementation. In 1989 it formed a Committee on Computer Interchange of Museum Information (CIMI) to develop a standard acceptable to the U.S. museum community.[27] MCN represents automation experts rather than the various professionals who create and use information within museums, such as registrars, curators, educators, or exhibit planners and because it does not represent the management or administration of museums, MCN has invited representatives from each of the major museum related professional organizations (AAM, AASLH, Association of Living Historical Farms and Agricultural Museums [ALHSAM], Association of Art Museum Directors [AAMD], and the Association for Systematic Collections [ASC]) to serve on CIMI. It has also invited representatives from the major museum networks (CIN/CHIN, MDA and RLG) to serve on the Committee.

The Committee, which received funding from the National Endowment for the Humanities and the Pew Charitable Trusts, began its work in July 1990. It held its first meeting in October 1990, at which it adopted a set of ground rules for its work. Consistent with the views advanced here, these group rules call on CIMI to serve as an "honest broker" and "intellectual cartographer," receiving definitions of required data elements from participating associations and mapping these to a data content technical standard.

CIMI envisions testing its approach to the task with two groups already organized within the museums community: the Common Agenda Project of the American Association for State and Local History, and the Art Information Task Force of the College Art Association, the Visual Resources Association and the Association of Art Museum Directors.[28] These two projects are defining and testing data content standards for cultural history and art museums respectively. A third project that is also underway, and which might feed into the CIMI protocol testing process, is sponsored by the Association for Systematics Collections. In each case, CIMI would make its services available to the other associations to map the data they want to interchange into a common protocol. The CIMI project officer would meet with task forces of these projects, identify their requirements with them, and bring a proposal to the Committee. The Committee would map the data onto the protocol, and provide incentives for vendors and networks to implement the solutions. Future requirements of other bodies representing different parts of the museum community would be met through a similar process in future years.

CONCLUSIONS

Although the bulk of time and money expended by museums is spent in the creation of information, information standards have not yet played a major role in museum professionalization. As a consequence, the museum community is highly idiosyncratic and it collectively wastes a tremendous amount of its resources discovering anew facts that others in the community already have researched, or making information that could be more easily made in other ways. In addition, museum management is currently automating its collections-related documentation without regard for the risk to which it is exposing its records over time – as long as there is no standard for information transfer generally accepted within the community.

The seriousness of these failings is being recognized, and efforts are now being made to correct the oversight, but the habits of years of quirky information recording practices will not be reversed unless demonstrable success follows from adoption of standards. The jury is still out on the first major informational standard adopted by U.S. museums, the Registrar's Committee Standard Facilities Report, but the prospects of its success are good, and the potential savings it brings with it if adopted by most American museums is so huge that it is certainly a strong suit to have led with. The more complicated enterprise launched by the CIMI committee of the Museum Computer Network promises no less in benefits, but will have a much more treacherous path. If it succeeds, it opens the way for museums to participate fully in the digital electronic revolution, the new literacy that will define the twenty-first century.

This new literacy, based in multi-media interactivity and the promise of large knowledge-bases easily navigated by individuals based on their own interests, will require adherence to a great deal more than simply the international standards developed by museums for the recording of their own information. Here the limited market importance of museums dictates that they will need to employ standards defined by others. Data representation decisions and technology standards choices made by museums will have long-term implications for the usefulness and the usability of their data. Already museums find themselves confronted by having to decide between analog and digital storage of images, the densities at which scanning should take place, and whether to store on magnetic disk or optical disks. In the near future, they will face many similar issues that will impress upon them the value of information standards established by other disciplines. In discovering the value of these standards, they are likely to better appreciate the value of their own standards, and to adhere more closely to them to achieve the promised benefits. The age of museum information standards has only just dawned.

Notes

1. National Association for Museum Exhibitions (NAME), "Code of Professional Standards and Ethics," *Museum News*, March/April 1990, p. 96; AAM Standing Professional Committee on Education, "Statement of Professional Standards for Museum Educators," *Museum News*, Jan/Feb 1990; American Society for Industrial Security, *Suggested Guidelines in Museum Security* (Arlington VA, ASIS, 1990) 21 pp.; AAM Registrars Committee, "A Code of Practice for Couriering Museum Objects – June 1986," in *AAM 1990 Annual Meeting Sourcebook* (Washington, AAM, 1990) ppp. 187-195; The Financial Accounting Standards Board (FASB) guidelines are still in a draft form.

2. Committee on Archival Description Standards, Report and position papers by members of the Committee, in *American Archivist*, vol. 52, #4, Fall 1989 and vol. 53, #1, Winter 1990.

3. Dorothy H. Dudley, Irma Bezold Wilkinson et al., *Museum Registration Methods* (Washington, AAM, 1979).

4. The American Museum Association, Museums Accreditation Process (MAP), dictates standards for gathering of program statistics so as to ensure comparability between institutions being accredited.

5. D. Andrew Roberts and Richard B. Light, "The Cooperative Development of Documentation in United Kingdom Museums," in R. B. Light et al. *Museum Documentation Systems: Developments and Applications* (London, Butterworths, 1986) pp. 113-130.

6. Jane Sledge and Betsy Comstock, "The Canadian Heritage Information Network," in R. B. Light et al. *Museum Documentation Systems: Developments and Applications* (London, Butterworths, 1986) pp. 7-24.

7. Deirdre Stam, "The Quest for a Code, or a Brief History of the Computerized Cataloging of Art Objects," *Art Documentation*, vol. 8 #1, Spring 1989, pp. 7-15. Also see: David Vance, "The Museum Computer Network in Context," in R. B. Light et al. *Museum Documentation Systems: Developments and Applications* (London, Butterworths, 1986) pp. 37-47.

8. Reginald A. Creighton and James J. Crockett; SELGEM: A System for Collection Management, *Smithsonian Institution Information Systems Innovations*, vol. 2 #3 August 1971. Also, Reginald Creighton, Penelope Packard, and Holley Linn; SELGEM Retrieval: A General Description, *Smithsonian Institution Procedures in Computer Sciences*, vol. 1, #3 (June 1975).

9. The history of the American Association of Art Museums joint venture with the Williamson Group, and the failure of the ARTIS software, has not been written, but when it is it should focus at least as much on the strategic error in trying to corner the market as it does on the numerous tactical errors that guaranteed the system would not function adequately.

10. D. Andrew Roberts, *Terminology for Museums: Proceedings of an International Conference* (1988) (Cambridge: Museum Documentation Association, 1990).

11. For an account of ICONCLASS, see the entire issue of: *Visual Resources*, vol. 5, #3, Autumn 1988.

12. James Blackaby, Patricia Greeno and the Nomenclature Committee, *The Revised Nomenclature for Museum Cataloging: A Revised and Expanded Version of Robert G. Chenhall's System for Classifying Man-made Objects* (Nashville, TN, AASLH, 1988) and *Social History and Industrial Classification (SHIC): A Subject Classification For Museum Collections*, Volume 1 The Classification (Sheffield, Centre for English Cultural Tradition and Language, University of Sheffield, 1983).

13. Following such basic standards can enable users of specialized databases, such as those in museums, to be linked to a broad range of commercial databases in order to enhance their meaning.

14. The Architectural Documents Advisory Group (ADAG) of the Getty Art History Information Program whose activities led to the Foundation for Documents of Architecture (FDA), insisted throughout its life on recording dates in the format 3 IV 1989 (DD MM YYYY with the month, MM, expressed as Roman Numerals), in spite of the international standard 19890403 (YYYYMMDD). Unfortunately this was not their only violation of norms.

15. *Art and Architecture Thesaurus*, vols. 1-3 (New York, Oxford University Press, 1990), see pp. 3-21 for a history of the project.

16. Standard Facility Report, Adopted by the Registrars Committee American Association of Museums, June 1988, 20 pp.

17. Jane Sledge and Betsy Comstock, "The Canadian Heritage Information Network," in Richard B. Light, D. Andrew Roberts and Jennifer Stewart. *Museum Documentation Systems: Developments and Applications* (London, Butterworths, 1986) pp. 7-24.

18. David Bearman and Richard Szary, "Beyond Authority Headings: Authorities as Reference Files in a Multi-Disciplinary Setting," in Karen Markey ed. *Authority Control Symposium* (Tucson, AZ, ARLIS/NA, 1986) pp. 68-78 Also Marilyn Schmidt's report on the demise of the J. Paul Getty Trust "Museum Prototype Project," available from the author at: J. Paul Getty Trust, AHIP, 401 Wilshire Blvd., Santa Monica CA 90401.

19. United Nations, Advisory Committee for the Coordination of Information Systems; Management of Electronic Records: Issues and Guidelines (New York, United Nations, 1990) GV.E.89.0.15.

20. David Bearman, Editorial, *Archives and Museum Informatics*, vol. 4, #1 (Spring 1990), p. 1 addresses the evolving business plans of the Museum Computer Network, Research Libraries Group, and the Canadian Heritage Information Network.

21. ISO 2709, called ANSI Z39.2 in the United States, is the parent of the MARC formats used by the international library community, and more recently by the archival community.

22. Walt Crawford, *Technical Standards: An Introduction for Librarians* (Boston, G.K. Hall, second edition, 1991).

23. David Bearman, "Archives and Manuscript Control with Bibliographic Utilities: Challenges and Opportunities," *American Archivist*, vol. 52 #1, Winter 1989, pp. 26-39; also: "Archival and Bibliographic Information Networks," *Journal of Library Administration*, vol. 7 #2/3, Summer/Fall 1986, pp. 99-110.

24. Electronic Document Interchange for Administration, Commerce and Transport (EDIFACT) is a framework for exchanging transactional data between businesses and business and government in order to directly effect the receiving system. This international standards effort, still in relatively early stages, could dramatically change the way in which computers are used in business, from recipients of recorded history to active participants. If the change does occur, museums will benefit from direct ordering of services as much as other institutions.

25. D. Andrew Roberts, *Planning the Documentation of Museum Collections* (Cambridge, MA, 1985) pp. 43-47 is the first serious piece on museum information standards I know of. It and the articles in the Light, Roberts, and Stewart volume (op. cit 17) are the best English language coverage of foreign developments.

26. Neville Houghton, "M-MARC: MARC for Australian Museums," Ms Thesis, Victoria College Melbourne, October 1982; Deirdre Stam and Ruth Palmquist, *SUART: A MARC Based Information Structure and Data Dictionary for the Syracuse University Art Collection* (Syracuse, MCN, 1989).

27. David Bearman, "CIMI:Computer Interchange of Museum Information," *Archives and Museum Informatics*, vol. 3, #2 (Summer 1989) 2-5.

28. For background on the American Association for State and Local History Common Agenda Project, see: *History News*, vol. 44, #3, May/June 1989. The Database Task Force of the Common Agenda project issued its "Final Report to the Field" in September 1989 (48 pp. typescript), after which a project was launched in Philadelphia to test the recommendations they made regarding the necessary data content of cultural history museum databases. The only publicly available source on the Art Information Task Force is an unpublished report available from the J.Paul Getty Trust, Art History Information Program (AHIP): Patricia J. Barnett, "Developing a MARC Format for Cataloging Art Objects and Their Visual Surrogates: Report and Accompanying Documents on the Workshop sponsored by the Getty Art History Information Program," chaired by Eleanor Fink, June 12-13 1989," 30 pp. typescript plus appendixes.

29. For information on the ASC effort the reader may write to: Dr. K. Elaine Hoagland, Executive Director, ASC, 730 11th St., NW, Washington DC 20001.

PART 6

Problems and Promises: Present and Future Trends

Future Directions in Standardization

WALT CRAWFORD, RESEARCH LIBRARIES GROUP

This article deals specifically with NISO, the National Information Standards Organization. NISO is the standards organization most directly relevant to publishers; it is also the one with which I have some familiarity. NISO has grown in strength and membership over the last few years, and should continue to grow. As with any other standards organization, its future success depends not only on development of new standards but on the way in which existing standards are handled.

NEW STANDARDS

NISO will develop new standards in a variety of areas, depending on the needs and desires of its members. For example, new standards are already being developed to facilitate transfer of patron and item information between libraries. Such standards raise potential problems in terms of patron privacy; there is reason to believe that those who see the need for these standards are also beginning to realize the need to build privacy safeguards into the standards. There will also be special-interest cases, where standards will be proposed that benefit one segment of the library and publishing community at the expense of another segment. NISO's membership and methodology should help to assure that attempts to impose such one-sided standards do not succeed.

I can't predict which areas will become hotbeds of standards activity. A few directions do seem clear, however, including the need to coordinate national and international standards, the likelihood of model and guideline standards, new standards to support OSI, and new standards to support preservation.

Originally published in *Book Research Quarterly* 4 (Fall 1988): 66-73. Reprinted with permission.

269

National and International Standards

We can certainly anticipate more direct attention to coordination of international and national standards. A recent case in point is standard Z39.60, Volume and File Structure of CD-ROM (the High Sierra Group standard). Approved by NISO and ANSI, it was not published by NISO because ISO, the International Standards Organization, was completing work on the equivalent standard, and some minor wording changes might be required. It made sense to hold the NISO standard so that the published national and international standards would be identical.

Other standards organizations find that a growing level of development activity takes place on an international scale, with meetings held abroad. Direct international development has real benefits but poses serious problems for voluntary standards organizations – particularly those such as NISO, whose members typically have limited budgets available for standards activity.

As a member of the American Library Association and its Library and Information Technology Association (LITA), which is currently a member of Accredited Standards Committee (ASC) X3, the standards agency dealing with information processing systems, I am perturbed that LITA's representative to X3 reports that the internationalization of standards may make it senseless for LITA to belong. LITA can't afford the overseas travel budget that would be required to be fully active in ASC X3. I would hate to see the same situation arise in NISO's area of activity. To avoid such a fate will require careful balancing between the need for international coordination and the need to operate within limited budgets.

Models and Guidelines

When an engineer thinks of technical standards, the standards involved tend to be clear-cut definitions. The thousands of standards written by the American Society for Testing and Materials (ASTM) are unequivocal: a material meets the standard or does not, and can be tested for compliance.

That isn't always true with NISO standards. Some existing Z39 standards really offer guidelines and are written in such a way that the question of compliance becomes meaningless. Does an index comply with standard Z39.4? It's virtually impossible to say. Does a thesaurus comply with Z39.19? It might be possible to demonstrate that a particular thesaurus violates certain guidelines within the "standard," but even that would be difficult. These and several other NISO standards offer advice more than rules.

We will probably see more such guidelines, but guidelines do cause difficulties when they are labeled as standards. NISO might consider adoption of some other name to help distinguish between distinct technical standards such as Z39.21 (Book Numbering, the ISBN standard) and guidelines such as Z39.19 (Guidelines for Thesaurus Structures, Construction and Use).

NISO may also develop models in various areas and should move to give such models equally distinct titles. OSI (discussed below) began as a model from ISO, not a discrete technical standard as such. Models can be enormously useful in guiding the development of other technical standards and in serving to focus thinking within an area. If models are confused with complete standards, however, they may not work nearly as well.

Standards for Open Systems

We will certainly see more standards supporting implementations of the Open Systems Interconnection (OSI) protocols within libraries and other fields. Some standards will come from NISO, others from the ASC X3. Still other OSI-related standards will be developed by other agencies within the United States and abroad.

OSI standards are slow and difficult to develop, and will probably be slow and difficult to implement. ANSI Standard Z39.50, Information Retrieval Protocol, the first NISO-developed OSI standard, has been approved after years of development; others will certainly follow. The advantages of open systems seem clear, and OSI has sufficient backing in the library community and within industry to assure that the work will continue. Although single-vendor "standards" may spread widely and early, unless those implementations become licensed standards and have clear definitions not actually dependent on a single vendor, they can betray those who rely on them. Open systems should prevent sudden abandonment or sudden shifts that favor one supplier over all others.

Standards for Preservation

Some of NISO's most important standards apply to preserving media or, if that is not possible, preserving the images of information contained within media. Efforts to develop and implement such standards will continue. For example, ANSI standard Z39.48-1984, Permanence of Paper, is being revised to incorporate coated papers. A recently formed NISO Standards Committee is working on environmental conditions for storage of paper-based library and archival materials; another new committee will work on a standard for physical preparation of printed theses and dissertations for long-term storage.

It is too easy to ignore the present and past in seeking out the future. Losing the dime novels and popular periodicals of the 1890s and 1910s will, if not prevented, severely limit future sociologists and historians who seek to understand the intellectual, social and cultural life of the time. It is not enough to assume that "important" works will be preserved because new editions will appear, and it is not enough to say that the "significant" texts will be preserved on CD-ROM or some other digital medium. It takes more than the classics of a generation to understand that generation.

That argument holds equally well for film, video and sound recordings, and electronic media. NISO and other agencies will and must continue to develop clear standards so that existing media can be retained where possible and so that preservation copies will indeed function properly in an archival role.

The best way to assure long life is to publish in a manner that builds in long life. With luck and persistence, publishers and libraries can work together to define standards that meet the needs of all concerned, so that publishers can produce books and other publications profitably and effectively, and libraries can expect to retain such publications longer than a generation or two.

DIRECTIONS FOR CURRENT STANDARDS

NISO, like every other standards organization, works with a body of existing standards. To some extent, NISO's future depends on how it deals with those standards.

Implementation

NISO's growing membership and broadening influence should mean that key NISO standards will be more widely implemented. Effective implementation is the key to technical standards. Without such implementation, the development and adoption process is wasted effort.

More publishers should use ANSI Z39.48, Permanence of Paper, the single most important current standard for the long-term survival of contemporary literature and thinking. Current estimates are that 15 to 29% of currently published monographs are available in editions conforming to the standard. That percentage may grow to 25% or 30% within the next few years. While I would like to see it grow to 50% or even 75% in the next few years, such a projection is probably too optimistic. NISO has done an admirable job of publicizing this standard, aided by at least one papermaker. Prices of permanent paper and acid paper are converging; publishers should move more rapidly to adopt permanent paper and clarify that adoption by using the circled-infinity symbol on back-of-title pages.

Standards in the Open Systems Interconnection area, such as ANSI Z39.50 (noted earlier), will be broadly implemented as they are developed. ANSI Standard Z39.60 (also noted earlier), the High Sierra Group standard, will surely be implemented almost universally for CD-ROM, for much the same reason that ANSI Z39.9 (ISSN) and ANSI Z39.21 (ISBN) have been implemented so widely: it meets a clear need, offers clear economic benefit, and has no serious competition.

Electronic Manuscript Preparation and Markup

We should see some implementation of ANSI Z39.59, Electronic Manuscript: Preparation and Markup, and possible extension of the standard in a way that benefits authors as well as publishers. Effective implementation should mean unobtrusive implementation, preferably embedded in word processing programs that authors already use. Several word processing programs for the PC environment appear suited to such development. For example, Sprint and Microsoft Word should both be suitable for embedded Z39.59 support in the form of new "style sheets," and it seems likely that WordPerfect 5.0, XyWrite/Nota Bene and WordStar 2000 have facilities that could similarly support Z39.59. NISO, the Association of American Publishers, and others with a real desire to see this standard implemented need to publicize its virtues and work directly with software publishers toward transparent implementation.

We will almost certainly see ongoing tension among authors, publishers and others in related fields as contracts and working arrangements are renegotiated to include use of Z39.59. Some publishers will write contracts that share the savings possible through intelligent use of word processing tools and make it worth an author's while to use those tools effectively. Unfortunately, some other publishers will view Z39.59 as a way to shift work to the author without compensation. I am optimistic enough to hope that most publishers and authors will arrive at mutually beneficial solutions to the problems of electronic markup and possible electronic publishing.

Common Command Language

I believe that ANSI Z39.58, the Common Command Language (CCL), will see wide usage soon after it is finally adopted – or, for that matter, even if it never achieves adoption. The "West Coast group" of online catalogs and technical processing systems (BALLOTS, RLIN, MELVYL, CARLYLE, ORION and others) have demonstrated for more than a decade that the syntax works well. OCLC has affirmed that CCL is the basis for its new system; my own implementation of a PC-based nonbibliographic database shows CCL to be a sturdy, broadly useful standard.

As commercial operators recognize that it is to their advantage to permit access through a common, widely known syntax, we should see CCL-based interfaces appearing for more and more catalogs and online databases. If CCL-based interfaces become available for CD-ROM products, presumably as alternatives to menu-based default interfaces, I would expect to see many users abandoning menus in favor of the efficient, effective command language.

Refinement

NISO will continue to refine existing standards and, where appropriate, combine similar standards into single, more clearly drawn standards. That trend will improve NISO's effectiveness in two ways: by making the standards more understandable and useful, and by making it more obvious that NISO is a coherent, effective organization.

In many cases, the best way to refine an existing standard is to reduce it to its essential elements. We can hope to see some NISO standards reissued in simpler form, containing those elements for which standardization has real benefit and eliminating elements where diversity does no harm. Such refinement would improve standards such as ANSI Z39.15, Title Leaves of a Book.

Other forms of refinement could also improve the standards and the organization. We can hope to see a version of ANSI Z39.21 (ISBN) that includes the algorithms for positioning hyphens in all cases, not merely in cases where the first digit is 0 through 7 (as at present). Some standards need better glossaries or simply need to be written for clarity.

Clearing Away the Deadwood

NISO should look particularly hard at standards that have not achieved wide implementation. Unless the problem is clearly a lack of publicity, NISO should consider such standards to be good candidates for refinement or abandonment.

The best reasons to abandon a standard are that the standard fails to serve a useful purpose, or that there is no likelihood of wide adoption. ANSI Standard Z39.29, Bibliographic References, may be the clearest case of the latter. Eleven years after its adoption, very few journals or publishers require the standard, and most will not accept references created according to the standard. After successfully arguing for Z39.29 style in two books, I have finally abandoned the fight; my current and future books will probably use *The Chicago Manual of Style*. Given that none of the organizations having their own styles for references adopted Z39.29, and given that *Chicago* is very nearly universal in most other environments, Z39.29 does not appear to solve a real problem, at least not in an effective manner.

Several other standards may fall into similar categories. What economic benefit derives from ANSI Z39.13, Describing Books in Advertisements [etc.] or ANSI Z39.22, Proof Corrections?

The success of a standards organization cannot be measured by the number of standards it develops. Success is measured by the number of standards that matter within the community and that save people time and money. Every trivial and irrelevant standard weakens NISO by diluting the impact of and publicity for the important standards.

Compliance

NISO standards are voluntary and will remain so. NISO has neither the resources nor the mandate to monitor compliance, but must generally rely on the good faith of those who assert that they follow standards.

When an organization says it follows standards, there is almost always an implicit ellipsis for *an unwritten caveat*. Depending on the organization, that caveat may be one of the following:

"Our organization follows standards . . ."

". . . *except* when we can gain a competitive advantage by following or promulgating a proprietary methodology."

". . . except when we already established procedures in an area and don't choose to reconsider those procedures."

". . . *when* it won't cost us anything to do so or when the payback for compliance is clear."

". . . when we stand to gain good publicity by doing so – and we're better at publicizing adherence than at maintaining full compliance over the long run."

". . . when we recognize them as standards – but we don't go out of our way to find standards to follow, and we don't distinguish between 'industry standards' and consensus technical standards."

". . . most of the time, but not always, and we don't publicize the exceptions."

". . . when it isn't too much of a nuisance or expense to do so."

". . . when we regard them as applicable and significant."

It's a rare organization indeed that would not follow the claim with one of those caveats or something similar. NISO efforts to eliminate deadwood and refine useful standards will surely not eliminate the caveats, but could result in more caveats that relate to relatively minor exceptions. When organizations must wade through a clutter of apparently trivial standards and provisions, they may reasonably tend to ignore the whole area or worry only about standards with high profiles.

Publicity and Availability

One safe prediction is that NISO will continue to provide good information on the status of standards, and that many in the community will find the information less than satisfactory. The *Voice of Z39* served American National Standards Committee Z39 and NISO well, providing periodic updates on the work of the organization and some useful information on the standards process. Leading from strength, NISO moved to an even more useful publication in early 1989, *Information Standards Quarterly*.

We may hope to see other changes that will make NISO standards more readily available and improve the level of awareness within NISO's areas of special interest. ANSI Z39.60, the High Sierra Group standard, goes far beyond NISO's traditional audience to reach the broader "information science" market. NISO should and, I believe, will move to solidify that extension and establish its role as a critical contemporary standards organization. Since lines of communication between ASC X3 and NISO are strong and should remain so, we expect to see more effective publicity and development from both organizations, with relatively little energy spent squabbling over territorial rights.

Urgency, Limits and Balances

One trend seems to be strong in NISO's international counterpart, ISO Technical Committee (TC) 46 (Information and Documentation): a sense that many standards are urgently needed and that the standards-making process needs to be streamlined to suit that urgency. The ISO "fast track" process makes adoption of a Proposed Standard automatic if 75% of those voting (excluding abstentions) approve the draft, as long as that 75% includes a majority of all TC members.

Some members of NISO will doubtless push for similarly streamlined techniques. At present, most NISO standards go through a fairly lengthy development cycle, offering members more than one chance to reflect on the implications of the standard and to raise objections and offer improvements.

It also seems unlikely that a NISO draft would be considered approved if 20% of the NISO members found it objectionable. The NISO process tends to limit fast adoption in favor of balanced consideration.

NISO has become more efficient in processing standards and we may see some fairly rapid standards efforts in the future. (By "fairly rapid" I mean eighteen months to two years from initial draft to publication.) I hope that we will not see the kind of "efficiency" that ignores serious objections in the rush to adoption, or that allows supposed urgency of need to override balanced, careful consideration. Standards for libraries, publishing and information science are not generally matters of life or death; we owe it to ourselves and to NISO's constituencies to take the time to produce the best possible standards.

Problems and Dangers of Standards

WALT CRAWFORD, RESEARCH LIBRARIES GROUP

Technical standards are fundamental to organized society. That doesn't mean that all standardization is good, or that all technical standards are positive achievements. Like most other instruments of civilization, technical standards can be good or bad.

STANDARDS AND COMPETITION

Technical standards development sometimes looks like collusion. Standards may lower or raise barriers to new competitors by making it easier or more difficult to enter an industry. In both ways, standards influence competition. While the historical record is generally good, there can be cause for concern.

Antitrust

When the major competing companies in an industry meet to decide on pricing or territories, it's called collusion. When employees of those companies meet to determine common specifications for parts used by the industry, it's called standards-making. The government has been known to object to the first type of meeting, but rarely to the second.

In 1964, antitrust questions were raised about an American Society for Testing and Materials (ASTM) standard on asbestos cement; it was suggested that the standard constituted a form of price-fixing. The District Court of Pennsylvania said that "because of the heavy reliance of federal, state and municipal governments upon ASTM for specifications, the Society may be regarded as an essential arm, or branch, of the government, and its acts may be entitled to the immunity from antitrust laws accorded governmental acts."[1]

Originally published in Walt Crawford, *Technical Standards: An Introduction for Librarians* (White Plains, N.Y.: Knowledge Industry Publications, 1986). Reprinted with permission. See also the second edition, published in 1991 by G. K. Hall.

Standardization organizations have generally been considered immune to antitrust laws. Such immunity is not inevitable and does not mean that technical standards development never functions in a collusive manner. The processes used by major standardization organizations should work to prevent standards that promote monopoly and oligopoly, but collusive standards are possible. Any standard that limits variety can potentially limit competition.

Competition

Uniformity standards can encourage illegal price-fixing. Technical standards that set minimum quality specifications may also be anticompetitive by raising barriers to new competitors. There are two ways to write minimum quality standards. One method concentrates on performance: to meet the standard, something must pass specified tests under specified conditions. Unfortunately, performance-based standards are not always feasible: technology to make proper measurement may be lacking, or the nature of "performance" may be such that any tests would be prohibitively expensive.

Minimum quality standards avoid such problems by specifying material and method. Such standards are prevalent in building codes and similar regulations. This form of standard can be directly anticompetitive. By barring different techniques and materials, the technical standard directly bars one form of competition. If the techniques or materials specified in a standard are proprietary, the technical standard is directly anticompetitive.

Totally unfettered competitive methods can include product adulteration, that is, cutting prices by reducing the size or quality of the product. Standards for weights and measures specifically work to eliminate the competitive thrust to charge less by selling less (and calling it more). Thousands of technical standards, including most of those developed by ASTM, are anticompetitive in that they work to prevent the sale of inferior materials. Such forms of competition endanger life and health; proper technical standards work to shift competition to more acceptable areas.

STANDARDS AND INNOVATION

Well-written standards encourage innovation allowing creators to focus on new tools, techniques and products. Timely standards for new techniques and products can also encourage widespread adoption, moving innovation into practice. While technical standards have aided innovation, technical standards can also work against innovation.

Premature Standards

When a new technology is developing, different developers may proceed along similar but distinct paths. At some point, one or more of the developers may initiate technical standards for the area. If standardization begins too soon, it can damage innovation in two ways:

1. Draining energy: Technical standards require time and energy. Time spent on standards committees may be time taken away from innovation and development. In some cases, standardization may be a deliberate attempt to slow development by draining the energy of competitors.

2. Establishing uniformity: If a standard is written and adopted, it will establish some level of uniformity. Innovation in those aspects will cease or at least be slowed for some time. The more successful the standard, the more innovation will be slowed.

Consumer videocassette recorders (VCRs) lack a single standard. This lack may have slowed the acceptance of VCRs, but seems to have increased the rate of innovation in VCRs. Beta, the minority format, typically led VHS in new ideas and techniques. Beta recorders were the first with special effects and high fidelity sound recording for VCRs. In each case, VHS engineers followed the innovative lead of Sony (the developer of Beta).[2] While consumers and prerecorded tape producers may suffer from the conflicting formats, consumers have benefitted from competitive innovation and sharply competitive pricing.

Established Standards

Well-established standards also pose barriers to innovation. In some cases, the barrier may be impossible to overcome. The QWERTY typewriter keyboard was created in the late nineteenth century as a way to keep type bars from jamming. The arrangement puts frequently used letters far enough apart that adjacent type bars are less likely to be in action at the same time. QWERTY was used on the first popular typewriters, and became familiar to the thousands, then tens of millions, of trained typists.

Technology eventually solved the jamming problem, but QWERTY faced no serious competition in the early twentieth century. More recently, electronic typewriters and word processing systems have totally eliminated mechanical jamming as an issue in keyboard design, but most students still learn QWERTY in typing class, and the system continues to maintain near-universal domination.

Some decades ago, the Dvorak keyboard promised to improve typing speeds and reduce typing fatigue. Typewriters with Dvorak keyboards have been available by special order for many years, but the system has never made any dent in QWERTY. Many microcomputers permit reassignment of keys; the Apple IIc has a switch to convert the keyboard to Dvorak arrangement. A few pioneers use the switch or reassignment programs and tout Dvorak's advantages, but no significant move away from QWERTY has happened, or seems likely to.

In the library field, some commentators assert that Z39.2 and the MARC formats are poor standards and should be replaced by more innovative standards. Though MARC is less than two decades old, the speed and extent of its success raise a major barrier against any replacement. (In this case, no replacement with any suggestion of improvement actually exists; unlike supporters of the Dvorak keyboard, opponents of MARC have nothing better to propose.)

OVER-STANDARDIZATION

Over-standardization damages the cause of standardization and can damage standards users. Over-standardization can occur for many reasons, and can take on several guises.

Overly Rigid Standards

Interchangeability standards enhance competition and reduce costs. Good interchangeability standards specify tolerances sufficient to assure real interchangeability; bad standards specify tolerances in excess of such assurance. A dimensional standard with no specified tolerances is incomplete; a standard with extremely narrow tolerances is anticompetitive or useless. Such a standard is anticompetitive when the tolerances are such that they can be met only by using equipment too expensive for a newcomer to obtain, or by using patented or licensed techniques.

Suppose that Z85.1, Permanent and Durable Library Cards, specified tolerances of +0 to -0.005mm for all dimensions. To meet such narrow tolerances under a variety of measurement conditions, the card stock might have to be a specially treated stock requiring patented equipment available only to one papermaker. A tolerance of 0.005mm (0.0002 inch) has no possible bearing on interchangeability of cards with an overall size of 75 mm x 125 mm; such a standard would be a deliberate attempt to prevent new papermakers from entering the market.

A standard is also useless when the tolerances are so narrow that it costs more to assure compliance than any realistic value for the item. For example, if papermakers were required to spend $1.00 per card to assure that each card met Z85.1 standards, papermakers would not attempt to meet the standards: the resulting products would not be saleable.

Standards of this sort tend to be self-limiting. When a standard appears to have been overstated in order to limit competition, courts may be inclined to ignore the traditional antitrust exemption of standards agencies. When a standard is uneconomically precise, it will be modified or ignored.

Overly Detailed Standards

The standard for ISBN's specifies how the numbers are formed, how they should be displayed and how they are assigned. It does not specify how they are to be stored in MARC records, the typeface that must be used to display them or precisely where on a publication they must be displayed. Such specifications would be overly detailed, reducing the use of the standard by overstating the requirements.

The library and publishing field seems prone to overly detailed standards. The standard for single-title orders, Z39.30, begins with a useful set of information to be included on an order. It then goes on to specify how many characters to allow for each item and exactly where on the form each item should appear. What could be a generally applicable standard, assuring that a certain amount of information is included in orders, becomes a rigid standard that some sensible agencies refuse to implement.

The tendency to excessive detail is quite natural, and one that requires care to avoid. Quite probably, standards committees build in too much detail because they fail to focus on the intent of the standard. For each detail, the committee should ask whether it is necessary to carry out that intent, and whether it is justified to carry out the intent. Requiring that a publisher's name and address appear on the title leaf is necessary to assure that catalogers have sufficient information; requiring that the publisher's name appear on the recto, no less than 3 and no more than 4 inches from the foot of the page, does little to serve the cataloger but much to restrict the book designer. The first is a necessary detail; the second, excessive detail.

Standards at the Wrong Level or at Mixed Levels

ENSUE Z39.30 is an example of excessive detail, but also of mixed levels. The list of data elements is a valuable checklist. The standard form with its detailed placement of elements may well be a valuable standard for typewritten orders. If these were separate standards, agencies producing computer-printed orders (or machine-readable orders) could follow the first, while ignoring the second. Examination of standards will reveal many with mixed levels. Inappropriate levels represent another issue, one more difficult to judge. A national standard for the size and threads of light bulb bases seems appropriate; a national standard specifying all physical characteristics of a light bulb would seem inappropriate.

Standards arise at too high a level through the assumption that if some standardization is good, then more is better. For example, the terminal at which these words were written uses many standards: ASCII, RS0232C, the QWERTY keyboard, a standard 3-prong plug, a standard P31 phosphor, and any number of materials, testing and component standards. All those lower-level standards helped a new company enter into competition with established terminal makers. The terminal also uses several "industry standards," with sets of switches to emulate the operation of several well-established terminals. So far, standards encourage competition.

All the standards referred to above are relatively low-level standards. A high-level standard might specify all characteristics of a terminal, creating an "ENSUE standard terminal." If such a standard had existed in 1975, it is unlikely that the author's terminal could have so many features for such a low price. In fact, a standard based on this terminal's qualities would have retarded improvements within the last two years. Inappropriately high-level standards slow innovation and discourage competition.

Standards with No Clear Scope of Application

Just as standards work best at a single level of specification, standards should always have a defined scope for application. Standards for the title page of a technical report would be inappropriate for the title page of a novel. Z39.2 is appropriate for bibliographic records, but would be inappropriate for full-text storage or transmission.

Standards sometimes lack clear scope definitions. A larger problem is misuse of standards beyond intended or appropriate scope. Well-drawn standards will frequently see use beyond original scope, and such extended use may be appropriate. The line between appropriate extension of scope, and inappropriate use out of scope, is a fuzzy line. Use of a standard outside of scope represents over-standardization in an ex post facto sense; while the standard may have been drawn correctly, it is being used incorrectly.

Verification Expense and Difficulty

Standards that are too expensive to verify are poor standards. Users at each level should be able to ascertain that producers at that level have followed appropriate standards. If such verification is unreasonably difficult or costly, adherence won't be verified. In such a situation, no certainty exists that any particular producer is actually following a standard. If an unscrupulous producer recognizes that the standard won't be verified, that producer may gain an unfair economic advantage by taking shortcuts, producing substandard goods.

Subjective Standards

Standards that involve subjective criteria are inherently flawed. If verification is only possible "in the mind of the beholder," the standard should be termed a guideline rather than a standard. Z39.6: Trade Catalogs, calls for body type 8 points or larger: an objective, easily verifiable standard. If the standard went on to state as a requirement that the type should be "attractive," the standard would be flawed.

Solutions to Trivial or Nonexistent Problems

Standards-makers can err on the side of overly ambitious standards. Similarly, standards-makers may err in the other direction. A standard should solve some problem; if the problem is trivial, or does not exist, the standard is a waste of time and energy.

Several Z39 and ISO standards appear to fall into this category. Z39.6 supposes that trade catalogs were being produced which failed to include sufficient information. Z39.13 must be based on the assumption that publishers don't know what information is needed in advertisements, and that publishers lacking such knowledge are likely to purchase and follow an American National Standard. Elements of ISO 8 appear to consider use of different typefaces for different articles in a periodical to be a problem; the nature of the problem is unclear.

The first question to ask when any new standards activity is proposed would appear to be, "What is the problem?" Standards should always be solutions, and should always be solutions to problems that deserve expenditures of time and energy.

DEFECTIVE STANDARDS

Defective standards come about for several reasons in addition to those mentioned above. Some standards are poorly written and misunderstood. Standards committees may lack appropriate expertise. Some standards may be approved despite legitimate objections, and others fail to retain compatibility with earlier versions. Finally, standards may fail to consider privacy issues or other issues affecting individual rights.

Poorly Written and Misunderstood Standards

Standards tend to be drawn by interested parties with specialized experience. When no one on a standards committee has good written English skills, the resulting standard may be poorly written. In extreme cases, poor writing may result in a defective standard, one that does not yield the intended results. Defective materials or safety standards can kill people. Preparing a clear standard requires a mix of skills: an editor without specialized skills may damage the standard in the process of clarifying its text.

Those who work on consensus standards or guidelines may know the difficulty of achieving good finished text. Many who work on such matters feel that committee time should not be spent on matters they regard as "simple editorial questions." Editorial questions frequently appear less important than "substantive matters." When people have spent enormous amounts of time in meetings to establish a standard, their reluctance to spend more time on "editorial questions" is natural enough. This viewpoint, while common, is unfortunate and shortsighted. Clear text allows standards-users to make the most of good substance. Standards-makers understand the details of their standard better than a later reader will; if those details aren't set down in clear, effective English, the standards-makers are weakening their own effort.

Insufficient Knowledge

Most standards develop from perceived needs, and standards tend to be developed by the community that perceives a need. That community may not contain sufficient expertise to prepare the best possible standard. ENSUE boards coordinate efforts of different agencies, partly to assist in this area. Good standards developers make special efforts to reach out for appropriate knowledge. Thus, Z39.48: Permanent Paper for Printed Library Materials, takes advantage of standards developed by ASTM and the Technical Association of the Pulp and Paper Industry, and representatives of paper companies served on the developing committee.

Standards developed without sufficient expertise may not be bad standards, but are unlikely to take advantage of the most current and complete information in special fields. Predictably, many standards will be developed without the best experts in some fields, either because the specialists are not well known or because the developing group is unable to enlist their cooperation.

Consensus Problems

Consensus implies more than simple majority, but is a far cry from unanimity. This distinction is necessary for any standardization effort to take place; otherwise, one determined agency could block all efforts to approve standards. For example, NISO makes a special effort to resolve every negative vote on a standard. ENSUE rules do not require unanimous approval; agencies can and do approve standards despite strong objections from members.

Consumer agencies claim that some standards organizations give little weight to consumer votes—while a negative vote from a single large manufacturer would doom a proposed standard, a negative vote from a consumer agency may be overridden. ENSUE instituted the Consumer Interest Council to deal with this problem; the question is still a valid one.

NISO includes many consumers and has stiffer requirements for consensus than some other standards developers. Such requirements do not assure that legitimate objections will properly block a standard. Politics plays a major role in NISO as in all organizations; negative votes can be resolved by political means rather than by resolving the technical problems. When standards are approved through political consensus rather than technical consensus, the standards begin weakly, have less chance of success and are less useful.

Compatibility

New versions of standards should encompass prior versions, but such is not always the case. For example, X3.9-1978, the standard for FORTRAN, makes illegitimate a data type permitted in previous versions. As a result, some programs developed following ENSUE standards require revision prior to compilation under new X3.9 FORTRAN compilers. The best argument for using ENSUE standard languages is portability; lack of upward compatibility limits such portability. According to those objecting to the changes, X3 language committees are imposing current ideas of "good language practice" on older languages, at the expense of compatibility and portability.[3]

PRIVACY

Standards can damage individual rights. Every few years, somebody suggests development of a national standard identifier for library patrons. After a recent attempt to initiate such a standard (turned down by the committee assigned to work on it), a column appeared in the LITA Newsletter which summarizes the problem:

National standard identifiers of one sort or another are neither uniquely a library idea nor particularly novel. The idea of assigning a number to each new U.S. citizen at birth or naturalization has been proposed many times. The idea has obvious merits: it would eliminate the maze of numbers with which we all deal, by substituting one simple number assigned at birth. It would be of enormous assistance to those attempting to find missing persons, very useful in tracing tax cheats, and so on.

"And so on. . . ." Thanks to the civil libertarians who remain active, "and so on" has so far been enough to prevent establishment of a single standard identification. What serves the IRS will also serve the police; what serves legitimate police will also serve witch-hunters and those setting up lists of enemies.

The problems with a national standard library patron ID are those of a national standard citizen ID. Libraries are places where people go for information – but not, properly, information about the reading habits of other individual patrons or who has read a particular book. At various times, the FBI and other agencies have attempted to use library circulation records to track down those with whom they have a quarrel. Libraries have been consistent in resisting such efforts, based on common understandings regarding privacy and the role of the library.

A national standard library patron ID implies some form of national registry. National registry ties in neatly with the national complex of computers; searches for borrowers and borrowing could be conducted far more efficiently and without all the bother of sending agents out to individual libraries. Paranoia? Perhaps; I once worked in a library which was the scene of a government attempt to inspect old circulation records, so I believe that such attempts are possible.

I've never seen a convincing economic justification for a national standard patron ID. There doesn't seem to be much need for such a standard on any grounds. Most library patrons don't skip from town to town charging books from different libraries – and most libraries would not blindly permit borrowing by out-of-area residents simply because they had a number. The ability to trace book thieves might be useful, but book thieves are unlikely to check out items using a single standard number. In any case, libraries which support confidentiality of patron records should be consistent in that support.

National standard library patron ID's are unlikely to come about in the next year or two; with luck, such standard numbers will never be established. If such a number [were] ever approved, it could well be part of a government trend toward monitoring of citizen activities, and the logical number would be the Social Security number. We've all heard the refrain that "honest people have nothing to hide"; quite apart from the somewhat extreme definition of "honest" this implies, the proper answer is that it all depends on who's looking or might start looking.[4]

Notes

1. *U.S. vs. Johns-Manville, et al.* Finding Fact on Application of ASTM. District Court for Eastern Pennsylvania. 1964 July 20. Cited in Hemenway, *Industrywide Voluntary Product Standards*, (Cambridge, MA: Ballinger, 1975) pp. 10-11.

2. Lyons, Nick. *The Sony Vision.* (New York, NY: Crown, 1976), p. 151.

3. Dvorak, John C. "Inside Track." *InfoWorld* (1984) October 8, p. 88.

4. Crawford, Walt. "Standard Fare." Reprinted by permission of the American Library Association from *LITA Newsletter* No. 19 (Winter 1985), copyright 1985 by ALA.

The Future of Standards

ALBERT L. BATIK, CONSULTANT

In 1986, a critical review of the standards effort in the United States was made. From that analysis, some projections were made about the future of standards. It was pointed out that international competition had placed a premium on doing things right, not only in old-line industries such as steel, but also in high tech industries such as computer chips. It was apparent then, as now, that superior quality was desired, not only by the average automobile owner, but also by industry at large, which must purchase materials, parts, and components. More than ever before, management was calling upon its engineering and manufacturing departments to control costs so that competitiveness was maintained.

In the background was the problem of environmental degradation. This part of the equation is no longer in the background. Dramatic changes in the ozone layer, clear evidence of global warming, mountains of toxic substances to be disposed of, and very slow improvement of the quality of air and water have demonstrated that time is limited and that the time for concentrated technological improvements is now at hand.

It was pointed out that these opportunities were a challenge that should be seized upon by the standards community to demonstrate that standards are indeed the wave of the future. There have been some notable successes. An example is the speed with which standards groups and industry have discarded old, adopted new, and modified older standards applicable to the use of chlorofluorocarbons (CFCs) in refrigeration and air-conditioning.

Despite these accomplishments, many problems outlined above continue to exist. Moreover, the technical problems seem to be getting worse, not better. As in any technological endeavor, new challenges have arisen.

Adapted and revised from *ASTM Standardization News* 14 (August 1986): 36-39. Reprinted with permission.

Engineering schools stopped teaching about standards in the early 1960s. Since that time, the pool of knowledgeable engineers needed to run or manage the standards process has shrunk. It has been suggested that the standards bodies undertake a concerted effort to improve this situation. To this end, a national conference sponsored by a number of major standards organizations, as well as by the Department of Defense, was held In July 1988. As a result, a comprehensive report (summarized in "Standards Engineering Education" in part 2 of this volume) was issued outlining steps that had to be undertaken to improve the situation. The American Society for Testing and Materials (ASTM) established an internal committee to review the problem and to make recommendations. In the years since the first projection of the future of standards, this is all that has been accomplished.

The results were predictable. Membership in the standardizing bodies has stabilized. Some important standards-writing committees are now finding it difficult to get adequate representation. The pace of the generation of standards is slowing, and indeed some efforts that were undertaken in new technologies ceased because of lack of support. Another result is that some of the standards bodies are now reporting for the first time that the sales of standards have not grown and indeed in some isolated cases have declined. This at a time when standards are needed more than ever.

One bright spot has been in the library and information sciences schools. A few important ones have now added a study of standards to their curricula. In addition, a major resource and reference book about standards sources, Patricia Ricci's *Standards: A Resource and Guide for Identification, Selection, and Acquisition*, was published in 1988 for the use of librarians and information specialists.[1] Still, as committees age and shrink, as sales of standards stabilize or even decline, some standards bodies face a very uncertain future.

Compounding the problem are two external factors that the standards community cannot control. First in importance is the harmonization of European standards under the EC 1992 program; and second is the advent of optical publishing. When first projections of the future of standards were made, it was pointed out that (unlike any other nation in the world) the United States has more than 500 standardizing bodies that go about their business in an uncoordinated manner. This is so despite the fact that the American National Standards Institute exists and is responsible for coordination of the standards effort in the United States. Many have defended this pluralistic standards approach, contending that it has worked in the past and that there is no reason to tamper with success.

This attitude was fine as long as the United States dominated world industry, as it did immediately following World War II. But gone are the days of American dominance in consumer electronics, automobiles, steel, textiles, and a host of other endeavors. Our friends now are issuing warnings. The executive director of the Canadian General Standards Board, John Woods, has said: "I think it would be fair to say that, from a Canadian perspective, we view the U.S. standards system with some fear and trepidation. While it is a system which has served the U.S. well in the *past*, and reflects almost perfectly the spirit of free enterprise and individualism so characteristic and so admired of the United States, its standards system is a model *not* imitated by any other advanced economic nation."[2]

In marked contrast, in Europe, where essentially there is but one standardizing body per country, additional consolidation is going on with a program designed to harmonize all EC standards into a common set of EC norms. The response from American standardizing bodies is interesting. Some have chosen simply to ignore the situation. Others are "observing closely"; still others hope to cling to the past by issuing statements that their standards are de facto "world standards." Peter Apostolakis, electrical engineer at the University of Illinois, has stated: "The great diversity of U.S. standards organizations should forge closer ties and try to achieve closer coordination in both domestic and international arenas."[3]

The National Institute for Standards and Technology recently proposed the formation of a United States of America Standards Council (or SCUSA), similar in nature to a like organization in Canada (SCC). The duties of such an organization appear identical to the now existing American National Standards Institute. An extensive set of public hearings was held in 1990 to discuss this and related issues of international standardization and competitiveness. Recognizing the antipathy of both industry and the standards-producing bodies to working under the auspices of the federal government, the fate of such an organization, if created, is not propitious. Still, retention of the status quo becomes increasingly difficult.

Charles Ludolph, director of European community affairs, Department of Commerce, has warned "that the U.S. voluntary and private system for standards, testing and certification does not fit their (EC) model for dealing with standards issues." More importantly, "the way that they have sold their program of creating a single market is that they will make the benefits of a single market available to the Europeans first, and then after time passes – after European companies have restructured and are more competitive – allow non-EC entities improved access. My frustration is that under that scenario, there is no time frame short of 10 or 20 years, in which to open the market to U.S. competition."[4]

Already there has been fallout. Some American companies with established plants in Europe are finding out that they must meet standards devised without their input and designed to make it difficult to compete. Some Middle East nations that have been traditional customers of the United

States are adopting EC standards as their own in selected technologies. A leading American business magazine has stated that the possibility exists that European standards may become world standards.

More often than not, federal government bureaucracies opt for the status quo. It is interesting to note that it is they who are now sounding the alarm. The assistant secretary for international economic policy of the Department of Commerce has voiced grave concerns, while at the same time the leaders of many important standards groups issue soothing platitudes. It has been contended that restricting access to the European market would generate possible reprisals, such as restrictions for Europeans to North American markets. Exports are far more important to Europeans than to North Americans. It is unfortunate, but there are two reasons why that scenario will not be followed. First, because the United States does in fact have no single coordinating standards body, it would be almost impossible to get a consensus on restrictive measures. Second, as has already been shown, other nations in the Middle East, North Africa and indeed South America can and will opt for European standards. That being the case, what will become of the standardizing effort in the United States?

Mr. Ludolph has put it plainly: "The more that the EC adopts international standards, the more U.S. business and others will find it less profitable and *less possible* to be insulated from the global market by just complying with the United States standards."[5] The flip side of this issue questions the use of American standards abroad. After spending several million dollars to harmonize their standards, why would EC countries continue to use American "de facto world standards"? The inevitable outcome will be a decline in the sales of standards, both domestically and overseas. With income going down and with a standards community in the United States divided into hundreds of entities that squabble and have no united policies, what can be the long-term outlook for these organizations? In a word, bleak.

The response to the greatest leap forward in the decimation of information since the introduction of television is typical of what occurs in a structure that is not unified and that can establish no coordinated policies. Optical publishing makes possible the storage, search capabilities, and application of information never before possible. Combined with the appropriate software, it is now possible to integrate words, diagrams, pictures, tables, and active mathematical equations into a single presentation. Multiple users can simultaneously work on a single project to develop drawings, working specifications, and bills of materials on computer-assisted design equipment. The standards community stands at the same crossroads as the sheet music industry did at the turn of the century. The sheet music industry, foreseeing the decline of its sales, fought the recording industry.

Finally, forced by the composers, the two industries joined forces under the supervision of their association, the American Society of Composers and Publishers (ASCAP). The net result was more money than they ever thought possible. When the broadcast industry came into being, however, the same battle had to be refought. Only the pressure of the Great Depression brought the two sides together. Broadcasting of popular tunes became so lucrative that at one point some record companies actually paid to have their records played on the air.

The lesson has been lost on American standards bodies. Instead of seizing the opportunity, instead of establishing some type of common policy to take advantage of the giant step forward, the organizations have chosen for the most part to stand in fear in a hopeless effort to hold onto paper sales. Instead of looking at total income, they have chosen to pit one source of income against another. This fragmented approach of course parallels the fragmented thinking of the entire standards process in the United States.

What is taking place in the European standards community is in marked contrast. It has been agreed that EC standards will become available in optical format. It has fallen to the Germans to do the software. DIN, the German national standardizing body, has formed a wholly owned subsidiary, DIN Software GMBH, to develop CAD-ready, 3-D solid models of DIN standards. It is anticipated that once the multimillion dollar project is completed, the same software will be applied to EC standards. The result will be that the engineering design costs for European companies will plummet. Is it any wonder that American companies are pleading for similar benefits?

If one combines the elements previously described of stable or falling membership, declining paper sales, and the erosion of support from American industry, one wonders what the future will be. Will the grand names of American standardization such as ASTM, ANSI, ASME, NFPA, and SAE follow the same road as the former grand names of American industry: Packard automobile, Philco radio, Republic Steel, City Service Oil, and Anaconda Copper? The United States is a very strange nation. It operates in ways beyond the ken or knowledge of an average person. Like a body at rest, it takes enormous energy to get it moving. History has proven that when the crisis becomes bad enough, the nation does move. And when it moves, it really moves. It has been proposed that a titan of industry, some charismatic CEO of a Fortune 500 corporation knowledgeable in standards, be recruited to head up a new, all powerful standards coordinating body. Using his or her contacts and powers of persuasion, he or she would gain contributions approaching almost half a billion dollars. (This is but one million from each of the Fortune 500). The money would be used to buy out the standardizing operations of most of those organizations now in the business, thus reducing the total to, at most, one dozen. Such a powerful organization could fund curricula in standards at major schools; it could license industry to make available standards in any format the market demands; it would provide one voice to work with the appropriate government officials to defend the international commercial rights of American industry.

The establishment of a new coordinating body for American standards, regardless of how powerful it might be, would not in itself change the direction of the European community with its EC 1992 program. In the late nineteenth century, a philosophy of military, economic, and political thought, known as Real Politik, arose in Germany. It stated that the one who ruled the center of Eurasia, basically the Berlin-Moscow axis, controlled the world. This philosophy was based on a projection of the world known as the Mercator projection. If, however, a polar projection is used and consideration is given to the geopolitical and economic changes now going on in the Soviet Union, this may lead to a greater community of interest between the U.S. and the USSR than between the U.S. and Europe (EC). A polar standards group, composed of the U.S., Canada, and the Soviet Union, would constitute the largest developed market in the world with huge natural resources, industrial potential, skilled labor, and gigantic consumer needs. Such an economic and standards block would be in an excellent position to negotiate open protocols with the EC harmonized standardization community. Everything is possible.

Notes

1. A new edition was published in 1990. See Patricia Ricci and Linda Perry, *Standards: A Resource and Guide for Identification, Selection, and Acquisition* (St. Paul: Stirtz, Bernards and Co.).

2. John Woods, "A Consensus Perspective on the Realities and Possibilities of Standardization in Europe: 1992," *ASTM Standardization News* (February 1990): 32.

3. Peter Apostolakis, "EC92 and Standardization," *ASTM Standardization News* (February 1990): 38.

4. Barbara Schindler, "Interview with Charles Ludolph," *ASTM Standardization News* (February 1990): 26.

5. Ibid., 30.

Appendix A: Recommendations of the Working Group on Standards for Archival Description (1989)

ARCHIVAL PARTICIPATION IN THE STANDARDS-SETTING PROCESS

The Working Group's first five recommendations focus on the role archivists should play in the development and implementation of standards, both in the United States and internationally. The most appropriate organizer and conduit for this participation is the principal professional archival association in the United States, the Society of American Archivists (SAA).

Recommendation 1:
The Society of American Archivists should establish a standards board to oversee the process of developing, implementing, and revising standards within the association and to provide an active liaison with other standards-developing organizations whose work affects archival practice.

Recommendation 2:
The Society of American Archivists should establish a full-time staff position devoted to coordinating the development, implementation, and monitoring of description standards and to the training of archivists in their use.

Recommendation 3:
The Society of American Archivists should provide sufficient resources to participate fully in the deliberations of organizations that control the development and implementation of those library standards that are also

---

The complete report of the working group, along with 13 background papers, can be found in *American Archivist* 52, no. 4 (Fall 1989), and 53, no. 1 (Winter 1990).

employed in archival description. SAA should require its designated representatives to these groups to report to SAA Council and the profession in a timely and effective manner.

Recommendation 4:
The Society of American Archivists should become a voting member and participate fully in the work of the National Information Standards Organization (NISO Z39).

Recommendation 5:
Archivists in the United States should establish formal links to the description standards working groups in Canada and the United Kingdom to work toward a broadly based Anglo-American agreement on standards for describing archives and manuscripts.

LEADERSHIP RESPONSIBILITIES OF NATIONAL INSTITUTIONS

The National Archives and Records Administration (NARA) and the Library of Congress (LC) have special leadership responsibilities in the archival community. Their particular roles in the areas of standards and archival description are addressed in the following three recommendations.

Recommendation 6:
The National Archives and Records Administration should work to develop more effective means for informing the professional archival community about its research in progress relating to description standards.

Recommendation 7:
The National Archives and Records Administration should take a strong leadership role in the development and application of standards that will ensure long-term access to and preservation of electronic records.

Recommendation 8:
The Library of Congress plays a critical role in the development and maintenance of standards used for archival description; the Society of American Archivists should communicate regularly with the offices in LC that conduct this work to ensure that archival needs and concerns are addressed.

ENDORSEMENT OF SPECIFIC STANDARDS FOR ARCHIVAL DESCRIPTION

In 1982 the Council of the Society of American Archivists endorsed the USMARC Format for Archival and Manuscripts Control and the NISTF Data Element Dictionary as the first and, until 1989, the only formally recognized standards for archival description. In October 1989, the Working Group sent a preliminary copy of the Recommendation 9, printed below, to Council for its consideration when it met at the SAA annual meeting in St. Louis. Council voted at that meeting to endorse APPM as a standard for archival description, for which the Working Group expresses its appreciation. Council has yet to act on the remainder of the recommendation, however, which deals with the need for establishing a process for the ongoing review and revision of APPM. The full recommendation is printed here to retain the full scope of the Working Group's conclusions.

Recommendation 9:
The Society of American Archivists should endorse Steven Hensen's *Archives, Personal Papers and Manuscripts* (APPM) (1989) as a standard for archival descriptive cataloging and establish a formal process for the continuing review and updating of APPM.

EDUCATION AND TRAINING NEEDS

As new standards are developed and implemented or existing ones revised, it is essential that new and experienced practitioners alike be informed of their content and purpose and trained adequately to use them.

Recommendation 10:
All archival and library education programs should include instruction in archival description that addresses the use of existing standards and the potential application of those under development.

Recommendation 11:
Archivists should seek funds to support the preparation of a basic handbook on standards and their application in the practice of archival description.

RESEARCH AND DEVELOPMENT NEEDS

During the course of these deliberations, the Working Group came to a better understanding about the processes of developing and implementing standards and about how certain standards function in an archival context. It also, perhaps inevitably, identified at least six areas in which significantly more research and development must take place in order to fully develop the potential of archival description.

Recommendation 12:
Since the purpose of archival description is to provide access to archival materials, research should be conducted to discover how users currently obtain access to materials to provide a benchmark for the improvement of archival description and the subsequent development of standards.

Recommendation 13:
In order to achieve a better understanding of the information management needs for the effective administrative, physical, and intellectual control of archival materials, archivists should give the definition of an archival information architecture a high priority on their research agenda and seek the resources for its development.

Recommendation 14:
Archivists should thoroughly evaluate existing description practices and systems in order to encourage development and implementation along the most effective lines.

Recommendation 15:
Archivists should explore the concept of authority control for archival materials, define the multiple types of authority records required in archival information systems, work for their acceptance through MARBI (Committee on Representation in Machine-Readable Form of Bibliographic Information, a joint committee of three ALA divisions, LITA, ALCTS, and RASD), and develop information systems that fully exploit the potential for authority control to enhance access and use.

Recommendation 16:
Developers of controlled vocabularies used for subject and name indexing should provide thorough guidelines for assigning terms during the description of records and for searching databases that employ the vocabularies.

Recommendation 17:
Archivists should explore further the integration of cataloging rules for archival materials, special media materials, library materials, and museum materials.

Appendix B: Standards Information Centers

Following is an alphabetical list of standards information centers from which it is possible to obtain information or purchase copies of standards and related documents. Included are addresses, telephone numbers, and brief descriptions of holdings of the major standards information centers.

American Institute of Architects
Building Performance and Regulations Committee
1735 New York Avenue, N.W.
Washington, DC 20006
(202) 626-7448

American National Standards Institute
1430 Broadway
New York, NY 10018
(212) 642-4900; telefax (212) 302-1286
Founded: 1918, nonprofit

Number of Standards:
9,700 U.S. nongovernment, 250,000 other.

Types of Standards:
9,700 American National Standards that deal with dimensions, ratings, terminology, symbols, test methods, and performance and safety requirements for materials, equipment, components, and a wide range of products.

Adapted and revised by the editors from Robert B. Toth, ed., *Standards Activities of Organizations in the United States*, (Gaithersburg, Md.: National Bureau of Standards, 1984).

7,000 international standards issued by the International Organization for Standardization (ISO) and 1,200 issued by the International Electrotechnical Commission (IEC). 250,000 standards of 75 national standards organizations that are members of the International Organization for Standardization.

ISO and IEC draft international standards; CEN and CENELEC/CECC proposals – draft standards and specifications. English translations of thousands of foreign standards.

American Society of Heating, Refrigerating and Air Conditioning Engineers
1791 Tullie Circle, N.E.
Atlanta, GA 30329
(404) 636-8400

American Society of Mechanical Engineers
Order Department
22 Law Drive
Box 2300
Fairfield, NJ 07007-2300
(201) 882-1167

ASTM Information Center
American Society for Testing and Materials
1916 Race Street
Philadelphia, PA 19103
(215) 299-5475 or 5585; telefax (215) 299-5576
Founded: 1898, nonprofit

Types of Standards:
U.S. nongovernment: all ASTM and ANSI standards. International: all ISO standards.

Building Official and Code Administrators International
4051 West Flossmoor Road
Country Club Hills, IL 60477
(312) 799-2300 and (800) 323-1103

Council of American Building Officials
5203 Leesburg Pike, Suite 708
Falls Church, VA 22041
(703) 931-4533

Department of Housing and Urban Development
451 7th Street, S.W., Room B258
Washington, DC 20405
(202) 708-1422

Document Engineering Co., Inc.
15210 Stagg Street
Van Nuys, CA 91405
(213) 873-5566 and (800) MIL-SPEC
Founded: 1958, private, for profit

Number of Standards:
75,000 U.S. government, 6,000 U.S. nongovernment.

Types of Standards:
All military standards, specifications, and related documents listed in the *Department of Defense Index of Specifications and Standards*. American National Standards Institute, American Society for Testing and Materials, SAE, Aerospace Material Specifications, American Welding Society, Institute of Electrical and Electronics Engineers, Electronic Industries Association, Institute for Interconnecting and Packaging Electronic Circuits. Automatic updating service, Military Sheet Fort Standards (MS, AN, AND series) Service, Qualified Products List Service.

Engineering Societies Library
345 East 47th Street
New York, NY 10017
(212) 705-7611
Founded: 1913, nonprofit

Types of Standards:
U.S. government, ANSI, IEC, ASHRAE, ASME, AWS, IEEE, NFPA.

Federal Construction Council
National Academy of Sciences
2101 Constitution Avenue, N.W.
8a-274
Washington, DC 20418
(202) 334-2842

General Services Administration
Public Buildings Service
18th and F Streets, N.W.
Washington, DC 20405
(202) 501-1406

Global Engineering Documents
Division of Information Handling Services
2805 McGraw Avenue, P. O. Box 19539
Irvine, CA 92714
(714) 261-1455 and California (800) 854-7777, 7179
Founded: 1968, private, for profit

Number of Standards:
40,000 U.S. government, 20,000 U.S. nongovernment.

Types of Standards:
All military and federal standards, specifications, handbooks, commercial item descriptions (CIDs), data item descriptions (DIDs), qualified products lists (QPLs), directives and regulations including armed services procurement regulations/defense acquisition regulations. Also all NATO standards and quality assurance publications, standardization publications of the Army, Navy, and Air Force, and federal acquisition regulations.

Standards and related publications of the following federal agencies are also stocked: NASA, NBS, Nuclear Regulatory Commission (NRC), COM, DOT, FAA, FCC, GPO, GSA, HUD, OSHA, and NTIS.

Nongovernment standards from most major standards developers; international standards of ISO, IEC, ECMA; and foreign national DIN, BSI, and JIS standards.

Government Printing Office
Superintendent of Documents
Washington, DC 20402
(202) 783-3238
Founded: 1895, governmental

Types of Standards:
Neither the GPO nor the superintendent of documents issues or publishes standards per se. However, as the principal sales agency for government publications, the superintendent of documents' inventory of available publications contains hundreds that relate to standards or contain standards issued by the various departments and agencies of the government. A few examples of the publications available are the *Department of Defense Index of Specifications and Standards*, Standards for Specifying Construction of Airports, Standard Specifications for Construction of Roads and Bridges on Federal Highway Projects, Government Paper Specifications Standards.

The DoD's military specifications and standards and GSA's federal specifications and standards are *not* available from GPO. Only the indexes for these publications are distributed by GPO. The standards and specifications are available from Naval Publications and Forms Center and the GSA Specifications Unit, respectively.

Illuminating Engineering Society
345 East 47th Street
New York, NY 10017
(212) 705-7916

Information Handling Services
15 Inverness Way East
Englewood, CO 80150
(303) 790-0600 and (800) 525-7052
Founded: 1959, private, for profit

Number of Standards:
170,000 U.S. government, 28,000 U.S. nongovernment, 35,000 other.

Types of Standards:
All military standards, specifications, and related documents; federal standards, specifications, and related documents; federal construction regulations and standards; Federal Aviation Administration standards; Veterans Administration specifications; Nuclear Regulatory Commission regulations and standards. Nongovernment standards developers are covered, including over 55 of the largest nongovernment standards producers. Also includes over 30 other national, regional, and international standards bodies. TECH DATA, an online database of citations of more than 140,000 standards, is available through IHS and Bibliographic Retrieval Service throughout the world. This enables users to quickly determine if pertinent standards exist.
    IHS provides access to:

- Industrial catalogs, spec sheets, and pricing data from around the world.

- U.S., foreign national, and international codes and standards.

- Unclassified federal and military specifications and other standardization documents.

- Federal personnel manuals, regulations, and case decisions.

- Federal supply schedules, contractors' catalogs, procurement regulations, and related publications.

- Safety and regulatory reports, publications, and documents.

- Technical reports and abstracts covering a multitude of engineering/scientific disciplines.

Institute of Electrical and Electronics Engineers
445 Hoes Lane, P. O. Box 1331
Piscataway, NJ 08855-1331
(201) 981-0060

International Association of Plumbing and Mechanical Officials
5032 Alhambra Avenue
Los Angeles, CA 90032
(213) 223-1471

International Conference of Building Officials
5360 South Workman Mill Road
Whittier, CA 90601
(213) 699-0541

James Jerome Hill Reference Library
Fourth and Market Streets
Saint Paul, MN 55102
(612) 227-9531
Founded: 1921, nonprofit

Number of Standards:
15,000 U.S. nongovernment.

Types of Standards:
Federal information processing standards (FIPS). 200 standards developers, including complete collections of ASTM, ANSI, IEEE, NFPA, UL, NEMA, SAE, ASHRAE, AWWA.

Library of Congress
Technical Report Section
Science and Technology Division
Washington, DC 20540
(202) 707-5655

Number of Standards:
310,000.

Types of Standards:
Military and federal, ANSI, ISO, IEC, CEE, CCITT, Soviet (GOST), Chinese (SBS). More than 70 U.S. nongovernment standards producers, including ANSI and others. Available for public inquiry and use.

Linda Hall Library
5109 Cherry Street
Kansas City, MO 64110
(816) 363-4600
Founded: 1946, nonprofit

Number of Standards:
100,000 standards total.

Types of Standards:
All military and federal specifications, standards, and related documents. Two hundred professional, commercial, or industrial agencies issuing standardization documents.

Morgan Technical Library
National Fire Protection Association
Batterymarch Park, Room 251
Quincy, MA 02269
(617) 770-3000, extension 445
Founded: 1945, nonprofit

Types of Standards:
NEMA, NFPA, UL. Partial files on approximately 30 other organizations, primarily those standards relating to fire safety. Partial files on approximately 15 federal agencies, primarily those standards relating to fire safety.

National Aeronautics and Space Administration
Kennedy Space Center
Code DE-C-1
Kennedy Space Center, FL 32899

National Center for Standards and Certification Information
National Institute of Standards and Technology, formerly **National Bureau of Standards**
Room A629, Administration Building
National Bureau of Standards
Gaithersburg, MD 20899
(301) 975-4040; telefax (301) 963-2871
Founded: 1965, government

Number of Standards:
NCSCI provides information on over 240,000 standards documents.

Types of Standards:

United States: industry and national (voluntary), federal agency (voluntary and regulations), state purchasing, federal purchasing. Foreign: national, international, and regional. Historical standards and specifications on microfilm (1970-date): ANSI, ASME, ASTM, API, NEMA, and NFPA historical, unclassified military, and federal specifications and standards.

Medium:
Paper, microfilm cartridges, and microfiche.

Indexing:
Computer-assisted indexing of standards titles in KWIC (key-word-in-context) format. An index of U.S. voluntary standards is available in microfiche or hard copy. Free product subject listings are often disseminated in response to inquiries.

Objectives:

To respond to the needs of government, industry, and the general public for information on domestic and foreign standards, regulations, certification, and other standards-related activities. To respond to foreign requests for information on existing U.S. standards and certification information. The objectives are accomplished by maintaining a microform and hard-copy collection of engineering standards and specifications, regulations, certification rules, directories, reference books, and special publications; responding to inquiries on the existence, source, and availability of standards and related documents; developing and publishing lists, bibliographies, and indexes of standards and related information; and conducting online search and retrieval of standards documents information. To the degree possible, respond to trade-related queries regarding regulations and other requirements of foreign countries for the export of U.S. products.

National Conference of States on Building Codes and Standards
481 Carlisle Drive
Herndon, VA 22070
(703) 437-0100

National Fire Protection Association
Batterymarch Park
Quincy, MA 02269-9990
(617) 770-3500 and (800) 344-3555

National Institute of Building Sciences

1015 15th Street, N.W.
Suite 700
Washington, DC 20005
(202) 347-5710

National Standards Association
1200 Quince Orchard Boulevard
Gaithersburg, MD 20878
(301) 590-2300 and (800) 638-8094
Founded: 1946, private, for profit

Number of Standards:
75,000 U.S. government, 29,000 U.S. nongovernment.

Types of Standards:
All military and federal standards, specifications, and related documents
listed in the *Department of Defense Index of Specifications and Standards*,
including ANs, MSs, QPLs, handbooks plus NATO and related standards.
AIA, ARI, ACI, ANSI, ASME, ASTM, AWWA, AWS, AFBMA, ISA, MSS,
NEMA, NFPA, RICA, SAE, UL, ISO, IEC, BSI, DIN, JIS.
   Military specifications and standards dating back to the early 1940s.
   A call-in order service, TECHINFO, can provide standards,
specifications, or government regulations – U.S. or foreign – and, if requested,
an automatic revision service for customers requiring document revisions in a
timely manner.
   Standards and Specifications (DIALOG File 113), an online index of all
U.S. government and industry standards, specifications, and related
documents. Over 100,000 records of U.S. military, federal, and
nongovernment standards, as well as over 29,000 cancelled military standards.
   Publishes the annual directory of *Identified Sources of Supply* listing
sources of products complying with standards.

National Technical Information Service
U.S. Department of Commerce
5285 Port Royal Road
Springfield, VA 22161
(703) 487-4636
Founded: 1970 (predecessor 1946), governmental.

Types of Standards:
Some military standards, nuclear, medical, environmental, food and drug.
American National Standards Institute publications cited in government
standards.
Retains all prior editions. Paper and microfiche.

Government Report Announcements and Index, annual, updated biweekly.

Naval Publications and Forms Center
NPODS
5801 Tabor Avenue
Philadelphia, PA 19120
(215) 697-5637
Urgent requests (215) 697-3321; Western Union (710) 670-1685

Type of Organization: governmental

Number of Standards:
41,584 U.S. government, 3,215 U.S. nongovernment, 1,212 other.

Types of Standards:
U.S. government: All military and federal standards, specifications, and related documents listed in the *Department of Defense Index of Specifications and Standards*.
U.S. nongovernment: Standards are provided to DoD agencies ONLY. These include AIA, NAS, ANSI, ASME, ASTM, AWS.

Medium: Paper.

Indexing:
The *Department of Defense Index of Specifications and Standards* is available in printed book form and microfiche. It is a three-part listing: alpha, numeric, as well as numeric within federal supply classes.

The printed edition is available from Government Printing Office, Washington, DC 20402.

The microfiche edition is available from Director, Navy Publications and Printing Service Office, 700 Robbins Avenue, Philadelphia, PA 19111. Both media are available to DoD activities from NPFC.

Related:
New and/or revised releases of military and federal specifications and standards (including qualified products lists) that are to be listed in the DODISS are available on a subscription basis for a single class or for as many individual classes as the subscriber chooses upon payment of a subscription fee per federal supply class. The subscriber will receive one copy each of all new or revised documents for a one-year period after the effective subscription date. Documents issued prior to the subscription date must be ordered individually from NPFC.

Naval Publications and Printing Service

Detachment Office
700 Robbins Avenue
Philadelphia, PA 19111
(215) 697-3321

Nuclear Standards Management Center
P. O. Box Y, Building 9204-1, M/S 10
Oak Ridge, TN 37831
(615) 574-5208

Type of Organization:
Government

Types of Standards:
211 nuclear energy (NE) standards are published under the auspices of the U.S. Department of Energy. The standards are available to United States government contractors and selected private industries engaged in the nuclear energy field. A "Nuclear Standards Master Index" listing standard number, title, facility, cognizant engineer, and status is published semiannually (January and June).

Southern Building Code Congress International Inc.
900 Montclair Road
Birmingham, AL 35213-1206
(205) 591-1853 and (800) 633-3876

Standards Council of Canada
Information and Sales
350 Sparks Street
Suite 1200
Ottawa, Ontario K1P 6N7
(613) 238-3222; in Canada, (800) 267-8220, telefax (613) 995-4564

Type of Organization:
Governmental

Types of Standards:
The Standards Council of Canada's Standards Information Service provides thousands of organizations in Canada and abroad with comprehensive, accurate information on standards, regulations, codes, testing, certification, and approval procedures effective in the global market.

The service's staff utilizes more than 400,000 national, foreign, and international standards publications as well as a complete collection of Canadian federal and provincial statutes and regulations. Through its affiliation with the International Organization for Standardization

Information Network (ISONET), the service can quickly obtain detailed information on the national standards and related documents of all International Organization for Standardization (ISO) member bodies.

For standards information, 24 hours a day, contact the Standards Information Service.

Part of the General Agreement on Tariffs and Trade (GATT), the Agreement on Technical Barriers to Trade (TBT) – known as the Standards Code – stipulates that each signatory must provide an enquiry point. Through a contract with the federal government, the Standards Council of Canada acts as the GATT TBT enquiry point in Canada.

Underwriters Laboratories Inc.
333 Pfingsten Road
Northbrook, IL 60062-2096
(708) 272-8800

Veterans Administration
Chief Architectural Specifications Division
(088B31)
Office of Facilities
810 Vermont Avenue, N.W.
Washington, DC 20420
(202) 233-4000

Glossary of Standards-Related Terminology

DONALD R. MACKAY, OFFICE OF STANDARDS CODE AND INFORMATION, NATIONAL INSTITUTE OF STANDARDS AND TECHNOLOGY (1985-1989)

OVERVIEW

This glossary provides definitions of terms and names for abbreviations commonly used in standardization, certification, laboratory accreditation, quality control, information technology, and archival activities. Multiple definitions are provided in some cases to identify organizational differences in the use of terms. In each case, the source of the definition is indicated. The terms are presented in a logically structured format, beginning with general terms and moving to more specific terms.

With the permission of Donald R. Mackay, this glossary was expanded by the volume editors to include two additional sections that provide full names for the numerous abbreviations, acronyms, and terms used in standardization for information technology and for archival and manuscript control. The editors also wish to acknowledge Michael B. Spring for contributions from his "Information Technology Standards," to be published in a forthcoming issue of the *Annual Review of Information Science and Technology (ARIST)*. D. R. Mackay is now Manager, International Standards for the Air Conditioning and Refrigeration Institute (ARI), Arlington, Va.

INTRODUCTION

With the increasing emphasis on trade throughout the world, the subjects of *standardization, certification, laboratory accreditation*, and *quality control* have greatly increased in importance. More and more organizations, companies, and individuals have recognized the value of standards and the benefits that can be derived from their use in the marketplace. Unfortunately, much confusion and misunderstanding stem from the imprecise use of many terms relating to standards.

The purpose of this glossary is to present commonly accepted definitions of various terms and phrases used in standardization, certification, laboratory accreditation, and quality control. An attempt has been made to include terms that are frequently misinterpreted.

The contents of this glossary are not "official" definitions, nor even "consensus" definitions, but are generally accepted by those in the "standards world." The source of each definition is indicated, and more than one definition is frequently provided for the same term to reflect differences in application, particularly between international organizations and U.S. organizations. The sources of the definitions are identified as follows:

"ANSI" indicates a definition taken from the American National Standard Z34.1 or Z34.2 published by the American National Standards Institute (ANSI) in October 1987.

"ARIST" indicates a definition or term described in Michael B. Spring, "Information Technology Standards," in a forthcoming issue of the *Annual Review of Information Science and Technology* (ARIST).

"ASQC" indicates a definition taken from the American Society for Quality Control (ASQC) Standard A-3, "Quality Systems Terminology."

"ASTM" indicates a definition taken from a standard published by the American Society for Testing and Materials. (The specific standard is identified after the ASTM acronym.)

"DOD" applies to a definition published in *Defense Standardization Manual DOD 4120.3-M* in 1982.

"IEEE" indicates a definition taken from the Local Area Network (LAN) Committee document 802.3 of the Institute of Electrical and Electronic Engineers (IEEE) published in October 1986.

"ILAC" indicates a definition taken from the report of Task Force C of the International Laboratory Accreditation Conference (ILAC) in 1979.

"ISO" indicates a definition taken from the fifth edition of ISO Guide 2, "General terms and their definitions concerning standardization and related activities," published by the International Organization for Standardization (ISO) and the International Electrotechnical Commission (IEC) in November 1986.

"EIPSC" applies to a definition initially approved by the Engineering and Information Processing Standards Council of the National Bureau of Standards (now known as the National Institute of Standards and Technology) in 1972. Some of these were edited slightly by the Office of Standards Code and Information (OSCI) in 1988.

"NTEP" identifies a definition established in the National Type Evaluation Program of the National Conference of Weights and Measures, which is sponsored by the National Institute of Standards and Technology.

"NVLAP" specifies a definition taken from NBSIR 79-1950, *NVLAP Glossary of Terms for Laboratory Accreditation, Product Certification and Standardization*, published by the NBS National Voluntary Laboratory Accreditation Program (NVLAP) in January 1980, with some minor editorial modifications by OSCI in 1988.

"OSCI" identifies a definition developed by the Office of Standards Code and Information of the National Institute of Standards and Technology in 1988.

"OIML" identifies a definition taken from the 1978 edition of the *Vocabulary of Legal Metrology* published by the International Organization for Legal Metrology, Paris, France.

"OMB" indicates a definition taken from OMB Circular A-119 "Federal Participation in the Development and Use of Voluntary Standards," issued in October 1983 by the U.S. Office of Management and Budget.

Comments on these definitions will be welcome as will suggestions for additional definitions. Please send them to:

Editor: Standards Glossary
Office of Standards Code and Information
Room A629, Administration Building
National Institute of Standards and Technology
Gaithersburg, MD 20899

The definitions are not alphabetically presented, as in a dictionary, but are in a logically structured format, beginning with general terms and moving to more specific terms in each of seven major areas: *standardization, types of standards, testing and certification, laboratory accreditation, quality control, information technology,* and *archives and manuscripts*. The alphabetical index will assist in locating definitions of specific terms and phrases.

This glossary should benefit those who have been unaware of the world of standards or who have been only casually acquainted with standards and standards-related activities or who have remained uncertain about the meaning of particular terms. It is recognized that increasing numbers of individuals have been exposed to the terms presented here when, as manufacturers, distributors, exporters, or others, they have been affected by the provisions of the GATT Standards Code, the European Economic Community directives, the U.S.-Canada Free Trade Agreement, or other domestic or international activities. For example, exports depend heavily on conformance to standards, acceptance of certification marks, and recognition of laboratory accreditation programs.

STANDARDIZATION

1. *Standardization*: Activity of establishing, with regard to actual or potential problems, provisions for common and repeated use, aimed at the achievement of the optimum degree of order in a given context. (ISO)

    NOTE: In particular, the activity consists of the processes of formulating, issuing, and implementing standards. (ISO)

    Standardization: The process of establishing by common agreement the engineering criteria, terms, principles, practices, materials, items, processes, equipment, parts, subassemblies, and assemblies appropriate to achieve the greatest practicable uniformity of products and engineering practices, to ensure the minimum feasible variety of such items and practices, and to effect optimum interchangeability of equipment parts and components. (The product of a standardization effort is a documentary standard.) (EIPSC)

2. *Simplification*: A form of standardization that reduces the number of types, sizes, capacities, or shapes of products, materials, and packages within a definite range to a number that is adequate to meet prevailing needs. (EIPSC)

3. *Harmonization*: The process whereby two or more nations (or standards bodies) agree on the content and application of a standard. Harmonization is accomplished by modification of a national standard (or agreement on a common document by two or more standards

bodies) so that it is consistent with the harmonized standard *or* by countries agreeing to accept products and services that are in conformance with the harmonized standard even if they do not conform to the requirements of their national standard. Furthermore, a standard may be said to be harmonized if its text is technically equivalent to another standard (e.g., a national standard that is technically equivalent to an international standard). (EIPSC)

4. *Consensus*: General agreement characterized by the absence of sustained opposition to substantial issues by any important part of the concerned interests and by a process that involves seeking to take into account the views of all parties concerned and to reconcile any conflicting arguments. (ISO)

    NOTE: Consensus need not imply unanimity. (ISO)

    Consensus: Substantial agreement of those concerned with the scope and provisions of a standard as judged by a recognized or duly appointed authority. Consensus implies much more than the concept of a simple majority but not necessarily unanimity. (EIPSC)

5. *Consensus procedures*: The rules and regulations of a recognized or duly appointed authority that pertain to the development of standards: (1) requiring that all interested and affected parties be given due notice of the initiation and development of a standard, (2) providing interested and affected parties the opportunity to participate in the development of each standard, (3) providing for the considerations of all significant objections to the standard, and (4) reaching substantial agreement in support of the standard with no unresolved objections, as judged by a panel of standards professionals. (OSCI)

6. *Subject of standardization*: Topic to be standardized. (ISO)

    NOTE: Standardization may be limited to particular aspects of any subject. For example, in the case of shoes, sizes and durability criteria could be standardized separately. (ISO)

7. *Field of standardization*: Group of related subjects of standardization. (ISO)

    NOTE: Engineering, transport, agriculture, and quantities and units, for example, could be regarded as fields of standardization. (ISO)

8. *State of the art*: Developed stage of technical capability at a given time as regards products, processes, and services based on the relevant consolidated findings of science, technology, and experience. (ISO)

9.   *Adoption of a standard*: The use of the latest edition of a voluntary standard in whole, in part, or by reference for procurement purposes and the inclusion of the latest edition of a voluntary standard in whole, in part, or by reference in regulation(s). (OMB)

10. *Reference to standards*: The inclusion of standards or parts of standards in specifications or standards, codes, rules, or regulations by reference to the identification of those standards and to the organization responsible for the standards. (EIPSC)

11. *National standards body*: An organization within a country that is recognized as a developer of standards that are widely used within that country. Alternatively, it may be a national organization that is generally recognized as the spokesperson for voluntary standardization activities of that country. In other countries, depending upon national political philosophy, national standards bodies may be governmental agencies, private organizations, or quasigovernmental or may have various degrees of governmental support and recognition. The national standards body is most often the organizational member of the International Organization for Standardization. (EIPSC)

12. *Secretariat*: The office that provides the administrative and secretarial services for a standardization activity. The secretariat function may include the calling of and arranging for meetings; distribution of agenda and documents; preparation of minutes and resolutions; conducting, recording, and reporting of letter ballots; control and circulation of official documents; conducting business of the standards activity between meetings; and carrying out the official correspondence and transactions of the standards activity. (EIPSC)

13. *Level of standardization*: Geographical, political, or economic extent of involvement in standardization. (ISO)

14. *International standardization*: Standardization in which involvement is open to relevant bodies from all countries. (ISO)

15. *Regional standardization*: Standardization in which involvement is open to relevant bodies from countries from only one geographical, political, or economic area of the world. (ISO)

16. *National standardization*: Standardization that takes place at the level of one specific country. (ISO)

NOTE: Within a country, standardization may take place in the national government, in state or provincial governments, within professional   organizations,   trade   associations,   or   standards development groups as well as within the nationally recognized standards body. (ISO)

17. *Company standardization*: Standardization that takes place within a corporation or company, including the development of specifications used for procurement purposes. (OSCI)

TYPES OF STANDARDS

18. *Normative document*: Document that provides rules, guidelines, or characteristics for activities or their results. (ISO)

     NOTE: The term *normative document* is a generic term that covers documents such as standards, technical specifications, codes of practice, and regulations. (ISO)

     NOTE: *Normative documents* are also referred to as *norms*. (OSCI)

19. *Standard*: Document, established by consensus and approved by a recognized body, that provides for common and repeated use, rules, guidelines, or characteristics for activities or their results, aimed at the achievement of the optimum degree of order in a given context. (ISO)

     Standard: A prescribed set of rules, conditions, or requirements concerned with the definition of terms; classification of components; delineation of procedures; specification of dimensions, materials, performance, design, or operations; measurement of quality and quantity in describing materials, products, systems, services, or practices; or descriptions of fit and measurement of size. (OMB)

20. *International standard*: Standard that is adopted by an international standardizing/standards organization and made available to the public. (ISO)

     International standard: A standard promulgated by an "international organization" (treaty or nontreaty) and recognized as having international applicability. An international standard promulgated by treaty organizations (e.g., the United Nations Food and Agriculture Organization FAO and its Codex Alimentarius) is generally mandatory in nature. An international standard promulgated by a nontreaty organization (e.g., ISO, the International Organization for Standardization) is generally not mandatory. However, the latter case implies a moral obligation on the part of the organizations' members to use "best efforts" in adopting international standards as national standards. An international standard may become quasimandatory,

mandatory, or a code, regulation, or rule as a result of its utilization or adoption by a regulatory authority. (EIPSC)

21. *Regional standard*: Standard that is adopted by a regional standardizing/standards organization and made available to the public. (ISO)

    Regional standard: A standard developed or adopted and promulgated by a regional organization (e.g., COPANT, the Pan American Standards Commission). Regional standards are generally voluntary in nature, representing the joint action of the national standards bodies of a regional group of nations. They may be regarded as voluntary harmonized standards. (EIPSC)

22. *National standard*: Standard that is adopted by a national standards body and made available to the public. (ISO)

    National standard: A standard promulgated by a national standards body (e.g., BSI, the British Standards Institution) and recognized as applicable to goods and services within a particular nation; it may or may not be mandatory. (EIPSC)

23. *Harmonized standard*: Standards on the same subject approved by different standardizing bodies that establish interchangeability of products, processes, and services or establish mutual understanding of test results or information provided according to these standards. (ISO)

24. *Voluntary standards*: Standards established generally by private sector bodies and available for use by any person or organization, private or governmental. The term includes what are commonly referred to as *industry standards* as well as *consensus standards* but does not include professional standards of personal conduct, institutional codes of ethics, private standards of individual firms, or standards mandated by law, such as those contained in the *United States Pharmacopeia* and the *National Formulary*, as referenced in 21 U.S.C. 351. (OMB)

    Voluntary standard: A standard that is usually developed by a consensus process for voluntary use and with which there is no obligation to comply. However, a voluntary standard may become quasimandatory or mandatory as a result of its use, reference, or adoption by a regulatory authority. (EIPSC)

25. *Quasimandatory standard*: A standard with which there is no legal obligation to comply but that is required in practice or under certain conditions, such as for a purchasing requirement or for compatibility with other products. (EIPSC)

26. *Mandatory standard*: A standard with which there is an obligation to comply by virtue of an action by government or by an authority endowed with the necessary legal power; called a code, regulation, or rule. In addition to *how* a product must conform, a mandatory standard usually prescribes *who* must implement the standard, to *what* products the standard applies and under what conditions, and *when* conformance is required. It may also prescribe how conformance is to be established and may define exemptions and deviation procedures and may impose penalties for nonconformance. (EIPSC)

27. *De facto standard*: A standard that has not been promulgated and adopted but has come into use by general acceptance, custom, or convention; may or may not be described in a published document. (EIPSC)

28. *Performance standard*: A standard that prescribes the acceptable functional or operational characteristics of a material, product, or system related to the circumstances of use to which the performance applies; includes or references the test methods by which these characteristics are measured. (EIPSC)

29. *Design standard*: A standard that describes how a required performance can be achieved by prescribing the physical or dimensional characteristics of a product, or system and its manufacture, construction, or fabrication; can describe a product that has been determined by product test to be in conformance with a prescribed set of performance standards. (EIPSC)

30. *Industry standard*: A standard developed and promulgated by representatives of an industry for materials and products related to that industry. An industry standard is generally oriented toward the industrial or institutional consumer and represents a consensus of the industry regarding the nomenclature, identification, standard sizing, and material, design, or performance specifications for materials and products of that industry. (EIPSC)

31. *Company standard*: A standard applicable to the design, manufacture, quality control, testing, installation, or servicing of products and services of a particular industrial organization. A company standard typically reflects implementation of industry or other standards and tends to be mandatory within the company; may be identified as an XYZ corporate standard, division standard, plant standard, manufacturing standard, and so on. (EIPSC)

32. *Proprietary standard*: A standard developed by a common-interest group and not generally promoted for use by the public. Company standards and many industry standards are generally considered to be proprietary standards. (EIPSC)

33. *Government standard*: A standard developed, adopted, or promulgated by a federal, state, or local government agency. A government standard is generally mandatory as applied to government procurements or when adopted as a code, regulation, or rule by a regulatory authority. (EIPSC)

34. *Federal standard*: A standard promulgated by the Federal Supply Service, General Services Administration, pursuant to the Federal Property Management Regulation 101-29.103 (41 C.F.R. 101-29.103) and applicable throughout the federal government. Federal standards provide standard data and test methods for reference in federal specifications and identify standard items for use in the Federal Supply Service. (EIPSC)

35. *Federal Information Processing Standard*: A standard developed by the National Institute of Standards and Technology, adopted and promulgated by the Department of Commerce, under the provisions of Public Law 89-306. Federal Information Processing Standards are applicable to federal information processing installations and government procurement of information processing equipment. They are generally mandatory in nature. (EIPSC)

36. *Military standard*: A mandatory standard developed and issued by the Department of Defense, used solely or predominantly for military activities. (EIPSC)

37. *Specification*: A set of conditions and requirements, of specific and limited application, that provides a detailed description of a procedure, process, material, product, or service for use primarily in procurement and manufacturing. Standards may be referenced or included in a specification. (EIPSC)

    Specification: A document prepared specifically to support acquisition that clearly and accurately describes the essential technical requirements for purchased material. Procedures necessary to determine that the requirements for the purchased material covered by the specification have been met shall also be included. (DOD)

38. *Technical specification*: Document that prescribes technical requirements to be fulfilled by a product, process, or service. (ISO)

39. *Federal specification*: A specification promulgated by the General Services Administration, Federal Supply Service, pursuant to Federal Property Management Regulation 101-29.103 (41 C.F.R. 101-29.103). It describes essential and technical requirements for items, materials, or services to be bought by the federal government. (EIPSC)

40. *Military specification*: A specification developed and issued by the Department of Defense and used solely or predominantly for military procurements and in Department of Defense contracts. (EIPSC)

41. *Code*: A collection of mandatory standards that has been codified by a governmental authority and thus has become part of the law for the jurisdiction represented by that authority. (EIPSC)

42. *Code of practice*: Document that recommends practices or procedures for the design, manufacture, installation, maintenance, or utilization of equipment, structures, or products. (ISO)

43. *Regulation*: Document providing binding legislative rules that is adopted by an authority. (ISO)

    Regulation: A standard or set of conditions and requirements that has been declared mandatory by a regulatory authority. (EIPSC)

44. *Model code*: A standard, a collection of standards, or another set of conditions and requirements that is recommended for adoption by regulatory authorities as a legal code. (EIPSC)

    Model code: A proposed code that is established within the procedural framework of a group of knowledgeable people and that is designed for adoption by governmental authority. (ASTM-E631)

45. *Superseded document*: A document that for new design of equipment is replaced by a new document or a revision to the existing document. It does not imply cancellation unless a specific notice of cancellation has been issued. (DOD)

TESTING AND CERTIFICATION

46. *Test*: Technical operation that consists of the determination of one or more characteristics of a given product, process, or service according to a specified procedure. (ISO)

    Testing: The determination, by technical means, of the properties, performance, or elements of materials, products, services, systems, or environments, which may involve application of established scientific principles and procedures. (ASTM-E699)

47. *Test method*: Specified technical procedure for performing a test. (ISO)

48. *Test report*: Document that presents test results and other information relevant to a test. (ISO)

49. *Interlaboratory test comparisons*: Organization, performance, and evaluation of tests on the same or similar items or materials by two or more laboratories in accordance with predetermined conditions. (ISO)

    NOTE: Specific, well-defined interlaboratory test comparisons are sometimes referred to as *round robin tests*. (OSCI)

50. *Proficiency testing*: Determination of laboratory testing performance by means of interlaboratory test comparisons. (ISO)

51. *Validation*: The process of determining the correctness of a standard as to its technical completeness and lack of ambiguity. (IEEE)

52. *Conformance*: The state of having satisfied the requirements of some specific standard(s) and/or specification(s). (IEEE)

    NOTE: *Conformance* is used with respect to voluntary standards and specifications, whereas *compliance* is used with respect to mandatory standards and regulations. (OSCI)

53. *Conformity*: Fulfillment by a product, process, or service of all requirements specified. (ISO)

54. *Verification*: The process of determining whether an implementation is in conformance with some specific standard(s) and/or specification(s). (IEEE)

55. *Compliance*: Adherence to rules, regulations, or other requirements. (IEEE) (See NOTE under *conformance*.)

56. *Certification*: The act of issuing a warranty, certificate, mark, or other appropriate evidence that attests that a product or service conforms to specific standards or specifications. (ILAC)

    Certification: The process by which recognition is obtained from an appropriate party that a product meets certain specified requirements. Prototypes or production models, or both, of the product(s) will have been tested and inspected to check that they do meet the requirements. Quality assurance programs are used to assure that the product(s) continue to comply with the specified requirements. Satisfactory tests, inspections, and quality assurance are the basis for certification. Certification may be evidenced by labeling of the product. (ASTM-E699)

Certification: The process of granting, by an authorized body, a statement of compliance, which may have legal ramifications, of some product(s), process(es), or service(s) to specific standard(s) or specification(s) requirements. (IEEE)

57. *Certification system*: System that has its own rules of procedure and management for carrying out certification of conformity. (ISO)

Certification system: The organizational and procedural process or the institutional mechanism for accomplishing product certification. (EIPSC)

58. *Certification scheme*: Certification system as related to specified products, processes, or services to which the same particular standards and rules, and the same procedure, apply. (ISO)

59. *Certification body*: Body that conducts certification of conformity. (ISO)

Certification body: An impartial body possessing the necessary competence and other qualifications to sponsor and operate a certification program. A certification body is that organization under whose authority a certification program is developed, promulgated, operated, and financed and with whose name the certification program is identified. (ANSI)

60. *Third-party certification*: A form of certification in which the producer's claim of conformity is validated (reviewed and verified) as part of a third-party certification program by a technically and otherwise competent body other than one controlled by the producer or the buyer. (ANSI)

61. *Self-certification*: A form of certification by a producer, on its own authority and not under the procedures of a third-party certification program, that a product or service is in compliance (conformity) with the designated standards or specifications. (ANSI)

62. *Certificate of conformity*: Document issued under the rules of a certification system indicating that adequate confidence is provided that a duly identified product, process, or service is in conformity with a specific standard or other normative document. (ISO)

Certificate of conformity: A tag, label, nameplate, or document of specified form and content, affixed or otherwise directly associated with a product or service on delivery to the buyer, attesting that the product or service is in conformity with the referenced standards or specifications. (ANSI)

63. *Mark of conformity*: Protected mark, applied or issued under the rules of a certification system, indicating that adequate confidence is provided that the relevant product, process, or service is in conformity with a specific standard or other normative document. (ISO)

    Mark of conformity: The sign or symbol owned or controlled by the certification body that is used exclusively by the third-party certification program to identify products or services as being certified and that is registered as a certification mark with the U.S. Patent Office under the Trade Mark Act of 1946. (ANSI)

64. *Certification mark*: A symbol, logo, hallmark, or other informative device adopted and authorized by a certification agency and affixed to a product to indicate that it conforms to or complies with the applicable or specified provisions of referenced standards, codes, or other requirements. (EIPSC)

65. *Certification label*: A symbol, certification mark, or other controlled mark or informative device affixed to a product to indicate that it conforms to or complies with the applicable or specified provisions of referenced standards, codes, or other requirements. The label may also indicate that a product has been approved by a specified organization or certification agency, that it has been tested and found to conform to or comply with the applicable requirements by an identified test facility, and/or that it is under the test and surveillance procedures of a specified certification system. (EIPSC)

66. *Approved product*: A product that has been inspected, evaluated, tested, or otherwise determined to be in conformance or compliance with applicable or specified provisions of referenced standards, codes, or other requirements and approved by an organizational entity for its own procurement or purposes or approved by a regulatory authority or governmental body for use within its realm of authority or approved by a third-party organization for use by other organizations. (EIPSC)

67. *Certified product*: A product that has been inspected, evaluated, tested, or otherwise determined to be in conformance or compliance with applicable or specified provisions of referenced standards, codes, or other requirements and certified by an authority that is recognized or that has the legal power to grant such certification. Certified products imply a guarantee or warranty of product conformance and the fact that

the product is under the test and surveillance procedures of a specified certification system. (NVLAP)

68. *Qualified product*: A product that has been inspected, evaluated, tested, or otherwise determined to be in conformance with applicable or specified provisions of referenced standards, codes, or other requirements and approved for listing in a qualified product list (QPL). (EIPSC)

69. *Qualified products list*: A list of products that have met the qualification requirements stated in the applicable specification, including appropriate product identification and test or qualification reference with the name and plant address of the manufacturer and distributor, as applicable. QPL is the accepted abbreviation for the term *qualified product list*. (DOD)

70. *Pattern evaluation*: The examination of one or more measuring instruments of the same pattern that are submitted by a manufacturer to the national service of legal metrology; this examination includes the tests necessary for the approval of the pattern. (OIML)

NOTE: *Pattern evaluation* is also referred to as *type evaluation*. (OSCI)

71. *Pattern approval*: A decision taken by a competent state authority, generally the national service of legal metrology, recognizing that the pattern of a measuring instrument conforms to the mandatory requirements. (OIML)

NOTE: *Pattern approval* is also referred to as *type approval*. (OSCI)

72. *Provisional pattern approval*: An approval, for a limited period, of a pattern of a measuring instrument to allow comprehensive and prolonged tests, under the normal conditions of use, of a sufficiently large number of instruments conforming to the pattern. (OIML)

NOTE: The decision of approval can, if necessary, prescribe the number of instruments to be constructed, their place of installation, and the verification accessories with which the instruments must be provided. (OIML)

73. *National type evaluation program*: A program of cooperation between the National Bureau of Standards, the National Conference on Weights and Measures, the states, and the private sector for determining, on a uniform basis, conformance of a type (of a measuring instrument) with the relevant provisions of National Bureau of Standards Handbook 44,

Specifications, Tolerances, and Other Technical Requirements for Weighing and Measuring Devices; and National Bureau of Standards Handbooks 105-1, 105-2, and 105-3, pertaining to reference standards and field standards used in weighing and measuring programs. (NTEP)

74. *Type*: A model or models of a particular measurement system, instrument, and element, or a field standard that positively identifies the design. A specific type may vary in its measurement ranges, size, performance, and operating characteristics as specified in the Certificate of Conformance. (NTEP)

LABORATORY ACCREDITATION

75. *Laboratory accreditation*: Formal recognition that a testing laboratory is competent to carry out specific tests or specific types of tests. (ISO)

    NOTE: The term *laboratory accreditation* may cover the recognition of both the technical competence and the impartiality of a testing laboratory or only its technical competence. Accreditation is normally awarded following successful laboratory assessment and is followed by appropriate surveillance. (ISO)

    Laboratory accreditation: A formal determination and recognition that a laboratory has the capability to carry out specific tests or types of tests. (ILAC)

    Laboratory accreditation: A formal determination and recognition that a laboratory has the capability to carry out a specific test(s) in accordance with a prescribed procedure(s). (NVLAP)

76. *Laboratory accreditation system*: System that has its own rules of procedure and management for carrying out laboratory accreditation. (ISO)

    Laboratory accreditation system: A system having its own rules of procedure for evaluating, judging, and recognizing testing laboratories that have demonstrated a competency to conduct specific tests. Such systems include (1) initial assessment of all aspects of laboratory management and operation by panels of expert assessors, (2) reassessment at prescribed intervals, and (3) proficiency testing programs on a regular basis. (ILAC-2)

77. *Laboratory accreditation body*: Body that conducts and administers a laboratory accreditation system and grants accreditation. (ISO)

NOTE: An accreditation body may wish to delegate fully or partially the assessment of a testing laboratory to another competent body (assessment agency). While it is recognized that this may be a practical solution to extending recognition of testing laboratories, it is essential that such assessment be equivalent to that applied by the accreditation body and that the accreditation body take full responsibility for such extended accreditation. (ISO)

78. *Laboratory accreditation agency (authority)*: An organization that conducts and administers an accreditation system to evaluate, judge, and convey in an appropriate manner that testing laboratories are competent to conduct specific tests. (NVLAP)

79. *Laboratory accreditation administrator*: A person or an organization that performs the executive duties required to manage a laboratory accreditation program. (NVLAP)

80. *Laboratory evaluation (assessment)*: Examination of a testing laboratory to evaluate its compliance with specific laboratory accreditation criteria. (ISO)

    Laboratory evaluation (assessment): The decision-making process, using information from laboratory examinations, whereby a laboratory's testing capability is assessed for conformance with general and specific criteria. Laboratory evaluation may be a basis for accreditation. (NVLAP)

81. *Laboratory evaluator (assessor)*: Person who carries out some or all functions related to laboratory assessment. (ISO)

    Laboratory evaluator (assessor): An individual of recognized professional competence and impartiality who assesses personnel, physical resources, testing procedures, and the quality assurance program of a laboratory to determine its compliance with specific laboratory accreditation criteria or requirements. (ILAC)

82. *Laboratory evaluation criteria*: Statements prescribing the organizational and technical resources, the equipment and facilities, the operational procedures, and the minimum technical, managerial, and ethical performance levels usually required of a testing laboratory for accreditation purposes. (NVLAP)

83. *Laboratory evaluation methodology*: Statements prescribing the process or procedures by which the organizational and technical resources of a test facility shall be examined and reported to an accreditation agency for a specific product test. (EIPSC)

84. *Monitoring*: The act of periodically observing or reviewing the functioning and proficiency of a laboratory or a certification program. (NVLAP)

85. *Evaluating*: The function of obtaining data developed by a testing agency and utilizing such data to perform calculations, determine suitability, project results, or otherwise draw conclusions resulting from an analysis of these data. (ASTM-E699)

QUALITY CONTROL

86. *Quality*: The totality of features and characteristics of a product or service that bear on its ability to satisfy given needs. (ASQC)

87. *Quality assurance*: A planned system of activities whose purpose is to provide assurance that the overall quality control program (see *quality control*) is in fact being effectively implemented. This system involves a continuing evaluation of the adequacy and effectiveness of the overall quality control program with a view to having corrective action initiated where necessary. For a specific material, product, or service, this involves verification, audits, and evaluations of the quality factors that affect the specification, production, inspection, and use of the material product, service, system, or environment. (ASTM-E699)

    Quality assurance: All those planned or systematic actions necessary to provide adequate confidence that a product or service will satisfy given needs. (ASQC)

88. *Quality control*: A planned system of activities whose purpose is to provide a level of quality that meets the needs of users; also, the use of such a system. The objective of quality control is to provide an overall system integrating the quality factors of several related steps including the proper specification for what is wanted, production to meet the full intent of the specification, inspection to determine whether the resulting material, product, or service is in accordance with the specification, and review of usage to determine necessary revisions of the specification. (ASTM-E699)

89. *Approved quality control program*: A quality control program that has been approved by a regulatory authority, a certification agency, or another user and accepted as fulfilling user needs for product conformance testing for a specific product. In addition to specifying requirements for the inspection, evaluation, or testing of a product, an approved quality control program may include requirements for the

maintenance, availability, or submission of quality control records and may prescribe specific sampling plans and procedures. (EIPSC)

90. *Product qualification testing*: The initial product test and analysis of a new product design or modification of a product design. Product qualification tests are the basis for the initial acceptance of a product as an approved or accepted product, approval as a certified product, or listing as a qualified product in a qualified product list (QPL) or as a product that has been granted type approval. (NVLAP)

91. *Inspection*: The process of measuring, examining, testing, gauging or otherwise comparing the unit with the applicable requirements. (ASQC)

    NOTE: The term *requirements* sometimes is used broadly to include standards of good workmanship. (ASQC)

92. *Recognition arrangement*: Agreement that is based on the acceptance by one party of results, presented by another party, from the implementation of one or more designated functional elements of a *certification system*. (ISO)

    NOTE: Typical examples of *recognition arrangements* are testing arrangements, inspection arrangements, and certification arrangements. (ISO)

    Recognition arrangement: A formal written agreement between two (or more) parties (e.g., companies, organizations, or national governments) to accept test data, the determination of product conformance to standards, product certification results, and/or the accreditation of laboratories to perform specific tests and issue certification certificates. (OSCI)

93. *Unilateral arrangement*: Recognition arrangement that covers the acceptance of one party's results by another party. (ISO)

94. *Bilateral arrangement*: Recognition arrangement that covers the acceptance of each other's results by two parties. (ISO)

95. *Multilateral arrangement*: Recognition arrangement that covers the acceptance of each other's results by more than two parties. (ISO)

INFORMATION TECHNOLOGY

96. *OSI*: Open systems interconnection standards, of the International Organization for Standardization, ISO. (ARIST)

97. *COS*: Corporation for Open Systems.

98. *MAP*: Manufacturing automation protocol.

99. *TOP*: Technical and office protocol.

100. *GOSIP*: Government open systems interface profile.

101. *ISDN*: Integrated services digital network, standards of the International Telegraph and Telephone Consultative Committee, CCITT. (ARIST). For related equipment standards, contact BELLCORE, BELL COMMUNICATIONS RESEARCH, in New Jersey, (201) 829-2000.

102. *ISP*: International standardized profiles.

103. *ODA*: Office documentation architecture, standards of the ISO. (ARIST)

104. *ODIF*: Office documentation information format.

105. *ISA*: Industry standard architecture, as in a computer bus. (ARIST)

106. *EDI*: Electronic data interchange. (ARIST)

107. *GUI*: Graphical user interchange. (ARIST)

108. *GKS*: Graphical kernel system. (ARIST)

109. *SQL*: Structured query language. (ARIST)

110. *ODS*: Open distributed processing. (ARIST)

111. *SGML*: Standard generalized markup language. (ARIST)

112. *IRDS*: Information resource directory standard. (ARIST)

113. *MOTIS*: Message-oriented text interchange service. (ARIST)

114. *CALS*: Computer-aided acquisitions and logistical support, program of the U.S. Department of Defense, DOD. (DOD)

115. *APPLE*: Apple Computer, Inc., a large manufacturer of smaller computers, including Apple, Lisa, and MacIntosh.

116. *ASCII*: American national standard code for information interchange, developed in the 1960s with U.S. government encouragement.

117. *CP/M*: A trademark of Digital Research, Inc., for a control program for microprocessors.

118. *DOS*: Disk operating system, developed by International Business Machines (IBM), Inc., for the operation of mainframe computers. Two later uses of the system came with the development by Microsoft Corporation of Microsoft DOS, commonly referred to as MS-DOS, or sometimes PC-DOS, since it is an operating system for personal computers.

ARCHIVES AND MANUSCRIPTS

119. *USMARC AMC*: United States machine-readable catalog format for archival and manuscripts control.

120. *AMC*: Archival and manuscripts control format. See USMARC AMC.

121. *MARC*: Machine-readable cataloging format. See USMARC AMC.

122. *MARBI*: Machine-readable form of bibliographic information.

123. *OCLC*: Online computer library center.

124. *APPM*: Archives, personal papers, and manuscripts.

NOTE: See Steven L. Hensen, *Archives, Personal Papers and Manuscripts: A Cataloging Manual for Archival Repositories, Historical Societies, and Manuscript Libraries,* 2nd ed. (Chicago: Society of American Archivists, 1989).

125. *AACR2*: Anglo-American cataloging rules, second edition.

126. *NUCMC*: National Union Catalog of manuscript collections.

Annotated Standards Bibliography for North America

STEVEN M. SPIVAK, UNIVERSITY OF MARYLAND
KEITH A. WINSELL, AMISTAD RESEARCH CENTER, TULANE UNIVERSITY

INTRODUCTORY ESSAY

John L. Donaldson, Standards Code and Information, National Institute of Standards and Technology

For many readers, a sourcebook presents an opportunity to end the search for the answer to some query. For others, it presents a place to start. The information gained in consulting a sourcebook can succeed in raising as many questions as it answers. To continue the pursuit requires knowledge of other source material. It is fitting therefore that this book should conclude with a comprehensive bibliography, which permits the serious reader to explore further the many facets of the subject of standards and their use. The bibliography that follows has been compiled so that any and all such facets of standards are covered. This is a complete standards bibliography.

In compiling the bibliography, its producers organized it for ease in reference and created a taxonomy that includes many useful headings. Of particular interest will be the references under "Regional and International Standardization," a subject of considerable current attention in view of the rapid rate of marketplace globalization. This section includes citations under "Trade and Commerce" that are equally pertinent. When considering commerce, the reader might also find the section, "Weights and Measures," worth consulting; all of commerce is subject to the standards and specifications governing commercial transactions. Of course, it is the consumer who is ultimately affected by these considerations. The consumer's perspective of these standards and, indeed, all types of standards – their development and use – is covered by the titles to be found under "Consumer

Representation, Consumer Interests." The public's interest is well served by the many sources identified under these various headings.

The background and development of standards are well documented under several headings. The listings under "Historical References" and "General Sources" provide ample opportunity for delving into the evolution and general nature of the subject, while titles found under "Standards Information," "Product Standards and Implications," and "Company Standardization" enable the reader to pursue the subject of standards per se. These sections, together with "Standards Guidelines, Procedures, Format," encompass much of the traditional literature and the focus of much of the documentation in the past. Of increasing interest recently, the *application* of standards is receiving more attention. The titles included under "Certification of Products Standardization, Testing and Certification" and "Laboratory Accreditation" indicate the availability of considerable documentation on conformity assessment and attestation of products' conformance to standards. Related to conformity assessment is the mandatory use of standards in complying with legal requirements; in "Regulatory Use of Standards," the reader can find citations of sources of information on mandatory standards or technical regulations. Besides using standards in this way, government is also a principal institutional user for purchasing goods and services; "Federal Procurement and Defense Standardization" covers this topic.

The consequences of the development and use of standards have been studied by many different parties but probably most often by those concerned with economic and legal implications. This literature is identified under "Economic Aspects of Standardization, Including Trade Issues" and "Legal Aspects of Standardization." Finally, whenever the implications of standardization are considered, the question of modifying the system is raised. The important writing on this subject is cited under "Reform of the Standards System/Future of Standardization." The reader reaching this point has learned to understand the system and is therefore ready to contemplate its modification; the sources cited in the last named section reflect this perspective.

A careful review of the contents of the bibliography will reveal that not all standardization subjects have received a great deal of attention. Some subjects need more study; they are sparsely represented in the bibliography, not because its producers overlooked references but because these are difficult topics and much more work is needed. One such area is the economic aspects of standardization. The benefits of participating in the development of standards is a major issue, but more research is needed before it is sufficiently well addressed to enable reasoned corporate decision making. The reader can form other observations from spending some time with the bibliography. Few of the authors cited are from the academic community; with the exception of one of the editors of this book, most educators have avoided standardization – that is, the process of development and use of standards – as a field of research and academic inquiry. Related to this is the small number of publications available that can serve as textbooks. Standards education needs more attention. The extent to which this bibliography enables research and academic progress will be a measure of its value. We in the field are grateful for its existence and potential contribution.

ABOUT THE BIBLIOGRAPHY

The books, monographs, reports, and other references collected here represent various aspects of standardization in the larger sense. The uniqueness of this offering is that not only is the selected bibliography organized by subject index, but also descriptive annotations accompany most citations. Following the brief descriptions collected by *subjects*, there is an *alphabetical* listing by author of all references, with complete citation, annotated comments or abstract, and keywords where available.

This annotated bibliography expands earlier standards bibliographies prepared by Drs. Spivak and Winsell using reference lists and bibliographies of Walter Cropper and Robert Toth; Maureen Breitenberg, Carol Chapman Rawie, Stephen Weber, Barbara Cassard, and others of the National Institute of Standards and Technology; and other annotations and publications. The assistance and contributions from these and other workers are gratefully acknowledged. The present work is not intended to replace but to expand and to supplement these and other very useful bibliographic works and information sources.

We will undoubtedly have missed some publications that are worthy of inclusion here, and we regret any omissions. The editors welcome information on citations or major works that should be included in a later edition of this book.

The various citations are organized into 16 separate subject categories to assist the reader in finding specific items of interest:

1. General Sources (Principles and Practices).

2. Standards Information (Bibliographies, Indexes, Databases, Directories, Catalogs).

3. Historical References (prior to 1970).

4. Standards Guidelines, Procedures, Format.

5. Certification of Products Standardization, Testing and Certification.

6. Laboratory Accreditation.

7. Weights and Measures.

8. Regulatory Use of Standards (Safety, Environment).

9. Economic Aspects of Standardization, Including Trade Issues.

10. Legal Aspects of Standardization (Due Process, Restraint of Trade, Authority and Responsibility, Liability).

11. Reform of the Standards System/Future of Standardization.

12. Regional and International Standardization (Germane to North America), Including Trade and Commerce.

13. Product Standards and Implications.

14. Company Standardization.

15. Federal Procurement and Defense Standardization.

16. Consumer Representation, Consumer Interests.

The selected readings are primarily books and monographs, reports, major collections, and information sources. The other major sources, periodical-journal articles, are cited in other indexes. With few exceptions, articles from periodicals are *not* included because of coverage elsewhere and the more general nature of this bibliography. A separate bibliography, and literature review, covering library and information services, is found in the earlier essay by Keith Winsell, "An Introduction to Library and Information Services Technical Standards Literature."

Note that the National Bureau of Standards (NBS) of the U.S. Department of Commerce has been renamed the National Institute of Standards and Technology (NIST). For better recognition, many citations continue to be shown as published under the former NBS moniker, except for recent publications now carrying the NIST imprimatur.

The editors wish to thank Alice O'Dea for assistance in preparing the bibliographic portions of the manuscript.

The annotations and many additional citations were originally developed by Dr. Keith Winsell under the overall direction of Dr. Spivak. This work was funded in part by an instructional improvement grant from the University of Maryland.

BIBLIOGRAPHY TOPICS

General Sources (Principles and Practices)

American Society for Testing and Materials, *Standards Make the Pieces Fit*, n.d.

Batik, Albert L., *A Guide to Standards*, 1989.

Breitenberg, Maureen A., *The ABC's of Certification Activities in the United States*, 1988.

Breitenberg, Maureen A., *The ABC's of Standards-Related Activities in the United States*, 1987.

Canadian Manufacturers Association, *Standards in Manufacturing: A Shifting Focus in the 80s*, 1981.

Cargill, Carl F., *A Guide to Information Technology Standardization: Theory, Organization, and Process*, 1988.

Cerni, Dorothy M., *Standards in Process: Foundations and Profiles of ISDN and OSI Studies*, 1984.

Congressional Research Service, *Voluntary Industrial Standards in the United States*, 1974.

Crawford, Walt, *Technical Standards: An Introduction for Librarians*, 1986. 2nd edition, 1991.

Glie, Rowen, ed., *Speaking of Standards*, 1972.

Grogan, Denis, *Science and Technology, An Introduction to the Literature*, 1973.

International Federation for the Application of Standards (IFAN), *Applying the World's Standards: Conference Papers*, 1986.

Interrante, C. G., and F. J. Heymann, eds., *Standardization of Technical Terminology: Principles and Practices*, 1983.

Legget, Robert F., *Standards in Canada*, 1970.

Preston, R. P., ed., *Putting Standards to Work*, 1977.

Preston, R. P., *Standardization Is Good Business*, 1977.

Sanders, T. R. B., *The Aims and Principles of Standardization*, 1972.

Standards Engineering Society (SES), *Proceedings of the 36th Annual Conference*, 1987, and other annual proceedings.

Sullivan, Charles D., *Standards and Standardization, Basic Principles and Applications*, 1983.

Verman, Lal C., *Standardization: A New Discipline*, 1973.

Standards Information (Bibliographies, Indexes, Databases, Directories, Catalogs)

American National Standards Institute, *Catalog of American National Standards*, annual.

American Society for Testing and Materials (ASTM), *ICPS Bulletin*, serial.

Breden, Leslie H., ed., *World Index of Plastics Standards*, 1971.

Breitenberg, Maureen A., ed., *Directory of International and Regional Organizations Conducting Standards-Related Activities*, 1989.

Chapman, Carol A., *Bibliography on the Voluntary Standards System and Product Certification*, 1979.

Department of Defense, *DoD Index of Specifications and Standards, DoDISS*, annual with periodic updates.

Folts, Harold C., ed., *McGraw-Hill's Compilation of Data Communications Standards, Including the Omnicom Index of Standards*, 1986.

Global Engineering Documents, *Directory of Engineering Document Sources*, 1986.

Grossnickle, Linda L., ed., *An Index of State Specifications and Standards*, 1973.

Houghton, Bernard, *Technical Information Sources: A Guide to Patent Specification, Standards and Technical Reports Literature*, 1972.

Information Handling Services, *The BRS Database for Industry and International Standards*, 1988, annual.

Information Handling Services, *The BRS Database for Military and Federal Specifications and Standards*, 1988, annual.

Information Handling Services, *Index and Directory of U.S. Industry Standards*, 1988, 2 vols., annual.

International Organization for Standardization (ISO), *KWIC Index of International Standards*, 1983 and thereafter.

National Bureau of Standards, *Publications of the Office of Product Standards Policy, Fiscal Years 1982-1985,* October 1985.

National Bureau of Standards, Institute for Computer Sciences and Technology, *Federal Information Processing Standards Publications (FIPS PUBS Index),* February 1984, updated periodically.

National Bureau of Standards, National Center for Standards and Certification Information, *Key-Word-in-Context (KWIC) Index of U.S. Voluntary Engineering Standards,* January 1986. (See citations under Slattery, William J., as well).

National Computer Graphics Association, *Standards in the Computer Graphics Industry,* 1986.

Omnicom, *The Omnicom Index of Standards,* for Distributed Information and Telecommunication Systems, 1987.

Ricci, Patricia, and Linda Perry, *Standards: Resource and Guide for Identification, Selection, and Acquisition,* 1991.

Slattery, William J., *Index of U.S. Nuclear Standards,* 1977.

Slattery, William J., *Tabulation of Voluntary Standards and Certification Programs for Consumer Products,* 1977.

Standards Council of Canada (SCC), *Directory and Index of Standards,* 1990, annual.

Standards Council of Canada, *Technical Information Centre Inventory,* Standards Information Division, 1990.

Standards Engineering Society, *Standards Engineering: Index (December 1961-April 1985),* 1985.

Toth, Robert B., ed., *Standards Activities of Organizations in the United States,* 1991, 2d rev. ed.

Historical References Prior to 1970

Association Francais de Normalisation (AFNOR), *La Normalisation dans L' Enterprise,* 1967.

Booth, Sherman F., *Standardization Activities in the United States,* 1960.

Brady, Robert A., *Industrial Standardization,* 1929.

Brady, Robert A., *Organization, Automation, and Society,* 1963.

Cochrane, Rexmond C., *Measures for Progress: A History of the National Bureau of Standards*, 1974.

Coles, Jessie V., *Standards and Labels for Consumers' Goods*, 1949.

Congressional Research Service, *Voluntary Industrial Standards in the United States*, 1974.

Edwards, Alice L., *Product Standards and Labelling for Consumers*, 1940.

Gaillard, John, *Industrial Standardization: Its Principles and Application*, 1934.

Gaillard, John, *A Study of the Fundamentals of Industrial Standardization and Its Practical Application, Especially in the Mechanical Field*, 1933.

Harriman, Norman F., *Standards and Standardization*, 1928.

Lansburgh, Richard H., ed., *Standards in Industry*, 1928.

LaQue, Francis L., *Report of the Panel on Engineering and Commodity Standards of the Commerce Technical Advisory Board*, 1965.

Martino, Robert A., *Standardization Activities of National Technical and Trade Organizations*, 1941.

Melnitsky, Benjamin, *Profiting from Industrial Standardization*, 1953.

National Bureau of Standards, *Report of the Panel on Engineering and Commodity Standards of the Commerce Technical Advisory Board*, 1965.

Perry, John, *The Story of Standards*, 1955.

Reck, Dickson, ed., *National Standards in a Modern Economy*, 1956.

Slattery, William J., *An Index of U.S. Voluntary Engineering Standards*, 1971.

Snider, Hazel S., *American Standards Association: Its Functions, History, and Relation to the Department of Commerce and the National Bureau of Standards*, 1958.

Struglia, Erasmus J., *Standards and Specifications, Information Sources*, 1965.

Struglia, Erasmus J., et al., *Standards and the Consumer*, 1964.

Suzuki, George, chairman and ed., *Report of the Voluntary Standardization Policy Study Group*, 1970.

Woodward, C. Douglas, ed., *Standards for Industry*, 1965.

Standards Guidelines, Procedures, Format

American National Standards Institute, *Procedures for the Development and Coordination of American National Standards*, 1987.

American Society for Testing and Materials (ASTM), *Form and Style for ASTM Standards*, 8th ed., 1989.

Mackay, Donald R., coordinator, *Guidelines for NBS Standards Committee Participants*, 1984.

Spivak, Steven M., *Implementation of OMB Circular A-119: An Independent Appraisal of Federal Participation in the Development and Use of Voluntary Standards*, 1985.

Swankin, David, A., *How Due Process in the Development of Voluntary Standards Can Reduce the Risk of Anti-Trust Liability*, 1990.

Swankin, David A., *Rationale Statements for Voluntary Standards – Issues, Techniques, and Consequences*, 1981.

Certification of Products Standardization, Testing and Certification

American National Standards Institute, *ANSI Global Standardization Report*, vol. 3, 1990.

American Society for Testing and Materials, *1990 ASTM Directory of Testing Laboratories*, 1990.

Breitenberg, Maureen A., *Directory of Federal Government Certification Programs*, 1988.

Breitenberg, Maureen A., *Directory of U.S. Private Sector Certification Programs*, 1989.

Chapman, Carol A., *Bibliography on the Voluntary Standards System and Product Certification*, 1979.

Federal Trade Commission, *Standards and Certification: Final Staff Report*, 1983.

Federal Trade Commission, *Standards and Certification: Report of the Presiding Officer on Proposed Trade Regulation Rule*, 1983.

Preiser, H. Steffen, and Robert S. Marvin, *Testing and Certification for Export Products in Industrializing Countries*, 1976.

Rawie, Carol Chapman, *Economics of the Product Certification Industry: Some Research Needs*, 1980.

Rawie, Carol Chapman, *A Guide to Papers Citing Antitrust Cases Involving Standards or Certification*, 1979.

Toth, Robert B., ed., *Federal Government Certification Programs for Products and Services*, 1986.

Laboratory Accreditation

American Association for Laboratory Accreditation (A2LA), *Directory of Accredited Laboratories*, and A2LA *Annual Report*, both annual.

Breitenberg, Maureen A., ed., *Directory of Federal Government Laboratory Accreditation/Designation Programs*, 1991.

Hyer, Charles W., *Principal Aspects of U.S. Laboratory Accreditation Systems*, 1984, new edition expected 1991.

International Laboratory Accreditation Conference (ILAC), the ILAC *International Directory of Accreditation Systems and Other Schemes for Assessment of Testing Laboratories*, 1990.

Locke, John W., ed., *Laboratory Accreditation: Future Directions in the United States, Proceedings of a Workshop Held at the National Bureau of Standards*, 1981.

Shock, Harvey, ed., *Accreditation Practices for Inspections, Tests and Laboratories*, 1989.

Shock, Harvey, ed., *Evaluation and Accreditation of Inspection and Test Activities*, 1983.

Standards Council of Canada, *Directory of Accredited Laboratories*, 1989, annual.

Standards Council of Canada, *Directory of Accredited Testing Organizations*, 1989, annual.

Trahey, Nancy M., Jeffrey Horlick, and Vanda R. White, *1990 Directory of National Voluntary Laboratory Accreditation Program (NVLAP) Accredited Laboratories*, 1990.

Weights and Measures

Ambler, Ernest, et al., *A Record of the Papers Presented at the Conference of Standards, Measurements, Quality Control and Production for Economic Support and Growth, Held in Cairo, Egypt,* 1983.

Brickenkamp, Carroll S., and Joan Koenig, eds., *Uniform Laws and Regulations in the Area of Legal Metrology and Motor Fuel Quality,* 1990, annual.

Cochrane, Rexmond C., *Measures for Progress: A History of the National Bureau of Standards,* 1974.

Oppermann, Henry V., ed., *Specifications, Tolerances, and Other Technical Requirements for Weighing and Measuring Devices,* 1990, annual.

Page, Chester H., and Paul Vigoureau, eds., *The International Bureau of Weights and Measures 1875-1975,* 1975.

Tholen, Albert, Carroll S. Brinkenkemp, and Ann Heffernan-Turner, eds., *Report of the 74th National Conference on Weights and Measures,* 1989, annual.

Regulatory Use of Standards (Safety, Environment)

Administrative Conference of the United States, *Guidebook Series on Alternative Regulatory Approaches,* 1981.

American Society for Testing and Materials, *ASTM and the OMB Circular A-119,* 1983.

Breitenberg, Maureen A., *Need for Economic Information on Standards Used in Regulatory Programs: Problems and Recommendations,* 1980.

Hamilton, Robert W., *The Role of Nongovernmental Standards in the Development of Mandatory Federal Standards Affecting Safety or Health,* 1978.

Harter, Philip J., *Regulatory Use of Standards: The Implications for Standards Writers,* 1979.

Settle, Russell Franklin, and Burton A. Weisbrod, *Governmentally-Imposed Standards: Some Normative and Positive Aspects,* 1976.

Spivak, Steven M., *Implementation of OMB Circular A-119: An Independent Appraisal of Federal Participation in the Development and Use of Voluntary Standards,* 1985.

Steiner, Bruce W., *An Institutional Plan for Developing National Standards with Special Reference to Environment, Safety and Health*, 1979.

Troy, Terrance N., *A Survey of Standards Activities of the U.S. Department of Energy*, 1982.

Economic Aspects of Standardization, Including Trade Issues

Breitenberg, Maureen A., *Need for Economic Information on Standards Used in Regulatory Programs: Problems and Recommendations*, 1980.

Dalton, James A., Peter Ashton, and Frank C. Graves, *The Impact of Private Voluntary Standards on Industrial Innovation*, vol. 1, 1982.

Fahnestock, Brian E., *Application of Cost/Benefit Analysis in the Development of Voluntary Standards*, 1986.

Faucett, Jack, Associates, *Principles and Practical Approaches for Evaluating International Standards*, 1975.

Hemenway, David, *Industrywide Voluntary Product Standards*, 1975.

International Organization for Standardization (ISO), *Benefits of Standardization*, 1982.

Johnson, Leland L., *Cost-Benefit Analysis and Voluntary Safety Standards for Consumer Products*, 1982.

Poulson, Barry W., ed., *Economic Analysis of the National Measurement System*, 1977.

Rawie, Carol Chapman, *Economics of the Product Certification Industry: Some Research Needs*, 1980.

Silberston, Aubrey, *The Economic Consequences of International Standardization*, 1967.

Toth, Robert B., ed., *The Economics of Standardization*, 1984.

Weber, Stephen F., and Barbara C. Cassard, *Economics Applied to Standards: A Guide to the Literature*, 1980.

Legal Aspects of Standardization (Due Process, Restraint of Trade, Authority and Responsibility, Liability)

American National Standards Institute, *Standards and the Law*, 1984.

Federal Trade Commission, *Standards and Certification: Final Staff Report*, 1983.

Federal Trade Commission, *Standards and Certification: Report of the Presiding Officer on Proposed Trade Regulation Rule,* 1983.

Hamilton, Robert W., *The Role of Nongovernmental Standards in the Development and Review of Mandatory Federal Standards Affecting Safety and Health,* 1978.

Harter, Philip J., *Regulatory Use of Standards: The Implications for Standards Writers,* 1979.

Rawie, Carol Chapman, *A Guide to Papers Citing Antitrust Cases Involving Standards of Certification,* 1979.

Reck, Dickson, ed., *National Standards in a Modern Economy,* 1956.

Swankin, David A., *How Due Process in the Development of Voluntary Standards Can Reduce the Risk of Anti-Trust Liability,* 1990.

Swankin, David A., *Rationale Statements for Voluntary Standards – Issues, Techniques, and Consequences,* 1981.

U.S. Congress, House, *The Effect upon Small Business of Voluntary Industrial Standards,* 90th Congress, 1968.

U.S. Congress, Senate, *Voluntary Industrial Standards,* 94th and 95th Congresses, 1976, 1977.

Reform of the Standards System/Future of Standardization

American Society for Testing and Materials (ASTM), *The Voluntary Standards System of the United States of America,* 1975.

Batik, Albert L., *A Guide to Standards,* 1989.

Hamilton, Robert W., *The Role of Nongovernmental Standards in the Development and Review of Mandatory Federal Standards Affecting Safety and Health,* 1978.

Harter, Philip J., *Regulatory Use of Standards: The Implications for Standards Writers,* 1979.

Locke, John W., ed., *Laboratory Accreditation: Future Directions in the United States, Proceedings of a Workshop Held at the National Bureau of Standards,* 1981.

National Bureau of Standards, *Report of the Panel on Engineering and Commodity Standards of the Commerce Technical Advisory Board,* 1965.

Spivak, Steven M., *Implementation of OMB Circular A-119: An Independent Appraisal of Federal Participation in the Development and Use of Voluntary Standards*, 1985.

Regional and International Standardization (Germane to North America), Including Trade and Commerce

American National Standards Institute, *ANSI Global Standardization Report*, vols. 1, 2, 3, 1989-1990.

American National Standards Institute, *Directory of International and Regional Standards Organizations*, 1982.

American National Standards Institute, *Standardization in the 90s: Success in a Global Market*, proceedings of public conference, 1990.

American National Standards Institute, *Voluntary (Private-Sector) Standards Programs and the GATT Code*, 1977.

Breitenberg, Maureen A., *Directory of International and Regional Organizations Conducting Standards-Related Activities*, 1989.

Cooke, Patrick W., *Benefits Perceived by U.S. Industry from Participating in International Standards Activities*, 1984.

Cooke, Patrick W., *A Review of U.S. Participation in International Standards Activities*, 1988.

Cooke, Patrick W., *A Summary of the New European Community Approach to Standards Development*, 1988.

Cooke, Patrick W., *An Update of U.S. Participation in International Standards Activities*, 1989.

Hemenway, David, *Standards Systems in Canada, the UK, West Germany, and Denmark: An Overview*, 1979.

International Federation for the Application of Standards (IFAN), *Applying the World's Standards: Conference Papers*, 1986.

International Laboratory Accreditation Conference, (ILAC), *International Directory of Laboratory Accreditation, Systems and Other Schemes for Assessment of Testing Laboratories*, 1990.

Leight, Walter G., ed., *Proceedings of Conference on Standards and Trade*, 1987.

Office of U.S. Trade Representative (USOTR), *Second Triennial Report to the Congress on the Agreement on Technical Barriers to Trade*, 1986.

Overman, JoAnne R., *1987 GATT Notification Activities*, 1987, annual.

Phucas, Charles B., *International Standards Activities: A Study of NBS Impact on International Standards Committee Activities*, 1975.

Phucas, Charles B., ed., *Symposium on International Standards Information and ISONET*, 1980.

Silva, Michael, and Bertil Sjögren, *Europe 1992 and the New World Power Game*, 1990.

Troy, Terrance N., *Barriers Encountered by U.S. Exporters of Telecommunications Equipment*, 1987.

Product Standards and Implications

American National Standards Institute, *ANSI Guide for Developing User Product Information*, 1990.

Breden, Leslie H., ed., *World Index of Plastics Standards*, 1971.

Bureau of Medical Devices, U.S. Department of Health, Education and Welfare (new Health and Human Services), *Bureau of Medical Devices Standards Survey*, 1979, national and international eds.

Cargill, Carl F., *Information Technology Standardization: Theory, Process, and Organization*, 1989.

Cerni, Dorothy M., *Standards in Process: Foundations and Profiles of ISDN and OSI Studies*, 1984.

DeChiara, Joseph, and John Hancock Callender, eds., *Time-Saver Standards for Building Types*, 1973.

Hemenway, David, *Performance vs. Design Standards*, 1980.

Hill, I. D., and B. L. Meek, *Programming Language Standardization*, 1980.

Hyde, William F., *Improving Productivity by Classification Coding and Data Base Standardization*, 1981.

International Laboratory Accreditation Conference (ILAC), *International Directory of Accreditation Systems and Other Schemes for Assessment of Testing Laboratories*, 1990.

Nagarajan, R., *Standards in Building*, 1976.

National Academy of Engineering, *Product Quality, Performance, and Cost*, 1972.

National Bureau of Standards, Institute for Computer Sciences and Technology, *Federal Information Processing Standards Publications (FIPS PUBS Index)*, February 1984, updated periodically.

National Computer Graphics Association, *Standards in the Computer Graphics Industry*, 1986.

National Machine Tool Builders Association, *Machine Tool Standards Index*, January 1986.

Nuclear Standards Management Center, DoE, *Nuclear Standards Master Index*, semiannual.

Ollner, Jan, *The Company and Standardization*, 1974.

Slattery, William J., *Index of U.S. Nuclear Standards*, 1977.

U.S. Consumer Product Safety Commission, *Handbook and Standard for Manufacturing Safer Consumer Products*, 1975.

Vogel, Bertram M., *Standards Referenced in Selected Building Codes*, 1976.

Williams, David, *Electrical Standards in World Trade*, 1982.

Company Standardization

Association Francais de Normlisation (AFNOR), *La Normalisation dans L'Enterprise*, 1967.

Ollner, Jan, *The Company and Standardization*, 1974.

Toth, Robert B., ed., *Standards Management: A Handbook for Profits*, 1990.

U.S. Congress, House, *The Effect upon Small Business of Voluntary Industrial Standards*, 90th Congress, 1968.

U.S. Congress, Senate, *Voluntary Industrial Standards*, 94th and 95th Congresses, 1976, 1977.

Federal Procurement and Defense Standardization

Department of Defense, *Annual DoD Standardization Conference*, 1981-1988, annual.

Department of Defense, *Defense Standardization and Specification Program Policies, Procedures and Instructions*, 1987.

Department of Defense, *DoD Index of Specifications and Standards, DoDISS*, annual with periodic supplements.

Department of Defense, *DoD Interaction with Nongovernment Standards Bodies*, SD-9, 1984.

Department of Defense, *DoD Specifications Development Guide*, 1975.

Department of Defense, *Enhancing Defense Standardization*, 1988.

Department of Defense, *An Overview of the Defense Standardization and Specification Program*, SD-8, 1983.

Department of Defense, *Standardization Case Studies*, 1986.

Department of Defense, *Standardization Directory (FSC Class and Area Assignments)*, SD-1, annual.

Department of Defense, *Status of Standardization Projects*, issued quarterly.

General Services Administration, *Federal Standardization*, 1981.

Grossnickle, Linda L., *An Index of State Specifications and Standards*, 1973.

Hagan, Norm A., *Implementing a Standards Program for Procurement*, 1985.

Information Handling Services, *The BRS Database for Military and Federal Specifications and Standards*, 1988, annual.

National Research Council, *Materials and Process Specifications and Standards*, 1977.

Society of Automotive Engineers (SAE), *An Equal Partner Approach, Proceedings of 1985 Conference*, 1986.

Consumer Representation, Consumer Interests

American National Standards Institute, *ANSI Guide for Developing User Product Information*, 1990.

American National Standards Institute, *Guidelines for Consumer Participation in Standards Development*, 1986.

Breitenberg, Maureen A., and Robert G. Atkins, *Consumer Representation in Standards Development: Literature Review and Issue Identification*, 1981.

Coles, Jessie V., *Standards and Labels for Consumers' Goods*, 1949.

Edwards, Alice L., *Product Standards and Labelling for Consumers*, 1940.

Johnson, Leland L., *Cost-Benefit Analysis and Voluntary Safety Standards for Consumer Products*, 1982.

National Academy of Engineering, *Product Quality, Performance, and Cost*, 1972.

National Consumers League, *Report on Consumer Representation in Voluntary Standard Setting*, 1978-1979.

Struglia, Erasmus J., et al., *Standards and the Consumer*, 1964.

ALPHABETICAL REFERENCES (BY AUTHOR)

Administrative Conference of the United States. *Guidebook Series on Alternative Regulatory Approaches*. Washington, D.C.: Administrative Conference of the U.S., 1981. Paperback. Six booklets. *Overview*, 24 pages. *Performance Standards*, 66 pages. *Tiering*, 56 pages. *Marketable Rights*, 56 pages. *Monetary Incentives*, 65 pages. *Information Disclosure*, 52 pages.

"This series is intended to provide a practical introduction – featuring both the theoretical and the proven limitations – to a special set of alternative regulatory tools: approaches that are generally more compatible with the market forces that govern business decisions. Booklets in the series are: overview; marketable rights; performance standards; monetary incentives; information disclosure; and tiering. The 'overview' explains that performance standards replace regulations that specify the exact means of compliance (usually detailed design standards) with general targets that the regulated firms can decide how to meet." (Page 3.)

Ambler, Ernest, et al. *A Record of the Papers Presented at the Conference on Standards, Measurements, Quality Control and Production for Economic Support and Growth, Held in Cairo, Egypt*. 29-31 October 1983. Washington, D.C.: National Bureau of Standards, Department of Commerce, October 1983. 75 pages.

A series of lectures was given by the U.S. participants in the Conference on Standards, Measurements, Quality Control and Production for Economic Support and Growth within the framework of the cooperation of NBS with Egyptian institutions. The Egyptian institutions involved were the Egyptian National Institute for Standards, the Egyptian Organization for Standardization and Quality Control, and the Office of Weights and Measures. NBS proposed the conference to explain the importance of standards, calibration, and reference materials to Egyptian industrial and government officials. The conference also provided a forum for describing the U.S. standards and quality control system.

Keywords: AID; calibration, certification; Egypt; fire research; measurements, quality control; reference materials.

American Association for Laboratory Accreditation, A2LA. *Directory of Accredited Laboratories*; and *A2LA Annual Report*. Gaithersburg, Md.: A2LA, annual.

American National Standards Institute. *ANSI Global Standardization Report: Providing the U.S. Standards Community with Information Important in Understanding the Access Process to CEN/ENCELEC.* Vols. 1-3. New York: ANSI, 1989-1990.

The third volume of the *ANSI Global Standardization Report* covers European developments affecting the United States standardization community. This edition presents the results of a private-sector delegation meeting with European standards officials from the European Committee for Standardization (CEN); European Committee for Electrotechnical Standardization (CENELEC); the European Commission; the Belgium Standards Institute; Oppenheimer, Wolff and Donnelly; the EC Committee of the American Chamber of Commerce in Belgium; and the U.S. Mission to the EC. The meetings in March 1990 resulted in increasing and continuing the cooperative understanding between U.S. and European interests in the fields of standards, testing, and certification.

The first volume of the *ANSI Global Standardization Report* focused on the results of private-sector discussions between CEN/CENELEC and ANSI in July of 1989. The second volume focused on practical strategies and tactics for U.S. industry to respond and represent its interests in the new European standards environment.

American National Standards Institute. *ANSI Guide for Developing User Product Information.* New York: ANSI, 1990. 20 pages.

"This ANSI publication is designed to help any professional, regardless of his/her field of expertise, to write effective user product information. This publication offers a 'one-stop shopping guide' on how to put together a coherent and usable instruction package by presenting an overview of the elements that might be included in the various types of instructional product literature.

The guide will be most helpful to small and midsize manufacturers who need to develop a wide range of instructional materials, such as Operator's manuals, Owner's guides, Instruction books and sheets, Instructions printed on blister packs or containers, Product labels, and Mixed media. (Page 1.)

American National Standards Institute. *Directory of International and Regional Standards Organizations.* New York: ANSI, 1982. Paperback. 15 pages.

"This publication identifies and describes the world's major international and regional standards organizations. The standards they develop or harmonize or, in many cases, accept for use in testing and certification programs have a significant impact on international trade. They can either facilitate market entry or pose barriers." (Page 2.)

American National Standards Institute. *Guidelines for Consumer Participation in Standards Development.* New York: ANSI, 1986. 19 pages.

ANSI's Consumer Interest Council prepared this publication to assist organizations and others that develop standards for consumer products in recruiting consumers and in training them so their input will be effective. It provides standards developers with some perspectives on what can be and is being done about the thorny problems of funding consumers and providing them with technical assistance, subjects on which there is not a great deal of unanimity.

"Helping standards developing organizations meet ANSI requirements that pertain to consumer participation is another goal of this publication. Also included in these guidelines is a section on consumer sounding-boards. This publication was prepared by a Consumer Interest Council task force." (Page 3.)

American National Standards Institute. *1990 Catalog of American National Standards.* New York: ANSI, annual.

American National Standards are listed by subject and designation. Information is also provided for obtaining copies of ISO and IEC catalogs and publications. Specialty catalogs are also available, such as the *1988-89 Catalog of American National Standards for Safety and Health.* (See the appendix "Standards Information Centers.")

American National Standards Institute. *Procedures for the Development and Coordination of American National Standards: Approved September 9, 1987.* New York: ANSI, 1987. 28 pages.

Many standards developers and participants support the American National Standards Institute (ANSI) as the central body responsible for the identification of a single consistent set of voluntary standards called *American National Standards.* ANSI approval of these standards is intended to verify that the principles of openness and due process have been followed in the approval procedure and that consensus of those directly and materially affected by the standards has been achieved. ANSI coordination is intended to assist the voluntary system to ensure that national standards needs are identified and met with a set of standards that are without conflict or unnecessary duplication in their requirements.

The purpose of this most recent revision, approved by the board of directors on 9 September 1987, is to provide clarification and consistency of language, update references, refine the canvass procedures, and add new information pertaining to standards planning panels, standards advisors, draft standards for trial use, substantive changes, and commercial terms and conditions.

American National Standards Institute. *Standardization in the 90s: Success in a Global Market.* Proceedings of ANSI 1990 Public Conference. New York: ANSI, 1990. 244 pages.

The American National Standards Institute's 1990 Public Conference depicted the importance of developing and executing strategic standards plans necessary for U.S. industry to remain competitive in light of the emerging global marketplace. The conference presented an inside look at the important domestic and international standards, testing, and certification concerns facing U.S. industry today. Proceedings from over 20 speakers at the conference are included.

Leaders from both sides of the Atlantic provided advice and experience as to how American interests can benefit from Europe's internal market initiative and other international standards developments. Discussions centered on the U.S. government's response to globalization, business-government relationships needed to strengthen U.S. competitiveness, and the opportunities and/or obstacles that the U.S. will face regarding certification, quality assurance, and conformity assessment. Also discussed were case studies on how standards awareness can increase profitability in the years to come.

American National Standards Institute. *Standards and the Law.* New York: ANSI, 1984. Paperback. 26 pages.

The four speeches contained in this booklet were presented at two sessions of the public conference on Standards and the Law of the American National Standards Institute. These sessions, "Regularity of Standardization" and "Antitrust Liability for Standards Developers," were part of a conference held 27 March 1984 in Arlington, Va.

American National Standards Institute. *Voluntary (Private-Sector) Standards Programs and the GATT Code.* New York: ANSI, 1977. Paperback. 34 pages.

The report includes recommendations on the private sector and governmental focal points, communications and a national standards registry, obtaining information and comment on national standards development in other countries, certification and quality assurance, and information and technical assistance.

American Society for Testing and Materials. *ASTM and the OMB Circular A-119*. Federal Participation in the Development and Use of Voluntary Standards. A seminar sponsored by ASTM, 18 May 1983. Philadelphia: ASTM, 1983. Paperback. 46 pages.

Seminar presentations printed here include "ASTM–The Basics," "The Genesis of OMB A-119," "The OMB Circular Makes Its Debut," "NBS–The Standards Coordinator," "Voluntary Standards Face the 1980s," "A Regulatory Agency's Use of Voluntary Standards," and "Legal Aspects of Voluntary Standards." Questions and answers are also presented.

American Society for Testing and Materials. *Form and Style for ASTM Standards*. 8th ed. Philadelphia: ASTM, September 1989. Paperback. 105 pages. Revised periodically.

"ASTM, founded in 1898, is a scientific and technical organization formed for 'the development of standards on characteristics and performance of materials, products, systems, and services; and the promotion of related knowledge.' It is the world's largest source of voluntary consensus standards. The purpose of this manual is to promote uniformity of form and style in ASTM standards. Such uniformity is desirable because it helps the reader to find what he wants more easily and to understand what he reads more quickly.

"This manual is the basic textbook for anyone writing an ASTM standard. A study of Parts A, B, or C will show the proper form for the principal types of standards including a detailed explanation of how to write each section, from the title to the appendixes. Included at appropriate places are examples and standard wording. Also included are examples of correctly written complete manuscripts of various types of standards."

American Society for Testing and Materials. *ICPS Bulletin*, International Coalition for Procurement Standards (ICPS) and ASTM: Philadelphia, serial publication.

International Coalition for Procurement Standards is a group of representatives of national and international purchasing associations and their affiliates organized to communicate, cooperate, and join in the coordinated activities of the recognized standards development organizations. This bulletin features reports of ongoing standard activities that are of interest to the purchasing community.

American Society for Testing and Materials. *1990 ASTM Directory of Testing Laboratories*. Philadelphia: ASTM, 1990. Paperback. Revised annually.

ASTM Directory of Testing Laboratories is completely new each year. All lab information is reverified or updated to reflect new capabilities and equipment.

Over 1,000 laboratories are featured. The majority are located in the United States, 43 in Canada, and several in 13 other countries. Each lab listing contains contact, specialty, fields of testing covered, materials and products analyzed, equipment, and staff. The listings are segmented by geographical location, with detailed subject and alphabetical indexes. The laboratories listed are performing services for a fee. They are not certified or endorsed by ASTM.

American Society for Testing and Materials. *Standards Make the Pieces Fit.* Philadelphia: ASTM, n.d. 16 pages.
This pamphlet is an introduction to standardization. A history of standards activity is included with emphasis on the role of ASTM. Other sections include the world standards forum and legal aspects of standardization (due process, restraints of trade, authority and responsibility, liability).

American Society for Testing and Materials, *The Voluntary Standards System of the United States of America.* Philadelphia: ASTM, 1975. Paperback. 31 pages.
This is a report of a 1973 committee "created to study the role of ASTM in the total standards system, the efficiency of the system, and the relationships of the parts of the system." Resulting from government and public criticism of the voluntary standards-making system, "this report represents ASTM's view of the existing system and the problems the system has now and will be facing in the future. The report also presents ASTM's concepts of an improved, more credible voluntary system, ASTM's role in such a system, and the way ASTM expects to interface with others who contribute to the system."

L'Association Francais de Normalisation (AFNOR). *La Normalisation dans L'Enterprise.* Paris: 1967. 295 pages.
The position of standardization in industry is dealt with in this volume, based on the degree of standardization achieved in different industries. The first part deals with standardization in general and the necessity in modern economies for standardization at all levels of industry. The second part treats the uses made of standardization by industry in its many branches. A concluding section considers the future of standardization in industry.

Batik, Albert L. *A Guide to Standards*. Parker, Colo.: A. L. Batik, 1989. 129 pages.

This book is designed to address the many facets of voluntary consensus standards. These standards have many other names, such as industry standards, private-sector standards, and commercial standards. What they are *not* are regulations or procurement documents, such as military or federal standards. A voluntary consensus standard may of course become a regulation or a governmental procurement document if the appropriate government entity takes the action to make it so.

The intent of this book is to help both the engineer and the supporting information specialist to gain a perspective about standards. Such a perspective leads to a better understanding of standards and aids in the use of appropriate standards to the benefit of the individual as well as to the organization that puts standards on its agenda.

Short chapters include history and development of standards, importance and application of standards, problems and solutions, involvement in standards, the major standards developers identified, plus other sources of information.

Booth, Sherman F. *Standardization Activities in the United States*. Miscellaneous publication 230. Washington, D.C.: National Bureau of Standards, 1960. 210 pages.

"This volume provides a descriptive inventory of the work of about 350 American organizations involved in standardization activities. It describes the organization and function of the societies and government agencies that are closely identified with standards activities. It should be of value to manufacturers, engineers, purchasing agents, and writers of standards and specifications."

Brady, Robert A. *Industrial Standardization*. New York: National Industrial Conference Board, March 1929. 306 pages.

An early comprehensive survey that is actually the unacknowledged Columbia Ph.D. thesis of Robert A. Brady. (See Brady, Robert A., bibliography.) The Conference Board president notes: "The principle of standardization, as it is expressed in the products, processes and practices of industry and trade, is now generally recognized as a fundamental characteristic of our modern economic system." (Page v.) There are 16 chapters and several appendixes. Chapter titles: "Historical Setting for the Standardization Movement," "Terminology of Standardization," "Company Standardization," "Standardization Work of Engineering and Other Technical Societies," "Trade Association Standardization," "The American Standards Association and Other

National Standardizing Bodies," "The National Bureau of Standards," "Standards in Government Purchasing," "International and Regional Standardization," "Agricultural Standardization," "Business Savings from Standardization," "Standardization and Marketing Technique," "Standardization and the Size of Business," "Standardization as an Aid in the Standardization of Business," "Standardization and the Ultimate Consumer," and "The Trend of Industrial Standardization."

Brady, Robert A. *Organization, Automation, and Society*. Berkeley, Calif.: University of California Press, 1963. 481 pages.

In the context of a broad international and interdisciplinary analysis, the author describes his work as "concentrated on industrial technology, with special attention to that level of development wherein the cleaning-up operations necessary to bring practice fully in line with scientific theory are already well along. It is essentially a sort of ground-clearing study. It stops short of any attempt to draw many conclusions. It seeks merely to answer one type of question, namely, what, in the light of certain well-accepted criteria, is the best way to organize the productive resources of an economy when decision makers are prepared to make full use of the potentialities opened up by advances in science and engineering." A detailed index shows the central role of standardization in the analysis.

Breden, Leslie, H., ed. *World Index of Plastics Standards*. Gaithersburg, Md.: National Bureau of Standards, December 1971. Paperback. 458 pages.

This computer-produced index contains the printed titles of more than 9,000 national and international standards on plastics and related materials that were in effect as of 31 December 1970. These standards are published by technical societies, trade associations, government agencies, and military organizations. The title of each standard can be found under all the significant keywords it contains. These keywords are arranged alphabetically down the center of each page together with their surrounding context. The date of publication or last revision, the standard number, and an acronym designating the standard-issuing organization appear as part of each entry. A list of these acronyms and the names and addresses of the organizations they represent are found at the beginning of the *World Index*. (See also Breden's *World Index of Building Certification Programs*.)

Keywords: Index of plastics standards; plastics standards, world index; standards, plastics.

Breitenberg, Maureen A. *The ABC's of Certification Activities in the United States*. NBSIR 88-3821. Gaithersburg, Md.: National Bureau of Standards, 1988. Paperback. 20 pages.

This report, a sequel to NBSIR 87-3576, *The ABC's of Standardization Activities in the United States*, provides further introduction to certification for a reader who is not entirely familiar with this topic. It highlights some of the more important aspects of this field, furnishes the reader with information necessary to make informed purchases, and serves as background for using available documents and services.

Keywords: certificates of conformity; certification; certification marks; conformance testing; inspection; product listing; quality assurance; standardization; standards; testing.

Breitenberg, Maureen A. *The ABC's of Standards-Related Activities in the United States*. NBSIR 87-3576. Gaithersburg, Md.: National Bureau of Standards, 1987. Paperback. 16 pages.

This report provides an introduction to voluntary standardization, product certification, and laboratory accreditation to a reader who is not fully familiar with these topics. It highlights some of the more important aspects of these fields, furnishes the reader with historical and current information on these topics, describes the importance and impact of the development and use of standards, and serves as background for using available documents and services.

Keywords: Certification; inspection; laboratory accreditation; standardization; standards; testing.

Breitenberg, Maureen A., ed. *Directory of Federal Government Certification Programs*. NBS SP 739. Gaithersburg, Md.: National Institute of Standards and Technology, 1988. 229 pages. Supersedes NBS SP 714.

This directory, which represents a joint effort of the U.S. Department of Agriculture (USDA) and the National Bureau of Standards (NBS), is designed to provide updated information on federal certification programs for products and services. This directory is a revision of NBS SP 714, *Federal Government Certification Programs for Products and Services*, edited by Robert B. Toth and published in April 1986.

This directory is part of ongoing NBS/USDA efforts to establish and maintain comprehensive databases on standards, regulations, certification programs, and related information in accordance with the requirements of the Trade Agreements Act of 1979. This material has been compiled to meet the needs of government, industry, and the public for information on U.S. government certification programs.

Keywords: Approved products; certification; grading; inspection; listing; pre-market evaluation; qualification; qualified products; specifications; standards; testing.

Breitenberg, Maureen A., ed. *Directory of Federal Government Laboratory Accreditation/Designation Programs*. NIST SP 808. Gaithersburg, Md.: National Institute of Standards and Technology, 1991. 105 pages.

This directory is designed to provide updated information on federal government laboratory accreditation and similar type programs conducted by the federal government. These programs designate a set of laboratories or other entities to conduct testing to assist federal agencies in carrying out their responsibilities. The programs generally include some assessment regarding the capability of the lab to conduct the testing. The type and degree of such assessments, however, vary greatly by program. It should be noted that the entries in this directory are based primarily on information provided by the federal agency and reflect the agency's view of its activities. Parties interested in this area may also wish to review NBS SP 739, *Directory of Federal Government Certification Programs*, which contains information on a number of closely related programs.

This directory is part of ongoing NIST efforts to establish and maintain comprehensive databases on standards, regulations, laboratory accreditation, and certification programs and related information in accordance with the requirements of the Trade Agreements Act of 1979. This material has been compiled to meet the needs of government, industry, and the public for information on U.S. government laboratory accreditation and related programs.

Keywords: Certification; grading; inspection; laboratory accreditation; listing; mutual recognition schemes; proficiency testing; qualified laboratories; standards; testing.

Breitenberg, Maureen A., ed. *Directory of International and Regional Organizations Conducting Standards-Related Activities*. NIST SP 767. Gaithersburg, Md.: National Bureau of Standards, 1989. Paperback. 366 pages. Supersedes NBS SP 649, 1983.

This directory contains information on 338 international and regional organizations that conduct standardization, certification, laboratory accreditation, or other standards-related activities. This volume describes their work in these areas, the scope of each organization, national affiliations of members, U.S. participants, restrictions on membership, as well as the availability of any standards in English.

International and regional organizations are listed in alphabetical order, and acronyms, national affiliations, U.S. participants, membership restrictions, scope of interest, and availability of standards in English are also included.

Keywords: Certification; international organizations; international standardization; international standards organizations; laboratory accreditation; metrology; organizational directory; standardization; standards.

Breitenberg, Maureen A. *Directory of U.S. Private Sector Certification Programs*. NIST SP 774. Gaithersburg, Md.: National Institute of Standards and Technology, 1989. 440 pages. Supersedes NBS SP 703, 1985.

The programs and activities of 132 private-sector groups that provide product certification services are cataloged in the newly revised *Directory of U.S. Private Sector Product Certification Programs* (SP 774), published by NIST. The directory is designed to serve the needs of federal agencies and standards writers, as well as product manufacturers, engineers, purchasing agents, distributors, and others concerned with product-related certification procedures. The listings describe type and purpose of each U.S.-based group, products certified, standards used, certification requirements, any accreditation or recognition by a U.S. or foreign private-sector or government agency, availability of services, and method used to determine cost of services. Information is indexed by organizational name, acronyms and initials, and by products certified.

Breitenberg, Maureen A. *Need for Economic Information on Standards Used in Regulatory Programs: Problems and Recommendations*. NBSIR 80-2123. Washington, D.C.: National Bureau of Standards, 1980. Paperback. 64 pages.

Government regulatory agencies are increasing the use of standards developed by the private sector. Federal regulators are, however, being required to provide increasing justification for their regulations, especially information on their economic desirability. If regulators are to use effectively voluntary standards in their regulations, rather than to develop standards in house, they will need the same types of economic information on the voluntary standards as they would on their in-house standards. This paper describes the types of requirements and pressures that regulatory agencies are faced with in justifying their actions and provides standards writers with guidelines on the types of economic information that may allow regulators to make greater use of voluntary standards.

Keywords: Economic information on standards; standardization; procedural history; rationale; federal use of voluntary standards; economic impact of standards; economic impact of regulations.

Breitenberg, Maureen A., and Robert G. Atkins. *Consumer Representation in Standards Development: Literature Review and Issue Identification.* Washington, D.C.: National Bureau of Standards, 1981. Paperback. 77 pages.

This report identifies for possible future study the major issues associated with the topic of consumer representation in the development of voluntary standards. The key terms (consumer and consumer representative) used in the report are defined, and background information on the Food and Drug Administration's medical device standards program is given. The report discusses important recent developments in consumer involvement in government and standards organization decision making and contains a review of federal public participation programs. The literature on consumer representation is reviewed from the perspective of standards-developing groups and consumer organizations, and the most salient documents are annotated. Based on available literature and supplemented by information obtained from personal contacts with affected parties, the major outstanding issues are summarized.

Keywords: Bibliography, annotated; consumer representation; literature review; medical device standards; public participation programs; standards development; voluntary standards.

Brickenkamp, Carroll S., and Joan Koenig, eds. *Uniform Laws and Regulations in the Areas of Legal Metrology and Motor Fuel Quality.* Washington, D.C.: National Institute of Standards and Technology, 1989. NIST Handbook 130, 1990. 172 pages. Revised annually.

This handbook, revised annually, compiles the uniform laws and regulations developed by the Committee on Laws and Regulations of the National Conference on Weights and Measures (NCWM). The compilation itself was approved by the NCWM in 1979, and this edition includes amendments adopted by the conference at its annual meeting in 1989. This edition also contains a completely revised Uniform Weighmaster Law.

The NCWM recommends adoption and promulgation by the states of these uniform laws and regulations as updated in this handbook.

Keywords: Basic weights and measures law; method of sale of commodities; motor fuel inspection; open dating; packaging and labeling;

pattern approval regulation; regulation of servicepersons; type evaluation; unit pricing; weighmaster law.

Bureau of Medical Devices, U.S. Department of Health, Education and Welfare (now Health and Human Services). *Bureau of Medical Devices Standards Survey 1979*. Silver Spring, Md.: Public Health Service, Food and Drug Administration, 1979. National and international eds.

The purpose of the *Bureau of Medical Devices Standards Survey* is to provide a comprehensive listing of current national and international standards promulgation activities in the fields of medical devices and diagnostic products. These standards include voluntary and regulatory standards, tentative and recommended standards, recommended practices, purchasing specifications, policy statements, glossaries of technical terms, and proposed standards. The standards identify criteria such as the safety and performance of medical devices and diagnostic products. Therefore, they will serve as a basis for the continuing review of the adequacy of existing standards and as guidelines for the development of new standards. The *Bureau of Medical Devices Standards Survey* was published in two parts: the international edition and the national edition.

Canadian Manufacturers Association. *Standards in Manufacturing: A Shifting Focus in the 80s*. Canadian Manufacturers Association: Toronto, Canada, October 1981. 45 pages. Out of print.

This paper is intended to identify the potential impact of different standards activities and to explain how Canadian standards system functions. It is intended to meet the needs of both senior management and middle management of manufacturing firms and contains the following sections: "Part 1–Standards, Business, and Marketing" outlines the different effects that types of standards can have on a firm's marketing strategies. "Part 2–The National Standards System" outlines the basic structure and procedures of Canada's major standards organizations. "Part 3–Issues" outlines the economic and public policy implications of several new developments in Canadian standards system. Appendixes provide how-to information, identifying and listing the specific responsibilities of Canada's major standards organizations and outlining the services they provide.

Cargill, Carl F. *Information Technology Standardization: Theory, Process, and Organizations*. Maynard, Mass.: Digital Press, 1989. 203 pages.

"This is a book about Information Technology Standardization–the theory, the organizations, and the process for them. It is an attempt to synthesize much that has been written about standards into a common whole and to provide a common base for future standards development, both actually and philosophically. The purpose of the book is not to act as a "how to" book for standards. Rather, it is an attempt to describe a process to show why the process happens, to explain the need and rationale for standards, specifically within the information technology industry. The concept of 'industry' is used to refer to all elements of that industry; suppliers, producers, and consumers. The book should be regarded as a companion piece to the book on standards authored by Dorothy Cerni, entitled *Standards in Process: Foundations and Profiles of ISDN and OSI Studies*.

"While it can serve as a source book for those wishing to begin a standardization effort, one of its functions is to lay the groundwork for a comprehensive look at standards as they relate to industry, including the role and expectations of the supplier, users, customers, and the government." (Page i.)

Cerni, Dorothy M. *Standards in Process: Foundations and Profiles of ISDN and OSI Studies*. NTIA Report 84-170. Boulder, Colo.: National Telecommunications and Information Administration Institute for Telecommunication Sciences, December 1984. 246 pages.

Telecommunication and computer technologies are merging, stimulating global communication projects such as the Integrated Services Digital Network (ISDN) and the Open Systems Interconnection (OSI) Reference Model. The systems of standards needed to ensure worldwide success of these projects are being developed. These efforts, of unprecedented complexity, are demanding an increase in knowledgeable, dedicated standards workers.

This report offers background material on the meaning, significance, and changing nature of standards and their development, both in the United States and internationally. The importance of international standardization to U.S. industry is stressed. Building on this foundation, the ISDN and OSI standardization efforts are presented as the consequences of converging technological advances worldwide. The increased cooperation among standards organizations such as the International Organization for Standardization (ISO) and the International Telegraph and Telephone Consultative Committee (CCITT) is documented. The report concludes with a summary of responsibilities and desired characteristics of standards writers.

Keywords: American National Standards; ANSI; CCITT; computer standards; FCC; GATT Standards Code: IEC; international standards; ISDN; ISO; OSI Reference Model; regulations; Study Group XVIII;

ASC Tl; TC97; telecommunication standards; voluntary standards; ASC X3.

Chapman, Carol A. *Bibliography on the Voluntary Standards System and Product Certification*. NBSIR 79-1900. Gaithersburg, Md.: National Bureau of Standards, 1979. 27 pages.

This bibliography lists references accumulated by the NBS Office of Engineering Standards in the course of its research into the workings of the voluntary standards system and the economic and legal effects of standards. The first portion of the bibliography lists references alphabetically by author. The second portion groups references by subject. Subject categories include standards system reform, regulatory use of standards (buildings, safety, environment), certification and laboratory accreditation, solar heating and cooling, product liability, and international and foreign.

Keywords: Bibliography; buildings; certification; economics of standards; legal aspects of standards; product certification; product liability; regulation; standards system; voluntary standards.

Cochrane, Rexmond C. *Measures for Progress: A History of the National Bureau of Standards*. Washington, D.C.: National Bureau of Standards, 1966, 1974. Illustrated. 703 pages. Out of print.

A comprehensive history of the bureau from the time of its founding in 1901 to the early 1960s.

Coles, Jessie V. *Standards and Labels for Consumers' Goods*. New York: The Ronald Press, 1949. 556 pages.

"Part I discusses the position of consumers as buyers, and the gradual development of consumer interest in their problems. In Part II, labels as they exist today are discussed and criteria for good labels set up. Part III covers some basic concepts of standards which are essential to an understanding of their use generally, and specifically in connection with consumer goods. How standards are used by producers in making, distributing, and describing consumers' goods is set forth in Part IV, while Part V deals with the manifold problems of getting standards: their development, establishment, terminology, and the procedures and agencies for securing standards and informative labels for consumers' goods. Part VI takes up the grade labeling of consumer goods in the United States and Canada, the controversies arising over compulsory grade labeling, and the general issues involved. Part VII is devoted to a discussion of the present status of standards and labels for consumers' goods." (Page iii.)

Congressional Research Service. *Voluntary Industrial Standards in the United States*. Washington, D.C.: U.S. Government Printing Office, 1974. Paperback. 122 pages.

The director of the Congressional Research Service introduces the document as an "overview . . . intended to give to Members of Congress highlights of the evolution of voluntary standards in the United States, in both the private and government sectors, and also to identify problems and issues that may merit fresh congressional attention, as well as an insight into advice and commentary received by Congress during the past 10 years." The last five pages are "selected recent references to standardization."

Cooke, Patrick W. *Benefits Perceived by U.S. Industry from Participating in International Standards Activities*. Gaithersburg, Md.: National Bureau of Standards, 1984. Paperback. 23 pages.

This report describes the results of a limited study to assess the extent to which U.S. industry profits by virtue of participation in the committee activities of international standardization organizations. The substantial trade benefits that can accrue are identified and evaluated in terms of the needs of the firms surveyed and the potential opportunities for new or increased foreign trade. Recommendations are given for industry to become more aware of the cost-effectiveness of participation and to extend the potential benefits to other firms and industries.

Keywords: Benefits; cost effectiveness; exports; foreign trade; international bodies; international standards; standards development; trade barriers; trade barriers; U.S. industry.

Cooke, Patrick W. *A Review of U.S. Participation in International Standards Activities*. NBSIR 88-3698. Gaithersburg, Md.: National Bureau of Standards, 1988. Paperback. 69 pages.

This report describes the role of international standards, their increasingly significant importance in world trade, and the extent of past and current U.S. participation in the two major international standardization bodies, ISO and IEC. The degree of U.S. participation covers the 20-year period from 1966 to 1986. An analysis of data indicates some correlation between U.S. participation and recent export performance for several major product categories.

Cooke, Patrick W. *A Summary of the New European Community Approach to Standards Development*. NBSIR 88-3793-1. Gaithersburg, Md.: National Bureau of Standards, 1988. Paperback. 13 pages.

This paper summarizes European Community (EC) plans to aggressively pursue its goal of achieving an "internal market" by 1992 and the standards-related implications of such a program on U.S. exporters. U.S. exporters will be affected by the harmonization of standards, implementation of EC directives, strengthening of European regional standards bodies, and other trade policy considerations affecting market access. U.S. government and EC contacts for obtaining additional information are provided.

Keywords: European Community; harmonization; international trade; regional standardization; Single European Act; standards; U.S. exports.

Cooke, Patrick W. *An Update of U.S. Participation in International Standards Activities*. NISTIR 89-4124. Gaithersburg, Md.: National Institute of Standards and Technology, 1989. 24 pages.

This report presents updated information on the current level of U.S. participation in the two major international standardization bodies, ISO and IEC. Data on the new ISO/IEC Joint Technical Committee 1 (JTC 1) on Information and Technology are also presented.

Keywords: American National Standards Institute; European Community; international standards; participation; standardization; U.S. exports.

Crawford, Walt. *Technical Standards: An Introduction for Librarians*. White Plains, N.Y.: Knowledge Industry Publications, 1986. 299 pages. 2nd ed. available, Boston: G.K. Hall, 1991.

"Standards aren't sexy–probably the best thing we can say about standards is that they are usually transparent." "Libraries must fight for the standards they want." So states the foreword to this important introductory treatise on standardization for librarians.

The first part of this book provides an excellent introduction to technical standards for librarians; the varieties and motives for technical standards; implementation, levels, and families in a standards hierarchy; and some problems and dangers.

A second part of the book concentrates on the standards process. Its key organizations are described (ANSI, Z39 Committee and NISO, Comm. X3, ISO), and there is in-depth discussion of the current standards developed by NISO (Z39) and Z85, X3, and ISO. Appendixes discuss the many layers of standards in a library catalog; discuss detailed organizational structures and committee members in NISO, ASC, X3, ISO TC46, and TC97; and contain a glossary of terms and useful bibliography.

Keywords: Library   science – standards;   technological innovations – standards; technology – standards; information science; information standards; NISO; ANSI; ASC; ISO.

Dalton, James A., Peter K. Ashton, and Frank C. Graves. *The Impact of Private Voluntary Standards on Industrial Innovation*. Vol. 1, final report. Gaithersburg, Md.: For National Bureau of Standards, November 1982. Typed copy. 30 pages.

"The objectives of this study are to develop a conceptual framework that describes the significant conditions and factors that could explain the impacts of standards on innovation; and to test and refine the framework through a series of case studies." The positive and negative effects of standards are reviewed.

DeChiara, Joseph, and John Hancock Callender, eds. *Time-Saver Standards for Building Types*. New York: McGraw-Hill, 1973. 1,065 pages.

"*Time-Saver Standards for Building Types* is intended primarily to meet the needs of those who are involved in the conceiving, planning, programming, or designing of buildings. It is intended to give basic design criteria for each major type of building. It will give those unfamiliar with a specific type of building a talking or working knowledge of its functions, organization, and major components.

"The material is intended to act as a guide or reference point for which the specific design solutions can be established. Absolutely no attempt is made in this book to present the final design solution for any building type, nor does it try to establish or influence the final aesthetic expression of the building. It is hoped that the designer or architect, by having at his disposal the widest range of information concerning a building type, will be able to design more functional, more meaningful, and more exciting buildings." (Page xiii.)

Subsequent related works edited by DeChiara include *Time-Saver Standards for Site Planning* (1984) and *Time-Saver Standards for Residential Development* (1984).

Department of Defense. *Annual DoD Standardization Conference*. Falls Church, Va: DoD, 1983. Proceedings, 753 pages. Executive summary, paperback, 63 pages. Annually from 1981 to 1988.

Synopses of the panel discussions, observations, conclusions, and recommendations are extracted from the full proceedings and reproduced in the executive summary. Recommendations and proposed office assignments are included. The initial session on developing standard subsystem is not included. Topics summarized are controlling the importance of contracted requirements, managing data in a constrained environment, identifying metric opportunities, updating qualification policies, automating the standardization and data management process, buying commercial for the DoD, disciplining the development of avionics architectures for the 1990s, planning for standardization management, and reducing the cost of spare parts.

Department of Defense. *Defense Standardization and Specification Program Policies, Procedures and Instructions, Defense Standardization Manual.* DoD 4120.3-M. Washington, D.C.: U.S. Government Printing Office, April 1987. 7 chapters. 100+ pages.

The chapter headings are organization and assignments, planning and programming, policies and procedures for standardization documents, qualified products lists, procedure for determination and implementation of item standardization coding, specifications for commercial products, and policies and procedures for the selective application and tailoring of specifications and standards in the material acquisition process.

Department of Defense. *DoD Index of Specifications and Standards. DoDISS.* Washington, D.C.: Government Printing Office. Updated regularly.

The *DoDISS* is a reference publication that lists all military and federal specifications, standards, handbooks, QPLs, commercial item descriptions, adopted nongovernment standards, international documents, and related publications. It includes approximately 38,000 specifications and standards and about 10,000 related documents. Printed editions are provided in (Part I) alphabetical, (Part II) numeric, and (Part III) federal supply classification listings. They are published annually with bimonthly cumulative supplements. Weekly bulletins called *DoDISS Notices* contain advance information about selected new and revised *DoDISS* listed documents.

Department of Defense. *DoD Interaction with Nongovernment Standards Bodies.* SD-9. Washington, D.C.: DoD, April 1984. 10 pages.

This document is intended to give voluntary standards bodies (VSBs) an understanding of the Department of Defense (DoD) Standardization and Specifications Program and explains how they can interface with DoD in the development, adoption, and use of voluntary standards. It describes how voluntary standards are adopted by DoD, provides the criteria used for adoption, and explains DoD participation in the document preparation process.

Department of Defense. *DoD Specifications Development Guide (History, Purpose, Disciplines and Technologies).* DMSSO-GB-1. U.S. Army Logistics Management Center. Fort Lee, Va: DoD, December 1975.

"This book is an effort to encompass under one cover the disciplines and techniques available for those personnel who develop or contribute to the development of specifications; and also to provide information for those personnel who manage the research, development, production, utilization, and support of specified products. It is intended to meet the needs, not only of the specifications writer, but all individuals concerned with the acquisition process and who either come into contact with or are influenced by specifications. Areas of disciplines include, but are not limited to, engineering, science, technology, industry, government, and consumerization.

"The material and information in this book are general and not intended to be specific doctrine of Government, industry, or the academic world."

Department of Defense. *Enhancing Defense Standardization: Specifications and Standards, Cornerstones of Quality*. Washington, D.C.: DoD, 1988. 49 pages.

This is a report to the Secretary of Defense by the Under Secretary of Defense for Acquisition, Dr. Robert Costello. This study builds on the earlier Shea report by the Defense Science Board in 1977 and the Toth report assessing the U.S. Defense Standardization and Specification Program completed in 1984. The current Costello report culminates from the Defense Standardization Study Team and offers results and recommendations of programs affecting the specs and standards used in defense acquisition. Recommendations and actions are provided to deal with needed revisions, updates, and streamlining of the defense standardization system. Major thrusts include establishing accountability, comprehensive review of all DoD specifications and standards, establishing closer ties with nongovernment standards bodies, automating standardization databases, line item budgeting of standardization projects, and expanded standards training.

Department of Defense. *An Overview of the Defense Standardization and Specification Program (DSSP)*. SD-8. Washington, D.C.: DoD, 1 May 1983. 16 pages.

The purpose of this publication is to provide government and industry managers with an understanding of the standardization process and insight into the Department of Defense program to manage military standardization initiatives. Included is a brief description of standardization principles, benefits, considerations, and documentation. A summary of the Defense Standardization and Specification Program

(DSSP) is presented to familiarize readers with the program's organization, policies, and procedures.

The term *standard*, as used in this document, can have three meanings. It can be a written set of technical, dimensional, or performance requirements. It can be an accepted process or procedure. It can also be a common product identified as a preferred item in a situation. The appropriate definition should be clear from the context of the coverage. Specifically excluded are those "standards" mandated by laws or regulations at the federal, state, and local levels. Such standards are not generally used to describe products and services but to establish requirements for meeting safety, environmental protection, welfare, and other national objectives.

Department of Defense. *Standardization Case Studies*. Washington, D.C.: DoD, March 1986. Paperback. 71 pages.

"This pamphlet . . . provides instructors with selected standardization case studies. . . . The pamphlet also contains applications which should be useful in the identification of cost-benefits and the preparation of additional case studies." (Page i.) Selected chapters include servicewide problems with tactical shelters, streamlining and tailoring standards and specifications, solving procurement problems through standardization, significant cost savings and other benefits with shipboard copier standardization, and developing a standardized system pays off.

Department of Defense. *Standardization Directory (FSC Class and Area Assignments)*. SD-1. Washington, D.C.: DoD, annual, updated quarterly. Paperback. 100 pages.

"This publication provides a convenient source of information relative to the name, address and responsibility of activities having interest in the conduct of the Defense Standardization Program. . . . Previous editions of this directory are superseded herewith."

Department of Defense. *Status of Standardization Project*. SD-4. Washington, D.C., DoD, quarterly.

This document shows the status of standardization projects for the development, revision, or amendment of standards, specifications, handbooks, and studies. The document has been compiled by the Air Force Logistics Command from data submitted by the military services and the Defense Supply Agency for use in the management of those projects. This document will be issued quarterly. (Page ii.)

Edwards, Alice, L. *Product Standards and Labelling for Consumers*. New York: Ronald Press, 1940. 134 pages.

"Various national agencies have set up special procedures under which different organizations and individuals work cooperatively in developing and promoting the use of standards and informative labels. Attention, in the material here presented, is given to the general procedures employed by a few outstanding agencies which foster cooperative activities of this type, and to some of the apparent weaknesses and strong points brought out by experience under them. Certain factors are pointed out which seem of special importance in insuring the practicability, as well as the economic and social soundness of standards established under the various procedures." (Page iii.)

Fahnestock, Brian E. *Application of Cost/Benefit Analysis in the Development of Voluntary Standards*. Master's degree thesis. Monterey, Calif.: Naval Postgraduate School, 1986. 129 pages.

The purpose of this thesis is to investigate the role and significance of standards to industry and society from an economic perspective. The decision-making processes of voluntary standards organizations such as the American National Standards Institute are examined within a framework of applied economic cost/benefit analysis. The findings of the study emphasize the need for nonengineering evaluation of standards and standardizing activities within single firms, industrywide organizations, or government.

Faucett, Jack, Associates. *Principles and Practical Approaches for Evaluating International Standards*. Report submitted to the National Bureau of Standards. Chevy Chase, Md.: Jack Faucett Associates, 1975. 42 pages.

The main text includes a concept for assessing welfare effects of standardization and the influence of the National Bureau of Standards on welfare with three case studies (computers, rubber and rubber products, nuclear instruments). Appendixes on the following topics: measuring changes in welfare, international trade and welfare effects of standardization, and a review of the literature on the economics of standardization.

Federal Trade Commission. *Standards and Certification: Final Staff Report, April 1983*. Washington, D.C.: Federal Trade Commission, 1983. Paperback. 382 pages.

In December 1978 the Federal Trade Commission initiated a rule-making proceeding to examine the extent of possible Federal Trade Commission Act violations (unfair methods of competition and unfair or deceptive acts or practices) in standards development and certification. The record of the proceeding contains extensive information on a wide range of factual, legal, and policy issues. This report summarizes the record evidence and presents staff's recommendations about appropriate commission enforcement action in the area. Based on the record, staff conclude that standards development and certification have the potential and in certain instances have led to competitive and consumer injury.

The sections of this report discuss the history of the proceeding and the remaining procedures that will be followed; the standards and certification industry, including reliance on the actions of standards developers and certifiers and potential positive and negative competitive effects on those actions; the practices on the record; legal theories that apply to those practices; and staff enforcement recommendations.

Federal Trade Commission. *Standards and Certification: Report of the Presiding Officer on Proposed Trade Regulation Rule.* Washington, D.C.: Federal Trade Commission, June 1983. Paperback. 315 pages.

The report contains a recommended decision based on the presiding officer's findings and conclusions as to all relevant and material evidence, taking into account the April 1983 final staff report. An introductory section includes posthearing matters and descriptives of the proposed rule. Finding of facts and conclusions are reviewed in the following sections: standards, how standards developers operate, how the proposed rule would affect standards developers, certificates, how the proposed rule would affect certifiers, appeals methods, alternatives and marketing. Legal issues are summarized.

Folts, Harold C., ed. *McGraw-Hill's Compilation of Data Communications Standards, Including the Omnicom Index of Standards.* New York: McGraw-Hill, 1986. 4,300 pages.

This compendium covers the field of data communications worldwide. The three volumes include the complete and unabridged standards set by CCITT, ECMA, EIA, ISO, ANSI, NCS, FIPS, and the U.S. government.

Gaillard, John. *A Study of the Fundamentals of Industrial Standardization and Its Practical Application, Especially in the Mechanical Field.* Doctoral Thesis (in English). Delft, Netherlands: Technical University, 1933. 132 pages.

Sections include essential functions of industrial standardization, definitions and characteristics of standards, practical applications, use in manufacturing concerns, organization of company standardization work, and further aspects.

Gaillard, John. *Industrial Standardization: Its Principles and Application.* New York: H. W. Wilson, 1934. 123 pages.

The author systematically describes the principles and functions of industrial standardization, taking most of his examples from the automobile industry. He starts with a brief account of events that led to the need for standardization, defining a standard as that which "should clearly and completely define, designate, or specify certain features of one or more of a number of concepts." He deals with standards from the point of view of management and views the standards movement as a stabilizing factor in the world economy.

General Services Administration. *Federal Standardization*. FPMR 101-29. Washington, D.C.: GSA, December 1981. Paperback. 7 chapters with distinct pagination.

This is GSA's counterpart to DoD's 4120.3M. "Federal agencies are expected to use this Handbook for guidance when they prepare and coordinate federal product descriptions under the Assigned Agency Plan described herein. They may also use it in development of departmental specifications and standards." (Page i.)

Glie, Rowen, ed. *Speaking of Standards*. Boston: Cahners Books, 1972. 302 pages. 29 articles.

This collection, sponsored by the Metropolitan New York Section of the Standards Engineers Society, is designed for engineering students as well as for general readers. According to the editor, several aspects of standardization are emphasized: "(1) learning or gathering of knowledge, (2) selecting or organizing knowledge, (3) promoting the use of standards or utilizing knowledge, and (4) communicating or spreading knowledge and know-how." (Page xxiv.) The special role of the standards engineers and the company standards department are identified by experienced practitioners. Although biographical sketches of each contributor are provided, the editor does not give exact citations for this collection of reprinted material. Major sections are introduction and standards (including reprinting of ANSI's illustrated brochure, "Through History with Standards"), standards engineer, standardization program, benefits of standardization, component selection and parts manual, and company standards departments.

Global Engineering Documents. *Directory of Engineering Document Sources*. 3d ed. A Consolidated Cross-Index of Document Initialisms Assigned by Government and Industry Organizations to Technical/Management Specifications, Standards, Reports and Related Publications. Santa Ana, Calif.: Global Engineering Documents, 1986.

Nearly 10,000 series of engineering, scientific, and management publications are included. Against each entry appears document series name, originating organization, index to the document series, and source of document.

Grogan, Denis. "Standards," in *Science and Technology, An Introduction to the Literature*. 2d rev. ed. London: Clive Bingley, 1973. 201-207.

Grogan, in the introduction to this edition, indicates that although "designated primarily as a textbook for students rather than a guide for practicing librarians, its adoption in universities over five continents would suggest that its particular approach to its subject fulfilled real need." Chapter 15, "Standards," covers types of standards, the British Standards Institution, United States standards, government specifications, international standards, and tracing standards.

Grossnickle Linda L., ed. *An Index of State Specifications and Standards*. NBS SP 375. Gaithersburg, Md.: National Bureau of Standards, 1973. Paperback. 394 pages.

This computer-produced index contains the printed titles of more than 6,000 state purchasing specifications and standards issued by 37 state purchasing offices through 1971. The title of each specification and standard can be found under all the significant keywords it contains. These keywords are arranged alphabetically down the center of each page together with their surrounding context. The date of publication or latest revision, the specification or standard number, and an abbreviation for each state appear as part of each entry. A list of these abbreviations and the names and addresses of the state purchasing officials are found at the beginning of the index.

Keywords: Index of state specifications and standards; Key-Word-in-Context index of state specifications and standards; purchase specifications and standards, state; specifications, state; standards, state; state specifications and standards.

Hagan, Norm A. *Implementing a Standards Program for Procurement*. Ottawa, Canada: Standards Council of Canada, June 1985. 19 pages.

This booklet was written for those who are creating standards programs as well as for purchasing officers and other managers. It is a guideline, and the author contends that "for the vast majority of the items you purchase, standards already exist." The value of standardization is recognized as permitting "economies of scale and minimization of an unnecessary variety of products that perform the same function." (Page 5.)

Hamilton, Robert W. *The Role of Nongovernmental Standards in the Development and Review of Mandatory Federal Standards Affecting Safety or Health*. Reprinted in booklet form from *Texas Law Review* 56:1328-1484, no. 8 (November 1978).

"In recent years the federal government has increasingly regulated the health and safety characteristics of products, processes, the workplace, and the environment. Since the middle of the nineteenth century, and particularly in the last half century, private organizations have developed tens of thousands of standards that serve to coordinate the productive efforts of American businesses. While many of these 'nongovernmental' standards apply to the same products and processes that have become the subject of federal regulation, the relationship between the private standards system and the many federal agencies responsible for developing federal health and safety regulations has not been formalized or even well defined. Many observers have voiced concern that nongovernmental standards do not adequately reflect the interests of consumers, workers, and small businesses.

"In this comprehensive article, Professor Hamilton examines decision-making in the most prominent private standards-writing organizations and suggests that they provide a valuable store of experience and expertise that federal agencies cannot readily duplicate, even though they do not, and perhaps cannot, adequately represent some interests. After analyzing the experience of several federal agencies that have attempted to use nongovernmental standards in developing federal health and safety regulations, Professor Hamilton argues for a more consistent approach to the use of these standards. To this end, he proposes a framework for the development of a uniform federal policy of coordination and cooperation with private standards-writing organizations that best utilizes the experience and expertise of the private organizations while ensuring adequate protection of health and safety interests consistent with the agencies' mandates." (Abstract.) Includes table of contents.

Harriman, Norman F. *Standards and Standardization*. New York: McGraw-Hill, 1928. 265 pages.

This is a basic source for one interested in the evolution of consciousness of the impact of standardization. The author, senior engineer-physicist at the National Bureau of Standards, notes that, despite recent interest in the subject "at the present time [August 1928] there is not a single book in the English language on this important subject." After surveying the "evolution" of standards, industry, and standardization, Harriman explains types of standards and makes predictions regarding the future.

Harter, Philip J. *Regulatory Use of Standards: The Implications for Standards Writers*. Washington, D.C.: National Bureau of Standards, 1979. Paperback. 286 pages.

The purposes of this report are (1) to help standards-writing organizations prepare standards that are acceptable to regulatory agencies for use in regulations or as an alternative to regulation and (2) to suggest how regulatory agencies might improve their relationships with private-sector standards organizations. The report describes how standards are used in regulatory programs and discusses the requirements imposed on agencies by administrative law. From this analysis, it is possible to make some general suggestions; for example, organizations writing standards for possible regulatory use should prepare an accompanying rationale and procedural history. The report summarizes complaints of standards organizations about regulatory agencies and suggests how agencies might improve their relationships with standards organizations.

Keywords: Administrative law; law; legal aspects of standards; regulation; safety regulation; standards organizations; voluntary standards.

Hemenway, David. *Industrywide Voluntary Product Standards*. Cambridge, Mass.: Ballinger, 1975. 141 pages.

"Except for the consideration of collusive conduct, economies have rarely analyzed industrywide activity, much less the role played by industrywide voluntary product standards and standardization in our society. This work examines this important aspect of intercompany behavior and offers, for the first time, an in-depth economic analysis of voluntary standards and standardization. Standards are classified and their benefits and costs discussed. The author shows how market structure determines both the incentives and the ability needed to create workable product standards within a given industry. The discussion includes prescriptions for public policy regarding industrywide standards." This book is a very comprehensive economic study of the U.S. voluntary standards system. Includes 170 bibliographical references.

Hemenway, David. *Performance vs. Design Standards*. NBS-GCR 80-287. Gaithersburg, Md.: National Bureau of Standards, 1980. Paperback. 35 pages.

This report compares and contrasts performance and design standards from an economic perspective. The research consisted of a careful examination of the literature and interviews with interested NBS personnel. The paper describes the characteristics of performance standards, explains why they are not used more often, and discusses particular areas where they may be appropriate. The report examines the design versus performance issue in automobile regulation and health care. There are suggestions for further NBS action to promote performance standards and a listing of areas for further research. Nine brief cases at the end of the paper illustrate points made in the main text.

Keywords: Performance standards; design standards; automobile standards; health care standards; standards; economies of standards; innovation.

Hemenway, David. *Standards Systems in Canada, the UK, West Germany, and Denmark: An Overview.* NBS-GCR 79-172. Gaithersburg, Md.: National Bureau of Standards, 1979. Paperback. 195 pages.

This report provides an overview of the voluntary standards systems of Canada, the UK, West Germany, and Denmark. The immediate purpose is to identify areas where further research might be useful. Ultimately, the aim is to gain a better understanding of national standards systems in other highly industrialized countries. Based on interviews and other research, the author discusses these aspects of the four standards systems: (1) history, (2) organization and finances, (3) standards development, (4) certification and accreditation, (5) international standards work, (6) consumer and labor participation, (7) metric conversion, (8) antitrust aspects, (9) research into economic impacts, (10) the government's use of standards and its role in standards work, and (11) other activities. The author concludes that further research is needed into standards systems of these and additional countries – for example, Australia, Japan, and Sweden.

Keywords: Antitrust; Canada; certification; Denmark; economics of standards; government policy; international standards; laboratory accreditation; standards systems; United Kingdom; West Germany.

Hill, I. D., and B. L. Meek. *Programming Language Standardization.* New York: John Wiley & Sons, 1980. 261 pages.

"The principal aim of this book is to dispel some of the confusion and misunderstanding which surrounds the subject of programming language standardization. Most programmers are aware that language standards exist, as least for Cobol and Fortran, but many are not very clear about what the existence of a standard means for them, or even whether particular features of their own implementation are standard or not; and relatively few could with confidence explain how language standards come about. We felt that there was a need for a book which would explain what the whole business is about – what has been achieved, how it has been achieved, what might be achieved in future, and the purpose of the whole exercise.

"The book is in two parts. Part 1 describes the current [1980] situation in the programming language standards field. Chapters are provided on each of the main languages in the standards arena at that time, and in some areas closely related to programming languages. The main criterion for inclusion has been whether a topic falls within the international (ISO) committee responsible for programming languages, and the emphasis throughout is on international standardization, rather than simply nations. Part 2 takes the form of a discussion of what programming language standards could be like, or should be like, rather than what they are like. Whereas the aim of Part 1 is to inform, the aim of Part 2 is to stimulate thought and discussion." (Preface.)

Houghton, Bernard. *Technical Information Sources: A Guide to Patent Specifications, Standards and Technical Reports Literature.* Hamden, Conn.: Finnet Books, Shoe String Press, 1972. 119 pages.

This work provides information on the bibliographical control of technical information, particularly relating to the British patent system. Chapter 6 covers the broader topic of standards and specifications: evolution and nature. Chapter 7 surveys standardizing bodies in the United States and England. Chapter 8 deals specifically with the bibliographic control of standards and should be helpful for those in the field of information services. There are ten chapters.

Hyde, William F. *Improving Productivity by Classification, Coding and Data Base Standardization.* New York: Marcel Dekker, 1981.

"An excellent reference on classification, written by one of the foremost authorities on the subject." Other related works by this author are also available.

Hyer, Charles W. *Principal Aspects of U.S. Laboratory Accreditation Systems.* Rev. ed. Gaithersburg, Md.: National Bureau of Standards, 1984. Paperback. 248 pages. Being revised for 1991.

The purpose of this report is to identify United States laboratory accreditation systems and to summarize the principal aspects of these systems. Previous reports were published in 1979 and 1980 under the same title. The latest adds 41 systems not previously reported and contains 109 systems. The most significant addition to the report over and above previous editions is the information on fields of testing and products covered for each system. The report places the systems in four separate categories: (1) federal government systems, (2) state government systems, (3) local government systems, and (4) professional/trade organization systems. A revised version of this report is due in 1990.

Keywords: Laboratory accreditations process; laboratory accreditation programs.

Information Handling Services. *The BRS Database for Industry and International Standards.* Englewood, Colo.: Information Handling Services. 1988. Annual.

The STDS Database contains voluntary engineering standards from private-sector societies and organizations. The standards in this database come from two secondary sources, the IHS/Industry and International Standards Database and the National Bureau of Standards (NBS) Voluntary Engineering Standards Database. Because each citation in STDS includes a location within the film of the full text, STDS can be used as an index to the IHS film. Alternatively, the full text of citations referenced in STDS can be ordered from Global Engineering.

Used in conjunction with the Military and Federal Specifications and Standards Database (MLSS), STDS provides the most complete online coverage available for published standards. To facilitate searching these complementary files, BRS has concatenated the STDS and MLSS databases; they can be searched together under the search label ISMS. File structure has been designed to promote complementary searching; refer to the MLSS Database Guide for complete information on this companion file to STDS.

Information Handling Services. *The BRS Database for Military and Federal Specifications and Standards.* Englewood, Colo.: Information Handling Services. 1988. Updated regularly.

The Military and Federal Specifications and Standards Database is the most complete source for active and historical standards and specifications of the DoD and the federal government. The full text of all the standards and specifications referenced in MLSS is available in microform as the Information Handling Services (IHS) family of products. Because each citation in MLSS includes a location within the film of the full text, MLSS can be used as an index to the IHS film. Alternatively, the full text of citations references in MLSS can be ordered from Global Engineering.

Used in conjunction with the Industry and International Standards Database (STDS), also produced by IHS, MLSS provides the most complete online coverage available for published standards. To facilitate searching these complementary files, BRS has concatenated the MLSS and STDS databases; they can be searched together under the search label ISMS. File structure has been designed to promote complementary searching; refer to the STDS Database Guide for complete information on this companion file on MLSS.

Information Handling Services. *Index and Directory of U.S. Industry Standards*. 6th ed., Englewood, Colo.: Information Handling Services, 1988. 2 Vols. Annual.

"With references to over 400 U.S. standards-producing societies, the *Index and Directory of U.S. Industry Standards* is the most comprehensive printed reference tool of its kind available today. Not only does it cover large organizations such as ANSI, ASTM, ASME, SAE, and NEMA, but it also references hundreds of smaller, lesser known, and specialized industrial societies." Volume one is the subject index; the second volume includes a society/numeric listing, ANSI number concordance, and society directory.

International Federation for the Application of Standards (IFAN). *Applying the World's Standards: Conference Papers*. Conference papers of 5th triennial meeting of IFAN and 35th annual meeting of the Standards Engineering Society (SES). Philadelphia: 28 September-1 October 1986. Paperback. Approximately 200 pages. Other triennial conference proceedings are available.

Sessions covered the following topics: standardization successes, critical issues in telecommunications and information processing, speeding up standards development by applying modern technology, applying international standards, techniques for measuring the effectiveness of standardization programs, finding and using standards, applying article characteristics, and new standardization developments around the world.

International Laboratory Accreditation Conference (ILAC). *International Directory of Laboratory Accreditation Systems and Other Schemes for Assessment of Testing Laboratories*. 4th ed. Chatswood, NSW, Australia: National Association of Testing Laboratories (NATA), 1990.

The directory is published by NATA on behalf of the International Laboratory Accreditation Conference (ILAC). It contains entries from 78 laboratory accreditation systems in 24 countries. It begins with laboratory accreditation systems by country. The information for each includes name of accrediting body, form of incorporation, funding, fees, geographic limitation, fields of testing, test methods, accreditation criteria, laboratory assessment, assessors, surveillance, proficiency testing, publications, international recognition, and point of contact.

International Organization for Standardization (ISO). *Benefits of Standardization*. Geneva: International Organization for Standardization, 1982. Paperback. 145 pages.

In an effort to help "quantify" the effects of standardization, this is presented as the "first attempt to propose methods that can be applied to all aspects of international standardization work, in addition to be applicable at national and company levels." The substantive chapters are how standardization benefits are generated, qualitative assessment, quantitative assessment, application of assessments, assessment examples, and benefit review of standardization areas. The methodology is explained, and definitions provided, in "annexes" to the preceding text.

International Organization for Standardization (ISO). *KWIC Index of International Standards*. Geneva: ISO, 1983 and thereafter.

This index contains the permuted titles of some 7,600 documents resulting from the standardizing activities of 24 international organizations. The documents include international standards, international recommendations, international conventions, technical annexes to international conventions, and international codes of practice. Some contain mandatory requirements (subject to ratification by governments) while in others the requirements are of a voluntary nature. Two criteria govern the selection of a document for inclusion in the index: It must establish technical requirements of importance to the international exchange of goods, services, or information, and it must emanate from a recognized international organization. Documents issued by regional organizations have not been included.

Interrante, C. G., and F. J. Heymann, eds. *Standardization of Technical Terminology: Principles and Practices*. Philadelphia: American Society for Testing and Materials, 1983. 148 pages.

"Of the many purposes that could be cited for this publication, the most important are to promote improvements in terminology used in technical standards and to foster communications among workers at various levels within the community that develops and uses technical terminology. (Page 1.)

"Contained herein are fourteen papers dealing with technical terminology topics from a broad range of viewpoints. These papers are complemented by a Summary and Commentary and a Glossary for the benefit of those not conversant with some of the terms found in this volume."

Johnson, Leland L. *Cost-Benefit Analysis and Voluntary Safety Standards for Consumer Products.* Santa Monica, Calif.: The Rand Corporation, 1982. Paperback. 71 pages.

This publication of the Institute for Civil Justice confronts issues such as "what view of the relative value of social investment in accident prevention is implicit in voluntary standards? Are they based on any formal analysis of the tradeoff between the dollar costs of preventive activity and the accident-related costs that are avoided? When such analyses are employed are they technically sound? How do standard-setters' price such intangibles as pain, suffering, annoyance and inconvenience? Is the information necessary to answer such questions now available to private or public decision makers?" The study "urges the more extensive use of cost-benefit analysis in establishing voluntary standards for product safety, even though difficult problems stand in the way. . . . (It) recommends several ways to promote the use of cost-benefit analysis." (Pages iii-vii.) A five-page bibliography is included.

Lansburgh, Richard H., ed. *Standards in Industry.* In *The Annals.* Vol. 137. Philadelphia: The American Academy of Political and Social Science, May 1928. 258 pages.

This survey of the topic is composed of essays written by individual authors. The four subject areas are standardization programs in industry (roles of national Chamber of Commerce, Europe, economic aspects, etc.), standardization programs of specific industries (textiles), standardization programs outside of industry, and standardization and the consumer. Volume 82 (March 1919) in *Industries in Readjustment* contains a six-article section on standardization of industrial equipment (national welfare, the work of the Bureau of Standards, etc.), pages 247-289.

The editor has divided the volume into four parts. Articles in the first part describe the contributions of early leaders in the standards field in the United States. The second part deals with the problems in standardization that have been met with in various industries, how they have been overcome, and the resulting progress. The remaining parts deal with nonindustrial and consumers' interest in standardization.

LaQue, Francis L. *Report of the Panel on Engineering and Commodity Standards of the Commerce Technical Advisory Board.* Washington, D.C.: National Bureau of Standards, 1965. 169 pages.

The report has been divided into two sections for purposes of reproduction. Section A contains the organization and activities of the panel, definitions of terms, major findings, concordance of recommendations made by the several task forces, references, and information on participants and meetings held by the panel and task forces. Section B contains the reports submitted by the task forces. Those having a special interest in particular aspects of standardization activities or in more detailed information should obtain both sections of the report.

The overall review was undertaken by task forces assigned to deal with seven areas of investigation. These task forces enlisted the aid of consultants having special knowledge and experience in the several fields that were explored in detail.

This overall panel report highlights the major conclusions and recommendations and constitutes a concordance of the principal features of the several task force reports.

The most important finding was the need for a more effective organization using improved procedures for voluntary coordination and promulgation of standards that would meet the requirements for recognition in "USA Standards" [American National Standards] both in national and in international standardization activities.

The development of standards should be left to the several private organizations already active in this field. These were found to be competent, effective, and aware of the continuing need of a dynamic standards activity responsive to the requirements of our freedom-oriented society.

Many additional recommendations are addressed to the government, to industry, to the organizations that develop and promulgate standards, and to the general public. We hope that these will stimulate enlarged and even more effective activities in this field with technical and financial support for them by both industry and government to the extent that the national interest requires.

Legget, Robert F. *Standards in Canada*. Ottawa: Economic Council of Canada, 1970. 248 pages. 16 chapters.

This survey is clearly intended to keep Canada in a leadership role in the field of standardization. In addition, "it is the purpose of this study to show how the concept of standardization pervades all parts of the national economy and to illustrate how powerful an instrument it is for good, but also how it can be turned to ill effect on occasion if not adequately controlled and directed." (Page 20.) Topics covered are industrial and safety standards, standard-writing bodies throughout the world, and national and international standards. Appendixes give bibliographical and organizational information.

Leight, Walter G., ed. *Proceedings of Conference on Standards and Trade.* NBSIR 87-3573. Gaithersburg, Md.: National Bureau of Standards, June 1987. Paperback. 109 pages.

The International Trade Administration and the National Bureau of Standards sponsored a one-day Conference on Standards and Trade on 5 May 1987. These proceedings contain the texts of speeches by government officials and representatives of the business and standards communities, summaries of question-and-answer periods, and reports of working groups that addressed participation in international standardization activities, test data acceptance, and adoption of U.S. standards.

The purpose of the conference was to identify and explore possible actions by the government and the private sector to enhance U.S. trade through promoting U.S. standards and the technology they embody in foreign countries and international organizations. Three U.S. government officials stressed the need to improve the national trade picture, described ongoing efforts by the government under the GATT Agreement on Technical Barriers to Trade (the Standards Code), bilateral negotiations on standards-related trade problems, participation in treaty organizations and other government-to-government international committees, and the status of the current Uruguay Round of Multinational Trade Negotiations (MTN) talks. They expressed receptiveness to private-sector views and their willingness to apply available resources to strengthen our trade position, especially in the international standards arena.

A second group of speakers addressed standards-related concerns of the business community. The third session considered the subject of private-sector participation in international standardization. Afternoon working sessions analyzed three areas: participation in international standardization activities, the need to accept the test data from other countries, and promoting the adoption of U.S. standards in other countries.

Locke, John W., ed. *Laboratory Accreditation: Future Directions in the United States Proceedings of a Workshop Held at the National Bureau of Standards.* Held in Gaithersburg, Md., 16-17 November 1981. NBS SP 632. Washington, D.C.: National Bureau of Standards, 1982. Paperback. 172 pages.

The purpose of the workshop sponsored by the National Bureau of Standards was to provide a public forum for the expression of views upon which recommendations could be developed to bring about a desirable and effective distribution of responsibilities between government and private sectors in the area of laboratory accreditation. The workshop was initiated in response to two related requests to change the Department of Commerce's (DoC) National Voluntary Laboratory Accreditation Program (NVLAP) to enable NVLAP's laboratory accreditation activities to be transferred to the private sector; DoC's role would be limited to that of an accreditor of accreditation systems.

As a basis for initiating public comment, 20 invited participants presented papers in five sessions: (1) background of U.S. laboratory accreditation, (2) international trade implications of laboratory accreditation, (3) need for laboratory accreditation, (4) criteria for recognizing laboratory accreditation systems, and (5) a mechanism to accredit organizations that accredit testing laboratories. Approximately 200 people attended the workshop, and the written and oral reviews of all who participated are summarized in these proceedings. Also included are written comments (letters) that were sent in by participants and other interested persons after the workshop was concluded.

Keywords: Criteria; definitions; history; international trade; laboratory accreditation; need.

Mackay, Donald R., coordinator. *Guidelines for NBS Standards Committee Participants*. Washington, D.C.: National Bureau of Standards, 1984. Paperback. 36 pages.

This document provides guidance to NBS employees who participate in standards development activities of private-sector organizations such as ASTM, ASME, and IEEE. It provides basic information concerning appointments to committees, funding of participation, and the need for coordination with other NBS participants and other federal participants. It also emphasizes the need to keep management informed regarding sensitive issues.

Keywords: Committee participation; federal standards policy; standards; standards committees; standards participation.

Martino, Robert A. *Standardization Activities of National Technical and Trade Organizations*. NBS publication SP 681. Washington, D.C.: Government Printing Office, 28 November 1941. 288 pages.

The volume, issued a few days before the attack at Pearl Harbor, is introduced by Lyman J. Briggs, director of the National Bureau of

Standards. He identifies it as "an effort to present an adequate picture of the standardization and simplification movement being carried on by national technical and trade organizations in the United States. It contains outlines of the activities and accomplishments of 450 American societies and associations in which standardization is a major or an important activity. It is hoped that the information contained will be helpful also to agencies who are engaged in carrying forward the program for national defense." The report also includes an extensive, partly annotated bibliography (pages 243-65). The bibliography includes Library of Congress call numbers for books and periodicals.

Melnitsky, Benjamin. *Profiting from Industrial Standardization.* New York: Conover-Mast Publications, 1953. 25 chapters. 381 pages.

Administrations from many different industries contributed information to this how-to book. "The underlying theme" is "to demonstrate that standards have value because they produce profits." Other benefits to firms of various kinds of standards (classification, materials, parts, design, testing, purchasing, etc.) are also described.

Nagarajan, R. *Standards in Building.* New York: John Wiley & Sons, 1976. 174 pages.

"The author has attempted to present an up-to-date review of the principles and practice of standardization in building, which have been greatly influenced recently by the principles of modular co-ordination, the theory of preferred numbers, research into functional requirements, the concept of performance standards, and industrialization in building."

National Academy of Engineering (NAE). *Product Quality, Performance, and Cost.* A report and recommendation based on a symposium and workshops, 29-30 April 1971, Washington, D.C.: NAE, 1972. Paperback. 154 pages.

The booklet includes 22 symposium presentations and a summary of five concurrent workshop sessions. "The symposium and workshops provided the medium in which the many diverse consumer, producer, and engineering interests were brought together. They concentrated on problems and corrective actions while increasing the awareness of all parties of the other person's perspective. The discussions encouraged a direct exchange of views of consumer and producer problems and recommendations for corrective action." (Page 2.) The introduction also includes specific recommendations in the following areas: consumer and producer information, consumer education, engineering education, design, professional societies, and safety standards and safeguards.

National Bureau of Standards. *Publications of the Office of Product Standards Policy, Fiscal Years 1982-1985.* NBSIR-84-2845. Gaithersburg, Md.: National Bureau of Standards, October 1985. 11 pages.

The Office of Product Standards Policy (OPSP) of the National Institute of Standards and Technology formulates and implements programs relating to national and international standardization, laboratory accreditation, and legal metrology. This report lists publications prepared by the staff of OPSP during the four-year period ending September 1985. Papers are listed alphabetically by author in six sections: "Standards, Guidelines, and Procedures"; "Standards Activities"; "Standards Information"; "Laboratory Accreditation"; "Product Certification"; and "Weights and Measures."

Keywords: Standards, guidelines, and procedures; standards activities; standards information; laboratory accreditation; product certification; weights and measures.

National Bureau of Standards. *Report of the Panel on Engineering and Commodity Standards of the Commerce Technical Advisory Board.* 2 February 1965. Part 1, PB166811. 41 pages. Part 2, PB 166812. Pages 42-290. Gaithersburg, Md.: National Bureau of Standards, 1965.

"This report is in three principal parts. The first covers major findings and recommendations based on a study by the panel as a whole of the findings and recommendations of its several task forces in the light of its over-all concern with the general subject. It brings together and emphasizes those aspects of standardization activities in the United States of America that the panel feels should receive major and most immediate attention. It serves, also, to coordinate the recommendations of its task forces which dealt with similar matters from different points of view.

"The second part is a concordance of recommendations made by the several task forces. It segregates them with relation to, and for the convenience of, the bodies to whom the several recommendations are addressed. It should serve as a guide to such action as may be taken by these bodies to implement the many detailed recommendations addressed to them. These recommendations are derived appropriately from their sources in the several task force reports.

"The third part includes the several task force reports and their appendices as they were presented to, and accepted by, the panel as a whole after prior approval by the membership of the task force in which a report originated."

National Bureau of Standards. Institute for Computer Sciences and Technology. *Federal Information Processing Standards Publications (FIPS PUBS Index)*. Gaithersburg, Md.: National Bureau of Standards, February 1984. Updated periodically. 37+ pages.

Included are standards, guidelines, and program information documents currently classified in the following categories: general publications, hardware standards and guidelines, software standards and guidelines, data standards and guidelines, and ADP operation standards and guidelines. Entries in the publication list include title, publication number, date of issue, and a short abstract for each *FIPS PUB*. Associated voluntary standards and federal telecommunications standards and guidelines are included, where appropriate.

National Bureau of Standards. National Center for Standards and Certification Information. *Key-Word-in-Context (KWIC) Index of U.S. Voluntary Engineering Standards*. Gaithersburg, Md.: National Bureau of Standards, January 1986.

This periodically revised KWIC index was last published in 1986, but no further revisions nor update are planned.

National Computer Graphics Association. *Standards in the Computer Graphics Industry*, Fairfax, Va.: National Computer Graphics Association, 1986.

Includes computer graphics references for ANSI, ISO, CGM, CORE, MAP, and other major developers.

National Consumers League. *Report on Consumer Representation in Voluntary Standards Setting*. Washington, D.C.: National Consumers League and the American Society for Testing and Materials, 1978-79.

A report of the demonstration project on consumer representation in ASTM's standards-setting work on consumer products. Report is in two parts, for years one and two, totaling 20 pages.

National Machine Tool Builders Association (NMTBA). *Machine Tool Standards Index*. 3d ed. McLean, Va.: NMTBA, January 1986.

This publication has been prepared by the NMTBA technical department as an aid to machine tool builders in their search for specific standards applying to the design, manufacture, sale, and use of their products. Included are lists of standards and specifications covering a wide range of subjects that are of interest to the industry, either directly or because they are referenced in other applicable standards or specifications. Much of the information pertains to standards promulgated in the United States; however, standards of the International Organization for Standardization (ISO) and the

International Electrotechnical Commission (IEC) have been incorporated because of the increasing interest in export sales and because of the expected future conversion of the United States to the metric system of measurements. The standards of individual foreign countries are not included because of the difficulty of obtaining the information and because of the great volume of these standards.

Part 2 is a listing of the pertinent standards known to NMTBA (2,000 standards of 80 U.S. organizations and ISO) at the time of publication. These are arranged under subject categories in alphabetical order by title. Following the titles are the identification codes assigned by the issuing agency.

Some standards are listed in several categories for the convenience of the user of this publication. Part 3 is a list of the U.S. Department of Defense machine tool specifications (approximately 250).

National Research Council. *Materials and Process Specifications and Standards*. Washington, D.C.: National Academy of Sciences, 1977. Paperback. 213 pages.

The Committee on Materials Specifications, Testing Methods, and Standards examined the present status of specifications and standards work in the Department of Defense and elsewhere, as appropriate. As a major item, the committee recommends that the U.S. voluntary standards system be extensively called on to rectify a growing deficiency in the DoD system. The impact of the present situation, as related to engineering education, industrial engineering, current domestic and international trade, and Department of Defense problems of cost, design, reliability, and procurement is assessed. Appropriate recommendations for a plan of action are made, aimed at producing a more efficient, effective, and nationally unified system.

Nuclear Standards Management Center, DoE. *Nuclear Standards Master Index*. Oak Ridge, Tenn.: U.S. Department of Energy, semiannually. Detailed citation is in Standards Information Centers appendix.

Office of the U.S. Trade Representative (USOTR), GATT Affairs. *Second Triennial Report to the Congress on the Agreement on Technical Barriers to Trade*. January 1983 to December 1985. Washington, D.C.: USOTR, February 1986. Paperback. 70 pages.

The Trade Agreement Act of 1979 requires that the administration report to the U.S. Congress every three years on its activities pertaining to the Standards Code. This is the second triennial report, covering the period January 1983 through December 1985. It concentrates on information about the code's implementation in the United States and in the other signatory countries, along with supplementary projections in some sections. One of the most significant elements of the Standards Code for U.S. exporters is the information network that has been developed to alert member countries of foreign standards-related activities.

The code establishes international principles by which signatories (currently 38) are to conduct their standards-related activities. Standards-related activities include the preparation, adoption, and application of voluntary standards, mandatory standards (i.e., regulations), test methods, packaging and labeling requirements, and rules of certification systems.

Ollner, Jan. *The Company and Standardization*. Stockholm: Swedish Standards Institution, 1974. Paperback. 87 pages.
    A general introduction to standardization in Sweden's companies. Chapters include the role of standardization, standards and products, the organization of standardization activities, practical formulation of company standards, and preparation of standards.

Omnicom. *The Omnicom Index of Standards*. For Distributed and Telecommunication Systems. Vienna, Va.: Omnicom, 1987. 710+ pages.
    The Omnicom Index of Standards, an annual publication, is a compilation of bibliographic citations with abstracts and ordering information covering currently published and pending standards related to Open Systems Interconnection (OSI), ISDN, and data communications. The standards covered reflect the efforts of 21 national and international organizations.

The standards are identified in two indexes—"Subject" and "Organization." The subject index is an abbreviated listing by subject, organization, and standard number. The organization index is alphabetical by organization, and within each organization citations are alphanumeric by standard or document number. Under each organization, published standards are listed first. A listing of technical reports also published by that organization may follow. The International Organization for Standardization (ISO), however, contains one continuous numeric listing of published standards, draft international standards, draft proposals, addenda, and technical reports.

Oppermann, Henry V., ed. *Specifications, Tolerances, and Other Technical Requirements for Weighing and Measuring Devices*. NIST HB44.

Gaithersburg, Md.: National Institute of Standards and Technology. 1990. 275 pages. Revised annually.

Handbook 44 was first published in 1949, having been preceded by similar handbooks of various designations and in several forms beginning in 1918. This 1990 edition was developed by the Committee on Specifications and Tolerances of the National Conference on Weights and Measures with the assistance of the Office of Weights and Measures of the National Institute of Standards and Technology. It includes amendments adopted by the 74th annual meeting of the National Conference on Weights and Measures in 1989. Handbook 44 is published in its entirety each year following the annual meeting of the National Conference on Weights and Measures. The current edition includes new standards for mass flow meters in the Vehicle-Tank Meters Code and the Milk Meters Code.

Keywords: Grain moisture; length-measuring devices; liquid-measuring devices; measures; scales; specifications; taximeters; tolerances; user requirements; volume-measuring devices; weights.

Overman, JoAnne R. (Debelius). *1987 GATT Notification Activities*. Gaithersburg, Md.: National Bureau of Standards, 1987. 25 pages. Annual.

This report describes the GATT notification activities performed by the Standards Code and Information Program, National Bureau of Standards, for calendar year 1987. The U.S. Department of Commerce designated NBS as the official U.S. inquiry point for information on standards and certification activities. NBS's responsibilities include notifying the GATT Secretariat of proposed U.S. federal government standards-based rules that may significantly affect trade, maintaining information on similar notifications made by other signatories, and responding to inquiries about foreign and U.S. notifications.

Keywords: GATT Standards Code; foreign regulations; notifications.

Page, Chester H., and Paul Vigoureau, eds. *The International Bureau of Weights and Measures 1875-1975*. SP 420. Washington, D.C.: National Bureau of Standards, 1975. 248 pages. Paperback. Illustrated.

This volume is a translation of the International Bureau of Weights and Measures (BIPM) centennial volume and celebrates the 1875 signing of the Treaty of the Metre. Following a historical introduction, several topics are examined in detail: mass, length, gravimetry, manobarometry, thermometry, electricity, photometry, measurement of radioactivity, X and gamma rays, and neutron measurements.

Perry, John. *The Story of Standards*. New York: Funk and Wagnalls, 1955. Illustrated. 271 pages.

This volume is a popular social history of standardization. The author, a Washington, D.C. management consultant, had a special fascination for the activities of the National Bureau of Standards.

Phucas, Charles B. *International Standards Activities: A Study of NBS Impact on International Standards Committee Activities*. Gaithersburg, Md.: U.S. Department of Commerce, National Bureau of Standards, 6 June 1975. 9 pages.

Includes as one of its appendixes the following report: Jack Faucett Associates, *Principles and Practical Approaches for Evaluating International Standards*. (Also included in this bibliography.) Includes 17 bibliographical references.

This appendix briefly outlines a conceptual framework for the economic evaluation of standards. The approach is applied in case studies of three areas of NBS international standards activities: computers, rubber and rubber products, and nuclear instruments. Two supplementary sections briefly discuss welfare changes as measured by consumer and producer surplus as well as the welfare consequences of changes in international trade as a result of standardization. Another supplementary section provides a useful review of some works on the economics of standardization.

Phucas, Charles B., ed. *Symposium on International Standards Information and ISONET*. Gaithersburg, Md.: National Bureau of Standards, 1980. Paperback. 61 pages.

The American National Standards Institute (ANSI) and NBS have been working cooperatively with the International Organization for Standardization (ISO) to provide United States input to the development of an International Standards Information Network, called ISONET. Symposium participants had an opportunity to learn more about existing international standards information systems as well as the plans for the further development of ISONET. Through question and answer discussions, participants were able to learn about new developments in U.S. trade policy, especially those policies pertaining to standards and certification systems.

Keywords: ISO; ISONET symposium; proceedings; standards information.

Poulson, Barry W., ed. *Economic Analysis of the National Measurement System*. NBSIR75-948. Gaithersburg, Md.: National Bureau of Standards, September 1977.

This report is a comprehensive summation of relevant work known to NBS on economic analysis of the national measurement system. It is written for a mixed audience of economists and physical scientists. The first part deals with the concept of measurement for economic analysis, the quantitative dimensions of measurement in the economy, and the relationships between measurement and economic change. The second part of the study examines the measurement system from the standpoint of the private sector, including the economic rationale for measurement by producers, by consumers, and in sales transactions. The third part deals with government's role of incorporating an economic rationale for measurement activities in the public sector and case studies of costs and benefits of activities by NBS. While none of the case studies satisfies the conditions of rigorous cost-benefit or cost-effectiveness analysis, they do provide insight into the economic role of NBS in the national measurement system.

Preiser, H. Steffen, and Robert S. Marvin. *Testing and Certification for Export Products in Industrializing Countries*. Washington, D.C.: National Bureau of Standards, 1976. 160 pages.

A regional seminar sponsored by the Singapore Institute of Standards and Industrial Research, the National Bureau of Standards, and the Agency for International Development was held in Singapore in May of 1975. The participants represented most of the countries in south Asia concerned with increasing their exports and concentrated on various problems connected with the testing and certification of such exports. Most of the prepared papers reviewed the practice and future plans of these countries. During the discussion, a number of specific problems and issues were raised, with a good deal of attention focused on the extent to which the standards and certification of goods by an exporting country can be and are recognized by the importer. This report includes both the prepared papers and a mildly edited version of the discussions following each.

Preston, R. P., ed. *Putting Standards to Work*. Ottawa: Standards Council of Canada, 1977. Paperback. About 100 pages. Out of print.

This collection represents the edited proceedings of a conference held in Montreal on 17 November 1977. Six distinct documents are included. The first, by the editor, presents an overview of the evaluation of standardization (17 pages). The second, by W. Bruce Dodd of the Canadian Government Specifications Board, explains the procedure for "finding standards information and obtaining standards" (9 pages and appendixes). A standards search plan is presented in outline form. A. P. Harris offers information on standards for quality assurance and certification (19 pages), followed by a review of the role of standards in trade by H. C. Douglas (11 pages). "Standardization Opportunities for Metric Conversion" is discussed by George O. Sanders (8 pages). The concluding paper is on standardization at the company level. It was prepared by B. G. Young and P. Emg (17 pages plus appendixes).

Preston, R. P. *Standardization Is Good Business*. Ottawa: Standards Council of Canada, 1977. Paperback. 27 pages. Out of print.

Basic introduction to the subject of standardization; includes discussion of the use and benefits of standardization to the individual organization.

Rawie, Carol Chapman. *A Guide to Papers Citing Antitrust Cases Involving Standards or Certification*. Washington, D.C.: National Bureau of Standards, 1979. NBSIR 79-1921. Paperback. 17 pages.

Since at least 1912, standards and certifications for products ranging from lumber to milk cans have been at issue in antitrust cases. Studying these cases may provide information about the economic effects of standards and certifications based on standards – in particular, their impact on competition and innovation. This paper describes several articles and reports that examine the antitrust history of standards. It is intended as a research tool to help economists and others decide which (if any) antitrust cases they should study to learn more about the economic effects of standards.

Keywords: Antitrust; certification; competition; economics of standards; law; standards.

Rawie, Carol Chapman. *Economics of the Product Certification Industry: Some Research Needs*. Washington, D.C.: National Bureau of Standards, 1980. Paperback. 74 pages.

A number of private organizations certify products for safety and other qualities. With the increase in safety regulation, product liability suits, and interest in encouraging the use of new technologies through certification, certification is likely to become more and more important as a way to show conformance with voluntary or regulatory standards. There has been a number of federal and state government activities related to product certification. However, the potential impact of past and proposed government actions is not clear. One reason may be that there has been insufficient study of the economics of the product certification industry. This paper asserts that such study is needed as a basis for setting government policy and raises issues that should be addressed concerning structure and performance of the product certification industry.

Keywords: Economics; certification; product certification; certification industry; government policy; standardization research needs; standards; accreditation of testing laboratories.

Reck, Dickson, ed. *National Standards in a Modern Economy.* New York: Harper and Row Publishers, Inc., 1956. 372 pages.

This book is a collection of 33 articles by various authors concerning the history and effects of standardization. It focuses primarily on technical benefits of standards in a number of sectors but also contains some qualitative comments concerning price and cost effects. A chapter by T. Richard Witmer discusses antitrust consequences of consumer goods standards, and a chapter by Corwing Edwards discusses the relationship of standards and product differentiation.

Ricci, Patricia, and Linda Perry. *Standards: Resource and Guide for Identification, Selection, and Acquisition.* St. Paul, Minn.: Stirtz, Bernards, 1991 revised edition.

This book is a very comprehensive worldwide directory of organizations that prepare and publish standards and similar works such as guides, recommended practices, handbooks, or specifications.

The directory sections emphasize purchasing requirements in addition to address and telephone number. International, multinational, regional, and single-nation standards bodies are included, along with information about major collections of standards publications in libraries throughout the world.

The bibliography section contains information on online databases, indexes, topical collections, and basic texts on standardization. There are several indexes: a subject index, an index to the acronyms for the standards organizations, and an integrated organization index. The index to standards publications' alpha designations is unique.

Sanders, T. R. B. *The Aims and Principles of Standardization.* Geneva: International Organization for Standardization, 1972. Paperback. 115 pages.

ISO Secretary-General, Olle Sturen, indicates that this volume is based on the assumed *"need* to standardize . . . particularly evident in the international field. . . . This book is an attempt to condense some of the general philosophy of these STACO [ISO standardization principles committee] studies, together with views expressed in certain other papers and documents emanating from leaders in close touch with international standardization." (Page 2.) Chapters cover the aims and principles of standardization, terms and definitions, measurement, standardization of products, tools of management, international level, national and company level, the consumer and standardization, the control of quality, and future trends.

Settle, Russell Franklin, and Burton A. Weisbrod. *Governmentally-Imposed Standards: Some Normative and Positive Aspects*. Prepared by the Department of Economics, Wisconsin University, for Assistant Secretary for Planning, Evaluation, and Research, U.S. Department of Labor. Washington, D.C.: June 1976. 55 pages. NTIS No. PB-256-274.

This report provides a conceptual discussion of the need for governmentally imposed standards. These mandated standards are compared with alternative policy instruments, such as taxes and public information programs. The conditions under which standards would be preferable to these other alternatives are studied. The analysis includes both equity and efficiency considerations.

Shock, Harvey, ed. *Accreditation Practices for Inspections, Tests and Laboratories*. ASTM STP 1057. Philadelphia: American Society for Testing and Materials, 1989. Paperback. 155 pages.

This peer reviewer volume lists many ASTM standards, international guides, and other publications relating to laboratory accreditation, the assessment of laboratories, quality systems, and associated test methods. Thirteen papers are divided into four sections: "General Concerns for Laboratory Accreditation," "Laboratory Accreditation Programs and Techniques," "Related Contributions to Laboratory Accreditation," and "Laboratory Accreditation in International Commerce."

Essential for persons operating inspection and test laboratories as well as for assessors, accreditors, regulators, suppliers, and customers of laboratories and accreditation.

Shock, Harvey, ed. *Evaluation and Accreditation of Inspection and Test Activities*. ASTM STP 814. Philadelphia: American Society for Testing and Materials, 1983. 195 pages.

Silberston, Aubrey. *The Economic Consequences of International Standardization*. Document ISO/STACO (Secretariat-54) 389E. Geneva: International Standards Organization, May 1967.

This report presents a list of possible economic consequences of both national and international standards, including costs and benefits to producers, consumers, and supplying industries. The importance of the distribution of benefits and costs is noted. A particular standard may benefit some parties (e.g., the long-run gains to producers resulting from a reduction of variety in production) while simultaneously resulting in a loss to others (e.g., a reduction of choice to consumers).

Silva, Michael, and Bertil Sjögren. *Europe 1992 and the New World Power Game*. New York: Wiley, 1990. 320 pages.

This stimulating work examines the new order that will result as the importance of national boundaries recedes in the face of a shared economic future after 1992. Calling it a "consumer era," he argues that world peace in coming years will have less to do with competing ideologies than with consumer products, and the European Community will play a central role in this drama. The first three chapters investigate the forces of a global market – capitalism, consumerism, and consortia. The actual mechanics of European unification and the obstacles to making it a reality form the subject of chapters four and five, while the decline of Japan, the revitalization of the U.S., and the technology explosion are the focus of chapters six, seven, and eight. A final section returns to issues of world realignment, exploring new directions in the relationships among Japan, Europe, and the U.S., with an eye toward the rapid consumerization of eastern Europe, the Soviet Union, and Communist China.

Slattery, William J. *Index of U.S. Nuclear Standards*. NBS SP 483. Gaithersburg, Md.: National Bureau of Standards, August 1977.

This index contains the permuted titles of more than 1,200 nuclear and nuclear-related standards, specifications, test methods, codes, and recommended practices published by 34 U.S. government agencies, technical societies, professional organizations, and trade associations. Each title can be found under all the significant keywords it contains. These keywords are arranged alphabetically down the center of each page together with their surrounding context. Each entry includes the date of publication or last revision, the standard number, an acronym designating the standards-issuing organization, any cross-reference standard number, and price.

Keywords: Engineering standards, index of; index of nuclear standards; nuclear standards; and KWIC index of standards.

Slattery, William J., ed. *An Index of U.S. Voluntary Engineering Standards*. Gaithersburg, Md.: National Bureau of Standards, 1971. 984 pages.

This computer-produced index contains the permuted titles of more than 19,000 voluntary engineering and related standards, specifications, test methods, and recommended practices, in effect as of 31 December

1969, published by some 360 U.S. technical societies, professional organizations, and trade associations. The title of each standard can be found under all the significant keywords it contains. These keywords are arranged alphabetically down the center of each page together with their surrounding context. The date of publication or last revision, the standard number, and an acronym designating the standards-issuing organization appear as part of each entry. A list of these acronyms and the names and addresses of the organizations they represent are found at the beginning of the index.

Keywords: Engineering standards, index of; index of standards, recommended practices, specifications, and test methods: Key-Word-in-Context index of voluntary standards; standards, voluntary, index of.

Slattery, William J., ed. *An Index of U.S. Voluntary Engineering Standards, Supplement 1.* Washington, D.C.: National Bureau of Standards, December 1972.

This supplement contains the permuted titles of more than 6,300 standards, specifications, test methods, and recommended practices published by 225 U.S. technical societies, professional organizations, and trade associations. Each title can be found under all the significant keywords it contains. These keywords are arranged alphabetically down the center of each page together with their surrounding context. The date of publication or last revision, the standard number, and an acronym designating the standards-issuing organization appear as part of each entry.

Keywords: Engineering standards, index of; index of standards, recommended practices, specifications, test methods; Key-Word-in-Context index of voluntary standards; standards, voluntary, index of.

Slattery, William J., ed. *An Index of U.S. Voluntary Engineering Standards, Supplement 2.* Washington, D.C.: National Bureau of Standards, May 1975.

This supplement contains the permuted titles of more than 5,700 voluntary engineering standards, specifications, test methods, codes, and recommended practices published by 164 U.S. technical societies, professional organizations and trade associations. Each title can be found under all the significant keywords it contains. These keywords are arranged alphabetically down the center of each page together with their surrounding context. The date of publication or last revision, the standard number, and an acronym designating the standards-issuing organization appear as part of each entry.

Keywords: Engineering standards, index of; index of standards, recommended practices, specifications, test methods; Key-Word-in-Context index of voluntary standards; KWIC index of standards; standards, voluntary, index of.

Slattery, William J. *Tabulation of Voluntary Standards and Certification Programs for Consumer Products.* Gaithersburg, Md.: National Bureau of Standards, 1977. Paperback. 187 pages.

This tabulation is a revised and enlarged version of NBS Technical Note 762, "Tabulation of Voluntary Standards and Certification Programs for Consumer Products," issued March 1973.

The original draft of the tabulation was developed by the American National Standards Institute (ANSI) in 1970. The product categories covered in the ANSI tabulation were based on those listed in the *Consumer Product Safety Index (CPSI)* of the National Commission on Product Safety, issued in July 1970. In 1971, at the consumer council's request, the bureau's Office of Engineering and Information Processing Standards revised the draft tabulation and issued it as NBS Technical Note 705. In March 1973, the tabulation was again revised based on the product categories developed for the National Electronic Injury Surveillance System (NEISS) of the Food and Drug Administration. The NEISS listings used in Technical Note 762 were an expansion and revision of the CPSI. The product categories in the current revision are based on the *NEISS Coding Manual* published by the Consumer Product Safety Commission in July 1975.

The tabulation lists over 1,000 product areas and over 2,000 standards titles covering products found in and around the home. (The major consumer product areas not included are foods, beverages, and drugs.) The tabulation also indicates the applicable national, industrial, and international standards that deal primarily with safety, performance, or both aspects of the products listed. For some of the product areas, there are no applicable standards.

Keywords: Certification programs; consumer products; household products; industry standards; international recommendations; national standards; product standards; recommended practices; specifications; test methods.

Snider, Hazel S. *American Standards Association: Its Functions, History, and Relation to the Department of Commerce and the National Bureau of Standards.* Washington, D.C.: National Bureau of Standards, 1958. Paperback. 13 pages and appendixes.

This study paper has been prepared to acquaint members of the bureau staff with the American Standards Association [now ANSI], which occupies a central position in domestic standardization and speaks unofficially for the United States in international standardization. The ASA is concerned primarily with *standards of practice*, such as codes and specifications, as distinguished from the *national standards of measurement*, which are the primary concern of the bureau.

The United States government leaves to private initiative many standardizing activities that in other countries are conducted by the government. However, various federal agencies participate actively in the technical work of ASA. In the case of the National Bureau of Standards (NBS), this participation is authorized by the fourth function, stated as follows in the organic act: "Cooperation with other governmental agencies and with private organizations in the establishment of standard practices, incorporated in codes and specifications."

Society of Automotive Engineers (SAE). *An Equal Partner Approach, DoD/SAE/ASTM, Conference on the Adoption of Non-Government Standards*. 4-5 December 1985 Conference. Warrendale, Pa.: SAE, 1986. Paperback. 10 pages.

The document includes keynote addresses, general session papers, and panel summaries of 15 presentations and panels.

Spivak, Steven M. *Implementation of OMB Circular A-119: An Independent Appraisal of Federal Participation in the Development and Use of Voluntary Standards*. NBS/GCR/85/495. Gaithersburg, Md.: National Bureau of Standards, 1985. 73 pages.

This study analyzes the implementation by government agencies of *OMB Circular No. A-119*, 1982. This circular established new standards policy for federal agency interaction with voluntary standards bodies and for government use of voluntary (nongovernment) standards. The report is based on interviews with knowledgeable individuals from the public sector, including federal procurement and regulatory agencies, and from the private sector, voluntary standards developers and standards users. A flow chart was also developed to illustrate the implementation provisions of circular A-119. Available data on federal agency adoption of voluntary standards are given to highlight the current level of implementation, and the expressions of those interviewed are used to analyze and critique the implementation of A-119 since 1982.

Keywords: Federal agencies; nongovernment standards; OMB circular; procurement agencies; regulatory agencies; standardization; voluntary standards.

Standards Council of Canada. *Directory and Index of Standards*. Ottawa: Standards Council of Canada, 1990. Paperback. Approximately 600 pages. Annual.

"The Directory, first published in 1977, is designed as a convenient reference document for users of standards as well as librarians and information centers in universities, government, industries and other organizations and professions. It was produced by the Standards Council of Canada, in cooperation with the accredited standards-writing organizations of the National Standards System.

"This cumulative Seventh Edition supersedes the previous six editions and Supplements No. 1 and 2 of the Directory. The current volume contains additions, deletions and revisions to data that appeared in the preceding volumes. The information provided in this edition was current as of March 31, 1986. For updating and verification beyond this data, users are urged to contact the Standards Information Service." [Shown in appendix, "Standards Information Centers."]

"The Directory is divided into two parts. Part 1 contains a brief explanation of the National Standards System and its components. Part II constitutes the major index of standards, published by the accredited standards-writing organizations, in two forms: a numerical listing of standards, classified under each standards-writing organizations; a KWIC (keyword in context) index of all such standards." (Foreword.)

The directory is issued annually, available from the sales division of SCC, and the cost changes each year.

Standards Council of Canada. *Directory of Accredited Laboratories*. CAN-P-1550. Ottawa: Standards Council of Canada, 1989. 73 pages. Annual with periodic updates.

Sections include list of registrants, indexes, acronyms, and keywords to this SCC/Canadian program of accredited laboratories.

Standards Council of Canada. *Directory of Accredited Testing Organizations*. Ottawa: Standards Council of Canada, 1989. Annual.

Standards Council of Canada. *Technical Information Centre Inventory*. Compiled by Anne J. Levesque. Ottawa: Standards Information Division, Standards Council of Canada, 1990. Approximately 200 pages. Annual.

This comprehensive guide to standards, directories, handbooks, and trade journals is divided into three major parts: a subject index, a keyword index, and an author index. Sources are not annotated.

The inventory guide is issued annually and in limited distribution.

Standards Engineering Society. *Proceedings of the 36th Annual Conference*. In Boston, August 1987. Dayton, Ohio: SES, 1987. Paperback. 206 pages. Annual conference proceedings are available from the society.

Standards Engineering Society (SES). *Standards Engineering: Index (December 1961-April 1985)*. Dayton, Ohio: SES, 1985. Paperback. 26 pages.

This is a chronological and alphabetical index of the articles that have appeared in the magazine. Supplements are issued periodically to update the index.

Steiner, Bruce W. *An Institutional Plan for Developing National Standards with Special Reference to Environment, Safety and Health*. Washington, D.C.: National Bureau of Standards, September 1979. 24 pages.

This plan was commissioned to provide a framework for the development of all essential nonnuclear energy-related, environmental, safety, and health (ES&H) standards for the private sector to coincide with the commercialization of new energy technologies. The development of such standards in the United States is a subset of the development of technological standards. Such standards consist of two basic types: limit standards, which establish system performance criteria, and compliance measurement standards, which establish methods for the demonstration of compliance with limit standards. The system addressed in this report encompasses four basic elements: (1) hazards, (2) limit standards, (3) evidence of compliance, and (4) compliance measurement standards. The unabridged version of the standards development process contains 39 discrete steps, each of which consists of intermediate stages. These are described here in the context of 10 essential standards management functions. Some essential components in a comprehensive system, such as the voluntary standards bodies, already exist. However, to carry out many of the other functions effectively, new organizations would be required. The operation of the entire process is described in terms of a hypothetical example.

Keywords: Energy standards; environmental standards; safety and health standards; standards development.

Struglia, Erasmus J., et al. *Standards and the Consumer*. Special report prepared by Consumers Union of U.S. Gaithersburg, Md.: National Bureau of Standards, 1964. Paperback. 84 pages. 3-page bibliography.

A contractual background report that outlines "the role of the consumer interest in standards of practice and define(s) the general problem of considering the consumer interest in the formulation of standards." (Preface.)

Struglia, Erasmus J. *Standards and Specifications, Information Sources*. Detroit, Mich.: Gale Research Co., 1965. 197 pages.

Included in this reference source are general sources and directories, bibliographies and indexes to periodicals, catalogs and indexes of standards and specifications, government sources, associations and societies, international standardization and periodicals, an author-title index, and a subject index.

Sullivan, Charles D. *Standards and Standardization, Basic Principles and Applications*. New York: Marcel Dekker, 1983. 94 pages. 19 sections.

A basic textbook summary of the major issues of standardization. "It is the purpose of this volume to introduce readers to standards and to provide information which will assist them in not only understanding such documents, but also the reason for standards and the influence they have on us and the world in which we live." (Page 1.) The need is indicated in the introduction: "Strangely, in almost all countries there is a surprising lack of information on standards in schools, even in countries where technology is highly advanced. There is a gross need for more knowledge of standards and their significance." (Page xi.) Following basic definitions and a historical review, other topics are types of standards documents, uses of standards, types of standards, application of voluntary and mandatory standards, standards for commercial products, mechanics of standards preparation, standards organizations, the Standards Engineering Society, standards in English-speaking countries, Canadian standards, National Conference of Standards Laboratories, and the factory mutual system. An index is also provided.

Suzuki, George, chairman and ed. *Report of the Voluntary Standardization Policy Study Group*. NBS report 10-391. Washington, D.C.: National Bureau of Standards, 1970. 172 pages and appendixes. Paperback.

"The aim of this study is to explore the issues associated with Bureau policies for participation in private voluntary standardization activities and to provide the basis for the formulation of new policies. The Panel's principal contribution is intended to be clarification of issues and options upon which new NBS policies and positions might be established." (Page 1.) Two categories of policy needs provide the basic format of the report: "(1) those that serve the general relationship between NBS and the voluntary standardization system and (2) those that will serve the management responsibilities within NBS in its participation in voluntary standards committee activities." (Page 7.)

Swankin, David A. *How Due Process in the Development of Voluntary Standards Can Reduce the Risk of Anti-Trust Liability*. NIST/GCR

90/571. Gaithersburg, Md.: National Institute of Standards and Technology, 1990. Paperback. 56 pages.

In view of two recent Supreme Court cases concerning potential antitrust liability faced by standards developers, this study identifies the key elements of due process that collectively constitute fairness. Eleven organizations, representative of a wide range of standards developers, were chosen for examination of and commentary on applicable portions of their rules. All standards-developing organizations are encouraged to reexamine their own rules periodically, testing them against appropriate criteria as discussed here.

Keywords: Antitrust; due process; liability; standards development; voluntary standards.

Swankin, David A. *Rationale Statements for Voluntary Standards – Issues, Techniques, and Consequences*. Washington, D.C.: National Bureau of Standards, 1981. Paperback. 90 pages.

This report provides an overview of the needs, practices, and consequences of providing rationale statements for voluntary standards. The research consisted of a literature review, a review of relevant court cases, the collection and assessment of examples of rationale statements, and discussions with those involved in standards writing. Six examples of rationales are analyzed, and a discussion of the most controversial issues associated with rationale statements follows. The report also contains a listing of product liability cases in which the issue of standards was raised and analyzes the legal consequences that rationale statements are likely to have on such cases.

Keywords: Legislative history; product liability; rationale statements; scope of standards; standards; standards writing.

Tholen, Albert, Carroll S. Brickenkamp, and Ann Heffernan-Turner. *Report of the 74th National Conference on Weights and Measures*. NIST SP771. Gaithersburg, Md.: National Institute of Standards and Technology. 1989. 259 pages. Annual.

Toth, Robert B., ed. *The Economics of Standardization*. Dayton, Ohio: Standards Engineering Society, 1984. Paperback. 112 pages.

This collection was prepared as the result of the need that "many managers of standards activities have felt . . . for procedures or techniques that would enable them to determine the value of their standardization efforts." Toth, in the introductory essay presents "a pragmatic approach." Other topics and contributions are a qualitative approach (A. J. Shearer), justification (C. E. Gastineau and D. L. Kear).

In chapter 4, Toth explains the "debits and credits" of National Aerospace Standard 1524, which is printed in the concluding chapter.

Toth, Robert B., ed. *Federal Government Certification Programs for Products and Services*. NBS SP 714. Gaithersburg, Md.: National Bureau of Standards, 1986. Paperback. 157 pages.

This directory presents information on 61 U.S. government certification programs for products and services. Entries describe the scope and nature of each certification program, testing and inspection practices, standards used, methods of identification and enforcement, reciprocal recognition or acceptance of certification, and other relevant details.

This directory is part of an ongoing NBS effort to establish and maintain a comprehensive database on standards, regulations, certification programs, and related information. This material has been compiled to meet the needs of government, industry, and the public for information on U.S. government certification programs in accordance with the requirements of the U.S. Trade Agreements Act of 1979.

Keywords: Approved products; certification; certifiers; grading; inspection; listing; premarket evaluation; qualification; qualified products; specifications; standards; testing.

Toth, Robert B., ed. *Standards Activities of Organizations in the United States*. NIST SP 806. Gaithersburg, Md.: National Institute of Standards and Technology, 1991. Paperback. 736 pages.

This directory is a guide to mandatory and voluntary standards activities in the United States at federal and state levels and by nongovernment (trade associations, technical and other professional societies). It excludes proprietary (company standards) and local levels of government (i.e., county and municipal). It supersedes the 1975 edition (NBS SP 417), "Directory of United States Standardization Activities," and the 1984 edition (NBS SP 681), and includes standards distributors, libraries, and information centers and union lists of standards repositories by regional areas. It also lists organizations that no longer develop standards or have become defunct since the previous directory was issued.

Over 750 current descriptive commentaries are formatted, with subject headings to facilitate access to specific information. The main sections cover nongovernment, federal government, state procurement offices, sources of standards documents and information, a subject index and related listings covering acronyms and initials, defunct bodies, and those organizations with name changes. Organizations have been included if they develop standards or contribute to the standardization process, whether voluntary or mandatory, or are sources of standards documents or information. An introductory section provides general information on federal (including military) standards activities, a list of 20 major nongovernment standards developers, some historical notes, and an overview of U.S. (national) standardization activities.

Keywords: Codes; government standardization activities; nongovernment standardization activities; overview of U.S. standardization activities; recommended practices; sources of standards; specifications; standardization; standards; test methods.

Toth, Robert B., ed. *Standards Management: A Handbook for Profits*. New York: American National Standards Institute, 1990. 510 pages.
This definitive and comprehensive guide was written to help manage company standardization programs cost effectively. It teaches how to organize a standards operation, get standards implemented, use standards in strategic planning and marketing, manage standards programs when companies merge, operate a company certification program, and set up and operate a standards distribution and information center. There are 24 chapters, and 37 authorities (including Spivak and Winsell) from a wide range of backgrounds.

This handbook takes the reader step by step through the planning, implementation, and management of a full standards program. Learn how to establish a standards program, evaluate your current program, or revitalize it in the face of intensifying global competition. Special features include case studies; how to achieve a 10 to 20 percent return on investment by using standards programs; chapters on the special needs of construction firms, service companies, and government contractors; sections on the special needs of small and medium-sized companies; and the first comprehensive treatment of government and regulatory standards programs.

Trahey, Nancy M., Jeffrey Horlick, and Vanda R. White, *1990 Directory of National Voluntary Laboratory Accreditation Program (NVLAP) Accredited Laboratories*. NISTIR 90-4280. Gaithersburg, Md.: National Institute of Standards and Technology, 1990. 69 pages.
This annual directory of NVLAP Accredited Laboratories provides information on the activities of the National Institute of Standards and Technology in administering the National Voluntary Laboratory Accreditation Program (NVLAP) during calendar year 1990. The status of current programs is briefly described, and a summary of laboratory

participation is provided. Indexes cross-reference the laboratories by name, NVLAP lab code number, accreditation program, and geographic location. The scope of accreditation of each laboratory, listing the test methods for which it is accredited, is provided.

NBS and now NIST have published the annual directory for the National Voluntary Laboratory Accreditation Program (NVLAP). The directory provides indexes to more than 140 laboratories nationwide that are accredited in one or more areas of testing. The indexes include a list of laboratories by name and NVLAP code number, test methods, accreditation program, and geographical location of each laboratory. There are laboratory accreditation programs for thermal insulation, ready-mixed field concrete, carpets, solid-fuel room heaters, acoustical testing services, processors of personal radiation dosimeters, and commercial products (paper and paper products, paints and related coatings and materials, and mattresses). Laboratories that test photographic film, seals and sealants, electromagnetic and telecommunications equipment, and other products are also included.

Keywords: Accreditation; acoustics; asbestos; carpet; computer applications; computer networks; concrete; directory; dosimetry; electromagnetic compatibility; laboratory; paint; paper; radiation; sealants; seals; stoves; telecommunications; thermal insulation.

Troy, Terrance N. *Barriers Encountered by U.S. Exporters of Telecommunications Equipment*. NBSIR-84-2845. Gaithersburg, Md.: National Bureau of Standards, 1987. 64 pages.

This report addresses the perceived institution of unreasonable technical trade barriers by major European trading partners to the export of telecom products and systems by U.S. companies. The DOC GATT technical office, which has responsibilities to assist U.S. exporters to take advantage of trade opportunities, informally contacted over a period of six months telecom companies and agencies to assess the extent of unreasonableness in foreign national standards, regulations, testing and certification requirements, and accreditation procedures. In each country, examples of requirements and practices were identified that allegedly blocked U.S. exports and other nondomestic products. Promises from our trading partners to revise their systems have yielded little, and each country continues to support unique requirements and practices that constitute trade barriers. Many trade barriers instituted by EC countries would be eliminated if EC regional and international telecom standards were harmonized, their adoption made mandatory for all EC countries, and results of testing for conformity from one government accredited laboratory were required to be accepted throughout the Community. Consequently, the United States should consider as an option supporting the development and implementation of European regional requirements and practices that promote uniformity.

Keywords: Certification; exports, GATT; international trade; trade barriers; regulations; standards; telecommunications; telecom equipment.

Troy, Terrance. *Survey of Standards Activities of the U.S. Department of Energy*. Washington, D.C.: U.S. Department of Energy, Office of Quality Assurance and Standards, August 1982. 97 pages.

The Department of Energy Standards Program, under the Assistant Secretary for Environmental Protection, Safety and Emergency Preparedness, is responsible for promoting standardization, increasing DoE's participation in voluntary standards bodies, and extending the benefits of standardization to the organizational units in DoE. To assist in designing and implementing needed programs, a survey was conducted to obtain information regarding ongoing DoE standards activities. The NBS Survey Team collected data on 17 information categories from a total of 63 DoE employees and DoE contractors in 36 separate interviews at 13 field locations and 15 headquarters offices. The survey team found that the flow of standards information within the infrastructure needs to be accelerated and that efforts must be directed toward providing DoE upper management with better understanding of standards programs. The data indicated considerable difficulty in maintaining necessary internal and external interface relationships and a need for guidelines for standards committee participation. The survey team suggested an "information focus" as a way for the Departmental Standards Program to help standards professionals at DoE, whose activities are closely involved in the development of energy technology, to improve their overall performance.

Keywords: Energy; standards; information; database; technology; policy; survey.

U.S. Consumer Product Safety Commission. *Handbook and Standard for Manufacturing Safer Consumer Products*. Washington, D.C.: U.S. Consumer Product Safety Commission, June 1975. Paperback. 68 pages. Out of print.

"Product Safety depends on purposeful planning and action, not on fortuity or mere hopefulness. This publication is intended to help minimize chance and maximize positive action through guidance for industry in answering safety-related questions.

"This Handbook was developed for use by persons in industry who are implementing or planning to implement the CONSUMER PRODUCT Safety Commission Standard entitled 'A System Standard for Manufacturing Safer Consumer Products.'" The term manufacturing is used throughout this publication as inclusive of all operations from design through production and distribution.

"The underlying premise of the Standard is that safety must be designed into and built into consumer products in conformance with the requirements of product safety systems planned, established, and implemented at the direction of executive management. The Standard identifies the elements of a comprehensive system approach to manufacturing safe products.

"Persons and organizations implementing the Standard have need of background information regarding the rationale of its requirements as well as suggestions and ideas for its implementation. This Handbook is a response to that need. It is intended to help industry establish product safety systems as an integral part of manufacturing, thereby serving the interests of industry and the public." (page vi)

U.S. Congress, House. Subcommittee on Activities of Regulatory Agencies of the Select Committee. *The Effect upon Small Business of Voluntary Industrial Standards*. 90th Cong., 1st sess., 1-2 June, 18-19 July, 24-25 August 1967. 1968. Vol. 1. 456 pages. U.S. Congress, House. Select Committee on Small Business, Subcommittee no. 5. *The Effect upon Small Business of Voluntary Industrial Standards*. 90th Cong., 2d sess., H. Rept. 1981. 110 pages.

The general theme of these hearings is the effect of voluntary industrial standards programs on small business. Specific attention is paid to the degree to which smaller firms are being denied minimum participation in the development of the techniques on which the standard is based or are denied full participation in the actual writing and promulgation of the standard itself. Possible violations of antitrust laws as well as other anticompetitive priorities are also discussed.

U. S. Senate. Subcommittee on Antitrust and Monopoly of the Committee on the Judiciary. *Voluntary Industrial Standards*. 94th Cong., final sess., 11-13, 18-20 March 1975, 511 pages; 2d sess., 22-23 March 1976, pages 513-696; 21, 25 June, 1, 22, 23 July 1976, 575 pages; part 2, 26 August 1976, pages 697-725. 95th Cong., 1st sess., 18-20, 25 April, 19 May 1977, 1,247 pages.

Verman, Lal C. *Standardization: A New Discipline*. Hamden, Conn.: Archon Books, Shoe String Press, 1973. 461 pages. 26 chapters. Out of print.

This volume represents one of the most comprehensive works on the subject of standardization, from a national and international perspective. The author identifies standardization as a "new discipline" and treats the subject "as a unit whole, with a view to bringing into perspective all such activities as may be directly or indirectly related to it, placing particular emphasis on organization, planning and direction, especially from the point of view of national development." (Page xiv.) He places special emphasis on the needs and problems of developing countries. A broad interdisciplinary approach is offered. Francis L. LaQue, the president of the International Organization for Standardization in 1972, adds in his foreword: "What recommends this book most is the philosophical approach taken by the author." (Page x.) Selected chapters include historical background, company standardization, national standardization (organization and procedure), international standardization, regional level activity, the consumer and standards, economic effects of standardization, interesting situations and solutions, education and training, and the future.

Vogel, Bertram M. *Standards Referenced in Selected Building Codes*. Gaithersburg, Md.: National Bureau of Standards, 1976. Paperback. 446 pages.

This publication provides a compilation of the standards that are referenced in the building codes promulgated by: (1) the three model building code organizations–that is, Building Officials and Code Administrators International, Inc. (BOCA), International Conference of Building Officials (ICBO), and the Southern Building Code Congress International, Inc. (SBCC); (2) the 20 states that have either mandatory or voluntary building codes; and (3) the 30 largest U.S. cities. In addition to identifying each standard referenced in the above-named codes, this publication lists the current date of the standard, its current title, the codes referencing it, the date of the code, the locations within the code where the standard is referenced, and the date of the standard referenced in the code. This publication is intended to provide a base for assisting the building community in updating, utilizing, and maintaining the standards referenced in building codes.

Keywords: Building codes; building regulations; building regulatory system; standards.

Weber, Stephen F., and Barbara C. Cassard. *Economics Applied to Standards: A Guide to the Literature*. Gaithersburg, Md.: National Bureau of Standards, 1980. Paperback. 86 pages.

This report provides a guide to the available literature on the application of economics to the analysis of standards and standardization. One hundred eighty-nine relevant articles, reports, and books were found and organized into four major categories of interest: (1) general methods of economic evaluation, (2) economics useful for standards analysis, (3) evaluation of specific developed standards, and (4) economics applied to the development of standards. The significant findings within each of these categories are briefly discussed in the text. The annotations that accompany the bibliographical entries provide more detailed information. The text includes a discussion of the approach followed in the literature search. An author index is also provided.

Keywords: Benefits; benefit-cost analysis; benefit-risk analysis; bibliography; costs; economics; evaluation; literature search; regulation; standards; standardization.

Williams, David. *Electrical Standards in World Trade*. Morden, Surrey, UK: IPC Middle East Publishing, 1982. 109 pages.

Electrical Standards in World Trade provides the first detailed survey of national, regional, and international standardization in the electrical and electronics industries. It looks at the work of the main electrotechnical standards bodies, describes their relationship with one another and with other organizations concerned with standards and testing, examines the nature and status of the standards they publish, and outlines relevant certification and approval activities.

Relevant certification marks are illustrated, and numerous address lists provide a valuable guide to organizations concerned with standardization and testing in each of the countries and regions covered.

Woodward, C. Douglas, ed. *Standards for Industry*. London: Heinemann Educational Books, 1965. 9 chapters and appendixes. 129 pages.

This collection relates to "the planned application of standards in industry. . . . The treatment ranges from a broad exposition of national and international standardization to detailed consideration of standardization in a basic industry." Among the chapter titles are "National Standards – Essential Framework for a Company Standards Program," "International Standards – Key to Smoother Foreign Trade," "Organizing a Company Standards Department," "Classification and Coding," "Product Standardization," "Standards in Measurement."

The Contributors

Albert L. Batik is a private consultant in Parker, Colorado. For over twenty years he was with the publishing and marketing departments of the American Society for Testing and Materials (ASTM). He later held several positions with Information Handling Services (IHS). He is the recipient of 29 awards and citations, including the SES/ASTM Robert J. Painter Memorial Award.

David Bearman, president of Archives and Museum Informatics, is a consultant in Pittsburgh, Pennsylvania. Previously deputy director, Office of Information Resources Management, at the Smithsonian Institution, he was in charge of computing and telecommunications. He was project director for the task force at the Society of American Archivists whose work during 1980-82 was responsible for the development of the USMARC AMC for archival information exchange, now used throughout the United States and Canada. His current activities include defining a format for the interchange of museum data.

Toni Carbo Bearman is dean, School of Library and Information Science, at the University of Pittsburgh. For six years prior she was executive director of the U.S. National Commission on Libraries and Information Science (NCLIS), responsible for policy and planning in the information field. She is a fellow of the American Association for the Advancement of Science and active in many national and international organizations, including the American Society for Information Science (ASIS), the National Information Standards Organization (NISO), the United Nations (UNESCO), and others.

Frank G. Burke is the incoming president of the Society of American Archivists (SAA) and president of the Association for Documentary Editing. For almost 30 years his federal career encompassed major archival positions with the National Archives, including 14 years as executive director of the National Historical Publications and Records Commission. From 1985 to 1987 he was acting archivist of the United States. He is now professor at the University of Maryland's College of Library and Information Services, with responsibilities for the double master's degree program in history/library science.

Walt Crawford is senior analyst, Development Division, with The Research Libraries Group. He has published nine books in the field of library automation and technical standards, edits the *LITA Newsletter*, and is founding editor of *Information Standards Quarterly*, published by NISO. Crawford writes and speaks widely on catalogs, desktop publishing, the MARC formats, technical standards, and personal computing.

Charles M. Dollar has been with the National Archives and Records Administration for 17 years. Currently he is assistant director of their archival research and evaluation staff. Dr. Dollar earned a Ph.D. in history from the University of Kentucky.

John L. Donaldson is chief for standards code and information at the National Institute of Standards and Technology (NIST), directing programs providing technical analysis, assistance, and reference publications. He represents NIST nationally and internationally in work on conformity assessment (certification) and has contributed widely to work in standardization, weights and measures, product standards policy, and standards education and research. He is active in management committees of ASTM and ANSI, in research planning and certification respectively. His career at NIST spans 25 years, including a brief leave during which he was at the American Society for Engineering Education (ASEE).

Cynthia J. Durance is director, archival standards, in the National Archives of Canada. She has held positions in the Government Records Branch responsible for coordinating disposition of all federal government records. She was also responsible for research and development of new computer and telecommunications technology at the National Library of Canada and for production of the national bibliography *Canadiana*. She is active in the IFLA and UNESCO and is author of several monographs and articles.

Norman Hagan is president of Norm Hagan & Associates, private standards consultants in Westport, Ontario. He served with the Alberta Public Works Supply and Services, where he was responsible for promoting standards use in procurement of goods and services. Mr. Hagan initiated the Canadian Committee for Procurement Standards, a joint effort among all Canadian jurisdictions, and previously had a long industrial career with the Iron Ore Company of Canada.

Patricia Harris is executive director, National Information Standards Organization (NISO), directing their activities and committee Z39 on standards for libraries, information sciences, and publishing. NISO is headquartered at NIST in Gaithersburg, Maryland.

Steven L. Hensen is assistant director, special collections, at the Duke University Library and author of *Archives, Personal Papers and Manuscripts*, the AACR2-based cataloging manual recommended by the Library of Congress, OCLC, RLIN and SAA as the authorized standard for all archival cataloging. He has worked with The Research Libraries Group, Yale University, and the Library of Congress and has also been active in the development of the USMARC AMC format with the SAA national information systems task force and their working group on standards for archival description.

H. Thomas Hickerson is assistant director of Olin Library for Special Collections and chair of the Department of Manuscripts and University Archives at Cornell University. He coauthored the first general review of archival information in the United States, authored the SAA basic manual on automated access, and wrote on the impact of library bibliographic networks on access to archival information and management. He is fellow of the SAA, chairs their standards board, and chaired its task force on archival standards. His work with The Research Libraries Group led to implementation of RLIN AMC.

Irving Louis Horowitz is Hannah Arendt Distinguished Professor of Sociology and Political Science at Rutgers University, The State University of New Jersey. He is also president and editor-in-chief of Tansaction Publishers.

Donald R. Mackay compiled the "Glossary of Standards Related Terms" in 1989 when he was chief, standards code and information, in the Office of Standards Services at the National Institute of Standards and Technology. He has been involved in standardization activities since 1960. He is now manager of international standards for the Air-Conditioning and Refrigeration Institute in Arlington, Virginia.

Jack L. Massau has served in various technical and supervisory roles for the Du Pont Company, including quality control, engineering computations, process monitoring manufacturing and laboratory automation, computer integrated manufacturing, and information systems architecture. He is author of Du Pont's "Document Management Architecture," forming the basis for Du Pont's program in creation, storage, retrieval, and dissemination of hypermedia documents. Currently, he is senior consultant with their Flexible Manufacturing Technology Center.

John McDonald is director, information management standards and practices, at the National Archives of Canada, where he has served in capacities related to the archival management of electronic records. Special interests also include the management of information in office systems and institutional management of records, regardless of their physical form. He has served on the Treasury Board task force on access to information and privacy legislation.

Neil McLean is associate librarian for management services at Macquarie University, Australia. Prior to his 1990 appointment there he headed library services and directed the Library and Information Technology Center at the Polytechnic of Central London for the previous decade. He has published widely in the field of information technology and libraries and was responsible for a large U.K. research program on the application of new technologies to information services.

Linda Musser is currently a faculty member and head of the Earth and Mineral Sciences Library at the Pennsylvania State University. She received her B.S. in civil engineering and M.S. in library and information science from the University of Illinois. She has previously worked for engineering consulting firms and the U.S. Army Corps of Engineers. She is involved in research on standards and other engineering information sources.

JoAnne Overman is supervisor of the National Center for Standards and Certification Information (NCSCI) at the National Institute of Standards and Technology. She has been involved with standards information at NIST since 1979 and in 1980 established the U.S. inquiry point at NIST for the General Agreement on Tariffs and Trade (GATT). Ms. Overman is a member of the Standards Engineering Society and the Special Libraries Association.

Paul Evan Peters is systems coordinator of the New York Public Library. He has been vice chairman of the National Information Standards Organization and representative for the American Library Association to the ANSI accredited standards committee X3 on information processing systems.

Michael B. Spring is a faculty member at the University of Pittsburgh in the area of information science. His research involves applications of technology to the workplace, particularly interface design and large-scale electronic document processing. He has a Ph.D. degree in education from the university and for more than a decade directed the University External Studies Program there. He has written numerous articles and book chapters on office automation, information technology standardization, and text and document processing and is the author of *Electronic Printing and Publishing: The Document Processing Revolution*.

Steven M. Spivak has served six years on the board of directors of the American National Standards Institute and over twenty years as professor in the Department of Textiles and Consumer Economics at the University of Maryland, College Park. He was recently named chairman of the Consumer Policy Committee (COPOLCO) of the International Organization for Standardization (ISO) based in Geneva, Switzerland. He has published widely on standardization for consumer products and on standards education and teaches courses on product standards, standardization, and international trade. He holds a certification in standards engineering and is a fellow of the Standards Engineering Society and the Textile Institute. His formal education was in textile engineering and in polymer and fiber science, the latter with a Ph.D. from the University of Manchester (United Kingdom).

Edward Steinfeld is professor of architecture at the University of Buffalo in the State University of New York. He is a registered architect and design researcher with special interests in design for the elderly and the disabled. He directs the Adaptive Environments Laboratory, conducting research on design for accessibility, safety, and health. He is internationally recognized for his research and is the recipient of awards for applied research from *Progressive Architecture*. Current research includes "barrier free design" and facilities for people with physical and mental disabilities.

James L. Teal is manager of the engineering standards program for the Du Pont Company in Wilmington, Delaware. Having been with Du Pont since 1967, he has more over 15 years of experience managing engineers and consultants from all disciplines. He is active in ANSI's Company Member Council and the Standards Engineering Society, and he chairs the Chemical Manufacturers Association codes and standards team.

Albert A. Tunis, consultant, retired in 1987 as founding director of the Education and Information Branch, Standards Council of Canada (SCC). Since then he has helped SCC coordinate and administer its international program of technical cooperation, both with the developed and developing countries. For many years he served as Canadian representative to INFCO, the information committee of the International Organization for Standardization. He also served as chairman of the management board for ISO/INFCOs information network known as ISONET.

Lisa B. Weber is assistant director for technological evaluation in the records program of the National Historical Publications and Records Commission, where she is responsible for the evaluation of funded work concerning archival automation. Her signal contributions to archival automation have been recognized by prizes from the Society of American Archivists(SAA), the American Library Association (ALA), and its Association for Library Collections and Technical Services. Previously, Weber held positions with the SAA and the State Historical Society of Wisconsin.

Thomas E. Weir, Jr., has been with the National Archives and Records Administration for 17 years. He currently works on the archival research and evaluation staff, with primary duties in standards for electronic documents. Mr. Weir has an M.A. in history from the University of Maryland and is completing doctoral studies in the university's College of Library and Information Services.

Martin B. H. Weiss is on the faculty in the Department of Information Science, University of Pittsburgh, with primary responsibility in their telecommunications program. His education included a Ph.D. in engineering and public policy from Carnegie Mellon University, with M.S. and B.S. degrees in the fields of computer/information engineering and electrical engineering. He has worked for Bell Laboratories, where he was involved in their design of the PBX digital telephone link for AT&T and of the DCP precursor to ISDN. He also served Bell Labs, MITRE Corporation, and others in telecommunications technology, integrated circuit design, and systems analysis.

Keith A. Winsell is associate director of the Amistad Research Center at Tulane University in New Orleans. He was previously consultant on the development of a special library on disability issues for the Paralyzed Veterans of America and librarian of the U.S. Architectural and Transportation Barriers Compliance Board. He has published reviews and articles on African American history and culture. Dr. Winsell studied political science and law, earned a Ph.D. in history (U.C.L.A.) and a master's degree in library and information services from the University of Maryland.

Index